THERESA MAY

THE ENIGMATIC PRIME MINISTER

ROSA PRINCE

Biteback Publishing

This updated edition published in Great Britain in 2017 by
Biteback Publishing Ltd
Westminster Tower
3 Albert Embankment
London SE1 7SP
Copyright © Rosa Prince 2017

ISBN 978-1-78590-273-4

10 9 8 7 6 5 4 3 2 1

A CIP catalogue record for this book is available from the British Library.

Set in Baskerville

Printed and bound in Great Britain by
CPI Group (UK) Ltd, Croydon CR0 4YY

THERESA MAY

For Conor

A NOTE ON THE SOURCES

Unless otherwise footnoted, all the quotes in this book are taken from interviews conducted both on and off the record during the summer and autumn of 2016. For ease of reference, individuals are referred to by their titles at the time the action of the book takes place, rather than those they currently hold.

CONTENTS

PREFACE

Theresa May was sitting in an ante-room preparing to go on stage when one of her closest aides, Fiona Hill, walked into the room with a mobile phone. The caller was bearing the most important news May would ever receive. It was 10 a.m. on Monday 11 July 2016, and the Home Secretary was getting ready to launch her campaign for the leadership of the Conservative Party. The reward for victory would be the greatest prize in British politics: to become Prime Minister of the United Kingdom of Great Britain and Northern Ireland. With May in the side room at the IET Birmingham Austin Court, a fashionable wedding venue and conference centre in the heart of the Second City, were her husband, Philip May, and Liam Fox, a long-time friend and former Defence Secretary, who was due to introduce her on stage. All three were immediately struck by the portentous look on Hill's face as much as by the words she spoke, as she informed May that Andrea Leadsom, her last remaining rival in the leadership race, wanted to speak to her urgently.

May glanced at the two men and quietly asked them to leave the room. Hill handed the phone over to the woman who had become her friend and mentor as well as her boss, and withdrew too, leaving May alone. In the long minutes that followed, the three waiting outside did not speculate out loud about what was taking place on the other side of the door, but it was impossible for their thoughts not to race ahead of them. Four days earlier, it had emerged that the contest for the Conservative leadership would come down to a straight fight between Leadsom and May. The race had been triggered on 24 June by the sudden resignation of David Cameron following the shock outcome of the referendum on Britain's membership of the European Union, in which the Prime Minister's Remain side had narrowly been beaten. The intervening sixteen days had seen a brutal bloodletting, with all the main contenders and expected favourites for the crown falling one by one until only Leadsom and May were left standing. The pair were now about to embark on a nine-week campaign before a ballot would take place of Conservative Party members. The result of the contest would be announced on 9 September.

Three days before May travelled to Birmingham to officially launch her campaign, Leadsom had given an interview in which she appeared to suggest that she was more in touch with voters' concerns than her rival because, unlike May, she was a mother. While Leadsom insisted her words had been taken out of context, she found herself facing a bruising barrage of criticism, with commentators and fellow politicians questioning her judgement. Shortly after the article appeared, she was forced to issue a humiliating apology to her rival. It had been the worst possible start to Leadsom's campaign and a boon to May, who maintained her dignity by refusing to respond. Now Leadsom was making a highly unexpected private telephone call to her fellow candidate – and those waiting outside the door could only wonder what it meant.

After a few minutes, May opened the door and invited Philip and Liam Fox back into the room. She said nothing about the phone conversation, and they did not ask what had transpired. May seemed perfectly calm and collected; her usual self, in fact. As always, she was immaculately turned out, in a navy zip-up jacket and matching skirt. Her shoes, inevitably the focus of attention, were red velvet with gold tips, and there were pearls at her ears and around her neck. If her companions had been wondering about the significance of Leadsom's phone call, they were no clearer now that they were back in the room with May. Her face gave away nothing. The three spent the next twenty minutes chatting quietly and making a few last-minute revisions to May's speech. At around 10.30 a.m., Fiona Hill returned to invite the group to enter the darkly intimate main hall of the IET so that the event could begin. Philip took a seat in the front row as Fox began his short introduction.

Then, just before 11 a.m., it was May's turn to speak. She formally launched her campaign with words which would later become famous, saying of the result of the referendum: 'Brexit means Brexit.' From there, May moved on to describe her vision for the future of the country, appearing to distance herself from the policies of her predecessor, David Cameron, by detailing a 'different kind of Conservatism'. If elected, there would be a new industrial strategy, a substantial house-building programme, and an end to corporate excess. 'There is a gaping chasm between wealthy London and the rest of the country,' she warned. The twenty-minute speech was followed by a press conference in which May was pressed in more detail about her plans. Asked by the BBC's deputy political editor, John Pienaar, for her response to Leadsom's apology, she said: 'I accept the apology, and, I'm here today, actually, ensuring that what I'm doing is talk about what I would do as Prime Minister and Leader of the Conservative Party.' Throughout her speech and the short press conference, May never once slipped up over her tenses or gave any intimation that her status had changed from being a candidate for the leadership to a Prime Minister-in-waiting.

Press conference over, May prepared to be interviewed on a one-on-one basis by a succession of journalists. First in line was Jonathan Walker of the *Birmingham Mail*. But before she could get to him, the phones of the other journalists still gathered in the hall began to vibrate with urgent demands from their news desks to question May about a series of messages that had just been sent by Laura Kuenssberg, the BBC's political editor, via Twitter. The first, issued at 11.27 a.m., read '@andrealeadsom making a statement at 12'. It was followed six minutes later by another: 'Westminster rumour mill going into overdrive over Leadsom statement and what it might be'. Finally, at 11.35 a.m., Kuenssberg sent the rumour mill off the scale: 'Source tells me Leadsom to pull out at 12 – not confirmed'. May's aides seemed as shocked by the news as the journalists were. May was hastily bundled back to the green room.

Once she was alone again with her husband and Liam Fox, May confirmed the suspicion they had held for the past ninety minutes. Leadsom had informed May by telephone that she would be pulling out of the leadership contest, and graciously wished her good luck for her future life as Prime Minister. She had asked, however, that May keep the news of her withdrawal confidential until she had the chance to make it public herself. May had taken her literally, not breathing a word to her close friend Fox, or even her beloved husband Philip, the man who is closer to her by far than anyone in the world. For an hour and a half, May had kept her composure, not betraying by a single word or facial expression the staggering reality that, with breathtaking speed, she was about to become Britain's second female Prime Minister. It was an honour she had long dreamed of; she could never have imagined the circumstances in which it would come about. Yet, at the very moment of her triumph, her self-control was such that she had not allowed herself even a moment's celebration.

It takes extraordinary strength of character to know for ninety long minutes that you are about to become the Prime Minister of the country you love, an honour you have craved from your teenage years, and not tell a soul. But, for Theresa May, there was no question that, having given her word to Andrea Leadsom, she would keep it. To understand how she could have displayed such composure at the very moment of her greatest success, it is necessary to go back, to an upbringing and family tradition that instilled in her a rigid sense of honour and the steely value of self-control.

CHAPTER I

BORN TO SERVE

Public service is in Theresa May's blood. Raised in a country vicarage in rural Oxfordshire, she was taught from a young age that it was her duty to help others. In her parents, she saw the concept of serving the community at first hand, their quiet religious faith and devotion to her father's congregation providing a guiding light that would lead her to dedicate her own life to helping others. With no brothers or sisters to dilute the intimacy of her relationship with her parents, May also learned the value and strength of small groups; throughout her life she would see no virtue in promiscuously forming friendships with large numbers of people, preferring instead to draw close to a tiny number of true intimates. Reflecting on her childhood, May once described a typical scene: she and her mother had joined her father at his church. Finding themselves alone, the family sank to their knees and sang a hymn together: mother, father and child, united, self-sufficient and ready to serve.[1]

The commitment to public duty has run through May's family for generations, taking various forms along the way. She herself has made clear the importance she places on it, saying in the speech in which she declared herself a candidate for the leadership of the Conservative Party in June 2016: 'I grew up the daughter of a local vicar and the granddaughter of a regimental sergeant major. Public service has been a part of who I am for as long as I can remember.' In some cases, her family's service was literal: both of May's grandmothers were maids in large Victorian houses, and one of her great-grandfathers was a butler. Her humble origins stand in stark contrast to her immediate predecessor as Prime Minister, David Cameron, whose ancestors were more likely to employ maids than to work as servants. May's antecedents were often not rich in monetary terms but the determination of her forebears to get on in life shines through her family tree. They were precisely the kind of ordinary working people she has pledged her premiership to serve.

Theresa May was born Theresa Brasier, and her father's branch of the family can be traced back to the late seventeenth century, to Limpsfield, in east Surrey, a village which appears in the Domesday Book of 1086 as 'Limenesfeld' and lies at the foot of the North Downs. Today, the village numbers around 4,000 people, and at least ninety buildings remain which would have been standing at the time May's relatives were living there, including their ancestral home of Brasier's Cottage. The amateur genealogist and former journalist Roy Stockdill has unearthed evidence of Brasiers in Limpsfield dating back to 1690.[2] He traces the first direct link to Theresa May to a Richard and Ann Brasier, whom he believes to be her great-great-great-great-grandparents, who baptised their son, James, in the nearby village of Oxted in June 1722. Generations of Jameses, Richards and Anns would continue the Brasier line through the eighteenth and nineteenth centuries. They were not well-off, but nor were they impoverished. The men were carpenters, joiners and builders, the women dressmakers and, in at least one case, a schoolteacher, suggesting that even in the Victorian era, the Brasiers had enough money, and enlightenment, to see that their daughters received an education.

At the end of the nineteenth century, a James Brasier broke the connection to Limpsfield, moving thirty miles away to Wimbledon, south-west London, with his wife Sarah-Jane. There the family stayed for the next few generations, living close to the edge of Wimbledon Common. It is an area where, a century later, their great-granddaughter Theresa May would make her home and serve as a councillor. May's paternal grandfather, Tom, and his five siblings were all born in the Crooked Billet area of Wimbledon. He was the youngest, coming into the world in 1880.

While his older brothers became carpenters and builders like their father, Tom went into the Army. He served with distinction for nearly twenty years, seeing service during the First World War at the end of his career, and it was he whom May referenced in her stirring leadership announcement. Roy Stockdill has speculated that Tom Brasier may also have fought in South Africa during the Boer War of 1899 to 1902, largely on the grounds that he does not appear in the British Census of 1901.[3] By the time of the 1911 Census, Tom was in India, a sergeant in the 4th Battalion of the King's Royal Rifles based in Chakrata, in the United Provinces of India, one of the many thousands of British men serving the Raj during the fading glories of the colonial era. Life for military personnel in India before the First World War was relatively jolly, in contrast to the plight of the indigenous population they ruled over. There were clubs and social events, outings and gymkhanas, military parades, cocktails on the veranda and a host of native servants to keep their gin and tonics topped up. As a sergeant, Tom Brasier was not close to the top of the social order, and his life would not have been as luxurious as that of higher-ranking officers, but he would still have enjoyed a standard of living far superior to that of his brothers and sisters back at home. This is almost certainly why he chose to have his family live with him at the barracks. At the time the Census was taken, Tom's wife, Amy, had recently given birth to a baby boy, James.

Amy Brasier, May's paternal grandmother, seems to have been an enterprising young woman. Her father, David Patterson, worked as a butler in a large house in Wimbledon, coincidentally not far from the Brasiers. The post was a prestigious one, but David's early death at the age of just forty-two in 1892 meant that by the turn of the century the family was struggling to get by. Perhaps it was for this reason that a few years later, Amy, by now in her late teens, was dispatched on the 12,000-mile journey to New Zealand, where she followed her father into service, working as a domestic maid for a family living in Christchurch. She stuck it out for just two years before homesickness got the better of her and, as the new century turned, she set sail again for England. On board was a young Wimbledon native – Tom

Brasier – who by then was already serving with the King's Rifles in India. Amy was striking, tall with dark hair; she soon caught Tom's eye. With their shared connection to Wimbledon, the couple had plenty to talk about, helping to while away the endless hours at sea. They struck up a romance and by the time the boat docked in India, where Tom returned to his regiment, they were in love.[4]

The relationship remained a long-distance one for nine long years, while Tom remained in India and Amy took up a new post as a maid in Ladbroke Grove, west London – the future power base of the Notting Hill set of well-heeled politicians whom her granddaughter would rub up against and ultimately overthrow. Even in Amy's day, Ladbroke Grove was prosperous. She found work as a parlourmaid, one of four servants in a large, four-storey villa owned by a wealthy middle-aged widow, Caroline Henderson, and her two grown-up daughters. Perhaps for practical as much as financial reasons, Tom and Amy did not wed until 1909, when he had returned from India and was living in the Rifle Depot in Winchester, Hampshire. The marriage took place in a Nonconformist chapel around twenty-five miles from Tom's barracks, in the town of Fleet, where Amy was living, having left the Hendersons' employment. Within two years, Tom was back in India, this time bringing his bride with him. Perhaps the long engagement rankled, or maybe she was sensitive about being older than her husband. Whatever the reason, in the 1911 Census, Amy lopped ten years off her age, claiming to be only twenty-four. In fact, she was by now thirty-four, while Tom was thirty-two.

During her time in India, Amy had two sons, the first of five children she would bear with Tom. Only one was still alive by the time she returned to England on the outbreak of the First World War in 1914. Once back home, she settled in Southfields in Wandsworth, south-west London, close to her in-laws in Wimbledon. Tom saw active service during the war, rising to the rank of sergeant major and being decorated for his valour. But by the time May's father Hubert was born in 1917, a year before the war's end, Tom had joined Amy in Wandsworth and was working as a clerk. He died there in 1951 at the age of seventy.

Amy lived to the ripe old age of eighty-eight. May's cousin Alan Brasier has said of 'Granny Amy', as she was known: 'She was kind and honest, a straightforward person who knew her own mind. And she was the type who would not tell anyone if she was feeling poorly; you had to worm it out of her.'[5] Another cousin, Andy Parrott, has said that, like her son Hubert and granddaughter Theresa, Amy took her charitable obligations seriously:

> She was always sending off cheques … though she didn't have much money of her own. But she cared. After she was widowed, she lived with us at my parents' house in Surrey for several years while I was at school. She would listen to the BBC Home Service with an earphone rigged up by my father and knit woollen squares to send to Africa and other poor areas.[6]

May's maternal grandmother, Violet Barnes, was no 'granny', insisting her grandchildren address her by the title of 'grandma',[7] Like Granny Amy, Violet had also been in domestic service in the early years of the twentieth century. Violet's father, William Welland, worked as a shop's porter; he moved the family from Devon to Reading in Berkshire when she was a small child. While still a teenager, Violet was taken on as a servant by a prosperous university physics professor, Walter Duffield, and his wife, Doris, who were originally from Australia and had recently moved to Reading. Before she was twenty, Violet, a diminutive figure who stood at only five feet tall, had begun walking out with Reginald Barnes, a travelling salesman and leather worker who originally hailed from Milton in Hampshire. Like Tom and Amy Brasier, 'Vie', as she was known, and 'Reg', as she called him, would be forced to endure a long-distance romance. On the outbreak of the First World War, Reg enlisted as a private in the Army Service Corps, and was sent overseas to fight in the East Africa campaign.[8] A photograph Violet gave to Reg when he set sail was passed down the family and still survives, along with the touching note she wrote to accompany her portrait: 'To Reg from Vie with fondest and truest love with all good wishes for great success in East Africa. "The ocean between lies such distance be our lot Should thou never see me? Love: forget me not."[9]

Violet's ardent wishes for Reg's safe return were to come true: he did not forget her and he did see her again, returning safely from the war to marry her in 1917. Their happiness would last less than a year, however. The end of the Great War was accompanied by the worst flu pandemic the world has ever known, resulting in the deaths of at least 50 million people, three times as many as were killed in the conflict itself. Among them, within a week of each other in 1918, were William Welland and his son, Violet's father and brother.[10] As well as the emotional trauma of the double bereavement, the loss of the Welland family's two main breadwinners was a major financial blow. After William's death, the couple moved in with Violet's mother. Geoffrey Levy of the *Daily Mail*, who has carried out extensive research into May's family tree, has theorised that, as well as prompting them to move into the Welland family home, a lack of money may explain why Violet and Reg delayed having their first child until she was thirty-three, relatively old for the time.[11] The terraced house was small, and would become even more cramped within a few years when one of Violet's aunts moved in as well.

May's mother, Zaidee, was born in 1928, four years after her brother Maurice. While there has been speculation about her exotic-sounding name, its roots lie in Violet's strong character rather than any foreign connection. May has said of her mother:

> Her brother was born first and my mother's mother wanted to call her son Kenneth and the father said he was going to be called Maurice. So she said when the girl comes along, 'I get to choose the name,' and she picked Zaidee, where from I know not. Even before she met my father, my mother was a regular churchgoer.[12]

In fact, Violet too was a regular churchgoer who, like her future son-in-law Hubert, was a devout Anglo-Catholic. It is likely that she found the name in her Bible: Zaidee, meaning 'Princess', was Abraham's wife in the Old Testament.

Both Reg and Violet lived long enough to know their granddaughter, Theresa. Reg died in 1970 at the age of seventy-eight, while Violet survived until she was ninety-four, outliving her daughter Zaidee by several years. For much of her widowhood Violet was confined to a wheelchair, having suffered an adverse reaction to a smallpox vaccination. Glynys Barnes, who is married to May's cousin Adrian Barnes, has said that Violet did not let her poor health slow her down. 'She was a tiny lady, but very positive, very determined and very, very forceful.'[13] Theresa May clearly inherited the strength of character of both of her former servant grandmothers.

While Violet Barnes's religious dedication was clear in her choice of name for her daughter, the extent to which Tom and Amy Brasier were fervent churchgoers is less certain. Like virtually all Victorians and Edwardians, they would have had some contact with the Church. Their decision to marry in a Nonconformist chapel, while perhaps taken for reasons of convenience, as it was close to where Amy was living, does suggest that their religious beliefs tended towards the 'Low Church', with an emphasis on personal morality and a family-centred view of their faith, as opposed to what may have been seen as an over-mighty organised church structure. Their son Hubert, May's father, would take an entirely different approach to his faith.

Hubert was an intelligent boy who in 1928 passed an entrance examination allowing him to attend the Wandsworth School, a grammar school close to his home in Southfields. It would change his life. Wandsworth had a reputation as one of the best state schools in the country, and Hubert was encouraged to try for university, an unusual path for a boy of his class at the time. Theresa May's long-running interest in the opportunities provided by a grammar school education to the bright children of low-income families may well have had their roots in her father's experiences at the Wandsworth School. Hubert was so well thought of by his teachers that in his final year he was named head boy. By coincidence, the head girl of the local girls' grammar school, Mayfields, was an eighteen-year-old Marjorie Sweeting, who would go on to become May's tutor at Oxford. Attending a function in Sweeting's honour in Oxford in 2014, May told the story of how, at the two schools' joint dance, it was a tradition that the head boy presented the head girl with a bouquet of flowers. Hubert somewhat unchivalrously gave Marjorie a cauliflower.[14]

In his teenage years, Hubert began to develop a deeper interest in religion. Two years after leaving the Wandsworth School, at the age of twenty, he became a theology student at the University of Leeds, a red-brick university born out of the original Yorkshire College of Science and Leeds Medical School in 1904. At Leeds, Hubert entered a hostel run by the nearby College of Resurrection, where he began training for the Anglican priesthood. Founded in 1903 in the nearby town of Mirfield, the college describes itself today as 'a Theological College like no other', and its 'High Church', Anglo-Catholic tradition was a world away from the Nonconformism that Tom and Amy had married within. The college is closely linked to the Community of the Resurrection, a movement which grew out of Christian Socialism and the Catholic revival that had taken place within the Church of England during the nineteenth century. All students were expected to attend Matins and Evensong six days a week. The location for the college, in the industrial north of England, was deliberate. The community's founders emphasised pastoral work in poor communities, and the college was set up in part to provide religious instruction to local men of little means – perhaps one of the reasons Hubert decided to train there. But Hubert also seems to have embraced the college's ethos of religiosity, conspicuous devotion and, perhaps most importantly, public service. During his last year in the Leeds University hostel, he became the Head Man. While worshiping at Mirfield, Hubert would have encountered both Lord Halifax, the then Foreign Secretary who regularly made his sacramental confession there, and Dietrich Bonhoeffer, a German pastor who led the Church's opposition to the Nazis and who stayed at the college before the war; he was later hanged in Flossenbürg concentration camp two weeks before its liberation in 1945.

Hubert graduated from Leeds with First Class Honours in Theology in the spring of 1940. It was perhaps the darkest time of the entire war. Britain stood alone against the Nazis, as Belgium, Holland and France fell one by one to the devastating German blitzkrieg over the course of just six weeks. With the United States yet to enter the conflict, the future of Europe itself hung in the balance. In desperation, the new Prime Minister, Winston Churchill, extended conscription to all British men under the age of thirty-six. As a student, Hubert had been exempt from service during the first year of the war. On graduating at the age of twenty-three, he joined another 'reserved occupation' – the clergy. Unlike his soldier father Tom, Hubert would do his bit for his country in time of war by serving on the home front. But World War Two was a war like no other, with the civilian population not spared the tortures of terror, violence and extreme deprivation. At times, the men, women and children at home faced death on a daily basis. The horrors Hubert would see in his ministry were scarcely less than Tom must have witnessed on the battlefield.

After undertaking postgraduate pastoral training at Mirfield, in 1942 Hubert became a curate at the Church of St Andrew the Apostle, in Catford, south-east London, in the diocese of Southwark. The church was an Anglo-Catholic one, built at the turn of the century in one of the poorest areas of London. By the time Hubert arrived, the community had already suffered dreadfully in the Blitz. Just six months into his time at St Andrew's, on 20 January 1943, Hubert would have witnessed one of the saddest tragedies of the war on the home front, when a local primary school, Sandhurst Road, took a direct hit from a German fighter bomber. While virtually all children in the capital had been evacuated to safety during the height of the Blitz in 1940 and 1941, and despite the continuing risk of random air raids, by the middle stages of the war many parents could no longer bear the heartache of separation, and had taken the difficult decision to bring their youngsters back to London. As a result, some schools, including Sandhurst Road, had reopened.

A single 1,100 lb SC500 bomb fell on the school at 12.30 p.m., just as many pupils and teachers had gathered for lunch in the dining room, which was totally destroyed. A local air raid siren went off too late, meaning those inside the school had no warning. It was later claimed that the German Luftwaffe pilot had deliberately targeted what he mistakenly took to be a residential block of flats, a scarcely more legitimate target, in retaliation for an RAF assault on Berlin three days earlier, as part of a strategy drawn up by Hitler called 'Terrorangriff', or 'terror raid'.[15] In total, thirty-two children were killed in the bombing along with six teachers. Most of them were buried together in a civilian war dead plot in Hither Green Cemetery, in a ceremony presided over by Bertram Simpson, the Bishop of Southwark. Hubert would have been at the service, and would have done his best over the following five years he stayed at St Andrew's, which was just 100 yards from the school, to provide some comfort to the dozens of grieving parents.

A few months after the disaster, Hubert was formally ordained in Southwark Cathedral. While many 'Mirfield Men', as graduates of the college were known, voluntarily took vows of celibacy, becoming 'oblates' who dedicated their lives to the ways of the brethren while taking their ministry to the wider community, Father Brasier chose not to adopt a monastic life.[16] The influence of Mirfield on his religious outlook would remain throughout his life, however. Appearing on *Desert Island Discs* in 2014, Theresa May named as one of her tracks the Anglo-Catholic benediction 'Therefore We Before Him Bending This Great Sacrament Revere'. Giles Fraser, the Church of England priest and journalist, has said of the hymn:

> This really is a fascinating choice. First, because no one who wasn't a proper churchgoer would ever have heard of it. And, second, because it betrays the enormous sacramental influence of her High Church father. Benediction, the worship of the blessed sacrament – or 'wafer worship' as Protestant scoffers often describe it – is pretty hardcore Anglo-Catholic stuff.[17]

The fact that Hubert did not marry until 1955, by which time he was already thirty-seven, in an era when couples tended to wed in their early twenties, perhaps suggests too that as a young man he had considered a life of celibacy.

At twenty-six, Zaidee Barnes was more than a decade younger than her groom on her wedding day. In 1948, Hubert had moved parishes to St Luke's in Reigate, a prosperous town in Surrey, still within the diocese of Southwark. Five years later, he moved again, to the seaside town of Eastbourne in East Sussex, where he worked as chaplain at the All Saints Convalescent Home. Unlike her roving husband-to-be, Zaidee had spent her entire life before her mariage in the same place, 156 Southampton Street, 'where Reading's trams trundled past the front of the terrace house and the loo was in the backyard'.[18] The couple were wed in a church on her street, St Giles, which is also in the Anglo-Catholic tradition. Zaidee's devout mother Violet must have been thrilled at her choice of an Anglican priest as her husband. After the wedding, the new bride moved with her husband to Eastbourne, where she joined Hubert in the Chaplain's House at the All Saints Hospital.

All Saints is in the Meads area of Eastbourne, a pretty, prosperous area. Built in the Gothic Revival style in 1867, it was an Anglo-Catholic convalescent home run by Anglican nuns. Today, the chapel is a wedding venue, while the hospital has been converted into luxury apartments. The Brasiers remained there until a shortage of nuns to nurse the patients and a lack of donations to provide the funds necessary for its upkeep meant the hospital was taken over by the NHS in 1959, before finally closing to patients in 2004. It was in Eastbourne, at a maternity home on Uppington Road, on 1 October 1956, just over a year after her parents' marriage, that Theresa Mary Brasier came into the world. Hubert is thought to have named her for Saint Teresa of Avila, a seventeenth-century Spanish Carmelite nun who advocated contemplative prayer and reform of the church.

The continuing influence of her parents' belief in the importance of both religion and public service is evident throughout Theresa May's life. Hers, however, seems to be a more traditional, Church of England faith than the Anglo-Catholicism they practiced. She has said of her religious belief:

> It is important. I'm still a practising member of the Anglican Church. I don't get as involved in church activities as I have done in the past, but I'm still a regular communicant. I think the point is that it is part of me. It is part of who I am and therefore how I approach things.

May has said that, while she never for a moment had doubts about her Christian commitment, she did enjoy engaging her father in lengthy debates as a teenager. Perhaps they discussed her inclination to move away from Anglo-Catholicism, towards a quieter, less ostentatious approach. She has said:

> It's interesting, because ... at no stage did I take issue with the Church, and I think that was partly because it was never really imposed on me by my parents. Obviously, in the early days, I was very much brought up in the Church, and going to church, but it was always understood that if I didn't want to I could make that decision, so I think precisely because of that I didn't feel the need to kick the traces in any way.[19]

As a parliamentarian, May has not shied away from taking decisions her parents may have found problematic due to their religious beliefs, including her radical move to bring forward legislation to allow gay marriage. She refuses to answer questions about whether her father would have approved. Other aspects of Anglo-Catholicism seem not to quite fit with May's character. It is hard to imagine Britain's second female Prime Minister, a woman who has worked tirelessly for over a decade to encourage more women into Parliament, supporting a teaching which, as many in the Anglo-Catholic tradition (although not Mirfield College) still do, shies away from the ordination of women priests.

Since becoming MP for Maidenhead in 1997, May has worshipped at the ancient parish church of St Andrew's, near her constituency home in Sonning, a beautiful and quintessentially English church with parts dating back to the medieval era. She wears her faith lightly and does not often speak of it. But her commitment to serving her community is clear – if kept private. In 2014, at a time when she was Home Secretary, one of the most challenging posts in the country, she cooked lunch for the residents of a homeless shelter run by the Samaritans in Westminster, without making it public,[20] a simple, low-key act of charity which would have made her parents proud.

A number of May's past and current colleagues reference her religion when describing her political philosophy. Cheryl Gillan, the former Welsh Secretary who has served alongside her in Parliament for nearly twenty years, says:

> That quiet faith that she has; not to over-egg the pudding, because she's not an evangelical Christian, but she's steady and has that underpinning, which you feel will give her a very strong … moral compass. I don't think she has to show off, or join in, she just does it; she goes to church.

John Elvidge, who served with May on Merton Council in the late 1980s, adds:

> There's a huge moral force behind [her philosophy]. I knew nothing [at the time] about her parents or her background, but obviously that's where it derives from. She obviously has a sense of corporate, public duty which drives her. It's not all personal politics, 'I've got to get to the top of the greasy pole,' she actually wants to do something once she's there.

It is a very Tory faith; low-key, traditional, steady, and without ostentation. Above all, Theresa May's religiosity has propelled her to seek ways through her politics to serve her fellow men and women in a concrete fashion. Her supporters and detractors may disagree over the extent to which she succeeds, but few doubt her sincerity.

CHAPTER II

CHILD OF THE VICARAGE

Hubert Brasier may not have become a father until more than a decade after the end of the Second World War, but when he finally did, his concerns were very much those of his peers, the parents of the baby boomer generation. Like them, having lived through the poverty of the 1930s and the horrors of World War Two, both Hubert and his wife Zaidee were keen to ensure their own child's life was one of comparative ease and comfort. It is this understandable desire that drove the couple to establish a safe and secure world for their only daughter, and would go a long way towards ensuring that her political, philosophical and religious outlook would be calibrated slightly differently from their own. Although his parents, Tom and Amy Brasier, had enjoyed a reasonable standard of living by the time of his birth in 1917, while growing up, Hubert would have seen real poverty among many of their neighbours in Wandsworth. He gained a further insight into the lives of the poor having undergone religious instruction at a college rooted in Christian socialism, and with a mission to train the sons of low-income families for the priesthood. From there, he had gone on to witness stark scenes of deprivation and suffering at close hand in his ministry in Catford during the war. Zaidee, raised with three generations crammed into the same terraced house in Reading, certainly understood what it was like to struggle to make ends meet.

These were concerns the Brasiers were determined that the young Theresa would be spared. And she was. Hers was a comfortable

childhood, played out in two idyllic villages in prosperous Oxfordshire. While they would never be rich, as adults the Brasiers
did not have to scrabble around for money as their forebears had.
There was enough in the bank for all Theresa's needs to be met,
including, when they felt it necessary, private education. The tran-
quil surroundings of her childhood would help to instil in May a
rather more conventional, conservative with both a big and a small
'C' mentality than her parents', slightly more socially liberal as
the times changed, perhaps, but with a harder edge economically,
and unafraid to pin her colours to the mast as on the right of the
political spectrum. Her future Cabinet colleague Liam Fox sums up
the influence on May of her upbringing and surroundings: 'She is
very much what it says on the packet. She is a vicar's daughter who
has a very traditional Conservative view.'

May was just two when her parents moved from Eastbourne following the closure of the All Saints Convalescent Hospital in 1959.
Her father's new posting was as the Vicar of Enstone, in the tiny
medieval hamlet of Church Enstone, a picture-perfect Cotswolds
village with thatched cottages dating back to the Saxon era, about
five miles from the market town of Chipping Norton and surrounded by corn fields. The vicarage was a few minutes' walk from the
village's Norman church, which is dedicated to the Anglo-Saxon
boy-king and martyr St Kenelm. Five years after Hubert's arrival in Enstone, his parish was extended to cover nearby Heythrop,
home of the fabled Heythrop hunt, and from then on he conducted
services every other week at St Nicholas's, another church dating
back to the Norman era.

May has said that as a young girl she was always aware that her
father's first duty was to his parishioners:

Obviously everything very much did revolve around the church.
[My] early memories [were] of, I suppose, a father who couldn't
always be there necessarily when you wanted him to be, but who
was around quite a lot of the time at other times when other
parents weren't, normally ... Some people would say sometimes

life as a vicar's daughter can have its ups and downs. But I feel hugely privileged, actually, in the childhood that I had.[21]

Elsewhere, she has said:

I remember one Christmas there had been a great car crash and a couple of families in the village had lost members of their families. That Christmas Day, after he'd done his services, my father went out and visited them and took them presents. I was about nine at the time, and because he was out doing his job, visiting those families, I didn't get my presents until six o'clock in the evening.[22]

The knowledge that her small demands were secondary to the needs of her father's parishioners would have been a strong antidote to any tendency for self-absorption as an only child. Growing up in the vicarage taught her other life lessons. She has said:

Being brought up in a vicarage, of course the advantage is that you do see people from all walks of life, and particularly in villages you see people from all sorts of backgrounds … and all sorts of conditions, in terms of disadvantage and advantage. What came out of my upbringing was a sense of service.[23]

May was aware that her father's role in the community placed expectations on her, too. She attributes her somewhat reserved nature to her early childhood, suggesting that, given her father's position in the parish, she could not be seen to behave in a way that would reflect badly on him. 'You don't think about it at the time, but there are certain responsibilities that come with being the vicar's daughter,' she once said. 'You're supposed to behave in a particular way.'[24] Elsewhere, May has added: 'You didn't think about yourself, the emphasis was on others.'[25] Hubert took his pastoral duties seriously. Speaking in 2016, one of May's cousins said:

The impression I got as a child was that Uncle Hubert was

more concerned about looking after his parishioners than he was himself. He was more interested in their welfare and spiritual well-being than he was in day-to-day things like, for example, cutting the lawn. He was very clever. He had a very quick mind and whenever I was in conversation with him, he seemed to be extremely knowledgeable. I'm guessing that's where Theresa got it from.[26]

May has said of her father:

He was hopeless at cooking or mending a plug but hugely respected for his pastoral work. He visited one family and heard scrabbling noises in the house before the door was opened. When he sat down he put his hand over the armchair straight into a bowl of jelly and ice cream. They had been sitting eating and tried to clear it away before the vicar came in.[27]

Hubert's parishioners were a mixture of the very wealthy inhabitants of the grand country houses which dot the area and local farm labourers. Today, Church Enstone is at the heart of the 'Chipping Norton set' – both David Cameron's constituency home of Dean Farm and the trendy retreat Soho Farmhouse are within five miles – and many of the country squires have been replaced by wealthy second-home owners. But in the 1960s, when May was a child, it still was something of a sleepy backwater. One inhabitant, John Sword, has said: 'It was a more remote area when Mrs May was growing up. It was rural but not backward. It's now a fashionable place to live.'[28] Another resident, John Watts, remembers the Brasiers well. He has described the young Theresa as a reserved and well-mannered little girl, and still has a couple of her old toy cars which her parents gave to his children. He has said: 'Her parents brought the toys down for my two boys in the 1960s after she had outgrown them. Theresa was a very pleasant and polite girl. As the daughter of the village's vicar she had a lot to live up to.'[29]

A few years after arriving in Church Enstone, when she was nearly five, May was enrolled at the state-funded Heythrop Primary

School. Her first day was not a success. 'I remember arriving at school screaming my head off because I didn't want to leave my mother,' she once wrote. 'So I had to be carried into the class in the arms of the headmistress, who announced to the rest of the class: "Look what a silly little girl we've got here."'[30] The shame of being singled out still clearly resonated with May forty years later. She soon thrived, however, in the school's tiny world. She wrote:

> Heythrop Primary was a very small school with only twenty-seven children in the whole school, and when I left there were only eleven children. Mrs Williams, the headmistress, was the only teacher. I also remember that when the sun shone we used to take our desks outside, and sometimes when the ice cream van came we all got an ice cream if we had been very good.[31]

May's school holidays were times of quiet happiness. She would later recall how the little family would take their annual summer vacation in the Lake District. 'I remember going to Seathwaite when I was eight,' she said. 'We had a cottage, and each morning I'd go across a field and collect fresh milk from a farm.'[32] Without siblings, May learned to be resourceful. 'Being an only child,' she says,

> you don't feel the same need to be in a big group, at least not in the same way as people who grow up with a lot of people around them. You're given more of a sense of … not 'making your own way', exactly, but relying on yourself a bit more, perhaps.

She enjoyed reading; *Swallows and Amazons* and the pony books of Pat Smythe were among her favourites.

After leaving Heythrop Primary School, May began her secondary education at St Juliana's Convent for Girls in September 1968, when she was a few weeks shy of her twelfth birthday. St Juliana's was about ten miles from Church Enstone, and Hubert and Zaidee's decision to send her there, rather than nearby state grammar schools such as Spendlove in Charlbury or Henry Box in Witney, is telling. As its name suggests, St Juliana's was a Catholic convent, and although fellow pupils at the time confirm that perhaps two-thirds of the girls who attended it in the 1960s were Protestants, as a Church of England vicar, Hubert's choice is yet another sign of his 'High Church' Anglicanism. Around half of the teachers at the school were nuns from the Sisters of the Servite Order, and the headmistress was the Mother Prioress. Although May was a day girl, St Juliana's accepted boarders, who went to chapel each morning. There was also a morning assembly, with prayers and a hymn. The most devoted could go to the Priory Church, across the street, to hear Latin Mass outside school hours. Priests would occasionally come into the school to take a Religious Education class. Grace was said – in Latin – before and after lunch.

St Juliana's was also fee-paying, although the rates were relatively low. One former pupil who attended in the early 1960s remembers that at one point the fees stood at £25 per term, equivalent to between £457 and £545 today. By 1982, when the ex-pupil enquired about sending her own daughters to the school, the rate was £185 a term, now worth £640. The fees were slightly lower for Catholic families. In her first years in Parliament, May made no reference on her CV to St Juliana's, which she attended for around two years before moving to a grammar school, which later became a comprehensive. It was only when the omission was spotted, and she was criticised for it, that she began to refer to St Juliana's publicly.

Nowadays, May makes a virtue out of her eclectic education, recently highlighting her unusual perspective in having experienced teaching in the independent, state grammar and comprehensive sectors to suggest she speaks with authority on the thorny issue of selection. 'I was incredibly lucky when I was a young girl growing up,' she wrote recently. 'My education was varied: I went to a grammar school that became a comprehensive – and, for a short time, I attended a private school … I want every child to have the kind of opportunities that I enjoyed.'[33]

Former pupils seem to have been fond of St Juliana's, which closed, 'due to a nun shortage', in 1984. On its Facebook page, created by an Old Girl, the school is described as 'probably the best convent in the world'. The former pupil who left just before May arrived remembers that discipline was tight. 'There were one or two girls who could be disruptive,' she says.

> If their behaviour continued to disrupt the class, they were sent out into the corridor and if necessary were sent to the headmistress, Mother Prioress. Occasionally a letter was sent home or a detention given. The most severe punishment that took place while I was at St Juliana's was when four boarders were expelled for leaving the premises at night; some of the day girls had told them that [the late 1960s pop star] Adam Faith ... was staying at the Bear Hotel in Woodstock. We never saw them again.

Sport was encouraged on St Juliana's extensive playing fields, and the school had a decent netball team that played other schools on Saturdays. Also at the weekend, one of the nuns would teach the girls to swim at a swimming pool in nearby Hinksey, walking the edge of the pool dressed in a full habit while bellowing out instructions. The former pupil remembers the teaching at St Juliana's as being 'enlightening and for the most part enjoyable', with a particular emphasis on Geography. May for one developed an early interest in the subject, going on to study it at university.

It was while she was still at St Juliana's, and on the cusp of becoming a teenager, that May began to develop an interest in politics. She had long been fascinated by current affairs. When she was a child in the vicarage, Hubert and Zaidee spoke to the young Theresa as an equal, and at an early age she joined in their discussions about the state of the world. '[I was] reading quite a lot, [and] probably at quite a young age started arguing, discussing things with my father,' she has said. 'I think part of being an only child was being exposed to much more of the adult world at an earlier age.'[34] As she grew older, her conversations with Hubert in particular turned into full-scale debates. 'He didn't sit you down and give you a lecture, it was more by conversation generally,' she has said. 'I was brought up in a vicarage where current affairs were talked about. Working with people and speaking were embodied by my father. It was a natural environment to seek a political future.'[35]

The late 1960s, when May's political consciousness was awakening, was a time of international turmoil, with the May 1968 student uprisings taking place in Paris, the My Lai massacre and escalating conflict in Vietnam, and the emergence of the civil rights movement and assassinations of Martin Luther King and Robert Kennedy in the United States. Closer to home, the Northern Ireland Troubles were beginning and racial tension stirring as Enoch Powell made his infamous 'Rivers of Blood' speech. Labour's Harold Wilson had been in No. 10 for five years, having promised a technological revolution to match the rapid social changes taking place. The global turmoil seems to have passed by sleepy rural Oxfordshire, however. May was determined, from the outset, that like most of her neighbours she was a Conservative. She has ascribed her early rejection of socialism to her father, saying: 'I wasn't an unthinking Tory. I was on the right because of individual freedom. I suppose standing on your own two feet was part of my father's ethos of public service.'[36]

As May began to take a deeper interest in politics, she raised with her father the prospect of joining the Conservative Party. Hubert was wary of politicising the vicarage, but gave permission for her to begin her involvement with the local party – with a few caveats. 'My father was very clear … that as far as he was concerned, he was the vicar for the whole parish, and so I shouldn't be out on the streets, sort of parading my politics,' May has said. 'It was important to him that I could be involved, but do it in that sort of behind-the-scenes sense.'[37] May now spent her Saturdays 'stuff[ing] envelopes in the Conservative office',[38] obediently taking care always to remain out of sight in a back room.

By the time May was twelve, she had decided she wanted to explore politics at a higher level. She would become an MP. 'I did want to be a Member of Parliament at a young age,' she has said.

And the reason I wanted to be a Member of Parliament, it can be summed up very simply, I wanted to make a difference. I wanted actually to be doing a job where I was making decisions that actually helped to improve people's quality of life. It's about making life better for people, I think that's fundamentally what drives me in politics.[39]

'Politics captured me,' she has said elsewhere.

I think it was because I wanted to make a difference to people's lives. That sounds terribly trite, but being involved in politics, being a Member of Parliament, and particularly being a government minister is a huge honour, a huge privilege but it also carries with it significant responsibilities … I wanted to be part of the debate.[40]

Life in the vicarage was not all about serious debate, however. The family was close and loving, the atmosphere in the kitchen in particular warm and cosy as Zaidee taught the young Theresa to cook – an art that would become one of her life-long passions. She has spoken particularly favourably of her mother's scones, using her first set-piece newspaper interview after becoming Prime Minister to share the recipe.[41] Hubert was no cook. 'I remember an omelette once. Didn't turn out right at all,' May has said.[42] There was usually a dog or two milling around, and classical music playing in the background. Zaidee was a fine musician, and May has said that refusing to let her mother teach her the piano remains one of her greatest regrets.[43] The conversations between May and her father were not entirely serious, either. May inherited Hubert's love of cricket, and the pair would spend long summer afternoons listening to Test matches on the wireless. They once got involved in a furious row over who the best-ever England batsman was – Geoffrey Boycott, as May argued, or John Edrich, her father's hero. It is an interest May has maintained throughout her life, often taking time away from Westminster to watch a match. Boycott remained a hero. She campaigned (unsuccessfully) for him to be given a knighthood, and was thrilled when, in 2013, he invited her to Headingley to watch Yorkshire play. Some interviewers have seen a metaphor in May's admiration for Boycott's somewhat stolid determination. She has said of the England player: 'I have been a Geoff Boycott fan all my life. It was just that he kind of solidly got on with what he was doing.'[44]

In 1970, when May was thirteen, Hubert was made Vicar of Wheatley, a large village about twenty miles from Church Enstone, to the east of Oxford. His new church was St Mary the Virgin, built in the mid-nineteenth century in the Gothic Revival style. It too was known as being 'very High Church'.[45] Hubert is remembered fondly by his former parishioners. He was still their vicar at the time of his death in a car accident in 1981, and a plaque in his memory has been placed on the wall inside St Mary's. One member of the congregation at the time has suggested that life in the vicarage shaped May: 'She was rather a serious young lady in those days. She was a very spiritual person. And has kept the faith.'[46] May was game enough to throw herself into village life, however, taking part in a local pantomime and getting a Saturday job in a bakery to earn pocket money, much of which she spent on clothes. May's fascination with fashion had begun. She has said: 'That was the era of flares and tank tops, I'm afraid. It would have been flared trousers; blouses used to have more sleeves in those days, voluminous sleeves. I had a yellow blouse which had huge, huge, voluminous sleeves.'[47] Elsewhere, she has said that the last time she experienced 'sartorial embarrassment' was 'in a pair of lime-green platforms as a teenager'.[48]

The Wheatley Vicarage, where the Brasiers now lived, was just around the corner from a girls' grammar school, Holton Park, which was well-regarded enough for Hubert and Zaidee to decide to place their daughter back in the state system. As it had been at St Juliana's, the teaching of Geography was particularly impressive. May passed the school's entrance exam and began attending as a third year. The school building was an old manor house, and rich in history. A Roman settlement existed under a playing field known as 'The Racks', which is now used as a tennis court, and the grounds contained a 900-year-old tree, called the 'Domesday Oak', so named because it dates back to the time of the Domesday Book. Oliver Cromwell's daughter Bridget is said to have wed at the house a few days before the fall of Royalist Oxford, in the middle of the English Civil War in 1646. In 1944 and 1945, the house was used by the American Army for the recuperation of servicemen wounded in the D-Day landings, and there were still Nissen huts in the grounds during May's time at the school. Three years after the end of the war, the building was purchased by the local authority, and the existing East Oxfordshire Girls' Grammar School was moved to the site and renamed Holton Park. In the years which followed, generations of girls passed down legends of the various ghosts said to haunt its passageways.

May has said she has 'fond memories' of her time at the school.[49] In 2011, when she was contacted by the Oxfordshire historian Marilyn Yurdan and asked to contribute to a book Yurdan was writing on Holton Park and other grammar schools, May agreed to write the foreword. 'This book brings back so many memories – from sherbet fountains to Corona, from Tommy Steele to *Z Cars*, from stodgy puddings to Vesta curries; and that's not to mention the education,' she wrote.[50] A few days before becoming Prime Minister, and to the surprise of the events' organisers, who assumed that she would have been forced to pull out, May returned to the school to open a garden made by children at John Watson School, a special needs school which stands in the extensive grounds of what was formerly Holton Park and is now Wheatley Park School.

May's new classmates at the grammar school found her a reserved character, a dedicated student who worked hard and was intolerant of those who took a lighter-hearted approach to their studies. 'I enjoyed reading, I did my homework, I was that sort of schoolgirl,' she has said.[51] Rosalind Hicks-Greene, who (as Rosalind Redmond) was at Holton Park with May, has said of her old classmate:

> She was very focused. She was the person that you knew would start to tut if we had a bit of an off-track conversation with the

history teacher. She was the one that would start to get a bit im-
patient because she wanted to get back on track. She was very
quiet, she was extremely studious, she was the person who always
did their homework, always came to lessons well-prepared.[52]

Tall for her age, by her teenage years May had developed a stoop
in her shoulders like her father, and has admitted she preferred to
keep in the background. 'I probably was Goody Two Shoes,' she
has said.[53]

A year after May's arrival at Holton Park, in 1971, the school
was swept up in the national education reformation which had
begun in the previous decade, when Oxfordshire County Council
decreed that the grammar school system should be abolished and
replaced with universal comprehensive education. Holton Park
was merged with a local boys' school, the Shotover School, and
renamed Wheatley Park School. As well as now taking pupils of
mixed ability, it also opened its doors to boys as well as girls. The
Holton Park site became the Upper School, while Shotover was
the Lower School, meaning May could stay where she was. Kevin
Harritage, who looks after the archive at Wheatley Park, says the
upheaval would have been immense – and suggests it has shaped
May's thinking on education:

> I think it was a huge change ... She was here at a time when it
> was probably the most difficult period in terms of the changeover
> ... I think she saw it at the worst possible time, and I believe that's
> why she thinks grammar schools are so good and that compre-
> hensive schools are not quite so good.[54]

While ex-pupils confirm that there was indeed 'chaos' at the school
for a time,[55] for the former grammar school girls, the disruption
was kept to a minimum. Most of the former Holton Park pupils
continued to be taught as they had been, in single-sex classes in the
old manor house. Martin Robinson, who became a pupil a year
after May left, has said:

The head teacher and senior leaders from the grammar school had remained in charge and the teaching for the top sets was mainly done by old grammar school staff ... Theresa would have been protected from the chaos due to her being educated away from the oiks, across the moat in the old manor, with the same staff and grammar school mores she had become used to. She ... was therefore untainted by the 'comprehensivisation'.[56]

The presence of male pupils at the school certainly did not intimidate the teenage Theresa Brasier. When a trip was arranged for the boys to attend an international rugby match, she made her feelings known at being left out. Hubert Brasier complained to the headmistress, Andrea Mills – and May got to go on the excursion. She has said: 'My parents' approach was very much: "Whatever you do, always aim to do the best." There was never any suggestion that because I was a girl there were things I couldn't do.'[57]

In September 1972, aged just fifteen, May entered the Wheatley Park Sixth Form. The previous summer she had picked up eleven O-levels and, given her clear intelligence and hard work, had been allowed to skip an academic year. She began studying for three A-levels and an S-level, a general studies exam taken only by the most able pupils, usually those on their way to either Oxford or Cambridge. By now, the tenacity and strength of purpose which her Cabinet colleagues would recognise were beginning to emerge. A few days after she became Prime Minister in 2016, a former schoolmate, Patsy Davies (née Tolley), wrote a letter to *The Guardian* saying:

In the early 1970s I found myself in the same class at school as a certain Theresa Brasier, now known as Theresa May. How we all sniggered when she announced to our form teacher Mr Montgomery that she wanted to be Prime Minister. Well, we're not sniggering now ... Immediately after O-levels I left that school to continue my education elsewhere. And why? Because, at the tender age of fifteen, Theresa had managed to persuade our headmistress to reconfigure the school's original A-level options to accommodate the subjects of her choice.[58]

Others recall May speaking of becoming Prime Minister in her teenage years (something she herself has denied). Her cousin, Andy Parrott, has said:

> I remember my parents had this tape, which they played me once … It was a tape Theresa had made, I believe in her sixth form, and this tape said that she wants to be the first female Prime Minister of Great Britain. My parents were very proud of this. They thought it was wonderful.[59]

Parrott says there was no sense that his parents thought May was being precocious, or that her words grated. Instead, the extended family was proud of her.

Unfortunately for May, her early attempts at forging a political career did not go to plan. For all her inner confidence, she remained somewhat reserved, even shy. Her first stab at public speaking ended in disaster. She has said:

> When I was at school we had a history teacher who decided he would set up a debating society … and he suggested a number of us went along one day into a classroom, which we all did, and he had some pieces of paper with different subjects on, literally in a hat, and everybody had to go up and pick a piece of paper and speak for two minutes … Funnily enough, despite the fact that I was quite used to discussing things with my parents at home, [when] … I went up and picked a piece of paper, and I turned round, I couldn't think of a single thing to say. So my career in debating started with silence.[60]

Her fortunes didn't improve later that year, when May stood as the Conservative candidate in a mock election held by Wheatley Park to coincide with the February 1974 general election. It was a tough contest – and May put up a good fight. The current head teacher of Wheatley Park, Kate Curtis, has said: 'There is a story about the school running an election and Mrs May standing as the Tory candidate. Apparently, she stood at the entrance to the old school house and gave a speech which was very impressive.'[61] May's Liberal opponent was the popular Rosalind Hicks-Greene, the school's head girl, who went on to win. She has said that while May's policies may have been considered sound by the electorate, she lacked the personal appeal to win their votes. It was a harsh introduction to the conundrum May and her fellow Tories would grapple with for much of her early career in Parliament.

In an early attempt at appearing modern, May was by now styling herself as 'Terri' Brasier. Hicks-Greene has said: 'I think she called herself that at school so as to be an approachable person. It was not hard to beat Theresa as she was not very charismatic.'[62] Elsewhere, Hicks-Greene has added: 'She was very serious and quite reserved and that probably didn't go in her favour. She was very quiet and studious but when she needed to make her views felt she certainly could do so.'[63] Recalling May's speech, Hicks-Greene has said:

> I can recall thinking to myself that it was a very typical, safe Conservative speech, very much grounded in safe Conservative policies as they were at the time … I'm afraid she was very quiet, very studious, she was not a charismatic person, but you felt that you could absolutely believe what she was saying and you could trust her.[64]

A photograph printed on the front page of the following week's *Oxford Times*, under the headline 'The New Prime Minister!' shows May smiling bravely as she watches Hicks-Greene throw her arms up in a victory celebration, while the unfortunate Labour candidate, Val Fortescue, who came last in the contest, beams at the camera. Despite her loss, however, the school's teachers were impressed by May. Rosemary Wain, a science teacher at the time, has said: 'I do remember standing here and hearing the results declared. And

I do remember that after the election, in the staff room, we talked about it, and what a good speech she'd given. She wasn't the winner, on that day, but she's the name that I certainly remember.'[65]

Six months after her disappointment in the mock election, and still only seventeen years old, Theresa May left Wheatley Park School bound for Oxford University to study Geography. It was time for the vicar's daughter to spread her wings.

CHAPTER III

OXFORD – AND PHILIP

Benazir Bhutto cut quite a figure on campus. Arriving at her women-only college, Lady Margaret Hall, as a twenty-year-old glamorous Harvard graduate in 1973, Bhutto was exotic, beautiful and self-assured. Her father, Zulfikar Ali Bhutto, had recently become Prime Minister of Pakistan, having previously served as its President. Benazir would follow him to Oxford, where he had studied history, and then into politics, her later career proving as turbulent and often blood-soaked as his. While her time in office was marked by great strides forward, particularly for women, allegations of chronic corruption dogged her until she was assassinated in December 2007. Long before she was murdered in a gun and suicide bomb attack as she left a political rally in Rawalpindi, Bhutto faced her first allegations of corruption and accusations of dynastic nepotism 4,000 miles away, amid the ancient quadrants and by-ways of Oxford University in the mid-1970s.

By the end of her first year at Oxford, Bhutto had set her eye on winning election as president of the Oxford Union, the university's prestigious debating society. The position changed hands every term, and competition was fierce. Serving as president was seen as a near-certain pathway to power in the real world; past holders of the office in the post-war era included such political giants as Michael Foot, Jeremy Thorpe and Michael Heseltine. While campaigning for the presidency, Bhutto often took to the road, driving around Oxford in what one of her supporters, the future Conservative

minister Alan Duncan, has described as a 'snot-coloured MG', seeking to drum up votes from fellow members. Another contemporary,
the journalist Michael Crick, adds that Bhutto also made a habit
of courting those of her classmates she considered up-and-coming
future politicians, regardless of their party affiliations, once taking
him out to lunch in an (unsuccessful) attempt to win his vote. 'Some
people thought she was using her name and money to buy the presidency,' he has said.[66] Barbara Roche, who would serve as a minister in Tony Blair's Labour government between 1999 and 2001,
was another wooed by Bhutto at this time. And so was a young
grammar school girl from rural Oxfordshire called Theresa May.

May had come to Oxford a year after Bhutto, in October 1974,
entering St Hugh's College, which, like Lady Margaret Hall, accepted only women students. St Hugh's was established in 1886, and
was granted full collegiate status along with the four other women's
colleges in 1959. (The college began to accept male students only
in 1986.) Fellow alumni include Aung San Suu Kyi, the Nobel Prize
winner and de facto head of state of Myanmar; Barbara Castle,
the late Labour Cabinet minister; and the suffragette Emily Dick-
inson. The first female students to take Firsts at Oxford in English,
History, Jurisprudence and Physics all studied at St Hugh's. May
has spoken in the past of how important all-female colleges were
to 'the advancement of women', in an era when 'they struggled to
assert their place at the male-dominated University'.[67] May's new
rooms were less than ten miles from her parents' home in Wheatley, but her life was now very different. May had always taken her
studies seriously. At St Hugh's, she found herself in the company of
similarly minded young women. 'We weren't girly,' one contemporary has said.[68] They wore the dark, formal academic dress known
as sub fusc to formal dinner, and were treated to wine from the
college's cellars. May's choice of degree, Geography, was rather
less showy than the PPE which many future aspiring politicians
studied, but her interest in politics was as keen as ever. She soon
joined both the Union and the Oxford University Conservative Association. It was at a disco organised by the latter, thanks to Benazir

Bhutto, that May met her future husband, Philip May, the love of her life.

It was autumn 1976, the start of May's third and final year at Oxford, and she was by now a fixture on the university's political scene. In contrast, Philip, two academic years behind her and eleven months younger, was still a relatively unknown freshman. But he had already come to Bhutto's attention, having won the freshers' debating competition at the Union. Philip had just turned nineteen, and was studying History at Lincoln College, when he wandered past Bhutto and her quiet friend May as they sat chatting together at the disco. May has described her first encounter with her husband-to-be: 'It was actually [at] an Oxford University Conservative Association disco, of all the things. I remember I was sitting talking to Benazir and Philip came over, and she said, "Oh, do you know Philip May?" And the rest is history.'[69] 'He was good looking and there was an immediate attraction,' she added. 'I think I quite liked him. We were jointly interested in politics. We were meeting at the Conservative Association, so we had some common interests to start off with.'[70]

The pair soon found they had a lot in common beyond their politics – including a shared love of cricket. They discussed the fortunes of Geoffrey Boycott and Theresa's new hero, West Indian fast bowler Tony Gray. And the quietly humorous Philip was able to make Theresa, seen as somewhat serious by some of her Oxford contemporaries, laugh. Damian Green, the future Cabinet minister who knew both Theresa and Philip May at Oxford, has said: 'Once they became an item, they [were] rock solid.'[71]

Like Theresa, Philip had attended a grammar school, Calday Grange in West Kirby on the outskirts of Liverpool, where he had moved as a small boy, having been born in Norfolk. Also like his wife-to-be, Philip's origins were respectably middle-class: his father, John, worked as a salesman for a shoe wholesaler, while his mother, Joy, was a part-time French teacher. Later on, the senior Mays would take a keen interest in their daughter-in-law's political achievements, expressing a pride which must have been important to her in the absence of her own parents. It may also have meant a lot to her that, sweetly, John, with his own background in the shoe business, encouraged and was amused by her soon-to-be famous love of fancy footwear. A former neighbour of the couple, Peter Curtis, has described how, in the 1990s, Philip's parents compiled a scrapbook of newspaper cuttings about their high-flying daughter-in-law. 'They showed me the scrapbook and at the end of it John started talking about Theresa being the next Prime Minister,' Curtis has said. 'At the time I didn't think she'd ever make it; I'm not sure she was even an MP at the time.'[72] When John May died in 2002, his wife moved south to be closer to her son and daughter-in-law. She died in September 2015. Curtis saw Theresa May at a memorial service held in Merseyside in Joy May's honour in January 2016. Her own parents were obviously on her mind. Curtis has said: 'We went to the service and Theresa May was serving the teas and coffees. We asked her what she was doing serving the drinks and she said, "I've served more teas and coffees than most people, being a vicar's daughter."'[73]

During her first two years at Oxford, before her encounter with Philip, May did not have a regular boyfriend, although over lunch with the journalist Zoe Brennan, a fellow graduate of St Hugh's, soon after arriving in Parliament in 1997, she did share 'some interesting tales … about smuggling men into the college, at a time when boyfriends were still nominally banned from undergraduate rooms'.[74] One of May's closest university friends, Alicia Collinson, has said: 'Theresa went out with other people. But none of them were quite what she wanted. None of them were special. Then in our final year, Philip came along. There was Philip and nobody else.'[75]

Instead of pursuing romantic adventures, May concentrated on her studies and her political activities. While most contemporaries insist that May was good fun, some admit she could come across as rather austere. The vicar's daughter dutifully continued to attend church on Sundays. There were no drugs and none of the alcohol-fuelled debauches enjoyed by the Bullingdon Club boys David Cameron and Boris Johnson a decade later. Indeed, what jinks there were to be had were somewhat muted. 'Theresa and I used to love watching *The Goodies* [a comedy sketch show starring Tim Brooke-Taylor, Graeme Garden and Bill Oddie],' one university friend has recalled. 'That was our sense of humour.'[76] Pat Frankland, who was at St Hugh's with May, has said:

> She's got a strong sense of humour, but I don't think she puts it out in public life. It's quite a dry wit, her father was the same. I will always remember coming back together from a party and we walked along the top of a wall outside the Ratcliffe [*sic*] Library together. I wouldn't say we were drunk. We didn't get drunk, because we didn't have the money to go and get drunk. We were slightly merry. We were just in high spirits.[77]

Like many aspiring politicians who attend Oxford, May began to draw close to a group who would go on to serve alongside her for much of the rest of her political career. Her circle included Alan Duncan and Damian Green, who began dating her St Hugh's friend Alicia Collinson and whom she would later appoint to her first Cabinet in 2016. Green has said of their time together at Oxford:

> I've known her since we were both eighteen. Theresa is perfectly good fun. She's been a friend of mine for more than forty years. The key to Theresa is what you see is what you get. Part of the secret of Theresa's appeal is that there's not a secret part of her character that the public doesn't see. Everyone sees a hard-working, hugely intelligent, hugely conscientious woman, and that's what she's like. That's what she's always been like. She has no side.[78]

Green and May met at the Oxford University Conservative Association; he would serve as the club's president in their final year. The association was an active one. In the real world, the Wilson government was gripped by industrial unrest and spiralling inflation. Safe in their cosy world in Oxford, the student politicians were certain they had the prescription to the turmoil outside. Green has said that his and May's 'was a generation that was very much turned against that left-wing nature of the '60s. We were the next generation up that became Thatcher's children. In that period when the Labour government was just running into the ground, the Conservative Association was very strong.'[79]

Alicia Collinson has said that from her first days at the college, May was overt in her political ambitions. The pair had begun their Oxford life within days of Harold Wilson's victory in the October 1974 general election, and politics was often a topic of conversation at the college dining table. 'My memory's hazy but it was the first term at Oxford in 1974,' Collinson has said. 'We were at breakfast and she said something about wanting to be Prime Minister.'[80] Pat Frankland too has said that May was always clear about her political aspirations, including her desire to be Prime Minister.

> I met her on our first or second day of college, when she was seventeen and I was eighteen. I was aware of that ambition from the very early days. She used to drag me along to political lectures. She wanted to be the first woman Prime Minister back in our Oxford days and she was very irritated when Maggie Thatcher beat her to it. It was just – 'I wanted to be first and she got there first.'[81]

Emma Saunders (now Hood), who also joined St Hugh's in the autumn of 1974, remembers that May was 'always very focused on going into politics. I remember her saying, "One day I will lead the [Conservative] Party." Theresa had this steely determination to make the grade at a very senior level in politics.'[82] Denise Patterson (née Palmer), who studied Geography with May, has said: 'Theresa was always interested in politics in a quiet, serious way. She wasn't a flamboyant character but she had this burning ambition.'[83] May's confident words – which she repeated to many of her friends at St Hugh's – show the steel of her early ambition. Interestingly, however, they are remarks she seems to have made only to her female contemporaries and Philip, with none of her male Oxford friends recalling any sense in her of a desire to run for the highest office.

May, Collinson, Patterson and a fourth member of the group, Louise Rowe, were taught political geography by tutor John Patten, who later married Rowe and went on to serve as Education Secretary under John Major. May came to see Patten, whose politics are on the right of the Conservative Party, as something of a mentor, and enjoyed discussing current events with him. While, as always, May worked hard at her studies, she was not considered to be particularly academic compared to some of her peers, and ended up with a Second in her 'Mods', the name given at Oxford to the first-year exams.

As Margaret Thatcher became Leader of the Conservative Party in February 1975, dashing May's ambitions to become the first woman to hold the post, she stepped up her involvement with the Oxford Union. In the cut-and-thrust, somewhat unreconstructed world of the Union, her quiet manner earned her a reputation as being 'sweet' but unlikely to make it to the highest level of politics. Michael Crick has said: 'Of all the political people at Oxford, she seemed the least likely to succeed.'[84] As would often be the case during her later parliamentary career, reports of her speeches focused on her appearance. In one debate, on abortion, she was described as 'the statuesque Miss Brasier burning with emotion in her red dress'.[85] May herself has said that the Union stood her in good stead for Parliament: 'Having been at Oxford and having the opportunity to debate in the Oxford Union Society is a very good preparation in a sense for the House of Commons, for politics.'[86]

If she was not rated as a star of the future by her Union contemporaries, May made more of an impression at Oxford's second debating club, the slightly less rarefied Edmund Burke Society, where the themes of the debates were more humorous in nature. In her last year at university, she was the club's president, overseeing proceedings while wielding a meat tenderiser in place of a gavel. Debates were held on Sunday nights in the Morris Room of the Union, and accompanied by liberal amounts of port wine drunk from tiny glasses. Among the light-hearted motions May suggested for debate as president were 'That this House thanks Heaven for little girls' and 'That life's too short for chess'.

Rajiva Wijesinha, the future Sri Lankan writer and politician who knew both Philip and Theresa May at Oxford and was a fellow member of the Union and the Edmund Burke Society, has said:

> I was very fond of Theresa Brasier at Oxford – she had a lovely sense of humour, vital in the Union – but never imagined that she would be PM. No one spotted any star potential in the fairly quiet blonde girl, but she was a good speaker at the Union and an active member of … the Edmund Burke Society … It would never have occurred to me forty years ago that she would be the most successful in politics of our contemporaries … Theresa laughed at most things in those days, with an equanimity un-usual in Union politicians. That was why perhaps she was not really one of the breed, giving way soon to her boyfriend, Philip May. They were an extraordinarily nice couple, far nicer than the other political couples of that time. I did find her mentor, Alicia Collinson, much more fun, along with her boyfriend Damian Green … But Alicia could be sharp when she wanted to be, and could make enemies, whereas Theresa had none.[87]

Busy with the Union and the Edmund Burke Society, and deeply in love with Philip, May's last year at Oxford was by far her most enjoyable. She must have felt some pangs of regret when she was forced to leave her happy life behind. But, in May 1977, she grad-uated with a Second Class degree, at the age of just twenty. While she immediately began working in London's Threadneedle Street, having been taken on as a graduate trainee at the Bank of England, her heart remained in Oxford, and she travelled back frequently to see Philip and their friends. At the start of his second year, Philip succeeded May as president of the Edmund Burke Society, and he in turn was followed by Damian Green, who next served as presi-dent of the Union, in the winter of 1977. During Philip's tenure,

May travelled back to Oxford to oppose the motion 'Sex is good…
but success is better'. Philip, speaking after her, declared he was
doing so to 'deny everything' she might say on the matter. In the
Union, too, Philip continued to play a leading role. He acted as
proposer during one debate in June 1978, arguing that the Callaghan government's 'industrial strategy will ruin British industry'.
At the height of the Winter of Discontent eight months later, he
opposed miners' leader Arthur Scargill on the motion 'That private
enterprise has failed the British economy'. He was seen as lacking
a little élan, however. The Oxford University student newspaper
Cherwell regularly described his contributions as 'boring', and he
was dismissed as a 'man of straw'.[88]

The following winter, with Philip entering his final two terms at
Oxford, *Cherwell* ran an item in its gossip column claiming, somewhat snidely, that May had issued him with an ultimatum: marry
her or break up, as other hot couples on campus had. 'I gather the
same fate awaits Philip if he hesitates any longer in announcing his
intention to make an honest woman of the vicar's daughter,' the
diary said.[89] Whether or not May had indeed issued an ultimatum,
by the spring term of 1979, the couple were engaged. She would
later describe 'saying yes when my husband asked me to marry
him' as the most important decision of her life.[90] Somewhat unexpectedly, Philip was by now president of the Oxford Union, having
emerged victorious from what was (as always with the triannual
Union elections) a hard-fought, somewhat murky contest, when
some low political skulduggery felled his more fancied opponents.

The Conservative side of the Oxford Union at the time was divided into factions: the 'Magdalen set', based around the college of
the same name, and a grouping known as the 'Dinhamites' after a
former president, Vivien Dinham, who had allegedly been 'knifed'
by Benazir Bhutto a few years earlier and forced to stand down.[91]
The Dinhamites included among their number Damian Green and
Chanaka Amaratunga, founder of the Sri Lankan Liberal Party
before his death in a car crash in 1996. But when the Dinhamites erupted into bitter infighting after Amaratunga unexpectedly

switched sides to support Magdalen's favoured candidate, Alan
Duncan, in the winter term of 1979, the various factions were left
in chaos and without an obvious candidate for the following term's
contest.

Much as his wife would be nearly forty years later, once all the
fratricidal bloodletting was finished and the bodies were being
counted, it was the unassuming, unfactional Philip May who was
best placed to come through the middle. He would go on to narrowly beat a Labour candidate for the presidency. Rajiva Wijesinha
has said: 'Philip was the obvious choice. I cannot remember anyone
else being elected president with such a near approach to unanim-
ity.'[92] Duncan was also impressed. He has described his successor
as a 'steady, logical speaker, sort of undemonstrative, thorough and
likeable. [He had] a dry, northern sense of humour, with a wry grin
rather than a belly laugh.'[93]

Theresa continued to take part in debates during Philip's tenure,
and was elliptically described in a pamphlet listing the events lined
up for the term as a 'presidential aide'.[94] Philip tempted some notable big names along to speak at the Union, including the disgraced
former US President Richard Nixon. For his farewell debate, he
selected the topic of the professionalisation of sport; he and Theresa lined up against Bobby Charlton, the former England football
captain, and a young Australian student called Malcolm Turnbull
– currently his home country's Prime Minister.

Some who encountered the Mays after Oxford are surprised to
learn that it was Philip who enjoyed the more glittering university
career of the pair – and wonder why he did not seek high political
office himself. John Elvidge, who met the couple in the late 1980s,
when they were active in their local Conservative Association in
Wimbledon, says: 'Philip was absolutely charming, very self-effacing.
It was a long time before I realised that he was president of the
Oxford Union, because, presumably deliberately, he had decided to
put himself in the background.' Alan Duncan has suggested that,
despite the apparent success of his time as president of the Union,
Philip did not feel comfortable in the spotlight. 'He had a different

approach to life. Theresa was prepared to step into the light of public gaze. Philip preferred to be more in the background. It's as simple as that.'[95]

Sandra Burling, who became a friend of the couple at around the time May was seeking selection for a parliamentary seat in the run-up to the 1992 general election, believes that Philip may have tried and failed to win selection himself in the early 1980s. It is a story the MP Keith Simpson also heard. He says:

> I remember Damian [Green] telling me years ago that because Philip was very active in university politics, the game plan with her and Philip was going to be that he was the one that was going to [try] to be an MP. They were both going to try for it, but she was going to go into the City [first] and earn the money.

Burling adds:

> By the time we met them [in the late 1980s], he was chairman of the local Conservative party and she a local councillor, and the one who got selected. I think he might have gone for selection earlier. They had already decided, I guess, or maybe things had just happened, that that's the way things were going to be. I think it was something that was already settled.

May herself has denied suggestions that she and Philip struck a 'deal' over who would take the more high-profile political career. 'No, there was no deal at all. I mean, yes, he was president of the Union, he's politically interested, which is a huge advantage – it means he understands campaigning and things like that. But no, it just happened...'

Philip graduated from Oxford in May 1979, joining May in the City of London, where he found work at the stockbroking firm de Zoete & Bevan. The following year, in September 1981, the couple were married at St Mary's Church in Wheatley; Theresa's father, the Rev. Hubert Brasier, presided over the ceremony. It was a traditional white wedding, with May, a few weeks shy of her twenty-fourth birthday, resplendent in a long, fitted gown and veil and holding a bouquet of red roses. Family and friends from Oxford filled the pews of the church she had worshipped in so many times as a teenager, and where she had listened to countless sermons from her father.

Shortly before May had left Wheatley for university, her mother Zaidee had begun to develop symptoms of multiple sclerosis, an autoimmune disorder which affects the central nervous system. May has said of her mother's disease: 'Multiple sclerosis is one of those things that can plateau for quite a period of time and then the condition can deteriorate. So at the end, and in fact by the time of my wedding to Philip, she was a wheelchair user.'[96] The Mays' wedding photograph shows Zaidee in her wheelchair, dressed in pink, clutching a large hat and smiling at the camera. Hubert, standing beside Theresa and behind his wife, is a stooped figure who looks far older than his sixty-three years. On May's other side, Philip and his father John wear identical smiles and traditional grey morning dress. Joy May is in yellow. It was one of the last occasions the family would all be together.

May had been married for just over a year and had turned twenty-five a few days earlier when her tight-knit family circle was torn apart by the death of her beloved father Hubert in a car accident in October 1981. The Rev. Brasier had been driving in his Morris Marina to conduct an Evensong service at a nearby church, St Nicholas's, in the village of Forest Hill, less than two miles from his home in Wheatley, on the other side of the busy A40 dual carriageway. As he approached the road, which connects Oxford and Gloucester with the M40, he edged his car forward onto the central reservation – and into the path of an oncoming Range Rover which was being driven at seventy miles per hour by Desmond Hampton, a stockbroker from London. Hubert suffered head and spinal injuries and died a few hours later in hospital. Following an inquest, Oxford coroner Nicholas Gardiner ruled his death an accident. An account of the inquest in the local paper at the time described the moments leading up to the fatal collision: 'I noticed the Marina stationary in the central reservation and it appeared to stay there for quite a bit of time,' the report quoted Hampton as saying.

It appeared to move slowly and then hesitate. 'I began braking and tried to get in the left-hand lane,' [Hampton added]. The Range Rover collided with the front off-side wing of the Marina … Mr Gardiner said it appeared that Mr Brasier had crossed from the slip road and was moving across the A40 in front of the Range Rover. It may have been difficult for Mr Brasier to see the Range Rover approaching head on. He said the crossing had to cope with slow local traffic and long distance fast moving traffic. 'That's never a good thing as far as road safety is concerned.'[97]

Emma Hampton, now Groslin, was in the Range Rover with her father, mother Kitty and sister Vanessa when the crash happened. Describing the accident recently, she said:

We were on our way from Gloucestershire on a dual carriageway back to London after visiting our grandparents. I was asleep in the back of the car with my younger sister and the next thing I knew, I woke up and it had happened. I knew it was a local vicar and he had been on his way to give his last service of the day. I had no idea he was Theresa May's father … It was an awful event.[98]

For most of her life, May has been reluctant to speak about her father's death, even to very close friends, viewing it as a highly private matter. Alicia Collinson did not find out about the accident until some years later, and members of May's staff confirm that it was a taboo subject.

Within a few months, at the beginning of 1982, Zaidee too had died, succumbing to her multiple sclerosis. Now May was an orphan, and the small circle that sustained her had shrunk to just one: Philip. It was enough. As the couple drew even closer, they lay down the foundations of a marriage which many of those who have met them have described as one of the strongest in politics. Philip became May's family; in the absence of both parents and children, all she would have for the rest of her life. While May does have friendships and an extended family of cousins, uncles and aunts, no one else would be particularly close to her until her fifties, when she met her two devoted advisers Nick Timothy and Fiona Hill. May herself credits Philip with getting her through the dark days after Hubert's and Zaidee's deaths: 'I think, crucially, I had huge support in my husband,' she has said. 'And that was very important for me. He was a real rock for me. He has been all the time we've been married, but particularly then, being faced with the loss of both parents within a relatively short space of time.'[99] May still feels the loss of her parents today, telling one interviewer of her regret that they never saw her become Prime Minister. 'I wish my parents could see it,' she said. 'I've had a number of letters of congratulations from people that I've known over the years and people who've known my parents in the past, all of whom have said the same thing: they would be extremely proud of me. I hope they would be.'[100]

CHAPTER IV

FROM THE CITY TO THE COUNCIL

The City of London was going through a turbulent time as both Theresa and Philip May arrived there in the late 1970s. These were the dying days of the Callaghan administration, its soundtrack the death-rattle of the post-war consensus with its basis in Keynesian economics. Governments of both stripes had failed to get to grips with the twin evils of industrial unrest and soaring inflation. In 1976, just before the young graduate Theresa May joined the Bank of England, James Callaghan had been forced to go 'cap in hand' to the International Monetary Fund (IMF) to request a £2.3 billion rescue loan to tackle the UK's soaring debt crisis. In return, the Labour government was forced to agree to cuts in public spending. The shame of having to endure outside interference in British economic policy would have a profound effect on both the nation's politicians and, perhaps even more so, the economists at the Bank of England. By the following year, when May began working at Threadneedle Street, where the Bank was established in 1694, inflation still stood at 15.8 per cent, lower than the 24.2 per cent reached in 1975 but still crippling for the economy.

The Bank of England was not the obvious career choice for a recent Geography graduate, but, given May's now established passion for politics, it turned out to be an astute move, as economics took centre stage in the nation's political life. She began working as a junior analyst. During her early career at the Bank, May's bosses were largely focused on dealing with the aftershocks of the IMF crisis. She was assigned to the Wilson Committee, a body headed by the former Prime Minister Harold Wilson, which examined the functioning of the country's financial institutions, which were thought to bear a heavy responsibility for the poor performance of British manufacturing by 'starving industry of the funds it needs'.[101] By the time the committee reported its findings, in June 1980, the entire economic landscape had changed, however.

In May 1979, just as Philip graduated from Oxford and prepared to begin his career at de Zoete & Bevan, the Conservatives had swept the sclerotic Callaghan government out of office. Under the guidance of her friend and economic mentor Sir Keith Joseph, the new Prime Minister, Margaret Thatcher, now began a free market revolution which would change the British economy for ever. Gone were the Keynesian orthodoxies of the previous thirty-five years, to be replaced with an exciting new economic approach: monetarism. Seven years later, on 27 October 1986, Philip's working world too turned upside, as the Thatcher government threw open the doors of the Square Mile in an overnight deregulatory revolution known as the Big Bang. It was a time of high drama. May has said: 'There was great excitement about the development of financial services when I worked in the City.'[102] Both Mays, therefore, had a ringside seat at perhaps the most exciting period in the City's long and tangled history. And while, in their calm and considered way, neither of them became too carried away by the excitement of it all, never falling into the trap of becoming money- and status-obsessed yuppies, what they witnessed during their time at the country's financial heart would shape their economic and political outlook.

By the early 1980s, and despite her lack of an economic background, May had gained a reputation as one of the most adept of the young analysts working at the Bank of England. She was moved to the Monetary Policy Group, a fascinating experience for a young Tory at a time when the Bank was grappling with the new Conservative government's radically different economic approach. Charles Goodhart, who would later become a member of the Bank's Monetary Policy Committee and is now a professor at the London School of Economics, headed the small team of four or five people working on the Monetary Policy Group at the time. He remembers May, who assisted with his research, as one of the brightest of the many young people he encountered during his long career at the Bank. Describing their work on the Monetary Policy Group, he says:

> [It] was practical rather than theoretical. We did forecasting. [This] was a government with a different viewpoint from the rather standard Keynesian analysis that had gone on before-hand. The Conservatives were trying to use monetary targetry [controlling money supply] as a way of steering the economy and of bringing inflation down ... and it was a period of quite a lot of difficulty between the Bank of England and the Conservative government.

Goodhart says May seemed not to be handicapped by not having studied economics at university. 'She was very competent, very reliable, very steady [with] a very clear mind,' he says.

> She was a very, very good research assistant. I admire[d] her very much. She was clearly one of the best people I had working for me in my many years at the Bank: competent, reliable, steady, adult, unflappable. I thought she was a very fine person. I enjoyed having her working for me.

Goodhart says that the team could not help but be aware of the high political drama being played out as they grappled with the raw data relating to the government's economic plans. In 1981, the then Chancellor, Geoffrey Howe, delivered a Budget that would prove one of the most controversial in modern political history. Its purist monetarist prescription for the chronic 'stagflation' crippling the economy (by controlling the money supply through tax rises and public spending cuts) was criticised in a letter sent to the *Times* newspaper and signed by 364 economists. While Howe was still delivering his Budget statement, a number of Conservative MPs walked out of the Commons Chamber in disgust. In his Budget response, Michael Foot, the Leader of the Opposition, described it as a 'Budget to produce over three million unemployed' – a prediction that would come true within two years.

'You couldn't really deal with the economic policy, including monetary policy, unless you appreciate[d] the political positions of those in power, and those who might come into power,' Goodhart says. 'The two [were] somewhat indistinguishable.' For the young Theresa May, long fascinated by politics, the opportunity to play a role in implementing the government's radically new economic policy must have been exhilarating. Goodhart is clear, however, that his team were too focused on their work to discuss their own views. Nor did Goodhart socialise with May, though as he was twenty-five years older than his young protégé, this was not peculiar. With May's attention largely focused on travelling back to Oxford during her early years at the Bank and, later, on her political activities in her and Philip's new home of Wimbledon, she does not seem to have found time for other friendships at the Bank. Despite this, Goodhart insists that May could be fun. 'She's not a stuffy person in any way,' he says. When Goodhart moved on, May wrote him a poem 'as a sort of leaving present'. It was devoted to the hilarious topic of monetary policy – an ode to the 'wayward mistress' of Sterling M3 – the term used by economists to describe the widest definition of money supply.[103]

Philip May also thrived in the City during the 1980s. In 1983, he moved from de Zoete & Bevan to Prudential Portfolio Managers, where he worked as a fund manager, investing money for the pension funds of major companies and managing relations with clients. While never seen by colleagues as among the flashier of the new breed of very successful traders, he was quietly successful, once receiving an award at the Extels, known as the City's Oscars. Philip would stay at Prudential until 2000, when his division was sold to Deutsche Asset Management, with whom he remained with for another five years. For the past decade he has been employed at the US fund managing firm Capital Group, where he no longer directly manages money but is in charge of client relationships. One colleague has said of Philip recently: 'Around the office, he is a fairly head down type of guy. There is a stereotypical investment manager with a big ego – he's not like that at all. He has very good integrity and never trades off his wife's name.'[104]

Back in the 1980s, it was now the turn of Theresa May to make her next career move. In 1985, a group of major banks, including the Bank of England, set up a new body called the Association for Payment Clearing Services (APCS), to oversee the smooth flow of money at home and abroad, including inter-bank clearing, debit and credit transactions, cheques and electronic transfers. May joined the new organisation, first as a financial consultant and senior adviser on international affairs, and eventually rising to become manager of the European Affairs Unit, which at the time looked after the new CHAPS system of transferring sterling and other European currencies.

As she had been at the Bank of England, and would be again for much of her political career, May was one of the few women at the association. Her friend Sandra Burling, who got to know her in the late 1980s, says that, like her at the time, May sometimes found this unsettling.

> We met from time to time for lunch, because she was in the City and I was working just outside the City. We talked about the general issue of what it was like being a woman in an organisation when you're trying to get up as high as you could.

May, however, has said of her time in the Square Mile:

> I have worked in two traditionally male-dominated careers, firstly in banking before moving into politics. In both professions I have never allowed being a woman to be an excuse or an obstacle. When I was working in the City I tried to see myself as a person, achieving what I did on my own merit not because of or in spite of my sex.[105]

During May's time at the APCS, she would gain valuable experience of negotiating within Europe, at this stage in her life relishing the challenge of working with our continental neighbours. One of the highlights of her time at the association came in April 1993, when her name featured for the first time in the national press, in an article in *The Guardian* headlined 'Transferring money abroad'. 'The banking industry in Europe is trying to develop better cross-border payment systems,' she was quoted as saying, somewhat dryly.[106] It was a quote of only fourteen words, but it would have been enough to start off her in-laws' scrapbook of press cuttings. May's role at the association was more senior than that she had held at the Bank of England, but it was clearly less exciting. With her political activities now taking off, that may not have been a bad thing.

Soon after their marriage, the Mays had bought a house on Replingham Road, Wimbledon, close to where both Theresa's father Hubert and her grandfather Tom had grown up. Perhaps it was this familial connection, coupled with the fact that neither of the young newlyweds knew London particularly well, which drew them to the area. Their new home was modest in size and located in a relatively unfashionable part of Wimbledon, but it was handy for work, with Southfields Underground station a ten-minute walk away and a connection straight into the City. By the end of the decade, thanks to the good money both were by now bringing in, the couple were able to move to a much larger house a mile away, on Dora Road, which, friends say, became their pride and joy. They hired an architect and converted the entire ground floor of the house into a large kitchen, where Theresa would cook up feasts for their new friends in the neighbourhood, leaving Philip to do the washing up afterwards.

The couple joined the local Young Conservatives soon after moving to Wimbledon in 1980. They stepped up their careers as local party activists shortly before the 1983 general election, not in Wimbledon but in the neighbouring parliamentary constituency of Mitcham and Morden. Wimbledon at the time was a safe Conservative seat which had been represented in the Commons since 1970 by Sir Michael Havers, usually with majorities of more than 10,000.

However, just across the border in Mitcham and Morden, which represented the other half of their local council area, Merton, and was therefore seen as something of a sister constituency, the battle-field was far more exciting.

The year before the general election, in June 1982, the Conservatives had unexpectedly snatched the Mitcham and Morden seat, riding a wave of patriotic fervour and enthusiasm for the Thatcher government inspired by the Falklands War, which was then in its final stages. The contest had been triggered by the defection of the sitting Labour MP, Bruce Douglas-Mann, to the new Social Democratic Party (SDP). Mann had decided to stand down and hold a by-election, which he assumed he would win with ease, a view shared by his Tory opponents. None of them could have predicted the Falklands factor. The Conservative candidate, Angela Rumbold, went on to win with a majority of more than 4,000, helped by her Labour and SDP rivals splitting the left-of-centre vote. Mitcham and Morden remains the last seat to have been gained by the Conservatives at a by-election when in government. The party was determined to hang on to it at the 1983 general election. And the Mays stepped forward to help them do just that.

Oliver Colvile, now the MP for Plymouth Sutton and Devonport, was working as Angela Rumbold's election agent and was in the party's office in a former haberdasher's shop when the Mays walked through the door. He says:

> She walked in with Philip, and they said, 'We're here to … help.'
> I was leafing my way through *The Sun* with my feet on the table.
> And I think I said: 'Oh, well, you'll find the leaflets over there.'
> I didn't know she was a future Prime Minister – she was just a
> voluntary worker who'd turned up to give us a hand.

Within days, Colvile came to see what a valuable asset the Mays were. He says:

> I became quite good friends with them. They were both very

young people, and I was quite young too, I must have been about twenty-two, twenty-three at the time. What was so wonderful was having some people who were different from the kind of crusty people we usually had around us. They were very keen, enthusiastic.

He adds: 'It was very nice to actually have some people who were normal.'

After the election, which Rumbold held comfortably, she too remained friendly with the Mays, becoming particularly close to Theresa. She would be instrumental in helping to secure May a seat of her own more than a decade later. Colvile says of Rumbold, who died in 2010: 'She and Theresa were quite close. I got the feeling they ended up talking to each other quite a bit. She ... was able to give her some good pointers. I think her time with Angela was quite important – she was very dynamic.'

For now, however, both Colvile and Rumbold encouraged the Mays to begin their Tory careers by becoming more involved in politics on a local level. Philip became party chairman in their council ward of Durnsford and May drew up plans to run for Merton Council, while serving in a variety of roles, including chairman of the party's social committee. Both were by now committed campaigners, spending their weekends knocking on doors and canvassing their neighbours. Still a dedicated communicant, May also became secretary of the Wandsworth Deanery Synod, helping to run the administration of Anglican churches in the area.

Oliver Colvile says that while he remembers the Mays as 'very sociable', their activities were largely focused on politics. There would be occasional Sunday lunches at their house, but trips out to pubs or restaurants were rare. The Mays would sometimes hold party meetings in their living room, which, fellow Wimbledon Tories remember, was covered in prints from the cricket bible *Wisden*. During the drinks afterwards, the talk was all of politics. 'They were very committed,' Colvile says. 'It was all part of that [time in the] 1980s when, frankly, there were still dragons to be slayed. Mrs Thatcher was about to start her second term. They were most certainly quite big players in Merton politics.' From her cosy suburban sitting room, papered with images of cricketing greats from the past two centuries, May now sketched out her plan to take her first big step on the political path that would ultimately lead to 10 Downing Street.

May won a seat on Merton Council at her first attempt, on 8 May 1986, representing Durnsford Ward. She was not yet thirty years old. The race had been tight, and her majority over her Labour rival was just 100. Overall, the contest for control of the borough between the Conservatives and their Labour opposition had also been closely fought, with the Tories emerging with a majority on the council of just one. May's hard work in securing her victory had been crucial to her party's success in capturing the balance of power. Merton was an interesting borough, containing pockets of deprivation alongside the handsome villas and large detached houses around Wimbledon Common. John Elvidge, who became the council's leader, says:

Merton is a very, very big borough. It runs all the way from Wimbledon Village with the All-England Tennis Club and multi-million-pound houses right down to the poorest parts of Mitcham. If you're on the council you do get a lot of correspondence, sometimes in green ink, complaining about this, that and the other.

With her arrival on the council in 1986, May brought a touch of glamour. Siobhain McDonagh, the future Labour MP who would go on to defeat Angela Rumbold in Mitcham and Morden in 1997, was herself just twenty-six and had already been on the council for four years when she first encountered May. She says the slightly older woman seemed to her to be completely alien, the age gap between them, in McDonagh's eyes, placing May in a different era. The Labour councillor also found May imposing, usually wearing high heels which added inches to her already statuesque height of 5 feet 8 inches. McDonagh describes May as different 'in terms of sophistication, and social class-wise, and just about everything. She was much, much better dressed; she had more money than I had.' Despite both being decades younger than most of their fellow councillors, the two young women did not bond. 'She didn't have small talk,' McDonagh says.

> She was four years older than me and I was [more concerned about] righting wrongs. This was a pre-feminist time for the Conservatives, they regarded women and any form of positive discrimination as anathema. She gave this strange speech about how the economy was going well, and that hem-lines had increased. And I remember looking at her and thinking, 'Do you really want to be talking this nonsense?' I thought she was very much a Tory ... I felt she would have regarded me as an oik.

Friends and fellow councillors from the time remember that May was always 'impeccably dressed' for council meetings, often wearing dresses in her favourite colour, red, accompanied by crimson lipstick. Arriving for meetings at Merton Civic Centre by Tube, direct from her job in the City, she sometimes adopted a pin-striped suit, and the blouses with large bows popular for a time during the 1980s. McDonagh adds: 'My memory of her is that she wore very fashionable clothes, but she wasn't part of that yuppie mindset. Her choices were more risqué than her personality would suggest. Perhaps you have to have a bit of your life which is a bit more jazzy and exciting.' May has said of her look at the time: 'When I was working in banking in the '80s, there was a lot of power dressing. Now the fashion is to look more natural, so I suppose my style has changed with the times.'[107]

Oliver Colvile remembers that May stood out from her fellow councillors from the start: 'She was the rising star, quite obviously. She was quite dynamic.' McDonagh adds, however, that May's clear ambition was not appreciated by everyone on the council, including some members of her own side. 'I think she was sincere in everything she did, but being on Merton Council wasn't the summit of her political dream, it was a step to somewhere else,' McDonagh says. 'She used to raise the hackles. Merton was very staid. The average age of councillors was much older. She was part of a generation of Tories who came in '86 who looked very different from the other members of their group, who were members of the local establishment.' McDonagh recalls an occasion when an older Conservative councillor, whose husband was a former leader and who was considered part of the 'Wimbledon establishment', turned to her while watching May address the council chamber to say: 'Who does that woman think she is? Look at us, we're here because we mean it.' McDonagh adds: 'I thought, "Blimey, you must feel strongly to say something nice to me."'

David Williams, a Conservative councillor at the time, has said, however, that on the whole May was popular with her Tory peers.

> Theresa was someone who did her homework. She took decisions with her head, even though she had a warm heart. She was also a very good ward councillor. We used to make fun of her for a voicemail message she left for her ward constituents. She would say, 'Your call is very important to me, please leave me a message and I will try and get back to you.' It's common nowadays but back then it wasn't. We all thought it was a bit over the top. But she truly meant it, and it showed how much her constituents meant to her.[108]

Oliver Colvile adds: 'She is incredibly polite. I never heard her interrupt anybody in making a point, and I've always been very struck by that. Being the daughter of a vicar, I think that must have been a very significant part of her view of life.' Philip Jones, a Labour councillor, has said: 'We all saw her as one of the more competent Tory councillors at the time. She made a positive contribution to the area and was quite a lively character.'[109]

In her second year on the council, in the autumn of 1987, May led the opposition to plans put forward by the authority's non-elected officials to cash in on its housing stock by mortgaging its property portfolio and investing the money on the stock exchange. A similar scheme had already been put into place in nearby Hammersmith, where councillors boastfully described it as 'liquid gold', garnering themselves a great deal of attention in the world of local government. But May was wary; rightly, as it would turn out. At a meeting of the Conservative Group in the autumn of 1982 which was expected to rubber-stamp the plan, it was agreed, at May's urging and despite the clamour of her fellow councillors to cash in on the expected bonanza, that a final decision would be deferred for a few weeks, until 20 October. 19 October 1987 has since gone down in history as Black Monday, with millions of pounds wiped off the value of UK shares. Oliver Colvile estimates that had May not fought the proposal, the taxpayers of Merton would have lost out on around £75 million. 'It was a bit touch and go,' he says. 'Theresa was very much against this. She is someone who knows the difference between right and wrong. She was very much involved in trying to stop this taking place.' The natural caution of the child of the vicarage had proved an invaluable check on the gambling instincts of many of those swept up in the excitement of the age of easy money.

John Elvidge was among those who was impressed with May's fortitude, and, in 1988, two years after she was first elected to Merton Council, he appointed her as deputy leader. He says: 'She was very dedicated, very hard-working. She stuck her nose to the grindstone and got on with the job. She was a pretty good public speaker, and you could absolutely rely upon her. That's why I made her my deputy.' Asked for his impression of May's politics at the time, Elvidge adds:

> She was quite practical. Certainly she was on the right-ish wing of our party. Merton is a very mixed borough, so you have to be centrist, really, but within that sort of right-wing leaning, she was actually very practical and pragmatic. I certainly am … a one Nation Tory and I just felt that Theresa was of the same ilk, and we worked together very happily. What you see now is what you saw then. She was fully rounded, I think, in her early twenties.

Elvidge says he found May a perfect deputy during what could be stressful times.

> We had a very tight majority of one, and there was no curfew on our meetings, so we ended up in the last year or so having council meetings that went on until one or three in the morning, so it was really quite tiring. [May] was very personable, and she was pleasant, and ... she was very collegiate. I had no trouble with her at all, we got on famously.

At the same time as he made her deputy leader of the council, Elvidge appointed May chairman of the Education Committee, one of the biggest jobs in local government. Her experiences on the committee led to an interest in education policy which continues to this day. The role was a challenge, as Merton was in the process of moving from what was known as a three-tier education system, made up of primary, middle and high schools, to a two-tier one, with youngsters spending a full five years at secondary school. Elvidge says of his decision to appoint May to the education role: 'It needed somebody who was prepared to talk to the parents and talk to the staff. Merton had always been a three-tier education system and moving to a two-tier ... was very difficult.' May also had to deal with anger from a group of parents opposed to the council's proposal to close a local primary school; with elections looming, it was a decision that was soon reversed. So keen was May to ensure that schools in Merton were able to attract the best talent that she insisted on paying teachers at the higher, inner London rate.

While May became increasingly involved with politics at a local level, she also began dipping her toe into the national scene, becoming a member of the party's London Area Women's Committee. Just as she would throughout her career, she began to seek out like-minded female Tories, now meeting another mentor, Jacqui Lait, who would soon become the MP for Hastings and Rye. Lait introduced her in turn to Sandra Burling, at the time an accountant and a neighbour in Wimbledon who had done some work for the party on women and taxation. Burling and her husband, Jeff Wehner, became close friends of both the Mays. She says of Theresa:

> She's very warm and amusing in private. Philip is a lovely guy too, and the four of us just really hit it off. We would see them on quite a regular basis. Our conversations ranged broadly, covering whatever was current at the time, not political in the sense of the politics and the people and the machinations of the various parties, [we were] just talking about the issues.

In 1990, May stood for re-election in Durnsford. Her campaign was run by another young local activist, a 26-year-old Chris Grayling, who would follow May first on to Merton Council in 1998 (by which time she had been elected to Parliament), and then, in 2001, into the House of Commons. Twenty-six years after he first ran an election for her, Grayling would serve as May's campaign manager during the 2016 Conservative leadership contest; she would go on to appoint him to her first Cabinet, as Transport Secretary. Grayling now joined the group of hard-working Merton Tories. He has recalled a characteristic incident which took place during one local election:

> She and I [were] standing on the doorstep side by side, canvassing in a [council] by-election in Wimbledon. At the end of it she told me off because I had only asked for the voting intention of the person who answered the door, not the rest of the household. That's Theresa, she's very thorough.[110]

May and Grayling's long association, with its roots in local government in south London, has led to suggestions of a Merton Mafia, not quite rivalling the Notting Hill set of the David Cameron era, but certainly providing a source of support May can rely on. John Elvidge says:

> There is something in it [although] I wouldn't want to call it

'Mafia'. I guess when you know people in your twenties and thirties and you trust them then, then you trust them when you get to higher things. You know their qualities and you can talk to them knowing it won't go any further.

With Grayling's help, May increased her majority in Durnsford in 1990, but on a borough-wide basis the Conservatives were less successful, and the council fell to Labour.

That same year, Philip May became chairman of the Wimbledon Conservative Association. The job became more challenging than expected when, in the run-up to the 1992 general election, the sitting MP, Charles Goodson-Wickes, an Army reserve officer who had succeeded Sir Michael Havers in 1987, was called up to serve in the First Gulf War. Philip was left to head the Conservatives' defence of the seat, helped by Oliver Colvile, who was still the local agent. 'Despite his very demanding City job, Philip took his job as one of my bosses very seriously,' Colvile says. 'We used to speak at least a couple of times a day. When I made the occasional mistake he would dismiss it as "fog of war, dear boy, fog of war".'

With the Conservatives in opposition on the council, May now concentrated on representing her constituents in Durnsford, raising their concerns about the increased traffic in the area on match days at Wimbledon Football Club's Plough Lane ground, and taking an interest in the development of a new shopping centre. She would later be criticised for opposing the football club's application to move to the former site of the nearby dog racing track. As a result, Wimbledon went further afield, first to a ground share at Crystal Palace's Selhurst Park stadium and, eventually, sixty miles away to Milton Keynes, a source of regret for many residents of south London then as now.

May cheerfully admits she is no football fan; she has never seen her current constituency's local club Reading play. Cricket was and continues to be her game. The Mays do also share a love of horse racing, however. In the mid-1990s, they co-owned a grey gelding called Dome Patrol, which racked up two wins at Lingfield Racecourse in Surrey. The horse's trainer, William Muir, has said:

> She came racing twice with her husband – they were in a small syndicate with a few other people from London. Dome Patrol did okay for them – he wasn't a world-beater but he did win us a couple of races. She was always very, very pleasant when she was at the races and always very nice when I met her.[111]

By now, the Mays had been married for ten years and were both approaching their mid-thirties. At the start of their marriage, they had naturally assumed that they would become parents before too long. It was not to be. For most of her career, May has been understandably reluctant to discuss her sadness that she could not be a mother. This has not stopped speculation about the reasons she never had children. It is one of the many examples of the double standards in politics that childless men do not receive anything like the attention that women who have either chosen not to or have been unable to become parents face. Men also seem to be spared the pointed insinuation that women who are not mothers lack some kind of maternal feeling, disqualifying them from fully empathising with those they seek to represent. It is perhaps a sign of progress that it was Andrea Leadsom's clumsy attempt to highlight May's childlessness during the final stages of the 2016 leadership race that led directly to the latter's coronation.

Over the years, the Mays' inability to have children was a source of sadness, but friends say they refused to be defined by it. They did seek the advice of doctors, but, in an era when fertility treatment was new, it was a route they either decided not to take or simply did not succeed with (May has always declined to say which). Her reluctance to discuss what she sees as a highly personal matter extends to her friends as well as the wider public. Sandra Burling says:

> That was not a conversation that we had. We did not touch on it. And, actually, I really understand that. It was such a private thing. People were much more private then than certainly the current generation, who share everything. If you had issues like that, it was something you dealt with [in private].

Burling is one of many of the Mays' friends and colleagues who stress how much both Theresa and Philip seem to enjoy the company of children. They are not the type of childless couple who go out of their way to avoid young people. Theresa May is a godmother many times over. Having been asked to take on the role for the first time at a young age, she once joked: 'I was a teenage godmother.'[112]

Until recently, on the rare occasions May was asked outright why she did not have children, she refused to answer. In 2002, she told the interviewer Matthew d'Ancona: 'I don't think it's an issue. And I don't think it should become an issue…'[113] To the *Telegraph*'s Rachel Sylvester the same year, she gave away only slightly more, saying: 'It wasn't a choice. But I'm not going to talk about it further.'[114] And there May was content to leave the matter, not discussing the subject in public for many years. It was not until 2012, while already Home Secretary, that she gave a wide-ranging interview to the *Telegraph*'s Allison Pearson, in which she said of the couple's hopes to become parents: 'It just didn't happen. This isn't something I generally go into, but things just turned out as they did. You look at families all the time and you see there is something there that you don't have.'[115]

May did not speak on the subject again until the 2016 leadership contest, when, in another interview, she made it clear that she did not expect any pity. 'Of course, we were both affected by it. You see friends who now have grown-up children, but you accept the hand that life deals you,' she said.

Sometimes things you wish had happened don't or there are things you wish you'd been able to do, but can't. There are other couples in a similar position. I'm a great believer that you just get on with things. There are lots of problems people have. We are all different, we all have different circumstances and you have to cope with whatever it is, try not to dwell on things.[116]

As so often in her life, May turned to her husband and politics to get her through the disappointment of not becoming a mother. As the '90s began, both Mays were spending much of their free time knocking on doors and campaigning on behalf of the party. It is a habit they continue to this day. John Elvidge says: 'They both worked extraordinarily hard. In those days we used to have a lot of ward functions. It was [a] highly marginal [area,] so there was a lot of campaigning to do all over the place. She was a very fierce campaigner for the Conservative cause.' Oliver Colvile agrees: 'What I would stress is that they come out very much of a grassroots political background. She is a very, very good, assiduous community campaigner. I was thrilled to see she still goes out knocking on doors in her constituency, despite being Prime Minister.'

Many of May's colleagues in Parliament also believe that her background in local activism gives her an understanding of the grassroots party that younger figures such as David Cameron and George Osborne, who entered the world of Westminster at a young age, lack. Liam Fox, whom May would appoint to her first Cabinet, says:

> Theresa wasn't one of those people who did [the Conservative] Research Department, [ministerial] special adviser [route]. She's been up through the fighting side of politics, through being in local government, and she understands the Conservative Party. One of my problems sometimes about Conservative politicians is those who've only been the professional politicians, they've never fought council elections in no-win areas, they've never had to face that hard pounding of the pavements, making the Conservative case where there's little resonance, and people forget that Theresa has done that. When they say, 'Oh, she's tough,' or whatever, well, what she is, is experienced. And she's had to be a fighter in a way that people [of] our age group who came through the fire of those early Thatcher years, when being Conservative was not flavour of the month, [had to be]. [A] lot of those who are younger, who have never experienced that, don't quite grasp the steel that [was] forged in those fiery times.

It was a steel May would need in her next political challenge.

CHAPTER V

THE CANDIDATE

Theresa May was driving, late at night and alone, through the windy County Durham countryside. It was March 1992, and May's mood was low. In a few weeks, at the forthcoming general election, her beloved Conservative Party seemed almost certain to be ejected from office after thirteen years in government. She herself appeared to be making little progress in her campaign to woo voters in the 'no-hoper' safe Labour seat of North West Durham she was fighting for the Tories. At the age of thirty-five, May's childhood dream of becoming an MP seemed further away than ever. Never one to give in to despair, however, May was determined to rally. As she continued on her journey back from an election meeting on the other side of the constituency, she reached over and switched on the cassette player. The uplifting sounds of Henry Purcell's Rondeau from *Abdelazer* filled the car. As she later said: 'I had to drive through the pitch black night and as I drove through on my own I put the tape of this music on and it lifted my spirits.'[117] The music was the theme for the Conservatives' 1992 general election campaign. It would prove to be an inspiring choice. By the end of the contest, the party was not only back in government but their intrepid candidate for North West Durham had taken a huge stride forward in her personal crusade to enter Parliament.

Just as many of her fellow councillors in Merton had long suspected, May had begun giving the idea of running for higher office serious thought by the end of the 1980s. She was encouraged in her ambitions by Angela Rumbold, who, fortuitously, had been appointed Tory vice-chairman for candidates. John Elvidge, the former leader of Merton Council, says:

> It was obvious that she wanted to become an MP. It wasn't an overwhelming ambition that she disclosed to everybody and talked about. [But] it was quite clear that she was going places. Angela Rumbold was the MP for Mitcham and Morden. Of course, there weren't very many female MPs in the Commons at the time, and she was very concerned to develop Theresa's political career as much as possible. I think they saw in each other a common drive and ambition.

Oliver Colvile adds: 'She knew exactly where she was going at that time. She was very good friends with Angela Rumbold. Angela was very keen to help women into Parliament. I would say that Angela was pretty fundamental in trying to make sure that Theresa did that.'

As a first step, May needed to get selected as a candidate for a parliamentary seat. This was not an easy task for any woman seeking to enter the Commons on behalf of any major political party at the time. Following the previous election, in 1987, there were just forty-one female MPs in Parliament, making up only 6 per cent of the House of Commons. In the Conservative Party, which had seventeen female MPs, the process for selecting parliamentary candidates had not changed for decades, with little adjustment made to encourage the entry of women into public life. Would-be MPs faced a somewhat bizarre approval process before their names could be added to the official candidates' list. Well into the late 1990s, prospective Tory MPs were still required to attend a weekend selection event, where they were grilled for their views on subjects such as the Common Agricultural Policy and observed by party officials to make sure they used the correct knife at dinner. Future Cabinet minister Cheryl Gillan entered Parliament in 1992. She says:

In the old days, to get on the list, you were given this two-day examination. You were given a number, your name was stripped out, and you were tested for everything, including your capacity for alcohol at the dinner, and you were given a soft interview and a hard interview. It was all based on military style. It was quite tough to get through.

Candidates deemed to have cut the mustard were then eligible to apply to Conservative associations with vacancies for a prospective MP, either because the incumbent was retiring or because the constituency had not returned a Tory at the last election. The local party would draw up a longlist and then a shortlist, and successful applicants were put through another round of interviews and assessments. These could again be a challenge, particularly for women. Keith Simpson, the MP for Broadland, who came into Parliament along with May in 1997, says:

You've no idea how the Conservative Party's changed. I thought I'd lost it in my final selection because the big question was where did I stand on capital punishment. There was a woman, a very clever councillor of mine, whose husband was a farmer, and she'd stood, and they had both gone for an interview. There was this dreadful drinks thing beforehand, and [a local] woman said to him, 'Well, what's going to happen if we select her? … She's going to be away in London.' And [a] man actually said to him: 'What are you going to do for sex?'

May's friend Sandra Burling recalls discussing the problem with her:

In general at the time it was so difficult to get women selected. It was often the local committee, who may well have been partly female, but were very traditional and were looking for the traditional husband with a wife who would get involved with the party. We had general conversations about how difficult it was. When

you look back, it's hard to believe that that was the environment
that we grew up in. There were still at that time Conservative
clubs which wouldn't allow women in the bar!

May herself has insisted that she never personally experienced discrimination when seeking a seat, although she heard the horror
stories at the time. 'Through my selection process, I never felt that
I was being treated differently,' she has said. 'Other people have
come across the awkward questions that shouldn't be asked. You
know, "How will your husband cope if you're a Member of Parliament – who's going to cook his dinner?"'[118]

May's gender was certainly a factor in her first attempt to be
selected, however, in the safe Labour seat of Holborn and St
Pancras, north London, in 1989. Those who were at the selection
meeting, where she lost out by just one vote to a civil servant called
Andrew McHallam, are divided over whether her sex was a positive
or a negative. 'The men all voted for her because she was wearing a
leather skirt – they loved it,' one local Tory said recently.

'It was too much for the women, however, and they voted against
her.'[119] On the night, May was given a sanitised version of events,
only to learn the truth many years later. 'I was told that I was wearing a bangle and it was irritating people by banging on the table all
night,' she said in 2011, while addressing a group of north London
Tories including an activist familiar with the Holborn selection.
'But tonight I've been told it was all about the length of my skirt.'[120]

May's wardrobe was clearly acceptable, however, to party
members in the constituency of Durham North West, where she
successfully won selection later that year. Like Holborn, it was a
'no-hoper', a safe Labour seat where an aspiring politician such
as May would be expected to cut her teeth and show off her talents before applying for a more winnable constituency next time
around. Sandra Burling says: 'I don't think there was much hope
or expectation she would win, but it was a rite of passage. She had
clearly committed herself to politics, because anyone who takes on
a seat in Durham when they live in Wimbledon and work in the

City is really very committed.' The constituency of Durham North West had been represented in Parliament since 1987 by Labour's Hilary Armstrong, who had succeeded her father, Ernest, who had occupied the seat since 1964. The area was far from Tory country. Armstrong says: 'It was seen as a fairly safe Labour seat. [The Conservatives] mainly saw it as a sort of testing bed for people who would go elsewhere and do other things, and this would be their first attempt at a parliamentary seat.'

Undeterred, May threw herself into the constituency with characteristic zeal, even purchasing a house in the smart village of Lanchester, about eight miles west of the City of Durham. This was a highly unusual move for a candidate with no local connections fighting a 'no-hoper', and raised a few eyebrows back on Merton Council. Siobhain McDonagh says: 'She went up to Durham and she bought a house, and we all thought, "How did you afford another house?" House prices weren't what they are today, but [Wimbledon] wasn't a cheap place to live.' Armstrong believes that in fact the house purchase was a canny move:

She bought a house in the constituency in one of my best villages. It's a commuter village to Durham, so plenty of university people living out in a nice part of the countryside. She kept the house for two years, from being selected until after the general election, then she sold it. And because it's a good village, houses are reasonably easy to sell.

The Mays spent the next two and a half years after her selection travelling between Wimbledon and Durham, often inviting friends north for the weekend to help them out campaigning. Burling says: 'She and Philip were going up there on a regular basis, which must have been quite a killer with all the travelling. She was up there every spare minute so I don't think anybody could have faulted her on commitment and effort.' Hilary Armstrong says that May had clearly thought strategically about how best to maximise her vote, and made the somewhat surprising decision not to take part in any public hustings. 'She set out, there's no doubt in my mind, to secure the Tory vote,' Armstrong says.

> She didn't do any public events, as it were. She didn't do any hustings, I never met her until the count, which was quite unusual. What she did was, she would meet Tory members in their houses and they would invite neighbours they thought might be interested in a chat with the Tory candidate. And that worked very well for her. She concentrated in the areas of the constituency where the Tory vote was, and she more or less sustained the Tory vote.

May's campaigning style may have [been] dismissed by her Labour opponent as chatting to Tory voters over 'tea and cakes',[121] but she assiduously put in the hours. It was not always an easy task. The journalist Anne McElvoy encountered May at this time. She has written: 'I watched May stand and lose in 1992 in my native Labour constituency: North West Durham. There she stood out as a rare breed of visiting Tory, on one occasion arriving to canvass farmers and finding herself ignored because two cows were about to calve.'[122]

May and Armstrong's Liberal Democrat opponent in Durham North West at the 1992 general election was a Newcastle University student who, at twenty-one years old, was the youngest candidate for any political party in the country. His name was Tim Farron and in 2015 he would become his party's leader. An election flier produced by the local newspaper at the time has become something of a collector's item as a result. It shows May with short, spiky hair and plentiful makeup, rather a metropolitan look for Durham at the time. Armstrong remembers being struck by May's appearance when the two finally met at the count on election night, 9 April 1992:

> She was very pleasant, she was very polite. She was in a very sharp, royal blue suit; very short skirt. She had short hair, which in those days was quite dramatic because it was short with the white streak. She looked … like a City lady. I … thought it was

interesting that by the time she went for Maidenhead [ahead of the next general election] she was looking very different. I think she'd realised that she wanted to soften the look of being a woman from the City.

No matter how obvious in advance the outcome of an election in an individual constituency is, gathering for any count on the night of a general election is always an exciting occasion. For May, fighting her first parliamentary seat, it must have been utterly thrilling. When the result came through, it was clear that her hard work in shoring up the Tory vote had paid dividends. While she had never been expected to win, she helped ensure that the Conservative tally dropped by only thirty-eight votes. At a time when the Conservative vote was falling nationally, it was an indication of how effective she had been as a campaigner. As the night wore on, all those present at the Durham count could not help but be aware of the drama taking place around the country, where, contrary to all predictions, the Tories were holding on. Defying expectations, Prime Minister John Major ended the night as he had started it, in power, winning a record number of votes and a majority of twenty-one. With or without the stirring music of Purcell, May's spirits must have been high as she drove away from Durham and back to Wimbledon. Her party was still in power in Westminster and she had acquitted herself respectably enough to be confident of winning selection for a more favourable prospect at the next election. Armstrong for one was sure she would see her again. 'I was fairly confident she would become a Member of Parliament at some stage,' she says, 'but I was fairly sure it would be in the south-east.'

The next seat May took on was indeed in the south-east, but the circumstances were even less propitious than in Durham. In February 1994, the campaigning Labour MP Jo Richardson died following a long illness, triggering a by-election in her constituency of Barking, in Essex. Barking had been Labour since the seat's inception in 1945, but at the time of her death, Richardson's majority stood at just over 6,000. In other circumstances, the Tories might have hoped to have scored a victory. However, when the by-election was announced, the Major government was in trouble. The party was still reeling from the disaster of Black Wednesday eighteen months previously, when Britain had crashed out of the European Exchange Rate Mechanism, the Chancellor, Norman Lamont, having squandered millions trying to sustain UK membership, destroying the government's economic credibility for good. An attempt by John Major to get his party back on track by using his 1993 speech to Conservative Party conference to urge the country to get 'Back to Basics' with a return to old-fashioned values backfired spectacularly. A string of sex scandals broke that winter and spring – including affairs by David Mellor, Tim Yeo and Stephen Norris – turning the party into a laughing stock.

The Back to Basics debacle reached its peak at around the time the Barking by-election was called. Essex Tories were now on the lookout for a candidate who, as the *Evening Standard* put it, was 'unlikely to have many skeletons in her cupboard'.[123] Step forward the vicar's daughter, Theresa May. Following her selection, one local activist was quoted as saying, 'proudly', 'She is very boring.'[124] As in Durham North West, the local association may also have seen the logic in selecting a female candidate to fight a Labour woman – this time her opponent was the formidable Margaret Hodge, a former leader of Islington Council who would go on to serve as a senior minister in the governments of Tony Blair and Gordon Brown. By the time the by-election got going in the spring of 1994, Barking's Tories were realistic about May's prospects. Brian Cook, a Conservative councillor on the local authority at the time, has said: 'Tory candidates who want to be MPs go for seats like Barking, where it would be a miracle if they won, as a testing ground.'[125]

A few weeks before polling day, which took place on 9 June 1994, tragedy struck – and May's task became even harder. Labour's popular leader John Smith died suddenly of a heart attack. Hodge was buoyed both by the wave of public sympathy over Smith's death and by the growing antipathy towards Major's government, as it began its death spiral into electoral disaster a few years later. With a new generation taking over the Labour Party – Tony Blair would be elected leader a few weeks later – it felt as if the country was ready for a fresh start. Labour threw everything it had at the seat, with big names including Blair, Barbara Castle and John Prescott turning out to campaign for Hodge.

Again, May chose not to take part in public hustings, preferring to concentrate on existing Tory voters. But, as ever, she put in the hours and worked furiously at her campaign. The local paper's coverage of her election launch reported her boasting of a full schedule of activities and achievements, remarkable given she had been in the area for only a few months. 'I've talked to people affected by the proposed Channel Tunnel link. I've put their fears to the Transport Minister … I have taken up traffic problems with the local council. I've put people's fears about the future of accident and emergency services in the area to the Health Authority…' she said.[126]

The voters of Barking were unconvinced, however. On the night of the by-election, as they gathered at the town's Broadway Theatre, May met Margaret Hodge and the Liberal Democrat candidate, Gary White, another 21-year-old student, for the first time. Hodge recalls: 'My memory of her at the count was of woman who chose to dress like an "Essex girl" and that she wore the most eye-catching shoes. So that trait was already there.' It was an impression shared by Jeannette Alexander, a Labour councillor who campaigned for Hodge at the by-election. She has said that May appeared to be trying to 'make herself look like an Essex girl, or what she assumed we looked like'. She went on: 'She had very blond hair [and a] short cerise-coloured suit. Within a couple of weeks of [the by-election] in Barking, she wore long skirts and pearls ready for the next seat she tried for.'[127]

When the announcement of the by-election's outcome came through in the early hours of 10 June, it was a humiliation for May and the Conservatives. The party's vote had dropped by an eye-watering 10,000 to just 1,976, falling to third place below White's Lib Dems. The *London Evening Standard* newspaper was scathing: 'The most pathetic Essex jokes today were the ones

wearing blue rosettes as the voters of … Barking delivered a humiliating by-election … blow to the Tories,' it said.[128] In her victory
speech, Margaret Hodge declared: 'What Barking has said tonight,
the people of Britain will say at the next general election when they
return a Labour government.' Her prediction would prove correct.
While the result was not entirely unexpected, May must have been
bitterly disappointed. She was, however, assured by Angela Rumbold and others at Conservative Central Office that the blame lay
not with her personally, but with the dying government. She was
encouraged to seek another seat.

May approached the forthcoming general election with as much
impatience as Hodge. Having earned her spurs in two no-hopers,
she focused on securing a safe seat, targeting only those with a realistic prospect of victory. As the months and years passed, with his
majority slipping away thanks to a string of by-election defeats and
New Labour under Tony Blair enjoying soaring opinion poll ratings,
John Major saw no value in going to the country early, however.
May, Hodge and the rest of the country would have to wait nearly
three years for the general election. In May's case, that turned out
not to be a bad thing. Despite her optimism about landing a safe
seat, as the months passed she was turned down by constituency
after constituency.

Her gender may well have been a factor. By late 1995, eighteen
months before polling day, the Conservatives had yet to select a
woman for a constituency considered safe. At times, May came
frustratingly close. She was the runner-up in the Gloucester seat of
Tewkesbury, and made it onto the final shortlist in two Kent constituencies, Chatham and Aylesford, and Ashford. In all three, a man
was selected in her stead, Ashford plumping for her old Oxford
friend Damian Green. 'I do remember her going through the process,' says Sandra Burling.

> That was what you had to do at the time. There were seats coming
> up, and there was a merry-go-round, and there were a bunch of
> people who were approved candidates, who had to go through

the same process every time: cocktail parties and selection meetings and all that kind of stuff.

Alarm bells began to ring at Conservative Central Office (CCO),
where party chiefs at least recognised that more women MPs were
essential to broaden the Tories' appeal, even if local party activists
were resistant. Concern rose further as it became clear that, following Labour's adoption of all-women shortlists for selection contests
in half of winnable seats, a large phalanx of new female Labour
MPs was likely to enter the Commons. With three 'Tory Dames'
due to retire – Jill Knight, Peggy Fenner and Janet Fookes – some
officials at CCO began to fear that the female representation on the
Tory benches after the election could look pitiful in comparison.
May's fortunes as she continued to trudge the constituency circuit
began to take on a greater significance. Briefed by a party insider
about the problem in October 1995, *The Guardian* wrote:

> Conservative election strategists are desperate to see a woman
> candidate selected to fight a safe Tory seat at the next election as
> a clutch of Westminster's 'Dames of the Shires' prepare to stand
> down – and Labour imposes a series of all-women shortlists. In
> the coming weeks officials will watch two women candidates in
> particular: Eleanor Lang [*sic*], former special adviser to cabinet
> ministers, and Theresa May, a Wimbledon-based councillor and
> City professional.[129]

In October 1995, May threw her hat into the ring for selection
in Maidenhead, a new constituency in Berkshire, to the west of
London, which was being formed from two existing constituencies,
Windsor and Maidenhead, and Wokingham. The new seat was
forecast to be a safe win for the Conservatives. As a result, competition for the candidacy was fierce, with more than 300 applicants,
including a number of sitting MPs who risked losing their existing
seats. But the local party was clear it had no interest in opting for a
'chicken runner', the derogatory name given to existing MPs who

abandon a marginal seat for a safer option just before a likely election defeat. Sir Paul Beresford, the MP for Croydon Central, Eric
Forth, representing Mid Worcestershire, and the late John Watts,
MP for Slough, all failed to make the Maidenhead shortlist. Other
candidates, including Sir George Young, whose Ealing Acton seat
was disappearing in boundary changes, and a 29-year-old former
special adviser turned media PR manager called David Cameron,
were also rejected. What the constituency wanted was a fresh, vig-
orous and committed MP. The final shortlist came down to May,
Nick St Aubyn, who would go on to become MP for Guildford,
and a tall, intelligent business consultant called Philip Hammond.
Twenty-one years later, May would appoint Hammond as her
Chancellor.

In November 1995, to her delight and the relief of Conservative
Central Office, May was selected to fight the seat of Maidenhead at
the forthcoming general election. Philip Love, who was a member
of the selection panel, has said it was May's long years of service in
local government that tipped the balance in her favour. 'We were
determined we wanted someone who'd been a councillor, as she
had been in Wimbledon,' he said. 'She was bright and articulate,
and once we'd appointed her we found we'd got two for the price
of one because Philip [May] has been brilliant for the area, too.'[130]
Emma Hobbs, another member of the panel, made clear to reporters at the time that May's gender was not a factor in her selection.
'When Theresa May walked into the room, there was this air of
total confidence. That was it for me. She has such a wonderfully
positive attitude. The fact that she is a woman made no difference,
as far as I was concerned.'[131]

Sandra Burling says May was overjoyed that her long search for a
winnable seat was over. 'She was really thrilled. It was not so far for
London, and worked for both of them really well. I think the only
thing she was sad about was they had to leave their beloved home
in Wimbledon.' In Tory HQ, there was also joy. Eric Pickles, who
was serving as a party vice-chairman, recalls Michael Trend – at
the time the sitting MP for Windsor and Maidenhead and due to

take on the new seat of Windsor when the constituency was split –
running into the office of Brian Mawhinney, the party chairman.
'We've got a woman!' Trend shouted. 'Yes! She's called Theresa
May.' 'We were so excited, as you can imagine,' Pickles adds.

Despite her own excitement, May, as usual, did her best to keep
her head, despite the growing press attention she attracted as one
of the few new female Tory candidates. 'It never changed her personally,' says Sandra Burling. 'She remained very grounded.' A few
days after her adoption, under a headline reading 'Candidate who
left ministers trailing', *The Guardian* produced the first profile of
May in the national press. In it, she resisted the temptation to blow
her own trumpet, saying of her selection over higher-profile candidates: 'At the end of the day the Association must have decided that
I had the right experience and qualities for the job.'[132] Elsewhere,
May said she was looking forward to life in Parliament with excitement 'but not a little trepidation', adding that she did not expect
the Commons to be 'an unfriendly place for women'.[133] Asked what
Philip made of the still novel experience of becoming the husband
of a Tory MP, May added:

> There's absolutely no question of my husband rustling up sponge
> cakes. He is completely supportive, but he has his own job to
> do. He knew of my interest in politics when we first met, and
> understands how important it is to me. He is well aware what the
> job will involve.[134]

As the general election approached, and the dramatic effect that
the introduction of all-women shortlists by the Labour Party would
have on the makeup of Parliament became increasingly apparent,
it was natural that May's views, as one of the few female Tory candidates standing in a safe seat, were sought. She was clear in her
stance. 'I'm totally opposed to Labour's idea of all-women shortlists
and I think they are an insult to women,' she said. 'I've competed
equally with men in my career, and I have been happy to do so in
politics too.'[135] Nor, at this stage, did she anticipate that she would

go on to become perhaps the most important campaigner in her party for increased female representation in the Commons, in fact sneering at the suggestion that she could use her new position to help other women. 'I became a candidate on my merits,' she said. 'I have no burning ambition to promote women's parliamentary rights.'[136] John Elvidge says of May's attitude towards women's equality before her election to Parliament: 'I don't think Theresa was a feminist in the sense we now understand it. But she was certainly somebody who thought that women in politics deserved to be there, ought not to be second class.'

Within a few months of her selection, the Mays had sold their beloved house on Dora Road in Wimbledon, and bought – for cash – a five-bedroom country house in the village of Sonning, on the banks of the River Thames and towards the west of her new constituency. Sonning was described by Jerome K. Jerome in his gentle late Victorian comedy novel *Three Men in a Boat* as 'the most fairy-like little nook on the whole river'.[137] Today the village is home to multi-millionaires attracted by the easy commute to London and celebrities drawn to its old-world charm. The Led Zeppelin guitarist Jimmy Page, former England football manager Glenn Hoddle and the illusionist Uri Geller have all lived in Sonning in recent years. The current biggest star in the village, however, possibly eclipsing even the Prime Minister in some fans' eyes, is the Hollywood actor George Clooney, who, with his wife Amal, bought a house there in 2014.

The Mays made Sonning their home in every sense of the word. They shop in the local high street (May famously refuses to have her groceries delivered because she enjoys pottering around the Waitrose store in nearby Twyford); she has her hair done at the local hairdresser, the Hair Company, a five-minute drive away in Wargrave, and they dine out at a posh curry house, Malik's, in another local village, Cookham. Naturally, she worships most Sundays at Sonning's church of St Andrew's, where Philip acts as a server at Holy Communion. It is said there are few people in Sonning whom May has not met.

Despite her gruelling schedule first as Home Secretary and now as Prime Minister, May maintains her reputation as a devoted constituency MP. Andrew Griffiths, currently the MP for Burton, who worked for May in the mid-2000s, says she memorised the entire rail timetable for trains running between Maidenhead and London 'so when a new timetable comes out, she knows whether [her constituents are] getting a better or worse service'. Griffiths adds:

I don't think there are many of my colleagues who are as dedicated in terms of time served and effort put in as a constituency MP than Theresa. Even though she was Home Secretary, even though in opposition she was a shadow Cabinet member, she would never jeopardise the time that she would spend knocking doors in [Maidenhead]. It always had to go in the diary, it was always the priority. She might be on the *Marr* programme, she might be dashing to Manchester to make a stump speech, but she'd still be absolutely determined that her door-knocking time in the constituency had to remain.

Philip Love, president of the Maidenhead Conservative Association, confirmed recently that May continues to work hard for the local party, despite her elevated status: 'She always joins us when we go out canvassing, even for the council election. You wouldn't believe people's faces when we knock on the door and say: "Would you like to have a chat with the Home Secretary?" They'll be even more surprised now.'[138]

May began her first campaign in Maidenhead as she would every other election she has fought in the seat since: with a tireless and dedicated relish. Over the following eighteen months, she launched flurries of press notices, knocked on thousands of doors and turned up to endless events. She even persuaded John Major to attend a birthday celebration in her honour a few days before she turned forty, in October 1996. Her hard work paid off.

On election night 1997, Theresa May turned up to her count wearing a royal blue skirt suit and matching rosette. (It was an outfit she would soon come to regret, saying just five years later: 'I was looking at a photograph of the 1997 election campaign yesterday … and I thought: "My God. Did I really have that hairstyle? And that Tory blue suit?"')[139] As the result was read out, she learned she had scored a resounding victory, capturing 25,344 votes, just shy of 50 per cent of the vote, and a majority of 11,981. Beside her on the stage, Philip beamed his approval. Their joy was not unadulterated, though; nationally, the Tories were on course for their worst defeat since 1906. By the end of the night, more than half their seats would be lost, and only 165 Conservatives would return to the House of Commons. May has said of her emotions on the night: 'I had won the seat, so there was celebration for that, but huge sadness of course for what had happened overall.'[140] That night, in an interview with her local paper, May made clear how eager she was to get to work. 'It's very exciting and also quite daunting because being an MP is quite unlike any other job,' she said. 'It's going to be important to get one's feet under the table fairly quickly. I will work hard and do my best to fulfil the expectations placed on me.'[141] It was a vow she would strive to fulfil for the rest of her political life.

CHAPTER VI

MEMBER OF PARLIAMENT

The House of Commons that Theresa May entered in May 1997 was a place radically transformed from any other time in its long history. Most obviously, there were now 120 female MPs, with women making up more than 18 per cent of those taking their seats on the green benches. But that was not the only change. With the arrival of New Labour, the Commons was suddenly younger than it had been, more reflective of society outside Westminster (although scarcely more diverse, with only three new ethnic minority MPs). The sheer scale of Tony Blair's landslide in winning 418 seats, a majority of 179, did not just mark Labour's greatest ever electoral victory; it also had profound implications for their Conservative opponents. The Tories relished their nickname of the 'natural party of government', a testament to their post-war domination. Having been in office since 1979, most Conservative MPs had never served in opposition, and many were appalled at the prospect. With the number of Tories in the Commons falling by more than half, from 343 to 165, there was also the human drama involved in watching so many friends and colleagues lose their seats overnight. For new MPs, such as May, there was a sense of 'there but for the grace of God go I', as promising candidates failed to capture seats assumed safe for the Tories. All those who took a place on the alarmingly empty opposition benches after the 1997 general election would experience a sense of survivors' guilt. The speed with which they were able to pick themselves up following the devastating election result would determine who would thrive, and who would sink, in the years to follow.

As a direct result of the Labour landslide, the 1997 Conservative intake of new MPs was far smaller than usual, and included only five women: Julie Kirkbride, Eleanor Laing, Anne McIntosh, Caroline Spelman and Theresa May. In total, there were now just thirteen female Tories in the Commons. While many of her fellow newbies were already familiar with Westminster, having worked at Central Office or as ministerial advisers, it was a foreign world for May. She did have a few friends in the parliamentary party, including her mentor Jacqui Lait (Angela Rumbold had not survived the election rout), and two new MPs she had met on the candidate circuit, Tim Loughton and Eleanor Laing. In her first days in Parliament, she was also able to stick close to a couple of Oxford friends; Alan Duncan had become an MP in 1992, while Damian Green was a fellow member of the 1997 intake.

May's high profile during the years she was seeking a seat, and Tory HQ's overt desire that, as a woman, she succeed in capturing a safe berth, meant that on her arrival in Parliament she was something of a celebrity. On her first day, she allowed a BBC camera crew to film her as she got ready to leave her home in Sonning for Westminster. Later that afternoon, she was asked by a reporter if her Tory bosses would be sending her to 'charm school' to prepare for life as an MP. No, she snapped, seeking to contrast herself to what she perceived as the new identikit 'Blair babes': 'We actually let people be themselves.'[142]

Many Tory MPs were aware who May was, although she did little to push herself forward. Cheryl Gillan says: 'It was very different to being a woman now. Because there were so few of us, we were entirely obvious. She did quite a bit of fighting of seats, she did a by-election, so she'd been knocking on the door.'

Andrew Lansley, who came into the Commons alongside May in 1997, adds:

When we arrived, it turned out there were far fewer of us than we had expected. People in what were thought of as safe Tory seats with majorities in double digits had fallen. I don't remember Theresa holding back, exactly, but certainly there were others who had done more in the way of networking than she had ahead of getting there.

Like many Conservative MPs who had survived the election, Gillan remembers the post-1997 period as an unhappy time. 'She came into a really depressed Tory Party. There weren't very many of us left; we had been wiped out. We were at the bottom of a canyon and the sides were very steep. You felt guilty: "Why should I survive when others didn't?"'

As she found her feet in the Commons, May would often be mistaken for one of the 101 New Labour 'Blair babes', an error she claimed not to mind,[143] using her maiden speech to describe how one Labour MP, Ernie Ross, had urged her to sign up for the ballot for Private Members' Bills. 'He was astounded when I looked at him and said, "Why?" Obviously, he had mistaken me for one of the ladies on the other side.' Sandra Burling says May's friendships with younger, more enlightened men from the new intake initially made up for the lack of women Tories:

> She had good relations with a number of people like Damian Green, people who clearly had a very different view of the world from perhaps the more senior people in the party … [They were] people who were used to having women as colleagues. So I'm not sure it would have been quite as isolating as it sounds, thirteen against [152], because to that number you could have added quite a few of the younger men.

Inevitably, however, May stood out. Cheryl Gillan says: 'We were so outnumbered by the Labour women. She struck me when she came in as being quiet and controlled and serious and sensible. I don't really remember anything negative except thinking she was very reserved. I almost thought she was slightly shy.' Michael Howard, who had just lost his job as Home Secretary, had met May before the election, and respected her from the start: 'I first came across her, and I remember it quite well … when she was still a candidate,' he says. 'I [had] gone to an event where she was … for candidates. And she made quite an impression, she asked quite a critical question … She was definitely someone with strong views and a strong personality who knew her own mind.'

If Howard had been impressed by May, the feeling was mutual. Following the election defeat, John Major had immediately announced his resignation, and the contest to replace him began at once. May decided to back Howard – although she played her cards close to her chest. Andrew Lansley says: 'I don't remember who Theresa was supporting. Not for the first time, she wasn't overtly committed.' As she went to vote in the first round of the leadership contest, on 10 June, May teased journalists waiting outside Committee Room Fourteen in the Commons, where the ballot boxes were held, saying: 'I haven't declared to anybody how I am voting.' 'Well, you won't get a job, then,' one reporter shouted back.[144] Unfortunately for both May and Howard, he came last in the first ballot and was forced to drop out of the race.

William Hague, who had served as Welsh Secretary in the Major government, now sought May's vote for himself. He says:

> It was a desperate situation in 1997. She was one of the new MPs, of whom there were only about twenty or thirty on the Conservative side, and they were thrown into a leadership election, which started immediately. So people like me had to get to know them quickly. I can't honestly remember the first meeting with her, but I will have met her during that leadership election, because I met all the MPs. As far as I was aware she wasn't supporting me in that leadership election. That was my first acquaintance, trying to get her vote in that leadership election, and probably failing to do so, as far as I'm aware.

By the end of the nine-day contest, Hague, despite his youth and relative inexperience (he was still only thirty-six) had emerged as the candidate seen by many Tory MPs as best-placed to stop the former Chancellor, Kenneth Clarke. Although Clarke was popular with the public and highly experienced, his attachment to Europe disqualified him from the leadership in the eyes of Conservative MPs still bruised from the battles over Maastricht of the previous parliament. As a new MP, it was a concern May felt less than her more established colleagues, and Hague believes she backed Clarke in the final rounds. He says:

> She was assumed to be supporting Ken Clarke in that election, rather than me … although since I got more votes than we were aware we were going to get, I don't really know who voted for me. It illustrates that she came from what one might regard as the moderate wing, if she came from any wing, of the Conservative Party. She wasn't coming from the right. The right wing, the very Europe-conscious MPs, were all supporting me to stop Ken Clarke: 'Don't let a pro-Euro person become the leader.' And clearly that wasn't an obstacle to her at the time.

If May was backing Clarke, she was to be disappointed for a second time. In the final round of the contest (which at this period was decided solely by MPs), William Hague was elected leader with 55 per cent of the vote.

Hague did not hold May's apparent vote in the leadership election against her. Instead, he paid attention to the early Commons performances of all the new MPs as he scrambled to assemble a front-bench team with a substantially depleted parliamentary party. Andrew Lansley was among those of the new intake who realised there were opportunities to be had, both to use the unreconstructed procedures of the House to hold an inexperienced government to account, and also for those new MPs who found themselves at least medium-sized fish in a tiny Tory pond to show off their talents.

> We were shell-shocked to start off with because there were so

many of those you knew who just didn't make it. A number of our older and senior colleagues were so devastated by it all that they retreated into their shells. In order to keep opposition going, the new intake had to get very involved. That shell-shocked aspect didn't last long for the new intake because there was so much to do. It was before family-friendly hours and guillotines, and it wasn't long before the Tories, as they got used to opposition, began to realise they could inflict damage if they worked hard at it. This was through-the-night stuff, keeping the government to account line by line in committee. We were very effective in the House, really forcing Labour to work hard. The idea was to build up credibility, to revive our thinking.

May was among those who realised the opportunities the changed circumstances of the House of Commons presented for dynamic new MPs. On 2 July 1997, she used much of her maiden speech to praise the concept of choice in education, particularly opposing Labour's plan to abolish the assisted places scheme, under which the government paid for free or subsidised entry to private schools for academically promising youngsters from low-income families. 'The assisted places scheme not only helps bright children, but is an important way of helping children from difficult family back-grounds or with particular social needs,' she told the House.

It was the first of a series of interventions in Parliament that caught the attention of her Conservative colleagues – including William Hague. Within a short space of time, May came to relish speaking in the Commons Chamber, finding something new in it each time. 'The interesting thing about the Chamber of the House of Commons is that you never quite know when you walk into it what the mood of the Chamber is going to be,' she has said.[145] Others came to enjoy listening to her. Vince Cable, the future Liberal Democrat Cabinet minister, who entered Parliament at the same time as May, says: 'She was quite a good performer in the House of Commons. Her voice helps; this quite mellow, nice without being too posh [voice] was very effective. Her manner and her voice make her look comfortable in that context, and she was always very self-assured.'

At the end of July, May was named by *The Times* alongside Eleanor Laing, Nick St Aubyn (the man she had beaten to the selection in Maidenhead), and John Bercow, the future Commons Speaker, as a 'Backbencher to Watch'. She was said to have 'impressed the whips with her willingness to attack…'[146] May was now appointed to serve on the influential Commons Education Committee, under the chairmanship of Margaret Hodge, who had defeated her in the Barking by-election three years earlier. Hodge too was impressed by May's contributions, and her interventions in committee attracted further attention. At the end of the year, *The Independent* singled her out as the most talented newcomer of her intake, saying she was 'turning heads'[147] and suggesting that Hague promote her to his front bench. He soon did just that.

In June 1998, just over a year after she had entered Parliament, May took her first step on the political ladder when Hague heeded *The Independent*'s advice and appointed her as a junior member of the shadow Education and Employment team. She was one of a number of the 1997 intake, including Eleanor Laing and Damian Green, who, thanks to the Conservatives' sheer lack of numbers following the election, were promoted to the front bench with dizzying speed. It was a role that suited her perfectly, given her previous chairmanship of the Merton Education Committee and long-standing interest in education policy.

May's colleagues largely felt that the promotion was deserved, although there were a few mutterings about the haste with which the new female MPs were being pushed to the front. Keith Simpson says:

No doubt about it, it was an advantage, because there were so few of them, to being a woman. William Hague was facing a blitz of criticism, both from the press [and] obviously the Labour Party [about the lack of women at the top of the party]. A lot of the men, not of the '97 intake but earlier, felt, 'Well, crumbs almighty. You just had to be a bloody woman with a short skirt and you got [promoted].' That was unfair, because two of the ones who were promoted almost straight away were [the able] Theresa and Caroline Spelman. [And we] were almost all catapulted into being front-bench spokesmen straight away.

Andrew Lansley adds:

She was quite clearly among the intake one of the most intelligent. There were a lot of bright people … but there was something about the niceties of those days that meant the women who were most likely to be able to carry a job were able to get preferment quickly.

Hague himself admits May's gender was a factor in his decision to put her on the front bench, but insists it was not the only, or even the principal, reason:

At that time, we only had about eleven or twelve [women] and I wanted to promote people much more quickly [than usual]. She [had] acquitted herself very well in Parliament as a new member. I was very impressed with her, and of course I wanted to assemble a front bench of many talents, of different opinions.

Along with the Education brief, Hague made May the party's spokesman on women, a role she would continue to play on and off for the next fifteen years.

The shadow Women's Minister appointment turned out to be an apt one. Within her first months in the Commons, May had come to two realisations: the first was that the lifestyle of an MP could, if she allowed it, play havoc on both her health and her relationships outside Parliament. The second was a growing sense that, despite her confidence before the general election that she would not struggle as a woman in a male-dominated arena, the Commons was in fact a deeply inhospitable place for female Tories in particular. The two were not unconnected. From the start, as a person used to exerting a high degree of control over every aspect of her life, May found the unpredictable ways of the Commons a challenge. A few weeks after entering Parliament, she admitted she was finding the adjustment difficult: 'It's an entirely different lifestyle … As someone who has come from a business background – well, the uncertainty, the chaotic nature of the diary…'[148] Sandra Burling says, however, that May did not grumble about her new life. 'She just got on with it. The thing about Theresa is she wasn't somebody who would say, "Oh my God, this happened today…" or "Somebody said this…" I don't ever remember Theresa complaining about anything or anyone.'

The demands on May's time were draining. While she purchased a small flat in Pimlico, a ten-minute walk from the Commons, to stay in when there were late votes, from the start, May was determined to travel back to Maidenhead as often as possible, a commute of at least ninety minutes. In part, this was down to necessity. Shortly after her entry into the Commons, the Liberal Democrats had launched a strategy known as 'decapitation', which involved targeting high-profile Conservatives. Despite her nearly 12,000 majority, May was a target. Keith Simpson says: 'Many of us, and she was one, within a year the Liberals were talking about "decapitating" her. So from the very beginning we were all not only working hard here, because there were so few people, but we were also working hard in the constituency.'

Faced with a gruelling schedule, unpredictable hours and a requirement to eat most of her meals away from home, May decided to take a practical step towards ensuring that she did not fall victim to the ill-health that can be the fate of many MPs. She imposed on herself a strict fitness regime which she continues to this day. She has said: 'When I first entered Parliament, within about six months I realised either I was going to start going to the gym or I would end up pretty unhealthy, because of the lifestyle and the invitations you get.'[149] May hired a personal trainer and began working out three times a week at a gym near her home in Sonning.

Perhaps unconsciously, May also took a second decision, opting early on not to be drawn into the drinking culture that dominated parliamentary life, particularly during her early years in the House, when, before the introduction by the Blair government of supposedly family-friendly hours, late votes were still the norm. Even following the shake-up of the Commons' daily schedule, MPs were still required to be available to vote late into the evening several times a week; many, then as now, whiled away the hours in Parliament's bars, taking advantage of the subsidised alcohol on sale. Even for those who are not big drinkers, the peculiarities of life as an MP mean that most are social beings, enjoying spending time with their colleagues. At all hours of the day and into the night, MPs socialise in the many dining rooms, tea rooms, smoking rooms, bars and various nooks and crannies dotted around the Houses of Parliament. May, however, took a different approach. Always somewhat reserved, if not downright shy, she saw no reason why her new place of work should also dominate her social life. As a result, she quickly attracted a reputation for being 'unclubbable', a categorisation that would dog her for much of her career.

Sandra Burling insists that the fact that she did not seek out her fellow MPs to socialise with does not mean May is an unfriendly person. Indeed, on entering Parliament, May made a point of keeping up with her old friends.

> She has this reputation for not being clubbable. It's such a male term, 'clubbability'. Women just don't do that kind of thing. Sorting things out by going down to the pub or going down to your club to have a nice chat about things, that's not something that most women ever do. If you have an issue to deal with, you deal with it in the office. You do your work, you give it everything, and when you finally go home, you go home, you don't have a stop between the office and home, which is the pub.

May has said of her attitude towards the lifestyle adopted by many MPs: 'When I came into the House of Commons, there was still a feeling that you sat in the smoking room and chatted to people, which I don't tend to do. I think: there's a job to be done, you get on and do the job.' Burling insists that, far from being unsociable, May is good company. 'Actually, she's very funny. I don't think that comes across often. She has always stayed really grounded and just a very normal person. She doesn't have that arrogance or that big ego that you see in some people when they become successful.'

Many of her fellow MPs, however, found May's approach hostile; they responded by leaving her out of the many clubs and societies which have sprung up over the decades to keep MPs entertained. Keith Simpson says:

> She was never invited to become a member of the One Nation Dining Club. Now, why is that? Well, is it because she's a woman? No, when I was invited to join in '98 we had at least two: we had Gillian Shephard and Virginia Bottomley. No, it's – would she contribute? Would she enjoy the discussion? There's a lot of discussion goes on and people probably thought no, she'd probably have said, 'Sorry, I don't have time.'

Andrew Griffiths says May simply felt it was more important to be respected for talent and drive than for connections.

> The interesting thing about Theresa, the key point about her, is that she doesn't play the game. Theresa does not do the clubbable thing, she never went to the tea room and did the tea room chat or ended up in the smoking room in order to ingratiate herself with colleagues. She just did her own thing, and some people found that difficult to understand and other people just dismissed her because of that, but she never felt the need to play the games in order to get up the slippery slope that other people did. To a certain degree, she did it the hard way. In this place, you see the cliques and groups, you see the patting on the back, the way that so often people coalesce around a rising star … Theresa just got on and did the work.

In her first weeks in the Commons, May continued to insist that she was no different from her male colleagues: 'I don't feel we stick out and I don't feel I'm sitting there as a woman,' she said. 'I'm just doing a job, having a role in the same way that anybody else has in the Party.'[150] It would not be long before she changed her mind, however. When May looked for examples from older women Tories for how to handle life as a female parliamentarian, she found two very different approaches. The first, embodied by the likes of Ann Widdecombe, the formidable former Home Office minister, and Teresa Gorman, one of the leading Maastricht rebels in the previous parliament, was definitely not for her. Andrew Griffiths says: 'The Teresa Gorman line is: "You've got to be more of a man than the men." Theresa [May] never did that. She didn't feel the need to be one of the boys.' Nor did May prefer the company of men, as Margaret Thatcher, the country's first female Prime Minister, had done. Anne Jenkin, who later helped May with her work promoting women within the party, says: 'Thatcher was the outsider. She was a man's woman, and that was the secret of her success. She liked men; she liked men more than she liked women. And I don't think that's the case with Theresa.'

Instead, it was the other approach, taken by older MPs including Jacqui Lait and the former Cabinet ministers Gillian Shephard and Virginia Bottomley, which appealed to May. These mentors acknowledged their different status as women – and sought to help those coming up after them. Shephard in particular proved an inspiration. The former Education Secretary had experienced much sexism during her years in politics – on being appointed to one ministry, she was told there were no lavatory facilities for women – and she had made a point of doing everything she could to encourage new female Tory MPs. Now the former Cabinet minister turned her attention to May. Keith Simpson says: 'Gillian was very protective and helped the new women MPs, there's no doubt about that, and wanted them to succeed and wanted to bring women on.'

It was support May appreciated as she navigated the challenging world of the Commons, an environment that would have been daunting for the most confident of new MPs, which, at that stage, Cheryl Gillan for one thought May was not. She says: 'I don't think that the confidence was there, I think that the confidence has grown. This is such a highly competitive atmosphere to be in, and any sense of weakness is jumped on by all and sundry.' Keith Simpson agrees about the challenges May would have faced in her early years. 'This is a sort of matey, manly place still. I think that at the very beginning, and she is a workaholic anyway, Theresa was determined to succeed. She knew that she would be judged by a higher bar than the men would.'

As she reflected on the invaluable support she had received throughout her political career from her three mentors, Angela Rumbold, Jacqui Lait and Gillian Shephard, May began to take more of an interest in women's issues, even attending the odd cross-party event at Parliament for female MPs. What she encountered shocked her. Not only was she invariably the only Tory in attendance, she could also witness at first hand the closeness of the many Labour women in the Commons, and how invaluable their strength in numbers was to boosting their confidence and standing within their party. Suddenly, despite the support of Lait and Shephard and her new friendships with Eleanor Laing and Julie Kirkbride, she began to be aware of how isolated she was.

Both Anne Jenkin and Professor Sarah Childs, who a few years later would help May found an organisation that would prove instrumental in boosting the recruitment of more female Tory MPs, say it was her experiences in her early years in the Commons which, despite her insistence before the 1997 election that she had no 'burning ambition' to help the cause, inspired her to become the champion for women's parliamentary representation she is today. Jenkin says:

> When she was elected ... there were thirteen [Conservative] women MPs, and there were no kindred spirits, no kind of modern women. When Theresa first arrived she started to do more of what you could call the feminist end of politics. Of course, in '97 Labour suddenly had hundreds of women ... So

Theresa would turn up to these meetings … on equality-type issues … and they were pretty snooty to her, and [said things] like: 'What do you think you're doing here? You're a Tory.' She would go to these things and be completely on her own. I bet that was quite instrumental. I bet she thought – we need more. It can't just be me that turns up to these things.

Childs says:

The Conservative women were obviously in a minority. There perhaps was less of a collegiate sense of group identity among the Conservative women at that time, given that they had come into Parliament at different times on the most part. The Theresa Mays, the Caroline Spelmans, the Eleanor Laings, were of a different generation to those that had gone by. Conservative women would have been looking across at a House of Commons that would have looked suddenly much more female on the Labour benches. They would have looked around their benches and seen very, very few women. I think those women began to realise some of the issues involved with being a woman in politics.

Sandra Burling adds that while May had enough friends and allies both inside and outside Parliament to avoid feeling completely isolated, there is no doubt she found the Commons somewhat hostile to women: 'I'm sure it was incredibly difficult and hard. When all the decisions are made by men, they tend to look for characteristics that are obvious in other men.'

In time, May would make the cause of advancing women in political life one of her main priorities. For now, however, as she entered her second year in the Commons, she was focused on her new responsibilities in the Education brief. In an interview given to mark her appointment to the shadow Education and Employment team, she admitted she was approaching her first outing on the front bench 'with trepidation', the same word she had used to describe her feelings on becoming an MP a year earlier.

When the big day arrived to make her debut as an Education spokesman, May took to her feet, stood in front of the Commons' Dispatch Box, and asked a tricky question about the removal of tax breaks for workplace crèches. Responding, Harriet Harman, then the number two in the Department of Education and Employment, answered with uncharacteristic warmth, congratulating May on her appointment before going on to say: 'I particularly welcome the point she made, about the tax treatment of workplace nurseries. I shall keep her informed about this. She has come to the Dispatch Box, and she has made an important point.' It was the first of what would be many exchanges between the two most senior women in their respective political parties for the next two decades. And it was an unusually cordial note to begin on.

The press response to May's first outing was warm. She was praised by both *The Guardian*'s and *The Times*'s parliamentary sketch-writers, the latter of whom called it 'crisp'.[151] Over the following weeks, before the long summer recess, she was generally seen by colleagues to have acquitted herself well. She took an early stand in opposing the government's decision to cut the budgets of grammar schools, an interesting intervention given her later, somewhat controversial, drive in her first weeks as Prime Minister to expand selection in the education system. Peter Craske was a Conservative press officer at the time on the Education and Employment team. He too found May impressive. '[She was] really good,' he says.

> She'd only been in Parliament just over a year, so still finding her feet there, and she mastered the brief very well. She was … always open to ideas or quite happy to get stuck into attacking the government or promoting the things we were working on, so I always found her easy to get on with.

By the time the political action resumed in the autumn, when the parties' annual conferences take place, May was firmly established as a rising star. In the press, she was now consistently referred to as a high flyer, with adjectives such as 'sensible' and 'measured' used to describe her performances. There were, inevitably, comparisons to 'a young Margaret Thatcher'. William Hague was faring less well, however. With New Labour at its peak, and no sign from the opinion polls that the Tories' fortunes were likely to improve any time soon, Hague's leadership had already begun to come under pressure. Having been in the Commons for just eighteen months, and no doubt to her own astonishment, May found herself included in the lists put about in the media of possible candidates to succeed him. Craske says:

> If you think about the MPs we had at the time, a lot of people had been around for a long time. She was new, normal – same as Damian Green. They were new faces, they came across normal and they sounded normal. Of the people who came in then, they were clearly the standout ones.

At the start of 1999, with Hague facing a number of departures of older faces such as Michael Howard from the shadow Cabinet, it became clear that a reshuffle was on the way. Speculation began to grow that May was on course for a promotion. In March, she was nominated for a 'Rising Star' award by *The House* magazine and Channel 4, but was pipped at the post by Labour's Oona King. Three months later, Hague heeded the cries of the press to freshen up his party's offering and promote new talent by elevating two members of the 1997 intake to his top team. They were Andrew Lansley – and Theresa May.

May was appointed shadow Secretary of State for Education and Employment on 15 June 1999. It was a meteoric rise for an MP who had been in Parliament for just two years. But Hague says that promoting May so early in her career was a decision he never regretted:

> At that time, more so than now, it was unusual to promote people in their first few years right into the shadow Cabinet, almost unheard of. But I thought we had to shake things up in such a small party

after the '97 election. There were good reports about her from the Chief Whip and others. Those who monitor the speeches from the dead of night in Parliament said she was always very competent, clear. It would mean we were promoting a new woman quickly, which would be good. But she would be good, actually, irrespective of being a woman. This was someone who could handle a difficult brief competently, and without making mistakes, and of course we really needed people who could do that.

Not everyone was convinced of May's talents, however. One backbencher passed over for promotion grumbled anonymously to a diary column: 'We call her Theresa May-be one day I'll express an opinion. She will be a huge success and a colour supplement phenomenon. Capable people who never commit themselves in politics always are.'[152] Lansley, who grew closer to May following their shared experience of rapid promotion, says, however, that she was perfectly suited to her new role. 'Because of her background in local government, her work on an education committee, I'd always had the impression that if Theresa was doing the job she wanted, it would be on education,' he says.

Hague was aware that he had given May a lot to take on, but he was confident in her abilities:

[It] was a big job … but I remember discussing it with the Chief Whip and we decided she was up to it. It wasn't like she had arrived in Parliament in her twenties; she was quite mature already, she was easily holding her own in debates. And, indeed, in … all the many troubles I had in that time, that decision never caused me any trouble. She never really put a foot wrong at that time. She was a very willing, constructive member of the shadow Cabinet.

May has remained on her party's front bench ever since.

CHAPTER VII

THE OTHER TERESA MAY

The two women sat side by side on the daytime television sofa, chatting politely about current events. Both were attractive and articulate; they were less than a decade apart in age. But there the similarity ended. One was an adult film star and topless model who had starred in more than sixty pornographic movies. The other was the shadow Secretary of State for Education and Employment. Strangers until that week, all that had brought them together that morning was the coincidence of their names. For the former was a 32-year-old called Teresa May – without an 'h' – from Beckenham in south London, and the latter was Theresa May; the 43-year-old vicar's daughter, former City high-flyer, and MP for Maidenhead. At the end of their friendly discussion for the TV cameras, the pair were said to have enjoyed their conversation so much that they kept it going over coffee in a nearby café.

Back at Conservative Central Office, the assembled party chiefs and press officers who had tuned into the family-friendly breakfast show rather than their usual morning fare of Radio 4's *Today* programme were beaming. Still reeling from the devastation of the 1997 election three years earlier, the party was not in a good place, with opinion polls consistently suggesting that William Hague's Tories were struggling to connect with voters. Compared to Tony Blair's New Labour, the Conservatives seemed stuffy and old-fashioned. Yet, with one appearance on the *GMTV* sofa, Theresa May was doing more than her colleagues had managed in years when it came to challenging voters' perceptions of her party. Here she was, a modern woman with a sense of humour, non-judgemental about her companion's career choice, well-spoken but not posh; light-hearted, approachable. What a contrast, not only to the traditional female Tory battle-axes, but also to what some saw as their somewhat po-faced, politically correct New Labour counterparts. This Conservative woman was in touch with 21st-century Britain, and wasn't afraid to have a little fun.

Thank goodness, satisfied Conservatives thought as they watched May chatting away on the *GMTV* sofa, that the press had picked up on the amusing coincidence of the two women's names… Except that the press hadn't, or at least not by themselves. The legend of 'the other Teresa May', as the story came to be known, has been passed down through the ages by Conservative press officers as an example of spin doctoring at its finest, achieving mass breakthrough and positive headlines for weeks, all by the simple planting of one small diary story in a broadsheet newspaper. For journalists did not stumble across 'the other Teresa May'; they were told about her by one of Theresa May-with-an-'h's press officers. And when the story tickled the interest of the public, making headlines first in Britain and, soon, around the world, the party's press officers pushed it for all they were worth.

May had been in her new post of shadow Education Secretary for only a few weeks when, towards the end of 1999, her secretary got into conversation with Peter Craske, who was still covering media for the Education and Employment team. He says:

> The person who ran her office at that time [said] they [had] got these weird letters, saying 'Congratulations'. The first one, it wasn't too creepy, it was 'Oh, we've been watching you on television for years, congratulations, good to see someone from that background getting into Parliament.' It didn't really make sense. And then another one came, similar but a bit more creepy, and we put it together and thought, 'Oh, God.'

The letters were from fans of the popular pornographic star Teresa

May who somehow, on hearing the news that Theresa May had been appointed to the shadow Cabinet, assumed their heroine had decided to enter politics. At one point, May's office even received a phone call from the Granada television channel Men and Motors seeking to book her, Teresa May having earlier played a nightclub hostess in a programme called *Lady Lust* for the station. May's response on being told she had been taken for a topless model with a similar name was one of amusement. Craske goes on: 'It became a story. If Theresa was speaking at a fundraising party or dinner, it was a good one to kick off with: "I'm being confused with a porn star."' May found that the story of 'the other Teresa May' won her laughs – something she sorely needed. Her first months in her new post had not gone well. The response to Hague's reshuffle was underwhelming. When May addressed her first Tory Party conference as a member of the shadow Cabinet in October, her speech barely raised a mention in the press. By the following month, there was speculation that May would be shuffled out of the shadow Cabinet after less than six months. *The Independent* suggested she had 'yet to make [her] mark',[153] and 'failed to live up to [her] promise',[154] while the *Daily Mail* described her as 'lacklustre'.[155]

Then Craske came up with a cunning plan, one which would both raise May's profile and win her brownie points by helping the party: he would give the story of 'the other Teresa May' a wider airing. Craske says: 'I gave it to the [*Daily Telegraph*'s] Peterborough column … and they put it as the lead one morning. It appeared on the Monday, and – blimey – you just couldn't believe it. Everyone picked up on it.' The story took off, winning space in newspapers members of the shadow Cabinet could usually only dream of at a time when the Blair government's dominance meant they were largely ignored. Craske goes on: 'It was on the front page of the *Mail* and the *Express* and *The Sun*; it was in every paper: "Shadow minister confused with porn star."'

Andrew Lansley, whom Hague had appointed shadow Cabinet Office minister, could only admire Craske's chutzpah – and how sporting May was, as she posed for photographs and gave quotes to accompany the story. Lansley's future wife, Sally Low, was also working on the Education team, as a policy adviser, and he often spent time in her office. He was therefore present as the story of the MP and the porn star became big news. 'It was Pete's idea to embrace "the other Teresa May",' Lansley says. 'At a time when you're in opposition and no one pays you the slightest attention, to own it and get noticed is rather brilliant.' At one point, as the story made headlines around the world, Lansley remembers being in May's office as 'Craske came in and said, "Thumbs up, result!" Theresa was in the *Singapore Times*.'

By the end of the week, the broadcasters had got in on the action. Craske says:

> It led to a funny piece on [Radio] 5Live, then on the Wednesday or Thursday, the *Today* programme picked it up and wanted to interview both of them. So that morning, both of them were interviewed … but not in the same place. Theresa was in Westminster and the other one was wherever she was.

In her part of the interview, Theresa-with-an-'h' said gamely:

> I have to confess I haven't actually seen any of the things that Teresa has been involved in. It's up to her how she wishes to earn her living. She may think it's slightly strange that somebody likes to earn their living as a politician. Teresa has chosen a career, she's working at it and I'm sure she does her job well.

Teresa-without-an-'h' was equally complimentary: 'Everyone has to do their job out there and I'm sure she does it very well, just like I do my job very well.' Within minutes, *GMTV* was on the phone. Craske says: 'They were both on the sofa together on *GMTV* and they got on really well and they were chatting away, and I think they went for a coffee together afterwards.'

The *GMTV* interview marked the official end of the 'other Teresa May' story, but the tale would continue to pop up from time to time in diary columns over the next few years. When May became Prime Minister in 2016, there was a new flurry of stories about her near-namesake, after shocked members of the public seeking information about the woman who had suddenly become their leader misspelled her name as they typed it into their search engines. Andrew Lansley believes that May's embrace of the story of the porn star is an example of what he would come to see as her clever use of visual imagery to raise her profile and portray herself as modern woman, something she would soon begin to do to even greater effect with her choices of clothes and footwear. He says: 'From quite an early stage, in a world when opposition politicians are congenitally ignored, Theresa managed to get noticed. It is not a small thing. A picture paints a thousand words.' Peter Craske agrees:

She got the piss taken out of her in the shadow Cabinet, but she got more publicity than anyone else in the shadow Cabinet in that week than they got in the previous month. It put her on the map, definitely. It put me on the map, certainly. It was very, very funny. When we catch up with people who were working [in the Tory press office] at the time we always talk about it: 'Do you remember that time…?'

May's fortunes would rise and fall over the coming months and years, but from now on the public would know exactly who she was. Craske believes that her insight in recognising the potential power of the little diary story he rustled up tells a deeper message about her understanding of the public. 'She did use it to talk about politics, and get people involved in politics and why it's important,' he says.

It was just one of those things to … break through, and it definitely worked. It definitely raised her profile hugely, but it did also get people watching *GMTV* at that time going, 'Oh, that's quite interesting.' She didn't look like a mad MP, she looked totally normal. [She] treated it like a funny story [because] it is a funny story. A lot of people would have run a mile from that, would have felt that it was demeaning, but she thought it was one of those things that have come along, grab it, use it, because it won't come along again, and use it to further what you want to do.

The story of 'the other Teresa May' provided some light relief in what were otherwise difficult times for the Conservative Party. William Hague had still not steadied the ship and his life was made more difficult when, in November 1999, Michael Portillo returned to the Commons in a by-election following an enforced two-year absence caused by the celebrated loss of his seat on election night 1997 (resulting in the catchphrase 'Were you up for Portillo?'). While Portillo was thought by most to be one of the finest political minds of his generation, and a stellar performer in the House of Commons, his arrival meant the 'prince across the water' was now firmly back on the other side of the channel, presenting a clear alternative to Hague should the leader stumble. The effect on the parliamentary party was immediately destabilising, with briefings against Hague and his team, including May, appearing regularly in the press. The leader was attacked – anonymously – for appointing the untested May to one of the biggest jobs in the shadow Cabinet, her promotion characterised as a sign of Hague's own inexperience.

In February 2000, in an unsuccessful attempt to quell the unrest by bringing Portillo inside the tent, Hague appointed his rival as shadow Chancellor. The briefings against him and his team did not stop. The following summer, one article suggested that (unnamed) colleagues felt May had been 'drastically over-promoted and will have to be moved before the general election campaign'.[156] One MP was quoted as saying: 'We have not shown any hunger or energy or gumption over the summer. Theresa May ... has not laid a glove on [Education Secretary] David Blunkett and we cannot go into the election scoring no points in such an important area.'[157] It would later be claimed that many of the hostile stories about Hague and shadow Cabinet members including Ann Widdecombe, Liam Fox and Michael Ancram as well as May were direct plants by Portillo supporters, if not by the man himself. A member of Hague's team claimed that the Portillo dogs were unleashed. 'Suddenly there were a rash of stories about the leadership being unhappy with their performances. It was a deliberate attempt to undermine them and clear the way for Portillo.'[158]

With many Tory MPs consumed by the whispering campaign against Hague, May preferred to sit out the drama. Peter Craske says:

At the time, it was Hague and Portillo, and it was really tedious, it dominated everything. But she wasn't interested in all that. She didn't really care about who was up and who was down, she was just getting on with what needed to be done, and serv[ing] the leader, whoever that was, and was a good team player.

Hague confirms that May took no part in the machinations behind the scenes. Instead, as she adjusted to life as a shadow minister, she became someone he could rely on:

She could handle a big portfolio, albeit in opposition, without making a mistake. I can't recall any occasion where I had to, as leader, rescue a situation that she had got herself caught up in, which leaders often have to with shadow Cabinet members … You could actually have confidence she would get on with it.

From the beginning, Hague says, May was a quiet but solid presence around the shadow Cabinet table. 'She would [speak up] but she was new, and generally the way these things work is most of the conversation in Cabinet or shadow Cabinet [is by] people who have been around for a long time,' he says. 'But she's never been shy at speaking up. I think sometimes she deliberately kept her own counsel about things, but she's never been afraid to speak up at all. She's always been competent and forceful from the beginning.' As she had as a schoolgirl at Wheatley Park, May was also assiduous about doing her homework. 'I used to require weekly reports of the shadow Cabinet, of what they were going to do, what they had achieved that week and what they were going to do the next week. And her reports were always very extensive,' Hague says.

> These always had to be on one page, that was my rule, but her page was always full. It was as much as you could fit onto one page, with all the meetings that had taken place, all the policy thinking that had been done, all the speeches she was going to give the next week. She was very, very systematic and conscientious about it.

May began working at a furious pace to get to grips with the Education brief and reconsider Tory policy in an area Hague felt was ripe for exploiting. Her ministerial team was made up of Tim Boswell, James Clappison and John Bercow; they were assisted by Peter Craske, the press officer, and Sally Low, as a policy adviser. As would so often be the case on the teams May has led during her time in politics, the non-elected support staff quickly came to like and respect her, Low in particular becoming a close friend. Some of the MPs working under her chafed, however, at what they saw as her tendency to micromanage her brief, which they felt left them little to do.

Peter Craske has nothing but praise for May's abilities, saying of her time at Education: 'It was the right job for her at that point, and she grew in confidence. I found her great to work for; she trusted you and had respect for you, and as a result you had respect for her and trusted her.' As a press officer, Craske found May's willingness to pursue some of his more unorthodox ideas, such as the 'other Teresa May' story, refreshing. She was also prepared to have fun with her Women and Equalities brief, in which she was shadowing Tessa Jowell, then both the Culture Secretary and the Minister for Women. Craske says:

> [Jowell] did this thing about there weren't enough women on television and there weren't enough normal-looking women, they

were all stick-insect models, so the government were planning to crack down. Theresa thought that was ridiculous. [The television host] Vanessa Feltz had been in the news at the time because she'd lost a lot of weight … I wrote this press release, just to see how it worked, and it was 'Maybe Tessa Jowell's going to ask Vanessa Feltz to put all that weight back on.' I didn't know [if May] would go for it, but she thought it was quite funny, and it was the right one for the story. She was always open to ideas, trusted you to do the job, and that's good to know if you're working with her.

Andrew Lansley, who became close to May at this time partly as a result of his relationship with Sally Low, agrees. He says of his wife-to-be's experience of working for May:

They got on very well. My impression is that is generally true of people who work for her, they find she is good to work with because she listens, she's willing to give people room to give advice, she's intelligent and hard-working, so you don't feel your work has been skated over or ignored. I have spoken to civil servants who all say she is into hard graft and clear decisions and they respect that.

Lansley remembers the shadow Education and Employment team as a jolly place, with Tim Boswell and John Bercow providing much of the levity. Later, when May was Home Secretary, by which time Bercow was the Commons Speaker, the pair would have some fierce exchanges in the Chamber as he blocked her from making points she felt relevant. For now, though, Bercow was a figure of amusement for the Education team. 'There were always jokes at Bercow's expense,' Andrew Lansley says. 'One day he came in with a red shiny face, and they all laughed about his "chemical peel".'

But the happy atmosphere felt by Craske and Low was not shared by everyone on the team. One member of the Whips' Office at the time recalls grumblings from more than one of May's juniors. The former whip says:

The impression in the Whips' Office, and I know that has continued, is that when Theresa became a member of the shadow Cabinet, she was incredibly difficult. I can remember one of the whips who was dealing with the team saying, 'They're all going to resign, she keeps things to herself, she never praises them. She can be very sharp.' So she had that reputation.

When complaints were brought to the attention of Patrick McLoughlin, then the Deputy Chief Whip, he backed May to the hilt – and compared her favourably to another hard taskmaster, Iain Duncan Smith, then the shadow Defence Secretary. The former whip says: 'I can hear McLoughlin saying, when someone would come in complaining: "I hear what you say, but we ain't got that many women, and she's good, and colleagues are just going to bloody well have to work with her. Try working with Duncan Smith, for Christ's sake."'

Cheryl Gillan believes that the charge laid against May by her junior shadow ministers that she micromanaged her brief was unfair.

I think that interpretation by any colleague of mine would be more about her communication skills. I don't think in the early days she was seen as a tremendously successful communicator, in running a team. She's a woman who's always played her cards quite close to her chest. She's not out to make people love her or like her. I don't think she cares.

Gillan points out that May had not been able to choose her ministerial line-up, and, given her rapid promotion, had not had much opportunity to get to know those now working for her. 'If you want to control things and you want to know what you're doing and be sure of what you're doing, you don't want to delegate to people who don't know what they're doing,' Gillan says. 'You don't pick your teams in this place. You get your teams given to you. That naturally makes you quite reserved, if you're serious about … doing a proper job. In a way, I think it was showing her caution.'

Eric Pickles, who would work under May a few years later, says of her reputation for refusing to delegate: 'I never really saw that side of her personality. I think if you get her trust and you say, "This is where I'm thinking of going," she's kind of OK. But I have heard those stories.' Pickles would grow to have great respect for May. 'She's the most interesting person to work with,' he says. 'She's very sparky, in the sense that you can talk things through and suddenly she kind of gets [it] when you go off on an angle. I found her a very creative person to work with.'

In the run-up to the 1999 Conservative conference, William Hague drew up plans for what would be a major policy document covering every aspect of government, intended to form the basis of the party's manifesto at the next general election. Having been appointed to her post only a few months earlier, May, aided by Sally Low, had to work furiously to get her section of the document, named 'The Common Sense Revolution', ready in time for conference in October. When it was her turn to speak, she announced a radical new education policy: free schools. A decade before David Cameron's Conservative Party made the concept of freeing schools from local authority control and putting power in the hands of parents and teachers a central plank of their offering to voters, a policy which would be enthusiastically introduced in government by then Education Secretary Michael Gove, May had dreamed up and done much of the thinking on the idea. Andrew Lansley says: 'Theresa invented free schools. This was not a Gove invention.' Peter Craske adds:

> That was the first idea of free schools. It was taking away all responsibility from the local authorities and giving it to the schools. That policy of free schools that was introduced in that document is what we have now. It was quite controversial at the time because it was new, but that's what came in, so she was ahead of the curve on that one.

In her largely unreported speech to Conservative conference, in which she introduced the notion of free schools for the first time, May said: 'We believe that heads, teachers and governors know what is best for their pupils and their schools, that local needs are best addressed by local decisions.' A few months later, May expanded further, writing in an article for the *Yorkshire Post*: 'We will make every school a Free School. The head and governors of the school would have complete control over their budget, be free to set their own opening hours, choose their own staff, decide their own pay packages and would have more freedom in implementing the national curriculum...'[159]

The teaching unions were not enthusiastic, but the reaction was not as adverse as might have been expected. Unusually for a Conservative politician, May had gone out of her way to meet with union leaders and brief them on her announcement in advance, winning over one, the National Association of Schoolmasters and Union of Women Teachers (NASUWT), with a separate pledge to introduce anonymity for teachers accused of misconduct by pupils until allegations were proved. 'That is quite indicative of how hard she worked in the Education brief, that capacity to work with trade unions,' Andrew Lansley says. 'It is not a natural role for Tories.' Not all the unions were convinced, however. When May addressed the annual conference of the left-wing National Union of Teachers in April 2000, her description of the Tories' plans for free schools was greeted with jeers.

As she settled into her brief, May also began to make a few noises about her belief in the effectiveness of grammar schools, although she was careful not to be too wholehearted given the vehement opposition of William Hague. One shadow Cabinet member at the time says:

William Hague was against the promotion of grammar schools. It would have been seen as toxic for the Tories, coming out of eighteen years of government, to have nothing more to offer voters than what were seen as old-fashioned grammar schools. If she privately favoured them, she did not say so even to colleagues.

If she had said something favourable about grammar schools, she would have been completely slapped down. And so she didn't. She probably still believed in grammar schools but the politics of it were undoable then.

Through the winter of 1999 and into 2000, May also worked hard on the other aspect of her brief, Women and Equalities. Having begun to take an interest in women's issues as a backbencher, the opportunity to delve deeper proved fascinating. Gone were her initial reservations about being pigeon-holed as a female politician narrowly focused on gender; instead, the Women's brief opened up opportunities to make a real difference to the lives of tens of voters. In the spring of 2000, assisted by Sally Low, May drew up a policy document reflecting her evolving thinking on the subject. Called 'Choices', and intended as a companion piece to 'The Common Sense Revolution', it was due to be launched with great fanfare at the end of March by May and William Hague. Unfortunately, at the last minute, Hague was called away to give evidence in a bizarre court case involving one of his constituents in his Yorkshire seat of Richmond, who had allegedly confessed during a constituency surgery to smuggling parrots from the former Yugoslavia. The case brought Hague unwelcome headlines referencing Monty Python's Dead Parrot sketch. And it proved a headache for Low, in particular, who was forced to watch her fiancé, Andrew Lansley, substituting for Hague at the launch, read a speech she had written. 'Sally thought it was very bizarre,' Lansley says.

Alongside eye-catching policies such as the introduction of scholarships to help women back into work after a career break to raise children, and a roll-out of CCTV cameras to make female pedestrians feel safer at night, the 'Choices' document included May's first thinking on how to attract more women into politics. She proposed a new scheme, to be called the Women in Public Life Initiative, which would advise constituency parties on the importance of including as many women as men on selection shortlists, and offer mentoring schemes for women interested in becoming

MPs or councillors. These ideas would later form some of the basis of May's hugely successful Women2Win campaigning organisation, but at this stage her proposals were not far-reaching. Andrew Lansley believes that now, at the turn of the century, May's interest in women's rights was not yet the driving force it would become: 'I didn't get the impression that this was some cause that she was pursuing from way back,' he says. 'It was a practical thing, as so often with Theresa. The need for the party to be perceived as much more responsive to the public was uppermost in her mind.'

William Hague now admits that he should perhaps have done more to tackle the problem of the lack of Tory women in the Commons, but says that the wider party was not yet ready for the fundamental reform this would involve. 'We started our efforts to change at this time, and in retrospect we didn't carry them out forcefully enough,' he says.

> I think we should have been more radical. But the radicalism built up in the party. It wasn't until … David Cameron became leader we could actually insist on quite a high proportion of the candidates being selected being women. But we couldn't have done that, there wasn't sufficient support for that, in the beginning of opposition. We were really starting on that when I was the leader. And [May] was an emblem of that.

From the beginning, May was clear that she did not favour all-women shortlists, a view she holds today. When, by the time of the 2000 Conservative conference in Bournemouth, and with a general election on the horizon, Tory associations again failed to select any women in winnable seats, the party was urged by two female would-be candidates who had lost out in a number of constituencies to consider positive discrimination. May's response was clear: 'In the Conservative Party we have always taken the view – and women have as well – they do not want to be selected on that basis of positive discrimination. But there is a long way to go. I accept that there is a lot of work to do.'[160]

Lansley suggests that May's sense of the need to introduce a level playing field, rather than imposing all-women shortlists, stems from a fundamental belief in equality for all. He says: 'She has never been a person persuaded by the merits of positive discrimination as such. What she was entirely convinced by was the need to explore the many reasons why women did not feel empowered. It's embracing the thought that everybody should be able to participate.' Lansley's unexpected involvement in the 'Choices' launch would have far-reaching consequences. He now began working with May on some of their mutual ideas on how to modernise the party, not only in its offering to women voters and by attracting more female MPs, but also, more generally, in seeking to transform the Conservatives' image. Along the way, like his fiancée Sally Low, Lansley became closer to May, forming one of the few friendships she had in Parliament. When Lansley and Low wed in September 2001, three days after the 9/11 terror attacks on the United States, May, accompanied by her husband Philip, was one of the only MPs to make the 'long trek' to Cheshire to attend their nuptials, on a day when most of her colleagues remained in London to take part in the recalled session of Parliament to discuss the atrocity. Lansley says: 'Partly because Sally was married to me, [Theresa and I] spent more time together and always got on. We have never really clashed on political terms, and I can't ever remember a discussion escalating into an argument.'

A few months after the 'Choices' launch, May took what the pair hoped would be both a practical and a symbolic step towards illustrating the Conservatives' capacity for change. Like many Tories, on becoming an MP, May had accepted an invitation to join the Mayfair private members' Carlton Club; unlike most, however, she was forced to take on only an associate membership, as the club continued to bar women from full membership status. Now May quit the club, declaring: 'I dislike the fact that lady associate members are treated as second-class citizens.'[161] The move was a bold one. The Carlton Club was a major donor to the Conservative Party, and any embarrassment could well have led to its withdrawing funding. Almost certainly for this reason, Hague refused to follow May's lead. In 2016, May accepted the offer of life membership traditionally extended to Conservative Prime Ministers, women members having been granted full rights six years earlier.

As the 2001 general election approached, the Tory ship was not a happy one. Spooked by the opinion polls and the conflicting advice he was receiving, Hague decided not to listen to those such as May and Lansley who were urging him to modernise, but shifted his focus to areas seen as traditionally strong for the Conservatives, such as immigration, Europe and law and order. In January of 2001, he un-veiled a list of seven 'sharp-shooters', who, he said, would head the Tories' election campaign. They included Portillo, Widdecombe and Lansley – but not May. Despite his inclusion, Lansley for one was not happy with the Conservatives' offering to voters. 'The 2001 election was a nightmare,' he says.

> The party went off on a save-the-pound gig. It wasn't William Hague's intention, but it was somehow hijacked. That made it very difficult to get the underlying message across. We were fling-ing proverbial stones at a tank, in terms of the Labour Party; just hopeless. There were moments when we thought we might break through … but under any rational analysis, there was just no way we could win.

So low was May's profile during the election campaign that at one point the *Mail on Sunday* described her as 'unknown and likely to remain so'.[162] Peter Craske did his best to push May out, sending her off on a regional tour. He found her an able campaigner. 'She was very good at having a message,' Craske says. 'She was one of the new MPs that had watched Blair in opposition and in govern-ment have a clear message and repeat it. Even if the [Conservative] Party's messaging kept changing, which it did, she would be: "Oh, OK, that's the message now," [and] she would speak to it.'

William Hague's spin doctor, Amanda Platell, barely commu-nicated with May during the 2001 campaign, instead dispatching

Sally Low to convey – unwelcome and unheeded – advice to the shadow Education Secretary about her choice of clothes. Lansley remembers:

> Amanda Platell just didn't speak to Theresa. She was very focused on William, and would ignore everyone else. She was inclined to sit in her office sending messages out telling people what to do. She was constantly sending messages out with Sally, saying, 'She should wear less leather and wear softer clothes.' Sally would convey the message, and Theresa would say: 'Get off out.'

The Tory general election campaign appeared doomed from the start. Going into the final week, at the end of May 2001, the party was running between fifteen and eighteen points behind Labour in the opinion polls. *The Guardian* went so far as to claim that 'when civil servants went to see Shadow Education Secretary Theresa May for the traditional pre-election briefing, asking what plans they should make for an incoming Tory administration, she kindly told them not to bother: there was no point'.[163] And so it proved. The result of the 2001 general election was scarcely better for the Conservatives than 1997 had been. The party's share of the vote increased by just 1 per cent, resulting in a net gain of only one seat. There were now fourteen female Tory MPs, one more than in 1997.

In Maidenhead, Liberal Democrat leader Charles Kennedy's tactic of targeting senior Tories had an impact, as his party's share of the vote rose by 11 per cent, resulting in May's majority plummeting to just over 3,000, her smallest ever. It would have been scant consolation that the Labour candidate fared poorly too. He was the novelist John O'Farrell, who once described Maidenhead, his childhood home, as 'Tory since the Bronze Age … [a] corner of Middle England [whose] tanned, Moschino-wearing inhabitants … somehow give the impression of having been nouveau riche for ten successive generations'.[164] As the sun rose on the morning after the election, and the party faced the prospect of another long spell in opposition, William Hague announced his immediate resignation.

The mood among Tory MPs as they returned to Westminster after the election was naturally low. A leadership contest began amid a bitter mood of recrimination, as leading figures sought to blame each other for the disastrous Hague years. Among the newer MPs, there was a growing realisation too that their prime could be spent in opposition. Andrew Lansley says: 'It dawned on my 1997 intake that we might end up doing the heavy lifting of opposition but never serve in government. The worst-case scenario is you slog all the way through opposition and the next lot inherit.' The candidates to replace Hague now began to emerge. As usual, the veteran Europhile Kenneth Clarke threw his hat into the ring, again with the effect that Eurosceptics on the back benches scrambled to find an alternative. They settled on Iain Duncan Smith, who based his pitch on opposition to Europe and a continuation of Thatcherism. Having completed his journey from the right to the left of the party, Michael Portillo made his long-anticipated challenge, focusing on modernisation and liberalism.

It is perhaps proof of how little attention May had paid to the reports that Portillo had briefed against her that she now firmly fixed her colours to his mast. Almost certainly she had come to respect his intelligence in shadow Cabinet and, unlike Hague, she appreciated that he was unlikely to bow to the right and reject the modernisation agenda she and Andrew Lansley had been working on. When, in an interview, the Tory grandee Lord Tebbit appeared to contrast the childless Portillo, who on returning to Parliament had been open about his youthful 'homosexual experiences', with Duncan Smith, whom he portrayed as a 'normal, family man with children', May sprang to the former's defence. 'It can be very hurtful if there are real medical reasons why somebody cannot have children,' she said. 'It is a difficult issue for a lot of couples. Some are childless by choice but for others there are medical reasons.'[165] Given her own history, they were words that clearly came from the heart.

To the shock of May and the other ten shadow Cabinet members who were backing Portillo, however, the long-time perceived leader-in-waiting crashed out of the contest in the third round, leaving Duncan Smith and Clarke to fight it out. Following reforms introduced by William Hague, the contest between the final two would be decided by the Tory membership, rather than the parliamentary party. On learning of his rejection by colleagues, the disappointed Portillo nonetheless fulfilled a promise to appear as guest of honour at a summer ball thrown by the Conservative Association in May's Maidenhead constituency.

May and Lansley used the lull before the result of the leadership contest to issue a call for whoever won the race to do more to encourage women to become Tory candidates. They stopped short of recommending all-women shortlists, instead proposing that the party's existing candidates' list be streamlined to include only individuals of the greatest potential. Crucially, half the spots on the list would be reserved for women, and a representative portion for ethnic minorities. In a document launching their proposal, they said: 'It is essential that, in future, we ensure constituencies make their selection from balanced lists … We wish to take this opportunity to urge upon our new leader that he should take immediate action to advance this objective.'[166] Neither Clarke nor Duncan Smith agreed to adopt the proposal, which would later form the basis of David Cameron's A-list – which in turn would transform the face of the modern Conservative Party.

On 13 September 2001, the result of the leadership contest was announced. While Clarke had emerged as the favourite of his colleagues, the Tory grassroots, more right-wing and Eurosceptic than the parliamentary party, jumped the other way, anointing Iain Duncan Smith – or IDS as he swiftly became known – by more than 60 per cent. May declined to reveal whom she voted for in the final round. Duncan Smith would never overcome the negative dynamic of the lack of support for his leadership among his MPs. The backbiting began at once, as the new leader appointed a string of right-wingers to his shadow Cabinet, including Michael Howard as shadow Chancellor. But while some senior MPs on

the modernising wing – Andrew Lansley among them – refused
to serve under him, when IDS extended the olive branch to May,
she accepted without question. More than that, unlike many of her
colleagues, both inside and outside the shadow Cabinet, she would
serve him loyally throughout his short, unhappy period in office.
Lansley says: 'I sat out the IDS years, unlike Theresa. But then
Theresa's a joiner.'

Assembling his team the day after his victory, IDS appointed May
shadow Secretary of State for Transport, Local Government and
the Regions. Her Labour opponent was Stephen Byers, a respected
figure in his party who had already served in several roles in the
previous Blair government. Within days, May would be handed the
greatest gift any shadow Cabinet minister can receive: the prospect
of her Secretary of State's head on a plate. It would be an agonisingly slow process, however, before May would finally succeed in
seeing Byers off, and her hesitation at times during the long, drawn-
out affair would attract heavy criticism.

In hindsight, it now seems inevitable that Byers would be forced
to resign from the moment it emerged that his special adviser, Jo
Moore, had sent an email on the day of the 11 September terrorist
attacks on the United States suggesting to his departmental press
officers that it was 'a good day to bury bad news'. In an era when
the Blair government was already perceived as overly reliant on
spin, her clumsy words resonated deeply with a disgusted public.
Incredibly, however, Byers fought for some months to prevent
Moore's dismissal. May led the attack, at one point telling *GMTV*:

> At a time when the world was transfixed by the horror of what
> was happening in New York, here was somebody whose immedi-
> ate reaction, her gut reaction, was not to say, 'This is a horrible
> tragedy, an incredible event,' but to say, 'Ah, good, this is the op-
> portunity for the government to [perform] some spin.'[167]

Somehow, Moore remained in post until the following February,
when another leaked email, sent by the department's head of

news, Martin Sixsmith, suggested that she was attempting to use the funeral of the Queen's sister, Princess Margaret, to again slip out inconvenient press announcements. In the ensuing furore, both Moore and Sixsmith were ousted.

A day before the emergence of the Jo Moore 'good day to bury bad news' email, in October 2011, Byers had suddenly announced that he was taking the struggling firm Railtrack, which managed Britain's rail infrastructure, into public ownership. His highly controversial decision was made without recourse to the rail regulator, and involved applying to the High Court on a Saturday to put Railtrack into immediate administration. Shareholders were not told about the plans until after they had received their annual dividend, which many had requested in shares, now of uncertain value. May had been in her post for only two weeks. Eric Pickles, who had been appointed May's deputy in the reshuffle, was impressed by the speed with which she got to grips with the matter. 'She made a fantastic fist in the response to nationalisation. It … happened as we were on our way to the [Conservative Party] conference. We talked a lot on the phone; when we got back she really took the Secretary of State to pieces.' With backbench Tory MPs behind her in the Commons Chamber chanting 'resign, resign', May told Byers: 'It is clear that you have been bent on destroying Railtrack from the start. As a result, schemes will be delayed, investment postponed and the industry placed in a protracted period of stagnation. You must go.'

Pickles worked with May for a year on the Transport, Local Government and the Regions brief until the massive department was broken up and he took over responsibility for Local Government in shadow Cabinet. He says:

I first really got an opportunity to work with her under IDS … She was bright, she was intelligent, but it's true it takes an awful long time to get to know her. I'm not sure anyone has ever entirely got to know her, and I don't mean that in a rude way. She's not even slightly clubbable.

Pickles was immediately struck by May's radically different approach to politics compared to most of their colleagues. 'She doesn't do the conventional things,' he says.

> Most business in this place is transactional: 'You do this for me, I'll do that for you. You want this thing through a shadow Cabinet? You want this thing through a Cabinet? Well, you know, let's talk about it, because there's something I want.' She won't do that. She will only do things on their merit. So even if life would be made easier for her, she won't do it unless you've got a reasonable case. But if you've got a reasonable case, yup, you'll never find a more reasonable woman.

Through the winter of 2001 and into 2002, May's weekly attacks on Byers became a feature of Commons life. At first, they were lauded as impressive. But then, as the minister dug in, she began to seem ineffectual. Calling an opposition debate on the Moore and Sixsmith debacle in February 2002, May told Byers he should resign immediately. 'Has he no pride?' she asked. 'Just what does it take for this Secretary of State to go?' Whatever it was, May hadn't yet found it. Despite her stirring words, her attack was felt to have lacked bite, with colleagues grumbling that she had let Byers off the hook by failing to raise the key question of whether he had lied about events during media appearances. Byers was able to turn the tables on May by pointing out that her statement did not address his own, suggesting she had prepared it beforehand rather than responding to what she had heard. As the reprieved Transport Secretary walked out of the Chamber, one crowing Labour MP said of May's performance: 'She acted more like a solicitor than a barrister.'[168]

And still Byers clung on. His eventual departure was like a death from a thousand cuts, as a series of issues which in other circumstances would not have seemed significant now took on a greater weight. Byers was criticised for first promising public money would not be used to bail out Railtrack shareholders and then reversing his position. Worse was to come when, in May 2002, a fatal rail crash took place at Potters Bar in north London; the accident was later deemed to have been caused by poor maintenance of the points on the track, which were the responsibility of Railtrack. Byers finally gave up the ghost three weeks after Potters Bar, over a seemingly innocuous issue about his muddled handling of a fair trading inquiry. He told friends he had come to the conclusion that he would never be trusted, and would always be seen by the public as a liar. May finally had her Cabinet scalp. Her response was one of relief rather than celebration, however. As one Tory insider briefed the press at the time: 'Had Byers survived, the knives would have been out for her. But as he has gone she can at least claim to have seen him off so she should be safe.'[169]

A few months later, on 23 July, May received her reward for dispatching Byers when Iain Duncan Smith used a reshuffle to appoint her to one of the highest-profile posts in his shadow Cabinet. It would come close to breaking her.

CHAPTER VIII

CHAIRMAN MAY

Theresa May had two big decisions to make. It was October 2002, and she was preparing to make the opening address at Conservative Party conference, her first as party chairman. She had been appointed to the post by the party's new leader, Iain Duncan Smith, a few months before, the first woman to hold the office and an unexpected choice made amid controversial circumstances. In this, her first major speech since taking on the job, May knew she needed to make a splash. She was also determined to finally go public with her concerns about the party's image, making clear her view that the Tories urgently needed to modernise if they wanted to regain power. Gathered in her suite in the Highcliff Hotel, Bournemouth, on the night before the speech, her team of her husband Philip, adviser Chris Wilkins, Conservative Party chief executive Mark MacGregor and press officer Katie Perrior worked late into the night, producing draft after draft. They kept coming back to one dilemma: identifying exactly the right phrase to hammer home the dire view May was convinced many voters had of the party. On top of that, she couldn't decide what shoes to wear.

The choices May would make in the early hours of the morning in a Bournemouth hotel room would have consequences none of those present could have imagined. The twin decisions would shape public perception of her for the next decade. Her first choice, to settle on the words 'nasty party' to describe to shell-shocked delegates how they were seen by the public would resonate perhaps more than any phrase uttered by a Conservative politician during the long period of opposition. In time, May's warning would be seen as prescient, the first sign of a senior Tory politician facing up to the scale of reform needed before the party could begin to break through electorally. At the time, however, any appreciation for what May was trying to convey in her speech was dwarfed by an overwhelming backlash against her frank use of words. May's second choice that night in Bournemouth, to don a smart pair of £110 leopard print kitten heels from Russell & Bromley, would prove of no less consequence to her image and future prospects.

It may seem preposterous that something as trivial as shoes should have played so important a role in shaping a future Prime Minister, but in fact May's interest in footwear – and the public's fascination with that interest – would ultimately speak to a larger truth about the role of a Conservative woman in modern politics. Just as she had with the story of 'the other Teresa May' a few years before, May was able to turn her genuine interest in fashion into a means of conveying a deeper message about herself and her party. Her adventurous shoe collection was designed to show she was modern and unstuffy. She saw no need to pretend to be a man, and, like millions of women across the country, acknowledged no contradiction in wanting to look nice and be taken seriously (and no one would ever suggest that May was not a serious person). Here was a woman, a Conservative no less, who was comfortable enough to embrace the term feminism while wearing bright lipstick, a low-cut blouse and pixie boots.

Professor Sarah Childs says:

Lots of women up and down the country care about nice clothes. If you're trying to connect with women in society, if you're trying to get out to people who don't listen to the *Today* programme or don't read the broadsheet press, actually doing a photo-shoot or talking about clothes and fashion is a way of connecting politics to women. I'm a bit suspicious sometimes when people say you can't be taken seriously as a politician if you like nice clothes.

Well, why not? I like the way that Theresa challenges the notion of who does politics.

May has said of her interest in clothes: 'I like clothes, I like shoes … One of the challenges for women in politics, in business, is an ability to be ourselves. You can be clever and like clothes, you can have a career and like clothes.'[170]

As a side effect, the attention May's shoes attracted also gave one of the most reserved politicians in Westminster some much needed cover. If she could talk about her latest shoe purchase to a journalist seeking to open her up about her private life, then she would be spared having to disclose anything more personal. If the first thing people saw when she walked into a room was a daring pair of black leather trousers, then it was easier to engage them in small talk. Zoe Healy, who worked as her press officer, says: 'They were a good ice-breaker. Whether she was visiting a prison or a town hall, people would always ask about the shoes. She would joke that she must have been the only politician in the Western world who, when she entered a room, everyone would look down.'

The kitten heels became a crutch for May, and an emblem, easy shorthand for journalists and the public to summon up when they referenced her. Before she became Home Secretary in 2010, it was rare for a newspaper article to mention May without also referring to her kitten heels. Even now she is Prime Minister, May's clothes and the sincere pleasure she takes in fashion are often remarked upon. Her friend Sandra Burling says: 'All politicians have something that people latch onto, and Theresa's been quite lucky that people latch onto something like that. Theresa's shoe thing is quite neutral to positive. Other politicians have been much less lucky, and people latch onto things that can be hurtful and destructive.'

Some believe, however, that, rather than being lucky, May's adoption of attention-grabbing footwear was a deliberate move to establish a safe, attractive narrative about herself. Sarah Childs says: 'Perhaps Theresa was more in control of her media image than some people recognise. I think she was quite astute with the shoes. It is interesting how people in politics get portrayed. With Theresa, I think there was some more active agency there.' Peter Craske adds: 'It became a thing: she likes to wear colourful shoes. Most MPs are male, wear black shoes, it helped her to stand out a bit.' Katie Perrior, another of her press officers, has said: 'She wears the clothes to show she is not the person you think she is. Her dress sense shows that risk-taking side. They are hidden signals. Her two fingers, a bit of control she has over her life.'[171]

Zoe Healy agrees that May both embraced and encouraged her image as a shoe-lover. She recalls visiting a farm with May during her time as party chairman:

> We had been told to wear wellies, so we both threw them in the back of the car. When we got out, Theresa's were green khakis, and mine were kind of flower power, festival boots. She looked at me and said [jokingly], 'Oi! You can't be outdoing Theresa – that's not in your contract.'

Over the years, May would establish a small number of 'safe' personal topics, including her love of shoes, which she would roll out for journalists in interview after interview. Read one after another, they are strikingly repetitive. May deployed the same anecdotes time and time again: she enjoys cooking but prefers Jamie Oliver to Delia Smith because the latter is too prescriptive; she likes cricket, particularly Geoffrey Boycott; she and Philip take an annual holiday in Switzerland but she is not a 'proper Alpinist' because she likes a hot bath at the end of a hike. In an era when the public and media demand to know everything about their politicians, the stories are engaging and appealing. Importantly for May, by wheeling out her safe stories, she also leaves little space for the trickier questions on personal matters that her reserved nature shrinks from. Andrew Griffiths says talking about her shoes or cookbooks gave journalists 'enough detail to add colour to the piece without [May] revealing too much of what she thinks is private'. 'She's just a very private person,' he adds. 'Her personality manifests itself in her shoes and her style of dress, she enjoys the fashionable things that lots of women enjoy … But her personal life was exactly that. She didn't share with anybody.'

There is no doubt that some of the coverage of May and her fashion choices, particularly the not uncommon remarks about her cleavage, drifted into sexism. They could also become hackneyed. Cheryl Gillan says:

> Although she quite liked the shoe thing at the beginning, and she liked the attention at first, it was a means to [an end]. I remember going into her office … and she'd got these shoe-themed cushions, people had obviously given her all this shoe stuff, and I always got the impression that she's very nice about it but in the end was really fed up with it.

May once said of the attention she received for her shoes following the 2002 conference:

> It is quite widely known that I like shoes. This is not something that defines me as either a woman or a politician, but it has come to define me in the eyes of the newspapers. I wore a pair of leopard print kitten heels to a Conservative Party conference a few years ago and the papers have continued to focus on my feet ever since. Quite apart from the fact that I can never wear boring shoes now, it is frustrating that they missed the reason I was there – as the first female chairman of a major political party.[172]

May's interest in fashion is genuine. From her teenage years in flares and hotpants to the crimson lipstick she wore as a City slicker and her blue suit on election night, she has always been very conscious both of how she dresses and of the messages she conveys. In her *Desert Island Discs* appearance in 2014, she chose a lifetime subscription to *Vogue* magazine as the luxury item she would like to take with her. As Prime Minister, May's interest in clothes and shoes is as strong as ever. She caused a stir in November 2016 for posing for a newspaper magazine interview wearing a pair of chocolate leather trousers by Amanda Wakeley costing £995, leading the former Education Secretary, Nicky Morgan, to say: 'I don't think I've ever spent that much on anything apart from my wedding dress.' She is due to appear on the cover of the April 2017 edition cover of American *Vogue*, having posed for the celebrated fashion photographer Annie Leibovitz. She does not employ a stylist or use personal shoppers, as several of the wives of recent Prime Ministers have done. Instead, while she continues to patronise upmarket high-street chains such as Russell & Bromley and L. K. Bennett, most of her purchases these days are made from a small boutique close to her constituency in Henley, named Fluidity, which stocks accessible designer clothes and upmarket casual wear.

Back when May was finding her fashion feet, and having toned down her look to win selection for Maidenhead in the late 1990s, it took a few years for her to feel confident enough to channel her inner clothes horse once she arrived in Parliament. It was the penetratingly astute Quentin Letts, parliamentary sketchwriter for the *Daily Mail*, who, peering down from the Press Gallery high above the Commons Chamber in the summer of 2000, first spotted that something exciting was going on with May's shoes. Describing May, then the shadow Education Secretary, as having the 'smooth hands of a City banker's wife and the longish legs of a moderate point to pointer', he gave an account of her clash with Estelle Morris, an Education minister, over a teacher bonus scheme, before concluding: 'A sartorial-minded critic might have given the bout to the Tory. Mrs May's Coventry City blue suit – a designer job? – was complemented by a pair of snazzy, blue-toed shoes.'[173]

Over the next few years, May's shoes became a regular item in the parliamentary sketches. By the time she was waging war against Stephen Byers as shadow Transport Secretary in the winter of 2002, May had begun to freshen up her clothes to match her newly flamboyant footwear. She went through a leather period, stunning viewers of *Newsnight* on the night of Byers's resignation by donning a lavender leather jacket. Addressing party workers at Tory HQ on the day of her appointment as party chairman, she joked that while she planned to introduce change, 'by that I don't mean everyone has to wear leather trousers and kitten heels'.

But it was her choice of leopard skin kitten heels to deliver her incendiary 'nasty party' speech to the 2002 Conservative conference three months later that really put May on the map. In a newspaper diary she wrote at the time, she said: 'I never thought my shoes would appear on the front pages of so many papers. I had worked out what I would wear a week before, but when I got to Bournemouth I changed my mind and the kitten heels came out. Very pleased with the coverage.'[174] The retailer Russell & Bromley was also very pleased with the coverage. Within days, the range of leopard print heels worn by May had sold out nationwide. She would later be credited with spurring a revival in the kitten heel style, and Russell & Bromley even presented her with her own range of shoes as a reward for boosting their annual profits.

In the first days of her appointment as chairman, it had been May's gender rather than her wardrobe that attracted the most attention, however. Iain Duncan Smith's first reshuffle, carried out ten months after he came to office, did little to quell concern within his parliamentary party about his leadership. Having won on a pledge to restore Thatcherism, and after less than a year in office, Duncan Smith turned on his first appointment as party chairman, the right-winger David Davis, who he judged was failing to carry out what he now decided was necessary modernisation. May, who had been talking about these issues for the past few years, seemed the perfect choice to take his place. Unfortunately for Duncan Smith, his decision to move Davis was made while the latter was out of contact on a family holiday in Florida. For nine long days, Davis failed to return increasingly anxious phone calls from officials eager to facilitate IDS's wish to get on with the reshuffle. Eventually, with Davis still AWOL, the leader went ahead and unveiled his changes anyway. On the day her new position was announced, May stood beside Duncan Smith on the steps of Conservative Central Office and delivered a short speech in which she declared: 'I believe that the Conservative Party is changing and my appointment as the first woman chairman symbolises that change.'

When Davis returned, he was furious; Duncan Smith was forced to announce publicly that his new role shadowing Deputy Prime Minister John Prescott was higher up the pecking order than May's. The chaotic nature of their appointments gave the reshuffle a general air of, as one MP put it, 'rearranging the deckchairs'.[175] May was described by the *Mail* as 'pleasant' but a 'lightweight'.[176] But her appointment made international headlines, with the *New York Times* even running a photograph of her alongside a short article headlined 'A New Look for Tories'.[177] May would come to love the job of chairman, enjoying the somewhat higher profile it gave her despite her natural reserve. The post required her to make frequent appearances in the media, something she had once dreaded but was now comfortable with. She said of her new-found fame at the time, not quite convincingly: 'The first time somebody recognises you in the street you think, "Ooh, gosh!" … But sometimes you wish you could get round Waitrose without somebody coming up and raising an issue.'[178]

May now met her new team, several of whom would play a key role in her life and career over the next few years. Katie Perrior, her press officer, would become one of her most trusted aides. Although Perrior would soon leave May's side to start her own PR company (which would mastermind Boris Johnson's successful campaign to become Mayor of London in 2008), the two women kept in close touch, and she remained a key if informal adviser. A decade after leaving May, Perrior returned to run the media side of her 2016 leadership campaign and eventually went into No. 10 with her as head of communications. Like all of May's closest members of staff, Perrior does not come from a privileged background. Her south London accent, down to earth manner and sense of fun set her apart from the Tory 'gels' at CCHQ, with their ponytails and pearls. Over the next few years, Perrior would become a touchstone for May, as well as a friend.

Along with Perrior, May would encounter two more young people at Central Office who would later become her closest advisers. They were Nick Timothy and Fiona Hill, employed at the time as a junior researcher and press officer respectively. They both caught May's eye, but would not begin working for her for another few years. At forty-one, Mark MacGregor, who had been appointed as the party's chief executive by Duncan Smith at the outset of his leadership, was also young for the heavy responsibilities he bore. Although he was known as an ally of Michael Portillo, he quickly struck up a rapport with May, sharing her interest in modernising the party.

Shailesh Vara, later the MP for North West Cambridgeshire but at the time working as a party vice-chairman, also now met May. He says he was struck by how, in her first days in the job, May did not allow herself to be affected by the row between Duncan Smith and her predecessor, David Davis. 'She had a job to get on with and she got on with it. To the extent there were issues, it would have been between David Davis and Iain,' Vara says. Although he had been appointed by Davis, Vara soon grew to have deep respect for May. 'I found her very committed,' he says.

> She's got an incredible capacity for hard work. Morale in the party was low. We had been trounced in 1997. We had made no progress in the 2001 election, and the job of party chairman is critical in such circumstances. She was determined to make sure we got working and started preparing to get back the votes we had lost.

From the outset, and with Duncan Smith's backing, May made clear that their focus should be on extending the party's appeal. Vara says:

> In every strata that you looked at in those days, it was male and white. Her view was that we should broaden the party both in view of the parliamentary level, the associations, and members of the ordinary public who were not Tories, and get them to vote for us.

May spent the run-up to the 2002 party conference, which she would oversee as chairman, thinking about the transformation she wanted to achieve. Above all, she believed that the Conservatives were capable of taking on the formidable force that was New

Labour – but only if they adapted to the changing times. What was needed was something to press home to the membership the necessity for reform. Her speech would serve as a wake-up call, setting out baldly exactly what was at stake. Eric Pickles says: 'At that time, Blair looked like he could go on for twenty, thirty [years], it could go on for ever. And the party still didn't get how out of kilter it had got with the public, how the party's values weren't really the public's values, and the public had noticed.' May has said of the motivation behind her famous speech:

> I started thinking about what I wanted to say about a month [beforehand] … This was to be a different sort of conference, and I wanted a different sort of speech. Jokes and gibes aren't me. The party has to understand how we are seen by the majority of the voters – that is what I meant by my reference to the 'nasty party'.[179]

Katie Perrior has described the scene as the team worked on the soon-to-be notorious speech on Sunday 6 October 2002. 'I remember going up and down the stairs with one draft, and there were about fifteen drafts, and they would say, "No way, this is definitely not it," and then they would go upstairs again and change it. It was pretty chaotic.' It was only at two in the morning that the speech was finalised and the Mays were able to get to sleep. May has never disclosed the identity of the person who came up with the phrase 'nasty party', although Perrior has insisted it was not her. While he has stressed that he did not write the speech in its entirety, there has long been speculation that Mark MacGregor was responsible for the sentence that would dog May for the next decade or more: 'You know what some people call us: the nasty party.' Perrior has since said that failing to persuade May to remove the 'nasty party' passage was her biggest mistake in her illustrious career as a spin doctor. 'I was only in my early twenties,' she has said.

> I realised at the time that this was going to be big, I didn't realise we'd still be talking about it ten years later. I was young, and

looking back now, I think I could have probably done more to tell her that she was right, but that she was delivering it at the wrong time, and the Tories weren't ready to be told that.[180]

As May prepared to take to the stage on Monday 7 October, she was, she later admitted, feeling nervous. She didn't let it show, striding forward in her Russell & Bromley kitten heels, exuding total confidence. Then she began: 'Ladies and gentlemen, you'll notice that there have been some changes to our conference this year. A new format. A new timetable. A new set. But most important of all, this conference marks a new approach from a party that is changing.' From the start, May took a stern line, warning that the public had become switched off by the antics of some Conservative politicians. Eyebrows rose as it became apparent that the chairman was referring to the string of scandals that had attracted embarrassing headlines in recent years. Only the week before there had been the admission by ex-minister Edwina Currie that she had had an affair with former Prime Minister John Major. There had also been recent embarrassment over the jailing of two former Cabinet ministers, Lord Archer and Jonathan Aitken, for perjury.

But it was May's warning about the Conservatives' image that would go down in history. 'Let's not kid ourselves,' she said.

There's a way to go before we can return to government. There's a lot we need to do in this party of ours. Our base is too narrow and so, occasionally, are our sympathies. You know what some people call us? The nasty party. I know that's unfair. You know that's unfair, but it's the people out there we need to convince – and we can only do that by avoiding behaviour and attitudes that play into the hands of our opponents … I want us to be the party that represents the whole of Britain and not merely some mythical place called 'Middle England', but the truth is that as our country has become more diverse, our party has remained the same … Ask yourselves: how can we truly claim to be the party of Britain, when we don't truly represent Britain in our party?

Reaction to May's speech was mixed to say the least. Vara says:

> I was in the audience listening. The party needed to change, and
> she had the guts to say so. Very brave. She's not afraid of saying
> things that are necessary, because she wants to achieve the best.
> And achieving the best means saying things that may not always
> be popular with everyone.

William Hague, however, says that the 'nasty party' phrase was un-
helpful: 'The mistake in it was that it was easy then for opponents to
quote: "Even she says that you're the nasty party." I wouldn't have
put it like that myself for that reason.' It is a view Andrew Lansley
shares:

> Any of us watching at the conference would have understood
> what she was saying: you have to understand the situation we're
> in, there's no use pretending otherwise. The trouble is, in the
> process, you hand a stick to your enemies. Given the reception,
> she probably regretted it straight away. But, then, we've all been
> there.

Eric Pickles was also in the hall in Blackpool. He says:

> I did have a sharp intake of breath when she talked about the
> 'nasty party'. I remember watching that and thinking, 'Mmm,
> we're going to have a bit of fun here.' But of course what she did
> speak was an inner truth … In a way it was a kind of a jolt. It was
> necessary, it was a kind of: 'Snap out it, get over it, move on, the
> times have changed.' Even though I kind of knew that, it didn't
> stop me going – 'gasp!' – when she said it.

While the backlash against May would soon be furious, it took a
little while to get going. The initial response to her speech in the
media was relatively warm. In the hall, too, stunned delegates had
applauded her enthusiastically as she finished, not appreciating

until later, perhaps, the starkness of her message. It took a few days before the full extent of the anger many senior figures in the party felt about the speech became clear. Kenneth Clarke was the first out of the traps, saying, within minutes of May concluding: 'She really did go on about the need to change the party and get more women. For me that's slightly unnecessary.'[181] Many MPs who expressed their outrage about May's remarks did so anonymously. But when both Lord Tebbit and Ann Widdecombe unequivocally entered the fray a few days later, the former insisting, 'This is a very tolerant and generous party,'[182] both May and Iain Duncan Smith, who had backed his chairman, were left in no doubt that the mood in the party was against them.

From the moment that the 'old guard', as the *Telegraph* put it,[183] turned on May in the days after her conference address, she faced hostility from large numbers of Tories both inside and outside Parliament. She was unrepentant, refusing to row back on her remarks, but did go out of her way to seek to reassure those at the grassroots level that she meant no disrespect. Zoe Healy, her press officer, says: 'I got the impression from party members when we would meet with them that she needed to explain what she meant by the "nasty party". Once people actually met her and spoke to her and she explained her thinking, they were always very positive.'

Some MPs were less forgiving, however. Eric Pickles says:

I don't think it did her any favours by telling the party where we were. She was branded by it. She was blamed for it. There were some [MPs] who kind of had a downer on her, and continued [to] in government. But it was a good thing to say, the right thing to say, and the doors to the modernisers wouldn't have really happened without that.

While she was prepared to put in the hours soothing local activists about her message in the speech, May worked less hard to put the media or her fellow politicians straight. Liam Fox says: 'It's quite Theresa, because most people would have spent quite a lot of time saying, "I didn't say that." She just, with an irritated shrug of her shoulders, brushes it off whenever it's mentioned.'

William Hague points out that the negative effect of the 'nasty party' speech on May's ambitions was not lasting. 'It did damage her a bit, because to MPs and many activists it was obviously giving something to opponents for them to say, and made them uncomfortable. But it didn't really hold her back. There's not been anything she's been unable to do.' By the time of her first Conservative conference as Prime Minister, in October 2016, May was able to make a joke of the infamous speech she had delivered almost exactly fourteen years earlier, using it to turn the tables on a Labour Party facing accusations of anti-Semitism and misogyny within its ranks: 'The Labour Party is not just divided but divisive … Do you know what some people call them? The nasty party!'

Back in the autumn of 2002, however, it soon became clear that May's words at conference had opened a Pandora's Box which would have disastrous consequences for her boss, Iain Duncan Smith. The parliamentary party had never warmed to their new leader, and his faltering Commons appearances, including an unfortunate tickle in his throat which seemed to emerge only when he faced Tony Blair across the Dispatch Box at Prime Minister's Questions, exacerbated their dissatisfaction. On MPs' return to Parliament after the conference break, it transpired that May's 'nasty party' speech had thrown a match into a tinder box. Following yet another poor performance by Duncan Smith at PMQs on 17 October, he was forced to face a hostile parliamentary party at a meeting of the backbench 1922 Committee. There, a number of angry MPs turned on him over May's 'nasty party' speech, one suggesting that it had been the equivalent of 'doing a Gerald Ratner' – a reference to the owner of Ratners, the low-price jewellers, whose disparaging description of his firm's products as 'crap' resulted in the near collapse of the business.[184] A few weeks later, a newly elected MP called Boris Johnson repeated the Ratner phrase in an interview, the first of many clashes between May and Johnson to be played out in the media over the next decade and a half.

Despite the furore, May did what she always did and got on with the task at hand: this time the self-imposed one of modernising the party, and particularly its approach to women and ethnic minorities. It was an uphill task. By November, it was clear that local Conservative associations were openly ignoring her call to select more diverse candidates. Only nine women had been selected in the fifty-eight seats which had so far made their choice; of these, just three had been picked during May's tenure as chairman, a worse record than David Davis's during his year in the post. May now proposed a variation on the scheme she and Andrew Lansley had drawn up ahead of the 2001 leadership election, to force local associations to select candidates from a curated list containing an equal number of men and women and a representative proportion of ethnic minorities. It would be known as the 'Gold List'. To her disappointment, however, with the grassroots and many MPs still reeling from her 'nasty party' speech, three weeks after conference Duncan Smith ruled that the party was not yet ready for any kind of positive action. He delayed the introduction of the 'Gold List' until at least after the following summer's local elections.

Duncan Smith's appeasing gesture was not enough to calm the mood of dissent. While it had been May who had actually voiced the offending words 'nasty party', it was Duncan Smith, who had backed his chairman fully following her speech, whose authority was now under attack. Within a month of the conference ending, he compounded his problems by taking a step that would alienate the left as well as the right of his party. Alarmed by the attacks he was receiving from traditionalists, Duncan Smith attempted to bolster his original reputation as a social conservative by imposing a three-line whip on controversial government legislation to allow gay couples to adopt, effectively ordering his MPs to vote against the reform. A number defied him, including John Bercow, who resigned from the front bench in order to do so, and Michael Portillo. Another thirty-five Tories, the shadow Cabinet ministers Damian Green and Tim Yeo among them, abstained. May dutifully followed her leader into the 'No' lobby to oppose the motion, a move which would come back to haunt her years later, when gay rights campaigners vehemently opposed her appointment as Equalities Minister. But, at the time, it was Duncan Smith who faced a firestorm. With insubordination raging on both his left and right flanks, the leader gathered his closest aides, including May, around him to debate how to handle the crisis.

On 4 November, just ten minutes before he had been due to set off for a press conference in east London on his party's plans to extend the 'right to buy' housing scheme, Duncan Smith scrapped the event and hastily summoned the media to Conservative Central Office to deliver what was described as a 'personal statement'. Over the years, the term had become a euphemism for 'about to resign' and many journalists turned up fully prepared to hear the leader announce his departure. Instead, with his closest advisers in the shadow Cabinet – May; Michael Ancram, the shadow Foreign Secretary; and shadow Home Secretary Oliver Letwin – sitting silently beside him in a show of loyalty and support, Duncan Smith issued an appeal for unity which later became known as his 'unite or die' speech.

Duncan Smith stood at a lectern in front of a banner reading 'Leadership with a purpose'. Letwin had written the words he now spoke:

A year ago the Conservative Party chose me overwhelmingly as its first democratically elected leader. Over the last few weeks, a small group of my parliamentary colleagues have decided consciously to undermine my leadership ... We cannot go on in this fashion. We have to pull together or we will hang apart. The Conservative Party wants to be led. It elected me to lead it in the direction I am now going. My message is simple and stark: unite or die.

The statement lasted for less than two minutes.

With unfortunate timing, Zoe Healy had been summoned to CCO to be interviewed for a job as May's press officer (replacing

Katie Perrior) just as the 'unite or die' press conference was about
to start. She says:

> It all looked a little bit chaotic. They were preparing for a press
> conference and during my interview people kept running in and
> out. It was almost as if they were quite keen to get me out of the
> way so they could get on with it. It was only then that they told
> me that the role was with Theresa May. Then I went over to the
> Houses of Parliament … and that's where I met Theresa for the
> first time. And she was so lovely.

Healy got the job.

But while May was enjoying a cuppa with her soon-to-be new
press officer, elsewhere in the Commons, Tory MPs were mutinous.
Within hours, a number of those who had defied the whip in the
gay adoption row had issued statements defending their actions and
refusing to apologise. Journalists doing the rounds of the Commons
bars found Tory MPs were in no mood to back down. But nor was
there much appetite for a challenge, particularly from Michael Portillo, who had been badly burned in the last leadership contest a
year earlier. All those with leadership ambitions were aware of the
reality of what Duncan Smith had made clear: he had been elected
with a clear mandate from the Tory membership; were he to be
challenged, he would simply run again and probably win.

What followed was stalemate. Duncan Smith still lacked the authority he needed to control his fitful party, but there appeared no
clear way to dislodge him. By Christmas 2002, the party's standing
in the polls had dropped to just 27 per cent, sixteen points behind
Labour. The atmosphere at Central Office became venomous, as
various factions blamed each other for the state the party found
itself in. One member of staff working at CCO at the time says:
'It was a tough time. To know that colleagues would be speaking
against you was difficult, you felt it. I couldn't understand why
people weren't rallying round the leader and the chairman.' Shailesh
Vara adds:

It was regrettable, because a lot of us wanted to concentrate on moving forward, and it was a distraction. [May] is very loyal. She'd been appointed by Iain Duncan Smith, he was the boss, she was going to do the best she possibly could for the boss, and she did. All the other things that were happening in the party were for others to get involved in.

Despite her desire to stay away from the drama, May found herself one of the targets for the backbiting. The CCO staffer says:

You couldn't be sure who was on your team. It was difficult. But she just got on with it. It couldn't have been easy. There was pressure from the media. I don't know where they were getting it from but there was always the suggestion that a stronger party chairman would not have let there be such pressure put on the leader from the parliamentary party. You couldn't ignore it, but her view was to avoid all the whispers and try to focus on the party members. Theresa always put the party first. She's a public servant. She's not interested in gossip and all that nonsense.

Vara adds: 'There were times when morale was low. But I for one went into politics to do things, and there's no point in moping around. Her attitude was likewise.'

May would later be accused of passivity for failing to fight back. Asked why she did not retaliate, she said: 'I got on with what I believed to be the job rather than the black arts. It was disruptive the way people kept opening papers and seeing anonymous sources making claims, and nobody knew who they were.'[185] Andrew Griffiths, who began working for her a year later, says May was temperamentally incapable of deploying the 'black arts'. 'In all the time I have known her, she would never publicly badmouth, she would never do the gossiping, I have never heard her brief against another politician, it just goes completely against her upbringing and approach.' Later still, in government, when May again found herself fighting intra-party squabbles, she would come round to the view that in politics it is necessary, sometimes, to stand up for one-self. If she would always be squeamish about deploying the 'black arts' herself, she would soon employ those prepared to perform a little dark magic on her behalf.

Amid the appalling atmosphere at CCO, May did her best to maintain staff morale while attempting to soothe the concerns of the membership at the highly public civil war taking place in the party. Healy says:

> She thought it was important to get out there as much as she could, going out on tours once or twice a week. She felt it was important to not be distracted. During those tough times, Theresa would come into the office and see if everyone was all right. She was sincere about asking how people were. People who may have been a bit miffed about the 'nasty party' speech soon warmed to her. After that, she gained respect. Researchers, who were always terrible gossips and eager to put people down, would come to enjoy preparing her for *Question Time* or whatever, because she was always very warm with them.

Healy, too, found May 'lovely to work with'.

> There were times I would get a bit of stick for being Irish: 'How can you have an Irish girl working for you?' That kind of thing. She would always stick up for me. If you talk to any researchers or special advisers, past and present, we are all very loyal to her. She believed in what she was doing, she was not interested in the politics of politics, she just wanted to get on with the job.

While she was friendly and pleasant to her staff, May did not social-ise with them outside of office hours. Healy says:

> We wouldn't be going out for a glass of wine together, it wasn't that kind of relationship, but she was fun. We spent a lot of time together, just the two of us. We would talk as we travelled

places in the car, we would chat about our lives. I was having a
long-distance relationship at the time with a Danish man who is
now my husband, and she would say, 'How's the Great Dane?'
She wouldn't share a lot herself. I don't think she thought it was
necessary.

As the New Year began, the mood within CCO became even
more toxic. Having first backed May over the 'nasty party' speech,
Duncan Smith began to listen to those who insisted she was to
blame for the ill-feeling it had engendered against him. He was also
irritated by the role Mark MacGregor had played, both in helping
to write the offending address and in supporting May's modernising agenda. Having been elected as a right-winger, Duncan Smith
now swung firmly back to his roots. A whispering campaign began
against May, with suggestions planted in the press that she was
likely to be replaced at his next reshuffle.

Then, on 14 February, IDS dramatically sacked MacGregor as
chief executive and appointed instead one of his cronies, Barry
Legg, a former right-wing MP who along with Duncan Smith had
been a Maastricht rebel. The assassination was carried out while
MacGregor was on holiday in Paris. He refused to respond to a
summons from Sir Stanley Kalms, the Conservatives' treasurer, to
return to London to hear the news in person, and so was informed
over the phone that his services were no longer required. Rick Nye,
the party's head of research and another moderniser, was also dispatched. When they heard the news, staff at CCO were shocked.
Zoe Healy says: 'We called it the Valentine's Day massacre. You
would look around and ask – who's in charge here? There was no
one there.'

After months of proving her loyalty to Duncan Smith, May found
his treatment of MacGregor and his rudeness in failing to properly
discuss the matter with her intolerable. She had been informed of
MacGregor's dismissal only a few hours before it took place, and
it had been presented as a fait accompli. As ever, though, May let
her displeasure be known only in private, refusing to rise to the bait

even when Michael Portillo said publicly: 'Changes have been made to the party that she should have been consulted about. She wasn't consulted about them. It looks very bad.'[186] 'I am the chairman of the party, and I am remaining the chairman of the party,' May said in response to speculation that she would – or should – resign.[187]

After holding a crisis meeting, the eight-person Conservative board, which IDS had also failed to consult before removing MacGregor and Nye, authorised May to carry a message to him that: 'Briefing against people and suggestions that they might be removed must cease.'[188] Three months later, Legg was gone. After waiting a decent interval for the fuss to die down, Duncan Smith had been forced to bow to the pressure of his chairman and the Conservative board. It was a quiet victory for May, her revenge carried out in private, away from the columns of the nation's newspapers. For Duncan Smith, however, it was too late to save his leadership.

With an uneasy truce now in place, May spent the summer pre-paring for her second conference as party chairman. This time, she was determined that the outcome would be nothing but positive, for her party and her leader. It was not to be. As May spent the evening of Sunday 5 October working on her speech in her hotel room in Blackpool, news was breaking of yet more trouble for Duncan Smith. The BBC's *Newsnight* had received reports that party staff had complained about the financing of the leader's office, including Duncan Smith's employment of his wife, Betsy. Earlier in the year, Michael Crick, the *Newsnight* reporter who been at Oxford with May, had been passed an email sent by Valerie Gearson, who worked in the leader's office, to a number of senior figures in the party including Mark MacGregor and May, expressing concern about the propriety of the arrangements. When the allegations were refuted in detail by Duncan Smith, *Newsnight* pulled the story. But reports of the programme's content were leaked to the press, and the scandal, which became known as 'Betsygate', first overshadowed conference and then consumed the leader.

The atmosphere in Blackpool became poisonous, with knots of

plotting MPs and journalists gathering in bars across the conference secure zone. May did her best to stay above the fray. A member of her team recalls the scene:

> The party chairman would traditionally speak on the Monday, so on the Sunday we were in the hall rehearsing. We were just trying to ignore everything that was going on. She saw her role as party chairman as being responsible for conference. Her priority was to deliver a good conference.

By now, May's feelings about Duncan Smith had cooled to the extent that she allowed herself a tiny, private joke at his expense. Zoe Healy says the team held a 'long debate' about what shoes she should wear to deliver her speech, eventually opting for a pair of kitten heels in material resembling Army fatigues. 'It wasn't quite "We're at war", but the message was clear,' Healy says. In her speech, May struck an emollient tone compared to the 'nasty party' harangue of the year before, saying: 'As the eyes of Britain focus on us this week, let us show them the real Conservative Party. A party of hope and aspiration, of freedom and social justice, of fairness and opportunity. A united party – for everyone, and of everyone.' But no one was really listening. All eyes were on Duncan Smith.

More details of the allegations involving Betsy Duncan Smith emerged in the days after conference. They centred on the claim that she had been paid around £18,000 a year from parliamentary funds to serve as her husband's official diary secretary while appearing to do little work. On 13 October, Parliament's sleaze investigator Sir Philip Mawer launched a formal inquiry into the affair – which would later fully exonerate the Duncan Smiths. It now emerged that May had advised Valerie Gearson to seek independent legal advice after she claimed Duncan Smith was seeking to pressure her into giving a false statement. Having stood by IDS in his time of crisis a year earlier, May now clearly felt little inclination to do so again following the lack of respect he had shown her over the sacking of Mark MacGregor.

Three weeks after conference, and with Betsygate still raging, Duncan Smith was fighting for his political life. On 26 October, amid reports that MPs were preparing to trigger a vote of no confidence in his leadership, he gave an interview in which he urged his fellow MPs to challenge him openly within the next three days or put the matter to rest. If a contest was held, he vowed he would stand. Under the party's rules, a vote of no confidence could be triggered once 15 per cent of the parliamentary party had written to the chairman of the 1922 Committee of backbench MPs expressing their lack of support for the leader. In 2002, this amounted to twenty-five MPs. Two days after Duncan Smith's bravado challenge to put up or shut up, Sir Michael Spicer, chairman of the 1922 Committee, announced that the threshold had been met. With Betsy and four members of the shadow Cabinet – Michael Howard, Michael Ancram, Oliver Letwin and May – standing beside him, Duncan Smith gave a press conference outside Central Office in which he welcomed the opportunity to end 'this ludicrous leadership speculation'.

The confidence vote was held the following day, 29 October 2003. Duncan Smith lost it, by seventy-five to ninety. Faced with the reality of trying to fight on in the face of such hostility from his own MPs, Iain Duncan Smith rowed back on his promise to fight on. He was gone. And, with dizzying speed, so too was May's dream job.

CHAPTER IX

GETTING ON WITH THE JOB

For someone who prides herself on her self-control, Theresa May was surprisingly emotional at the departure of Iain Duncan Smith. As she stood beside him while he brought the curtain down on his disastrous 26-month reign, triggering an immediate leadership contest, the third of May's short career in the Commons, she was said by those watching to be 'visibly upset'.[189] It was an unexpected response, given the battles she and IDS had become embroiled in during the six months since the 'Valentine's Day massacre' of Mark MacGregor, and particularly given her failure to back him over 'Betsygate'. But May was also a loyalist, and very conscious that Duncan Smith had given her a seat at the top table, sharing confidences and inviting her to be involved in many of the important discussions facing the party. It was a proximity to power she would not feel again until she became Prime Minister, the next two leaders she would serve keeping her outside of their inner circles. While she could not foresee the dynamics of her future position within the party, May clearly sensed the loss of something important with the departure of Duncan Smith. It also swiftly became apparent that she was about to lose her job.

Before Duncan Smith had finished giving his farewell address on 29 October 2003, with the unseemly haste that accompanies all political interregnums, Tory MPs and the media began to speculate about who would replace him. There was only one name on everyone's lips: Michael Howard, the shadow Chancellor. Howard held a press conference launching his leadership bid just eighteen hours after IDS's forlorn farewell announcement. No other candidate stepped forward. The speed with which the party coalesced around the former Home Secretary outpaced even that with which Conservatives were drawn to May in the chaotic aftermath of the 2016 European referendum thirteen years later. By the time of Howard's launch, he had attracted the support of ninety MPs, including all but three members of the shadow Cabinet. Eight days after Duncan Smith announced his departure, Howard was installed as leader.

Only May stood apart from the collective surge to anoint Howard. Using the cover of her role as party chairman, which, by convention but not always practice, required her to stay neutral, she was one of the three shadow Cabinet ministers who failed to express support for Howard the day after IDS's resignation (the other two, Tim Yeo and Michael Ancram, later issued statements saying they would not run). Instead, May went out of her way to attempt to prevent a coronation, arguing that, under the existing rules and regardless of the lack of any opponent, Howard should present himself for formal election by the grassroots membership. 'I think the parliamentary party does need to understand how angry the voluntary party were about the deposing of Iain,' she said.[190] While May's dedication, as chairman, to the rights of ordinary members was no doubt sincere, her stance was also somewhat ridiculous, and the Conservative board ruled against what would have been a largely meaningless and expensive exercise. In 2016, May would be elected to her party's leadership unopposed, meaning she too never faced a ballot of party members, let alone the wider electorate, before becoming Prime Minister.

A less charitable view of May's attitude to Howard's swift installation might be that she was aware she was unlikely to remain as party chairman under his leadership. Howard himself insists that he bore May no hostility, but she would have suspected that, while they had always got on, he did not share her views on modernisation. She was probably also conscious that Howard had not been a fan of her 'nasty party' speech. He says today: 'I was critical of that.

I thought it unnecessarily gave ammunition to our critics. There was a truth in [the speech], it was the phrase I objected to.' From the moment the abbreviated leadership contest began, the press speculated that May would be moved from the chairmanship. The only question was whether she would retain any role in the shadow Cabinet.

On 6 November 2003, Michael Howard was elected leader of the Conservative Party, its fifth in thirteen years. Welcoming him to the post, May said: 'I am delighted to pledge my full support for the leader of the Conservative Party, Michael Howard … I look forward to working with Michael and doing all I can to ensure that this party is ready to win the next general election.'[191] Three days later, he sacked her as party chairman. In her place, Howard appointed not one but two 'joint chairmen': Liam Fox, who had been shadow Health Secretary under Duncan Smith, and Lord Saatchi, a Treasury spokesman in the Lords and one of Howard's closest friends in politics. Howard says of his decision: 'I had my own people that I wanted to bring in to become party chairmen … It wasn't an adverse reflection on her, it was just I knew who I wanted to do that job.'

May put on a brave face, joking that 'Yes, it takes two men to step into the shoes of one woman',[192] but there was no doubt she was bitterly disappointed. 'It was difficult to leave, I really enjoyed being chairman,' she admitted soon afterwards.[193] Shailesh Vara was also sad to see May go. He says:

> It was a pretty tense time. I had built up a very good rapport with her, and given that we were trying to change the party, to make the party have a broader appeal, more women, more ethnic minorities, this was the person who was really driving the agenda, and then she moved on. But then that's politics.

May was now forced to get to grips with a shadow Cabinet role no one outside Howard's inner circle could have anticipated. The new leader had come up with a radical approach to the formation of his front-bench team: instead of simply shadowing their counterparts in government, his line-up would take on 'super portfolios', covering briefs he felt sat better together than those traditionally delineated by Whitehall. Just as novel, his shadow Cabinet would be slimmed down to only twelve from the customary twenty or more, with some members responsible for briefs shadowing more than one, or parts of several, departments, while other posts usually represented at shadow Cabinet level were reduced to more junior status. Following speculation that May might be shunted out of his top team altogether, on 10 November, Howard announced the makeup of his new shadow Cabinet of eleven men and one woman. The sole female at the table was Theresa May.

May now boasted the title of shadow Secretary of State for Transport and the Environment, responsible for shadowing not one but two of Whitehall's most complex departments, represented in government by the formidable Alistair Darling and Margaret Beckett respectively. Zoe Healy says: 'I think she would have liked to have stayed on [as party chairman], definitely. But she didn't take it emotionally. It was: "I have got to get on with Transport and Environment so I will get on with Transport and Environment. That's what I have got to do."' Howard says he was never in any doubt that he would retain May in the shadow Cabinet throughout his time as leader. 'She was thorough, she was hard-working, and she was quite reliable. I did see her as a high-flyer,' he says. But the press viewed May's new role as a demotion. In an insightful article, Benedict Brogan of the *Daily Telegraph* set out the reasons May's star was now seen as being on the wane:

Mrs May was the first female Chairman, and in her leopard print kitten heels and lilac leather skirt she was supposed to be the embodiment of a new, trendy Tory party. But to the dismay of the party's modernisers who hoped she might emerge as a standard-bearer for their cause, she turned out to be an excellent communicator but a terrible politician. Outside Westminster, and in particular outside the party, people responded enthusiastically to her. So much so that when focus groups were shown footage of Mrs May's interviews and speeches, they compared her admiringly to Margaret Thatcher. But among colleagues she failed to build a network of friends who would back her when things went wrong … It was noticeable in the past week that no one came forward to argue for her to be kept on, or even promoted.[194]

May's staff confirm that she took no interest in courting either the media or her fellow MPs, and that this may well have affected her standing at the time. Zoe Healy says: 'A lot of people would say she would keep herself to herself. She wasn't a gossip, she wasn't interested in the Westminster bubble. I never saw her socialising with MPs, beyond what she would be expected to do.' May's opponents found that she did not participate in the bonhomie that many rival politicians engage in away from the cameras. Vince Cable recalls his impressions of her during the opposition era: 'She was not one of the Tories you tended to develop a chatty relationship with. I suppose I saw her as … a bit tribal, a bit aloof. You never, ever saw Labour, Lib Dem people wandering up to her and having friendly chats.'

But if her parliamentary colleagues viewed her as unsociable, those who have worked alongside May often insist that that she is good company. Liam Fox says: 'I've never found Theresa cold. She's quite reserved but there's a big difference. She doesn't wear her heart on her sleeve, she's not somebody who is obsessed with getting profiles in the media, being talked about. She gets on with her work.'

Rather than schmoozing in the bars of the House of Commons, May put in long hours at her desk. Shaya Raymond, who now joined her team as a researcher, says of his experience of working for May:

I remember that time as being a time of working really hard, working until eight o'clock, half eight, nine o'clock, it was very busy. But we always felt that we were a good team and we would support each other. We felt we had a good boss and a good team and were very loyal to her.

Andrew Griffiths began working as May's chief of staff in 2004, soon after she was given the Transport and Environment brief. He says of her commitment:

She was first at her desk, she was always in the office before I was, and would plough through the work, nose down, until it was time to go home. What was really interesting was her ability in the Chamber and her command of the brief, and that's where her personality came to the fore, and her approach to politics won through. Theresa was a detail person, she would go through every single line of every single document until she was happy. Many of our colleagues get on with a wing and a prayer ... whereas Theresa delves deep into the detail.

It is a dedication which Griffiths believes can be traced back to May's upbringing in the vicarage. He says:

She ... takes her obligations very, very serious[ly]. And that runs through everything. It runs through making sure she reads every document, it runs through being at her desk as early as possible in the morning and not leaving until all the work's done, it runs through making sure that she treats people with respect. She gets the politics, absolutely, but she just doesn't play the politics.

While May is said by friends and many former colleagues to be amenable company, there is no denying her reserve. Shaya Raymond says:

The problem with Theresa is she can come across as slightly cold. She would never do a meeting on a sofa; when it comes to work, business ... it's professional to the umpteenth degree. She wasn't the sort of person to go for team drinks. It was a very formal working relationship; we never really had a relationship where we would send each other friendly chatty emails.

Anne Jenkin confirms that May does not have much in the way of small talk: 'Honestly, no. You can't really have that chit-chat, because her time is too precious, she's too serious, and she would feel I was wasting her time. I'm sure she wouldn't feel that, by the way, it would just be the way I would feel. Everything was very business-like.'

Another young May staffer from the time adds:

She was very good to work for, she was very nice, she was very friendly, but she was never, certainly for myself, someone you could have a warm, open relationship with. Some MPs and their researchers, they go out drinking together, they go to the pub, and obviously for Theresa's character that's not who she is at all. She's very focused, she's obviously very hard-working, but she also keeps a professional distance as well. You can be a bit kind of cold and formal and not very warm but still be a nice, interesting person.

May's sense that her staff were there to work for her and not to be her friends is reflective of a general attitude towards her relationships. Once asked who her 'best mate' in politics was, she responded by naming not a fellow MP but 'my husband, who is a great supporter in everything I do'.[195] All of those around May confirm that, rather than relying on a wide support network, either inside or outside Parliament, once her parents died her emotional needs were fully met by her husband. Anne Jenkin says: 'Philip is obviously her rock … I'm sure she talks it all through with him, and so she should. He's a political person, in the same way Denis [Thatcher] was for Lady T, he's a good honest listener who will give advice and support.'

So comfortable was Philip May in his role as a supportive husband to his politician wife that he did not flinch at attending meetings and coffee mornings organised for the spouses of Tory

MPs, at which he was invariably the only man present. Andrew Griffiths says: 'I never saw him feel awkward about that. He was always relaxed about his role and her role. He's just completely supportive.' The MP Keith Simpson says his wife, Pepita, made a point of seeking out Philip May at meetings of the spouses' support group: 'He was always on his own as the only man, and she used to go and sit with him.'

At the height of the 2003 leadership contest, May, then still party chairman, had gone ahead with announcing one of her proposed major reforms, the holding of US-style open primaries for selection contests, with all voters in the area, and not just members of the Conservative Party, eligible to take part. The first of the primaries was set to be trialled in the safe Labour seat of Warrington South. By the time the primary was held on 13 November, May was out of the job, but the contest went ahead anyway, resulting in the people of Warrington South selecting a female candidate in Fiona Bruce, a local solicitor and mother-of-two, to fight the forthcoming election. The outcome must have given May enormous satisfaction, but the open primary system was not taken up under Michael Howard's leadership. In a small sign, however, that May's efforts as party chairman had been appreciated, she was named Opposition Politician of the Year at the 2003 Political Studies Association Awards a few weeks later.

As May worked tirelessly on her huge brief of Transport and Environment through the first half of 2004, she would have been aware that, in contrast to her days with Iain Duncan Smith, she was no longer involved in the day-to-day running of the party or in framing its offering to voters. Instead, two bright new members of the 2001 intake, David Cameron and George Osborne, seemed to have leapfrogged her and others of the class of 1997 to take a seat at the top table. Although strikingly young at thirty-seven and thirty-two respectively, Cameron and Osborne had long experience in Conservative politics, the former having worked as Howard's special adviser in government and both with time served at the Conservative Research Department (CRD). The pair had helped in

the difficult task of preparing Iain Duncan Smith for his weekly tor-
ture of facing Tony Blair at Prime Minister's Questions, a role they
continued under Howard. By the middle of 2004, both Cameron
and Osborne had reached the shadow Cabinet, the former with a
role coordinating policy ahead of the general election, the latter
as shadow Chief Secretary to the Treasury. Both were involved in
daily discussions with Howard about the party's strategy, direction
and approach.

Andrew Griffiths believes that, as long as Howard was happy
with her work, May would not exactly have minded that he had
chosen two young, inexperienced (and privileged, public school-educated) men as confidants. Her lack of allies around the shadow
Cabinet table would, however, have been starkly highlighted by the
tight unit Cameron and Osborne formed. He says:

> I think Michael just respected her for her ability to do the job. I
> don't think Theresa has ever asked for more than that. She's very
> happy to just be judged on her output and her work rate. [But] I
> think it was difficult for her. You would sense when you would go
> to bigger meetings that other people around the room would have
> their allies. We would go to a meeting with George, David, when
> they were MPs but were advising Michael at that time, and they
> would be close. Theresa didn't have that, she would have to fight
> to make sure her voice was heard, and fight for her principles.

Zoe Healy adds:

> I got the impression from MPs and Central Office that they com-
> pletely underestimated her. I don't think they would have seen
> her as a future Prime Minister, or would have appreciated how
> far she would have gone. I think she had been underestimated for
> a long time. I always thought she was very able and capable, but
> that certainly wasn't the view in the party.

On 14 June 2004, after just seven months in the Transport and

Environment post, May was pitched into another of Howard's 'super departments', to the newly created role of shadow Secretary of State for the Family. The move was briefed out as a demotion, a form of punishment for what was seen as a failure to make her mark on shaping policy in the meatier realm of Transport and the Environment. Two days later, the *Sun* columnist Jane Moore wrote: 'In his shadow cabinet reshuffle, Michael Howard has appointed Theresa May as "spokesman for the family". Ms May has no children. Politicians never learn, do they?'[196] May hit back, telling a diarist from the *Sunday Telegraph*: 'I used to be shadow Transport Secretary, but I'd never been a train driver. There are many types of families. A couple can be a family.'[197]

As usual, May got stuck into her new brief, drawing up policy on helping children in care and on giving fathers a presumed right of shared custody. While the portfolio cut across several government departments, including Health, the Home Office, and Work and Pensions, her main opponent was Margaret Hodge, the Minister for Children, her old adversary at the 1994 Barking by-election. As she drew up plans to improve the rights of separated fathers, somewhat to her alarm, May found herself lauded by groups such as Fathers4Justice, at the time involved in a campaign of direct action which included staging a citizens' arrest on Hodge and pelting Tony Blair with purple flour bombs during Prime Minister's Questions. One member of her team at the time recalls: 'I remember Fathers4Justice sent her a Christmas card, and we were joking and saying, "Let's not tell anyone we got that Christmas card!"'

In addition to her brief, May was forced to devote much of 2004 and the run-up to the general election in 2005 to her Maidenhead constituency. The Liberal Democrats had run her close in 2001, and her 3,000 majority looked more vulnerable than ever as opinion polls suggested many Labour supporters were likely to defect to the Lib Dems to register their opposition to the 2003 war in Iraq. One of her staffers says:

Round about that time, there was a lot of concern that Theresa could lose her seat ... It was still the aftermath of the Iraq War [and] Charlie Kennedy was quite popular. It was uncertain whether Theresa was going to make it through 2005. There was a sense that we all had to pitch in hard and we were quite driven as a result of that.

As polling day approached, it became clear that while Labour's standing was indeed adversely affected by the issue of Iraq, Tony Blair's party was maintaining a lead over the Conservatives. By April, a month before the election was due to take place, the Tories were still lagging three points behind. For May, it was a time of frustration as well as anxiety over the result in Maidenhead. Having risked so much in public as party chairman to try to persuade the Conservatives of the need to change their image, on leaving the role she had been forced to make the case in private that the Tories could not win against New Labour unless they did something radical to alter voters' perceptions. Above all, May felt, the Conservatives were going into the 2005 general election with little to offer women; half the voting public. It was a problem compounded by the fact that, once again, the vast majority of constituencies would be fought by Conservative candidates who were male.

Michael Howard has no memory of May seeking to persuade him that female voters needed something more, however. He says:

The process of change had started. The number of female candidates was increasing, the number of ethnic minority candidates was increasing, a lot of us thought we'd have liked the pace to be faster, but there are practical limitations to what you can do over a short period of time.

Nor does Howard believe that the Conservatives' offering at the 2005 general election was a turn-off for women voters. 'I think that's absurd when you consider that our most prominent promises were cleaner hospitals, with a particular emphasis on getting rid of the disease in hospitals of MRSA, discipline in schools, more police; these were all policies which were very close to the hearts of women and families.'

Andrew Griffiths says, however, that Howard's belief in the Conservatives' appeal to female voters was not shared by May.

Michael Howard had a set view about what he thought voters were interested in and what motivated them to go to the ballot box and he didn't get, I think, that the sort of issues Theresa was talking about were key, not just to getting out the women vote but actually key to changing the perception of the party and what we care about and our priorities.

Griffiths recalls May becoming enraged by an edition of *Newsnight* in which voters in a focus group were asked for their reaction to a set of policies. They were broadly positive – until they discovered that the policies were those of the Conservatives. Griffiths says: 'It wasn't the message [that was the problem], it was how the message was received. That was the kind of thing she was talking about, and keen to address.'

Tony Blair won his third general election victory on 5 May 2005. While Michael Howard had steadied the ship, proving largely successful in bringing to an end the civil war within the Conservative Party that had raged under Iain Duncan Smith, the challenge of seeing off the still-formidable New Labour machine was too much. Under his leadership, the Tories had made inroads, however. Blair's majority was reduced to just sixty-six, with Howard adding thirty-three seats to the Conservatives' tally. In Maidenhead, May overcame the Liberal Democrat threat with ease, almost doubling her majority to 6,231. All her hard work had paid off – locally, at least.

CHAPTER X

WOMEN2WIN – AND LOSE

In the summer of 2005, Theresa May launched two campaigns. The first would end in abject failure. The second would change the face of British politics for ever. She has never spoken publicly about her attempt to run for the Conservative leadership following the party's third consecutive general election defeat. Her run remained so secret that, while she did not seek to quash speculation in the media, she never declared it publicly. Ultimately, her ambitions came to nothing when she failed to garner the support of more than a handful of MPs. A woman who, a decade later, would win the backing of 60 per cent of her colleagues in the final round of her second run for the top job could count the number of supporters at her first in single digits. From the ashes of her leadership bid, however, was born a project that would prove perhaps her greatest achievement in politics before her entry into No. 10. Almost by accident, May would launch a campaign that would transform her party into a modern, inclusive and forward-looking organisation which, although much work remains to be done, is attracting increasing numbers of women, ethnic minorities and working-class candidates – and voters. It is said that no Conservative woman elected to Parliament since the launch of the group she helped found, Women2Win, has got there without its help. Their triumphs and glories over the coming decades, as well as those who follow them, will stand as one of May's great legacies.

Back in 2005, May came out of the general election campaign

feeling dejected. Once again, the Conservatives were facing a long spell in opposition. May was also deeply troubled by the fact that, despite her work as party chairman to encourage the selection of more women and ethnic minority candidates, the party's female representation still stood at only seventeen out of 198, just three more than at the previous election and four more than when she herself entered Parliament in 1997.

There were some successes; although the net gain was three, thanks to the resignation of two sitting women MPs there were five new female faces on the Tory benches, including such promising prospects as Justine Greening, Theresa Villiers and Maria Miller. In addition, Adam Afriyie and Shailesh Vara had become the party's first ethnic minority MPs. Vara recalls how May, encountering him at a Tory ball soon after his selection in 2004 for North West Cambridgeshire, gave him a big hug, a celebration, he felt not just of the fact that a man she liked was on his way to Parliament, but of the broader achievement in securing a safe seat as an Asian candidate. As May would go on to point out, however, following the 2005 election there remained more men called 'David' in the shadow Cabinet than women. At that pace, it would be 400 years before the party achieved gender parity. A photograph of the 2005 Conservative parliamentary party would have appeared remarkably similar to one taken a century before.

In the hours following the election defeat, on 6 May 2005, Michael Howard announced that he would be standing down as leader. He added, however, that he would remain in place until a review had been held of the rules governing the contest. The race would not formally begin until October, with the result due two months later. The delay gave time for some of the party's rising stars to test their support, and for all the potential candidates to weigh their options. Howard now promoted within the shadow Cabinet both David Cameron and George Osborne. To the surprise of many, Osborne, still only thirty-three, was given the plum portfolio of shadow Chancellor, while Cameron, an also youthful thirty-eight, was made shadow Education Secretary. With a higher-profile brief, Cameron was able to take steps over the summer to burnish his leadership credentials, a task he was ably assisted in by his close friend Osborne, who ruled himself out of the contest within a week of the general election defeat. In deferring to his older friend, Osborne made clear that Cameron was to be considered the senior of the pair, despite his lowlier position in shadow Cabinet. May, who already bore the heavy load of shadowing the non-existent Department of the Family, had the Culture, Media and Sport brief added to her portfolio.

It is the stuff of Conservative folklore that Howard's decision to delay the 2005 contest gave Cameron the opportunity to grow in stature and prepare the viable bid for the leadership that would not have been possible had his predecessor stepped down immediately. Howard denies that this was his motivation, but agrees he did want the party to make a considered choice. He says:

> My thinking was that I was the fourth leader of the Conservative Party in six years when I took over; I did not want, six months down the road from the choice of the new leader, people to say, 'If only we hadn't rushed it, we wouldn't have made this mistake.' So I was determined to take some time over the process … so that the party had a chance to take a good, long, hard look at all the candidates.

The long summer months did indeed give May for one an opportunity to reflect. She began to consider her own position, to observe the strengths and weaknesses of those around her, and to decide what she felt was of primary importance to her politically. Still incensed by the lack of progress made by women candidates at the general election, she determined that this was the greatest challenge facing the Conservatives. Eric Pickles says: 'I think it was that relatively brief phase as party chairman that made her kind of understand [the need to modernise] and apply that to Women2Win.'

May's sense of the importance of change was twofold: as she had warned in her 'nasty party' speech two years earlier, without a dramatic transformation she feared the electorate would never entrust the Tories with their votes in sufficient numbers to beat New Labour.

Secondly, it was wrong in principle that a major political party, one she loved to its bones, was unable to attract, and propel to Parliament, candidates from a range of backgrounds. Her own political struggles, and the help she had received from mentors including Gillian Shephard and Angela Rumbold, had instilled in her a desire to help other women. Andrew Griffiths, then working as her chief of staff, says: 'She's always been committed to this idea of getting more women into politics and changing the face of politics, I think because she had to battle the "male, stale and pale" … Tory benches looking incredibly similar, and had to fight her way through.'

As she sat in the post-election shadow Cabinet, May was discouraged. Howard, she felt, had never heeded her warnings about the need to change the party by making its policy offering more attractive to female voters and encouraging more women to stand as candidates. And there was little indication that any successor would prove more receptive. While she liked and admired a number of the likely candidates, who at this early stage included Ken Clarke and David Davis, considered to be the favourites, as well as Liam Fox, Alan Duncan, Malcolm Rifkind and Tim Yeo, none of them had taken a lead on equalities issues. Nor did the young bloods of Cameron and Osborne particularly impress her. Griffiths says:

> I remember her desperately trying to get Michael Howard to support policies for more flexible maternity leave for women, increased maternity pay, and getting real difficulty in [persuading] modernisers like David and George, who when they were in power might have done a lot of these things, but at that stage she had to really battle to get them to understand these issues and take them seriously.

More generally, May feared that a six-month leadership contest between six or seven white men would prove a turn-off to voters, highlighting the lack of progress in the Conservative Party. She began to give the thought of running for the leadership herself serious consideration. Griffiths says that she knew she could not win, but felt that it was important to have a female presence in the contest nonetheless.

> There had been in the run-up to that leadership [battle] some really, really bad stories about how the Conservative Party had treated some of their women candidates ... some pretty depressing stories, from Theresa's perspective, about how we treated women and how we valued women. She felt that there was a need for a woman to be in the race. She felt that the issues that she cared about needed to be aired.

Like most of those considering a run, May kept her cards close to her chest as the party lurched into a self-destructive discussion about the rules under which the contest should take place. She became a leading opponent of Howard's broadly unpopular proposal that the right to vote for leader be taken away from grassroots members and transferred back to MPs. As some within the party began to agitate for Howard to quit immediately, Cameron confirmed his intention to stand, even as the still undeclared David Davis emerged as the bookies' favourite. Privately questioning both candidates' interest in the question of women's advancement, these developments further solidified May's view that she should take a tilt at the job herself.

On 15 June, May gave a speech to the Adelaide Group, a gathering of senior businesswomen, which she tacitly considered the launch of her leadership campaign – even if the audience were never told so. In her address, she said: 'I think the Conservative Party needs more women. We need more women candidates, more women MPs, and more senior female faces on television, on the radio and in the newspapers,' adding that, 'as things stand, the modern Labour Party is far better than we are at speaking the language of the woman voter'.[198] She called for positive action to get female Tories into Parliament, in later interviews expanding on this to suggest that 50 per cent of the parliamentary party should be made up of women. Griffiths says: 'She ... called for a 50/50 Parliament, and that was her point of differentiation as all these runners and riders were preparing themselves for this leadership campaign. That was clearly something that she felt passionately about, so she went on the front foot about it.'

Opaque though it was, May's speech generated interest in her leadership intentions. In words dubbed 'intriguing' by *The Guardian*, she had concluded with the words: 'Are we really saying there is no prospect of a woman leading any of the political parties in the near future?'[199] Now journalists began to ask, on and off the record, whether she intended to stand. Her team was careful to neither confirm nor deny she would be a candidate. Zoe Healy, who was splitting her time working as a press officer for both May and Francis Maude, now party chairman, at Central Office, remembers journalists trying to get her to spill the beans over drinks in a nearby pub. 'There was a bit of an over-reaction by people. Theresa did not discuss it. At all. People having drinks in the Marquis of Salisbury would be asking me about it, and I would just say: "We're not discussing this." People in Central Office certainly thought she might stand.'

A week after her speech, May inadvertently gave the game away herself when she misspoke during an appearance on Radio 4's *Today* programme. Asked outright if she would be running, she said: 'Let's wait and see what happens when the autumn comes and candidates actually declare our…' before correcting herself to go on: '… themselves'. Further confirmation of her intention came when she granted a rare full-length interview to *The Times*, in which she criticised her fellow candidates for lacking ambition in their plans to modernise the party, saying: 'There is more to this than appearing on television without a tie.' Asked why she was not considered a front-runner in the contest, she did not deny the suggestion that she was a candidate, instead musing that she was 'not terribly popular'. 'I don't do my politics in the way many people here do politics,' she added. 'I'm much more interested in getting on and delivering, rather than debating in smoke-filled rooms.'[200]

Not long after the general election, May had been invited to take part in a panel discussion on BBC Radio 4's *Woman's Hour*. The topic was the low level of female representation in the Conservative parliamentary party, and her fellow guests were Professor Sarah Childs, an expert on gender and politics, and Anne Jenkin, whose husband, Bernard, father, grandmother and great-grandfather all were or had been MPs. Now a member of the House of Lords, Jenkin remained active in Conservative circles despite her own failed bid to be elected to Parliament in 1987, and had begun hosting lunches for Tory-supporting women in the hope of persuading them to run for office. Jenkin has since said of the *Woman's Hour* discussion:

> I remember sitting in the green room at the BBC when the re-searcher came in to talk to the woman following on after me, a comedian I think. 'You are on after a piece about women and the Conservative Party,' she said. And they both chortled. I felt ashamed of my party. That confirmed to me there was much work to do.[201]

Perhaps to the surprise of the programme's producers, however, what followed was a spirited discussion in which neither May nor Jenkin pulled their punches or sought to make excuses for the party's lack of progress. Jenkin had met May a few times in the past, but the pair were not close. As they sat together in the *Woman's Hour* studio, Jenkin now realised she was in the presence of a kindred spirit – on women's issues at least.

Not long afterwards, on 7 July, Jenkin again found herself sitting next to May, this time at a sixtieth birthday brunch held by Michael Ancram, then the Conservatives' deputy leader. The atmosphere was strange and sombre, with most of the guests in shock at the horrific events that had unfurled in central London a few hours earlier, when four suicide bombers had detonated devices on public transport, killing fifty-two passengers. Like the other guests, May and Jenkin could talk of little apart from the terrible devastation that had been wrought a few miles from where they met. It was only towards the end of the gathering that they moved on to discuss the state of the Tory Party. Jenkin soon learned that, like her, May was sceptical about the leadership candidates' commitment to the cause of women's representation. May did not, however, reveal to Jenkin her own interest in the job. Jenkin says:

> I can … remember sitting next to Theresa and saying, 'What is going to be done?' At that stage it looked like David Davis was going to win the leadership. We said to each other: 'Well, is there any point when he's not going to understand our agenda, and do I really want to spend my summer campaigning on something that's not going to get anywhere?'

The two women discussed what they felt was the root of the problem: even if, partly as a result of May's work as party chairman, constituency parties were now shortlisting female candidates, when the final selection was made they tended to go for a man, who better fit the image they had of an MP. This was especially true in safe seats. All too often, women candidates were complaining, they would perform well at selections and get down to the last two or three, only to find themselves pipped to the post. What they needed was practical help to get them over the final hurdle. The pair agreed that the answer lay in a priority, or 'Gold' list, such as that May and Andrew Lansley had first suggested at the time of the previous leadership election, in 2001. Despite their reservations about the likely commitment of the next Conservative leader, the two women began making tentative plans for a new pressure group to advance the cause of women within the party by providing practical help to get them selected in safe seats. Jenkin says: 'That first conversation we had at that Michael Ancram breakfast was so crucial. I remember thinking, "Oh God, she's prepared to get stuck in, fantastic." We … agreed that I would do the running around and getting things done and she would turn up and be the spokesperson.'

That August, the Mays holidayed in Switzerland as usual, where they spent much of their time discussing the question of whether she should run for the leadership, ultimately agreeing that if she could get enough support then she had a duty to run. May still did not share her thoughts even with friends such as Jenkin or more junior staff including

Zoe Healy; only those closest to her, including Griffiths, her press secretary Katie Perrior and husband Philip, were let in on the secret.

When Parliament returned in September, a small group began meeting on a weekly basis to discuss the project to help female candidates, usually gathering in May's Westminster office. Among the regular attendees were May's staffers, Perrior and Griffiths, who would both become hugely influential in the campaign, and the late Shireen Ritchie, a long-time advocate of increasing diversity within the Conservative Party (and for ever known in the press as 'Madonna's mother-in-law' thanks to her connection to the pop star through her stepson Guy Ritchie). Other attendees included Laura Sandys, who would go on to be elected to Parliament in 2010, but who at the time was struggling to get a seat. Sandys regaled the group with a story of how she was narrowly beaten to a selection in Arundel and South Downs by Nick Herbert, the openly gay future Home Affairs minister. As she left the selection meeting, she overheard one 'old trout' telling another: 'Well, he may be a homosexual, but at least we didn't get a woman.'[202]

Margot James, who would go on to become MP for Stourbridge, was another prospective candidate who attended some early meetings, having herself experienced difficulty getting selected ahead of the 2005 election. She says that although by now it was clear there was a desire for change at the level of the national party, the message had yet to filter down to the Tory shires. 'The associations had more control and they had less training,' she says.

> They had a lot of autonomy and a lot of freedom to select in the image of the retiring MP if they liked him, and it always was a him, of course, so it was harder for women to get selected. I remember I applied to Reading and I got a very nice, polite letter outlining what the procedure would be … and if I got through to the last stage, I'd be very welcome to join them for cocktails – and bring my wife.

After trying out and rejecting a series of 'dreadful' alternatives, the group settled on the name Women2Win. Margot James goes on:

There was a debate about whether we should embrace positive action. Theresa felt very strongly that nothing would change unless we started to assert ourselves and make waves. She felt strongly that if we left it to just gentle encouragement, and what had been happening before, then it would be hopelessly slow and really nothing would change. I think she felt probably that she had been battling away on this issue with her predominantly male colleagues in the Commons and felt really that she wasn't getting very far, and certainly not fast enough.

At the same time as Women2Win was being formed, May began to ramp up the rhetoric of her still covert leadership campaign, focusing almost exclusively on her critique of the party which, she suggested in one speech, would face sex discrimination litigation were it an international company. She again called for positive action, accusing those who opposed the idea of 'living in the dark ages'.[203] In a speech to the Fawcett Society, which campaigns for women's rights, she went on: 'We cannot just pay lip service to the need to elect more women and members of ethnic minorities as Conservative MPs,' adding that the party 'will have to throw away traditional stereotypes and accept new ways of doing things'.[204]

At the end of September, the question of the rules under which the leadership contest would be run was settled, with Howard failing to secure enough support for his proposal to give the final say back to MPs. May had been a staunch opponent, repeatedly stressing the importance of allowing the grassroots a stake in the selection of their leader. Howard had hoped to avoid a repeat of the 2001 leadership election, when the MPs' clear favourite, Kenneth Clarke, had been defeated by Iain Duncan Smith's appeal to the more right-wing (and anti-European) membership. Unlike Howard and his young advisers Cameron and Osborne, however, May had done time as a local party activist, and felt strongly that the voices of ordinary members should be heard. The system introduced by William Hague in 1998, of members selecting from a shortlist of two voted for by MPs, remains to this day.

As the 2005 Conservative Party conference approached at the start of October, May still considered herself a candidate, even though she had yet to declare her intentions. When a meeting was called of the contenders' campaign teams, to draw up a timetable for a series of hustings, she sent representatives along. Griffiths says that while she was not yet ready to announce it officially, her purpose in making clear she was likely to run was twofold:

> Theresa absolutely was in that race, I think not with any expectation that she would win, but [with] a clear determination to make sure that the issues she cared about were heard. But also I think … that by raising those and being an effective communicator and a good politician, [she] was making sure that her place around the [shadow] Cabinet table was secured.

Many of her colleagues failed to pick up on the subtle signs that May was hoping to run. Michael Howard says: 'I'm not sure I was aware she was wanting to put her hat into the ring … It was quite a crowded field, and there wasn't room for many more candidates.' The MP Andrew Robathan, who was working on David Cameron's campaign, was, however, well aware that May was mulling over a bid. He has said: 'She was contemplating standing for the leadership in 2005, and it's no criticism of her to say that she had that ambition.'[205]

Delivering her conference speech in her capacity as shadow Culture Secretary that October, May set out her stall, warning delegates:

> … for the small minority who don't accept women – or black or gay people – as their equals, I've got a message: don't think you'll find a refuge from the modern world here; there is no place for you in our Conservative Party. Because every day that we are unwilling to embrace a future in which all men and women respect each other as absolute equals is another day we will be out of government.[206]

But the scale of the attitudinal change needed within the party was made clear as, outside the hall where she was speaking, David

Davis, who in the run-up to the conference had become the leadership front-runner, paraded two busty supporters dressed in tight T-shirts emblazoned with the words 'It's DD for Me'.

Still a few weeks away from its formal launch, May and Jenkin held an event at conference for Women2Win. Among those attending was May's future leadership rival Andrea Leadsom. Jenkin says:

> I remember Andrea Leadsom getting up and saying: 'I've got all the qualifications that any man would be expected to have, I fought my [unwinnable] seat in Liverpool or wherever it was, and what more have I got to do? Although I hate any form of positive action I am beginning to think we might have to go down the route of all-women shortlists.'

Jenkin too had begun to think that all-women shortlists, such as Labour had adopted, were the answer to the Conservatives' equality problem. May remained opposed. Griffiths says: 'She never called for all-women shortlists. I think that Theresa believes in meritocracy and she believes in levelling the playing field. My reading of it is that she doesn't think that women need special treatment, they just need the same treatment as the men.'

Professor Childs says that, while the need for fundamental reform of the Conservative Party had been obvious for some time, particularly following the introduction of all-women shortlists in the Labour Party and the resulting surge in female Labour MPs in 1997, it was the involvement of a high-profile politician such as May that made all the difference to the success of Women2Win. 'The party did need to act because the evidence in the House was just so embarrassing,' Childs says.

> But, obviously, the Conservative Party and its ideology and its ethos found anything that smacked of positive action – not even positive discrimination but just positive action – it made a lot people uncomfortable. She [May] was somebody who was publicly known, quite often through her shoes and her clothing, and that support

was important. Without that, I think there would have been less media coverage. She clearly felt seriously enough about it that she would not only speak about the problem, but suggest the solution that would be criticised by a lot of members of her party.

For May, that solution was not all-women shortlists, but her Gold List.

The contest to replace Michael Howard formally began the day after conference ended, on 7 October, when nominations opened. By now, May was coming under increasing pressure to make clear whether or not she would stand as a candidate. Boxed into a corner during a conference appearance on the *Today* programme, she had said she would make an announcement the following week. The reality of the situation was that, while she was desperate to become a candidate in order to voice her opinions and help shape the debate about the party's future in the forthcoming hustings, she was struggling to find fellow MPs to back her. May's famous 'unclubbability', her refusal to put in long hours socialising with colleagues in the many Commons bars, or to show off her wares as a political heavyweight in the television studios, meant that, in Shailesh Vara's words, she had no 'natural following'. In addition, a sizeable number of the small electorate of (male, pale and stale) MPs found May's repeated warnings about the change needed in the party off-putting. Eric Pickles says:

I used to nag her to go into the [House of Commons] Dining Room. She wouldn't do that, she wouldn't do the [Commons] Tea Room. It's not she's not a pleasant person, it's not like she's not rather good company, it isn't like she isn't actually a laugh. I just think she found it uncomfortable and superficial.

Vara agrees: 'Those who knew her and had worked with her realised that this was a formidable politician. But she didn't go out of her way to show that to other people, because that's not Theresa.'

May's discomfort at the prospect of wooing and glad-handing her fellow MPs, and, having never cultivated strong friendships, the fact that she lacked a strong ally in the Commons to do it for her, meant she struggled to ask even those well-disposed to her to actually give her their vote. Despite being as close as May came to having a friend in Parliament, she did not approach Andrew Lansley, he thinks because she suspected he too was hoping to run. He agrees that May's lack of a coterie was an issue for her campaign, saying: 'I don't think she ever had a network.' Cheryl Gillan adds:

> I don't honestly know when I became aware that she had leadership ambitions … but I probably did [then] because I've always known that she was wanting to go for leader. [But whereas] Cameron had a clique going all the way through … she's not that cliquey. She's not got this 'I'm born to rule' attitude, and that was what came through with Cameron.

Having delayed for as long as possible, by the time MPs returned to Westminster after the conference break, May knew she had to make a decision. In the final tally, her level of firm support from her fellow MPs numbered no more than a handful out of nearly 200. One MP has suggested she got the backing of just two of her colleagues. Rather than risk humiliation, May and the team agreed that she should gracefully retreat from the field. In keeping with her below-the-radar campaign, no formal capitulation announcement was made. Instead, on 12 October, May again went on the *Today* programme and disclosed that she would be backing David Cameron in the contest. Saying he 'understood the depth of the change which is needed', she described Cameron as 'somebody who is a fresh approach for the Conservative Party and somebody who is willing to address the issues that matter'. If the slight from her fellow MPs smarted, May never let even those closest to her see she was upset or disappointed.

Her own leadership ambitions having ended in failure, May concentrated on two new projects: encouraging the next Tory leader to support the advancement of women and ethnic minorities in the party, and building up the fledgling Women2Win. In the first, she was encouraged by the noises coming from Cameron's camp. The young challenger was now established as the favourite to win the contest, thanks largely to an electrifying speech at conference which, to her approval, stressed his credentials as a moderniser. In contrast, Davis had stumbled, with a lacklustre address which focused almost exclusively on his Home Affairs brief and failed to set out his broader vision. Griffiths says:

> The first goal was to force the new leader of the party, and by then we knew it was going to be David Cameron, to take the issue of women seriously, and to stake out some territory. It was the women parking their tanks on the new leader's lawn. The whole idea was we would commit David to taking the issue of women seriously, and particularly women's representation.

Women2Win was formally launched with an event on 23 November at Westminster's Millbank Tower, chaired by Jackie Ashley of *The Guardian*, at which May, Professor Childs, Katherine Rake of the Fawcett Society and Jenny Watson, then head of the Equal Opportunities Commission, spoke. Figures were released illustrating the dismal pace of progress: just 9 per cent of the Conservative parliamentary party was female, and there were only three more women Tory MPs than in 1932. Briefing the media ahead of the launch, May described a new sense of 'militancy' in the party, and called for the next leader to ensure that half of winnable seats were fought by women. She went on: 'If we don't do something now, we are going to lose out and carry on losing out. A lot of constituencies still have a stereotypical view of what an MP should be – and that is often male.'[207]

The group had asked all Conservative MPs to sign up to a pledge supporting Women2Win. The inclusion of men in the project was a deliberate strategy. Childs says: 'It felt very professional from the start. They were prepared for the criticism they were likely to get, and their strategy of having supportive, high-profile men associated with it was a very astute one.' A number of sympathetic MPs, including Maria Miller, Eleanor Laing, Caroline Spelman,

Peter Viggers and Bernard Jenkin, were in the audience along with would-be female candidates who had tried and failed to get selected. Sandra Howard, wife of the outgoing leader, and Shireen Ritchie also attended. Sitting alongside them was Steve Hilton, one of Cameron's key advisers and an avowed moderniser. On returning to Cameron's campaign headquarters, he is said to have described the Women2Win launch as 'the first meeting with normal people I have attended in the Conservative Party'. Hilton persuaded Cameron to get behind Women2Win.

Two weeks after the launch, on 6 December 2005, Cameron was declared the winner of the leadership contest and the new Leader of the Opposition. His team immediately contacted Women2Win, and together they drew up plans for a priority list, which Cameron called the A-list, and which he announced just six days later. Griffiths says:

> David signed up to the A-list, which was massively controversial. There were all these male barristers from the shires who got incredibly upset about the fact that they weren't going to be able to apply for these seats. What we were finding was that women would quite often get into a final, and then the local Nigel, the barrister with 2.4 children and a spaniel, would end up getting the seat. Our representation in terms of women candidates was acceptable, but when you drilled down and worked out the chances of those women ever becoming MPs, it was laughable. So the whole point of the A-list was … it prevented marginal seats from selecting candidates from anywhere other than the A-list, and the A-list was 50 per cent men and 50 per cent women. It made a massive difference in terms of the selection of women.

Once both Women2Win and the A-list were up and running, in Jenkin's words, 'we were then off'. As agreed at the outset, while Jenkin worked behind the scenes, drumming up financial support and organising events, May was the public face of Women2Win, as well as providing an invaluable source of support to would-be candidates. 'Introduction to politics' sessions were held, where leading Conservatives such as Virginia Bottomley advised how to 'navigate the maze to the green benches', as Jenkin put it. Would-be candidates were helped with their CVs and tutored on getting through selection interviews. Financial help was made available for those fighting winnable seats, which Jenkin sourced by contacting major commercial donors. Griffiths says:

> They … set up a mentoring programme and support network to try and replicate, if you like, the old boys' network. You would find with other candidates that all the boys would go off and drink wine and smoke cigars into the evening, and help each other through the tribulations of getting selected in a seat, whereas the women would be isolated and on their own and have nobody to talk to. And so the whole point of the networking was to try and support those women, give them that network of other women to help each other along, to share information, chat, share their experiences of how selections worked, what was successful, what wasn't successful. We set up a training programme to help women with … what to say at selection. It wasn't just tea and sympathy, it was direct support in terms of the nuts and bolts of their election campaign.

Margot James adds:

> The quality of the coaching was very good … A lot of the men put in a lot of time to do mock interview panels, really put women into real-life, getting selected-type scenarios. The trouble … with doing general candidate events is they become very male-dominated. The culture changes, the atmosphere changes. It's not every woman who blossoms in that environment.

May's parliamentary staff were in no doubt that Women2Win, and the wider project to modernise the Conservative Party, was her central priority. Researcher Shaya Raymond says:

The Women2Win initiative was so close to her heart. Anyone who worked for Theresa had to help out with Women2Win events. Every week there was a different event in support of a female PPC [prospective parliamentary candidate], or a female candidate. She would give up so much of her time to help women firstly win the nomination, then win the seat in the run-up to 2010.

Margot James confirms that May's commitment to Women2Win was wholehearted.

Theresa was a presence, definitely, during those years. She would attend quite a few of the events, she would speak, she would be across all of the selections, monitoring how effective we were being. Every time there was a selection she would want to know who was standing, what was happening, were women getting on the shortlist?

Over the following months and years, a record number of women were adopted in promising seats for the Conservatives, including several who remain at the highest levels in politics today. Jenkin says:

They all got selected incredibly quickly: Margot [James, now a Business minister] and Amber [Rudd, currently Home Secretary] and Andrea [Leadsom, the Environment Secretary] and Harriett Baldwin [a Defence minister]. They were seats we had to gain back from Labour, but they were seats we knew we were likely to win.

Other future MPs adopted at this time included Karen Bradley, now the Culture Secretary, Jane Ellison, a Treasury minister, and Tracey Crouch, the Minister for Sport. Jenkin says:

Theresa looked after that whole generation. She would take a call from anybody, she would send letters to people saying 'keep going', she was very much a personal mentor to that generation … who were elected in 2010. I can picture her office … and her being on the phone and saying to individuals: 'Go on, keep going, don't worry, there's a seat with your name on it.' She would make time for coffees. She was absolutely proactive.

For such a private person, the role of providing a shoulder to cry on might have seemed a chore. But Griffiths says:

I've seen her spend a huge amount of time with women, trying to convince them that they've got what it takes to become an MP, cajoling them, massaging their ego and making them feel they've got the ability to do what needs to be done. [She] would spend hours and hours with them. But [she] would never feel the need to divulge anything about herself. That kind of paints a picture of her as either a closed person or not a very warm person. Actually what you find is that she is hugely warm, that she takes a great interest in other people, but she doesn't ever give anything of herself of a personal nature.

May has told how she personally mentored her future rival, Andrea Leadsom.

I first met Andrea when I mentored a number of female candidates as part of the help I offered when we set up Women2Win. It would have been before she was selected as a parliamentary candidate – we helped with training and general advice about how to get on in politics, which can be an intimidating place for some.[208]

While Leadsom has not discussed the help she received from May, others have. Amber Rudd has said:

For women candidates competing for seats and for election in 2010, like myself, Theresa was an inspiration. Not just because she was so evidently a successful Conservative woman politician, but because she made a personal effort to meet candidates, advise them and then quite often call us on the day of selection to give us a motivating pep talk and push.[209]

Chloe Smith, who got to know May at an early Women2Win event before being selected for Norwich North, which she went on to win in a 2009 by-election, says the older woman proved an invaluable mentor. Describing May as 'supportive and warm', Smith adds: 'She has consistently struck me as someone calm, competent and with the rare skill of an instinctive listener.'

Even following her elevation to the post of Home Secretary, May continued to make Women2Win a priority, finding time to speak at events despite the most gruelling schedule of perhaps any minister in government. While the A-list survived for only a few years before being quietly shelved by Cameron, Margot James believes that the numbers of women selected ahead of the 2010 election formed a critical mass which meant others were encouraged to come forward. Women2Win continues to offer them help, support and advice. James says: 'I don't think we do need the A-list any more. The changes have been permanent.'

The results of both the A-list and Women2Win speak for them-selves. At the 2010 general election, forty-eight women were elected to Parliament on behalf of the Conservative Party. Following the 2015 election, the Tories had sixty-eight female MPs. While the level of representation in the Tory Party still trails that of Labour, at 20 per cent compared to 43 per cent, Andrew Griffiths says May and all those involved in the founding of Women2Win have been instrumental in transforming the Conservatives in Parliament: 'I would say that both in the 2010 and 2015 intake there wasn't a woman elected who hadn't benefited from the Women2Win net-work.' Professor Childs adds: 'It's had a huge impact. Without it, the number of Conservative women would be much, much lower.'

Some believe that May has not received the credit she deserves for inspiring the A-list. She herself told Women's Parliamentary Radio in 2007:

Some of us have been going on about this for some time … The priority list approach … was first suggested by myself and Andrew Lansley in summer 2001. I have been speaking about the need to change the party, the need to adapt to the new politics, for some years; particularly when I became party chairman in 2002, I took that forward. My party conference speeches show that. The 'nasty party speech', as it's known, that was saying that we've got to change ... So it's taken several years for it to be actually brought forward and put into practice.

Lansley agrees that it was long years of work which brought about the transformation. 'The party and the country shifted dramatically when David Cameron became leader,' he says. 'Previously, under William Hague, Michael Howard and Iain Duncan Smith, the party membership somehow still believed that if only they carried the party torch, it would all be fine. It was a big shift. Hopefully Theresa and I were providing ammunition to those pushing this.'

Eric Pickles adds:

If you were to say in terms of party organisation what's her big achievement, it's Women2Win. She was the driving force behind that, put an enormous amount of effort into it, and made the difference. And it wouldn't have been possible for the number of women we see in the Conservatives without Theresa, for sure. David got a lot of credit for that, but it wouldn't have been possible without that training, without that help, without that network. I think if she'd done nothing else in politics, she's actually reshaped the face of the Conservative Party.

In 2006, May, by now the shadow Leader of the House, posed in a T-shirt provided by the Fawcett Society proclaiming 'This Is What a Feminist Looks Like'. Cameron refused an invitation to follow suit. But despite her unabashed claiming of the term, and the work she would go on to do as Home Secretary to tackle violence and intimidation against women and girls, not all are convinced she is in actual fact a feminist. Labour's Harriet Harman, herself a long-time advocate for the advancement of women in politics, has criticised May's consistent opposition to all-women shortlists, saying she is 'no sister'. Speaking after May's appointment as Prime Minister, Harman said:

> Theresa May is no supporter of women. When we were pushing for more Labour women MPs, she chased me round TV and radio studios decrying us, joining the men in her party and some in ours who called it 'political correctness gone mad'. Theresa May is woman – but she's no sister.[210]

Privately, however, many female Labour MPs are more positive about May's contribution. Most objective observers agree. Trevor Phillips, the former head of the Equality and Human Rights Commission (which often came under attack from May during her time as Home Secretary), has said: 'Theresa May, in my opinion, is just as aggressive as Harriet Harman was on women's equality. Equality is an issue that can transcend politics, and we should judge people not on their political label but what they are doing and what they deliver.'[211] The Liberal Democrat Vince Cable, who in the coalition government worked with May on encouraging more female representation on company boards, says she is 'genuinely' a feminist. He adds:

> She was one of these top women who believe in promoting other women. She wasn't like [Margaret] Thatcher. She supported the sisterhood. It wasn't phony. Sometimes with the Labour people it's a bit of a banner-waving exercise, but in her case I think it was just instinctively, 'This is the right thing to do.'

Lynne Featherstone, another Liberal Democrat, who served under May as Equalities Minister during the coalition, agrees. 'Labour regarded women as their pitch,' she says. 'Theresa, on women's rights, violence against women, you couldn't really fault her. She changed the face of the Tory Party single-handedly, to bring women in and encourage women.'

CHAPTER XI

OUTSIDE THE CHARMED CIRCLE

Theresa May and the new Conservative leader David Cameron may have grown up in picturesque villages either side of Oxford, where they both attended the town's illustrious university, but there the parallels ended. Cameron was still only thirty-nine when he became leader in December 2005, the privileged second son of a family of four, whose stockbroker father and Justice of the Peace mother had sent him to Eton, the most exclusive public school in the country. His childhood had been happy and secure; his home prosperous and comfortable. In his marriage to the glamorous Samantha Sheffield, the daughter of a baronet, he sought to recreate his parents' strong relationship and the family's life of ease. At the time of his election as leader they had two children (the oldest, Ivan, was born profoundly disabled and died four years later at the age of six; another son and a daughter would be born during his leadership). The Camerons were a warm and outgoing couple who tended to surround themselves with friends who, like them, were bright, young, self-assured, politically engaged and socially comfortable. This gilded group would go on to dominate Conservative politics for the next ten years. Like much in his life, politics had come easily to Cameron. Having entered Parliament less than five years earlier, he and his close friend George Osborne now stood at the pinnacle of their party. Theresa May would not be alone in finding the fact that it was Cameron's well-manicured hand on the tiller, however benign his captaincy, somewhat irritating.

By now May was established as a senior figure in the party. Although viewed as something of a workhorse, she was respected by the new team, not least for her drive to modernise the party. But she would never become a member of the inner circle. Cameron appointed her to the post of shadow Leader of the House, her sixth shadow Cabinet portfolio in as many years. It was not a key role, considered among the lowlier jobs within the shadow Cabinet in terms of importance, and May was no longer the highest-ranking woman, that honour falling to Caroline Spelman at Communities and Local Government. The job must have been something of a disappointment.

As May settled in to her new role, however, it soon became apparent that, despite any initial reservations, it was a good fit for her. Unlike most portfolios, there was little or no requirement to formulate new policy. Instead, shadowing the Leader of the House, whose job it was to get government legislation through the Commons, she had to be across the full range of government policy and was in charge of presenting her party's opposition to proposed new laws. While not terribly high-profile in terms of media coverage, it did mean she would be required to spend a great deal of time in the House of Commons, which would stand her in good stead by honing her skills in the hand-to-hand combat that was the cut and thrust of parliamentary debate.

Blessed with strong characters as her opposite numbers in the form of first Geoff Hoon, then Jack Straw and, from 2007, Harriet Harman, May would go on to become one of the strongest parliamentary performers in her party, not declarative or given to speechifying, but clear and effective. Despite her reputation as being somewhat humourless, she even learned how to throw in the odd joke. May's weekly verbal jousts against Straw and Harman at the Thursday session of Business Questions became must-see events for lovers of parliamentary debate. Shaya Raymond, who joined her office at around the time she was appointed shadow leader, says:

> She did enjoy the fact that every Thursday she got to go up
> against Jack Straw. There was a bit of 'Who can get in the

most jokes?' And she was always very comfortable, enjoyed the sparring match every Thursday. She actually had a very good relationship with Jack Straw.

But while she did her best to display a light touch in the Commons chamber, May was deeply serious about her new role. She was now reunited with Shailesh Vara, who had worked with her at Central Office and who, six months after entering Parliament, was appointed her deputy. Vara says:

> We had our Thursday morning session when we would be on the floor of the House [for] Business Questions, and they had to be topical. We would work towards preparing her speech. If somebody made a suggestion and she liked it, she'd say, 'Happy to take it on board.' There wasn't any element of 'I didn't think of that so it's not going in.' She was very inclusive. Theresa always outclassed Harriet. There's just no two ways about it. Theresa's also got a sense of humour, which you really see on the floor of the House sometimes, and that came out when she was dealing with Jack Straw and Harriet. By God, she certainly did hold the government to account, she would ask some seriously probing questions, which would make both Jack and Harriet have to think, and they couldn't just fob us off.

While May was more comfortable in her brief than she had been for some time, and despite the assumption that the shadow leader's role entailed coordination of the parliamentary party, she was now no more interested in socialising with other MPs than she ever had been. Instead, as her stock rose and the Conservative Party's fortunes appeared to rally, she drew even closer to her husband, Philip. The Mays had always been a close couple and Philip grew increasingly important to her on a political level. Rather than mix with colleagues in the evenings, May preferred to dine with her husband. Unusually for the spouse of an MP, he would often come into the Commons, where the pair would take a table in either the

Members' Dining Room or the Adjournment restaurant in Parliament's Portcullis House. There, the pair would thrash over the issues of the day. Philip's political antennae were sharp, and May came increasingly to rely on him. Andrew Griffiths says:

> I don't think they needed anyone else. They must undoubtedly be the tightest couple in Parliament. They do share things, they do talk about things, about politics. For Theresa, Philip has been there throughout it all, the door-knocking, the black-tie dinners, the late nights in Parliament, he has been there with her.

Philip's input could be influential. Griffiths goes on:

> Many's the time when I would spend days and days toiling on a party conference speech, honing every word, going through it with her, perhaps putting together a little team, and we would draft the speech exactly as she wanted it, and then she would get in the car and drive to party conference with Philip, and I would get the call, knowing there would be a re-write. She'd discussed it with Philip, it just didn't feel right, and she wanted to re-write the speech. He was her sounding board, and she valued his opinion. There would then be a late-night drafting session with maybe myself and some of the other people who had worked on the speech, which would then result in Theresa practicing the speech using an ironing board in the room as a make-shift lectern. It would be 2 a.m. grafting. And Philip would be there and part of it. So they're not just a couple, Philip is part of her politics.

William Hague agrees: 'Philip is a really nice, interesting and convivial chap and politically astute himself. I've a lot of time for him, a lot of respect for him.' Cheryl Gillan adds: 'Philip has always supported Theresa. This is a very lonely job as an MP. It's an even lonelier job as a Prime Minister. Philip is like a rock to Theresa.' The importance to May of her husband cannot be underestimated. In the days after she became Prime Minister, following the appointment of Philip Hammond as Chancellor of the Exchequer, a joke circulated Whitehall that Hammond was now 'the second most important Philip in government'.

Soon after May's appointment as shadow leader, Andrew Griffiths was replaced as her chief of staff by Nick Timothy, whom she had come to know during her time as party chairman. Timothy had then been serving time in the Conservative Research Department, the finishing school for young Tories, whose alumni include both Cameron and Osborne as well as the former Cabinet ministers Andrew Lansley, Michael Portillo and Chris Patten. Perhaps more than anyone, Timothy would go on to transform May into one of the leading politicians of her age, giving her an ideological heft and strategic focus which some believe she lacked until then. Now performing the same role at No. 10, Timothy, thirty-seven, remains one of the closest people to May, not just in politics but in life.

If May, particularly in the early years of Cameron's leadership, never allowed any frustration she may have felt at being outside the inner clique to show, Timothy was overt in his irritation from day one. Raised in the working-class district of Tile Cross, Birmingham, the son of a steel worker and a school secretary, both of whose education ended at the age of fourteen, Timothy himself attended a grammar school. It was here that he decided to become a Tory as a twelve-year-old during the 1992 general election, on being told that a Labour government would close the school. A year after joining the Conservative Party as a seventeen-year-old, he became the first member of his family to attend university. He chose Sheffield because the living costs there were more affordable than in other university towns, and went on to get a First Class degree in Politics. Timothy is a fervent supporter of Aston Villa Football Club, and behind closed doors would mock David Cameron's somewhat questionable claim to be a fellow long-term fan (giving a speech during the 2015 election campaign, Cameron referred to himself as a supporter of West Ham, who play in similar colours to Aston Villa, only to row back, blaming 'brain fade').

Timothy's impatience with the privileged cabal at the top of the

party (despite later forming a romantic relationship with George Osborne's adviser Poppy Mitchell-Rose) expressed itself in a coherent
political vision which advocated the cause of the aspirational working and middle classes. He was and is a devoted advocate of selective
education, saying that his own experience at a grammar was 'trans-
formational', and a follower of the philosophy of the social reformer
Joseph Chamberlain, a fellow Brummie. His influence over May's
thinking on class and social mobility has meant that, unlike Cameron, she is seen by many as being more attuned than her predecessors
to the concerns of 'blue-collar Tories' and communities who might
in the past have voted Labour but in recent years may have been
attracted by the ideas articulated by the UK Independence Party
(UKIP) and the Vote Leave campaign during the EU referendum
debate. It is no coincidence that one of May's biggest disagreements
in government would be with George Osborne over the impact of
immigration, or that in her speech on becoming Prime Minister she
would pledge herself to 'the service of ordinary working people'.

Timothy would work for May in her role as shadow leader for
only a year, but he would leave and return to her employ several
times over the following decade. While he gained a reputation for
being tough, particularly with civil servants, fellow advisers and
even some ministers, he was kind to more junior staff, and is uni-
versally considered an impressive character. Shaya Raymond says:

> I think Theresa's career changed the minute she met Nick. The-
> resa had her own passions, but he came at it with a far more
> political brain of how to work the political system, and how to
> make sure Theresa was positioned in the right sort of way that
> supported her career in keeping it in the higher level. Nick was
> the brain behind her, for sure. With Theresa, it's quite difficult
> to work out her ideology; she's more driven by a moral compass
> than anything else. But that's why she worked so well with Nick,
> because Nick's given her the political brain.

During one of Timothy's spells away from May, in the run-up to the EU referendum, he wrote a column for the ConservativeHome website, which gave further clues to his thinking and personality. Many of the policies he espoused, including the expansion of grammar schools, wariness of Chinese investment in British infrastructure, and curbs on vested interests in the banking and business sectors, have already borne fruit in terms of policy and the new Prime Minister's rhetoric since their entry into No. 10.

The columns are also remarkable for the naked disdain in which Timothy clearly held both Cameron and Osborne. In one post, he wrote:

> … While the majority of Conservatives want to help people to get on in life, there is undoubtedly a small minority of people in our Party who frankly do not care very much about others. They might be involved to protect narrow commercial interests, to defend certain class values as they see them, or they might simply be in it for their own careers, but their lack of interest in others is unmistakable. We all know the kind. They reveal themselves through minor acts of snobbery, strange comments that betray a lack of understanding about the lives of ordinary people…[212]

While Timothy did not mention Cameron or Osborne by name, the context of his article, written in response to the resignation of Iain Duncan Smith from the Cabinet following a row with Osborne over the 2016 Budget, made clear who he was referring to. Now married to a German woman, Timothy opposed Cameron (and, to some extent, May) by supporting the Leave campaign during the 2016 referendum.

Timothy's influence over May is somewhat controversial. One current minister has compared him to Rasputin, the mysteriously charismatic and dissolute priest who dominated the ruling Romanov family in the years before the Russian Revolution (and who, like Timothy, sported an impressive beard). The minister said: 'Before Nick came along, Theresa was a clever and attractive politician in search of a distinctive world view. He provided her with one.

She doesn't make any decisions without him being involved. He has too much power for some of us. She does not need a Rasputin.'[213] Ameet Gill, a former Cameron adviser who is friendly with Timothy, has said, however:

> I think the Rasputin charge is extremely unfair. He has not got Theresa in some sort of hypnotic charm … they are very much a team, he very much works to her. When you work for senior politicians … you often do believe in the same things, otherwise you wouldn't be working for them.[214]

While May was still shadow leader, and with an eye to her future prospects, Timothy set her one task which she obediently abided by but struggled to master: to become more clubbable. Her diary secretary, Jenny Sharkey, was ordered to reserve a spot in her schedule to work the tea rooms and get to know her fellow Tory MPs on friendly, informal terms. She dutifully sallied forth each week, but never grew any more comfortable making small talk and gossiping with her fellow MPs. One member of her team at the time recalls: 'Theresa never seemed overly keen to socialise with other MPs in the party. Nick made sure we put it in her diary every Wednesday after PMQs, forcing her to go to the Members' Tea Room to socialise with MPs, every week, like clockwork.' The aim of the charm offensive was to ensure that the attention-shy May maintained a high enough profile to remain in front-line politics, with an unexpressed longer-term plan to stay at a level where, should the opportunity arise again, she would be in a position to run for the leadership. In the monthly opinion poll run by the ConservativeHome website which ranked the performance of the shadow Cabinet, May usually languished near the bottom. Timothy's instructions to raise her profile were a first step towards tackling this.

The staffer says:

> From Nick's perspective, I don't think it was 'Let's get Theresa to do this to make sure she's the next Prime Minister.' She's always wanted to be Prime Minister, but at the time there was

no guarantee that Theresa would even be a senior member of the party. Shadow Leader of the House was not a serious brief at all. So the aim was to keep her at the top of the party as much as possible, to make her as relevant as possible, and to help build bridges with other MPs. She probably did find it a bit of a chore. If you're not as popular in the party as others are, it's quite tough to socialise with other MPs and show that common touch.

Timothy also encouraged May to adjust her approach to the media, concentrating on offering a smaller number of bigger stories, with a clear message and theme. While the project to socialise with MPs was quietly dropped after Timothy's departure, she maintained her clearer message to the media, and although she would never develop relationships with individual journalists, as most senior politicians do, she and her team became adept at planting interesting stories and maintaining her profile.

Over the following few years, as Cameron and Osborne began the process of 'detoxifying' the party, by hugging both huskies and hoodies, May concentrated on Women2Win and her role as shadow Leader of the House. By now, despite the help she had given Cameron with his key reform of the A-list, it was clear that she would never form part of his inner circle. She was not a 'Cameroon', a member of the Notting Hill or Chipping Norton sets, which were dominated by a cabal of usually young, usually public school-educated men including Cameron himself, George Osborne, Oliver Letwin, Steve Hilton, campaign director George Bridges, chief of staff Ed Llewellyn, Michael Gove and, although less so on a social level, William Hague. From 2007, the spin doctor Andy Coulson would join the close-knit band, and was valued for his common touch precisely because so many of the others lacked it. Many of the group had forged their friendships at the CRD a generation before Timothy, in the 1990s, putting in long hours trying to work out how to blunt the New Labour attack – and learn from it.

The Cameroons deny that May was kept at arm's length, however. One now says:

It has since become clear that Theresa's people at least felt that she was in some way undervalued or overlooked. But if Theresa did feel resentful at the time, then she never let that show to David in opposition. It just didn't seem to be an issue. And, anyway, she was heavily involved. She was always at the top table when the important decisions took place.

This source adds that at this stage, the scale of May's ambitions was not clear to anyone involved in politics. 'If it was something that David overlooked, then it's not like he was alone,' the source says.

It wasn't like there was a narrative anywhere, in the press, in the wider public, in Parliament, that Theresa May was a Prime Minister of the future. That didn't begin until much later, well into her time as Home Secretary. In fact, probably the only person who saw Theresa May as a future Prime Minister was Theresa herself – and that's to her credit. She sensed in herself that capacity, and she always allowed herself to be open to it.

If May's lack of access to the centre rankled, she did not share her frustration with colleagues. Andrew Lansley says:

She was always treated with respect but not affection. She was never part of the clique. They would have felt that Theresa was never part of that group that grew up together at the CRD. I don't think that worried her. Her concern would have been that they weren't listening. Her view would be 'Can I tell them what I need to tell them?'

May responded to her position on the outside in characteristic fashion, by dedicating herself ferociously to her responsibilities within the shadow Cabinet – and by building up a wall of mistrust which would shape her relationship with Cameron and Osborne, probably without their fully realising it until much later. Keith Simpson says:

Look at what happened when she became Prime Minister, and what appears to be a ruthless dispatch of the Cameroon clique and all the Old Etonian boys. For lots of reasons … I think bubbling up, suppressed inside her, was twenty years of being patronised. She was quite determined, and burst forth: 'It's not going to be about what school you went to, or a chumocracy … I'm just not going to put up with that.'

Eric Pickles jokes that May's relationship with the Cameroons, nearly all ten to fifteen years younger than her, was 'bound by two steel bands of trust and understanding: they didn't understand her and she didn't trust them'. But despite them perhaps not understanding her, Shaya Raymond says everyone who worked for her was aware that Cameron was canny enough to realise that he needed May. 'She was not in the Notting Hill set, she was not in the inner circle, in some respects she did not want to be. But she was probably the most prominent female MP the Tories had, there was no one else … so Cameron had to use her.' And as she got on with the job, the Cameroons swiftly perceived what an effective operator May was, an impression which grew through the early years of his leadership. Pickles goes on: 'She was never on the inside, but only a very small group were on the inside … I think they always respected her.'

Vara insists that May was unaffected by being outside the charmed circle, and prioritised attacking Labour over worrying about her role in the Conservative hierarchy. 'We were in opposition and our main aim was to get into government,' he says.

And from Theresa's point of view, it was important that whatever job she had she could not be faulted on it. I think she was more concerned about doing the job than whether she was invited to this or that function. Whether she was in or out was not something that would have troubled her. What would have troubled her was: 'I have this job to do, and am I going to do it?' And she would have been desperately keen to do it well and deliver. She was somebody who rose above it. If you've got confidence in yourself, which she clearly had, then you can say, 'Well, whether I'm in a set or out of a set, it doesn't bother me. I'm in a job and I'll get on with it. And I'll be judged at the end of the day on that.'

While May's reputation was growing in the set around Cameron, she was less popular in the media and among her fellow MPs, many of whom still viewed May with suspicion following her time as party chairman. Raymond says:

She was still very much looked down on because of the 'nasty party' tag. A lot of the MPs at the time, the old right wing of the party, didn't think the party needed to change. In a way they kind of blamed her for the Cameron modernisation programme, the husky stuff.

A leaked private email from Desmond Swayne, Cameron's parliamentary aide charged with being his 'eyes and ears' in the Commons, warned the leader in July 2006 in blunt terms that May was not highly thought of by her peers, suggesting it would be unwise to give her responsibility for representing the Tories in ongoing cross-party talks on reform of the House of Lords, despite the matter falling under her brief. 'This is a sensitive issue and Theresa is neither liked nor trusted across the party. A tight rein will be necessary,' the email read.[215]

May was not highly rated by party members, either. Soon after becoming shadow leader, in January 2006, her approval rating in the monthly survey by ConservativeHome was among the lowest in the shadow Cabinet, at 29 per cent. Just under a year later, in December 2006, she had fallen to the bottom of the rankings. The few references to May in the press at the time focused on her appearance, her shoes and, often, her 'embonpoint', as the diaries put it. After sending columnists into apoplexies when she wore a low-cut wrap-around dress in the Chamber, an outfit she had picked because she was going on to a dinner for her husband's birthday, she joked that she had triggered 'cleavage wars'.

May continued to play a leading role in Cameron's project to modernise and detoxify the party. She was appointed to the key panel that decided which candidates would and would not be appointed to the A-list, a process which would make and break the careers of the next generation of would-be Tory MPs. She also maintained her support for Women2Win, speaking around the country and even hosting a networking event at a branch of one of her favourite shoe stores, L. K. Bennett, entitled 'An Evening of Shoes, Shopping and Politics'. At the 2006 party conference, Cameron's first as leader, she was roundly mocked in the media for wearing a pair of leopard skin wellies to deliver her speech, having come, she informed delegates, straight from a community garden which senior party figures had been encouraged to show off to the media to highlight the Tories' green credentials.

The day before she arrived in Bournemouth, where the conference took place, May had celebrated her fiftieth birthday with a 'quiet dinner' at a smart restaurant with Philip.[216] A week earlier, she had thrown a large party for, as a spokesman briefed, 'friends, staff and colleagues'.[217] Anne Jenkin, who was among the guests, noticed there were very few of the former in attendance. 'I remember her having a lot of constituents there, and thinking, "I'm not sure I'd have a lot of constituents [if it were my party]." My guess is she doesn't have a very wild social life.' Other guests ranged from Peter Jennings, her local butcher in Sonning, to David Cameron himself.

In 2007, Cameron appointed May shadow Women's and Equalities Minister in addition to her role as shadow Leader of the House. She began exploring policy to help women beyond the narrow cause of parliamentary representation, speaking out on issues including the gender pay gap, sex trafficking, maternity and paternity leave, and lap dancing clubs. Asked the following year who the next female Prime Minister would be, she replied coyly:

Well, I hope that the next Prime Minister is David Cameron and I hope that the next female Prime Minister, whenever that is, will

be Conservative too. We've got so many great women, not just
in the parliamentary party but also running as candidates, that
it would be impossible and unfair to name just one. We may be
spoilt for choice![218]

While she still may not have been rated by the media, Cameron and
Coulson began to rely on May to lead the charge against Labour.
Her brand of forthright seriousness meant she could be trusted to
deploy the more personal attacks the party wished to fire at the
opposition, without appearing grubby. When Tony Blair finally
made way for Gordon Brown in July 2007, the Conservatives, just
nineteen months into Cameron's leadership and with little in place
to fight an election, readied themselves for an early campaign –
which never came. Despite his early popularity, Brown became
spooked by an unfavourable opinion poll over the party conference
season and called off Labour's plans to reinforce his mandate with an
early election. The fiasco became known as 'the election that never
was'. As the country plunged into recession, the chance would not
come again for Labour before the mandated time at which Brown
was forced to go to the country, May 2010. Early in Cameron's
reign, May had been deployed, with effect, to attack Tessa Jowell,
the then Culture Secretary, over her husband's links to a scandal
involving the Italian former Prime Minister Silvio Berlusconi. Now
she was let loose on Brown. In one memorable phrase, she taunted
the troubled Prime Minister in the Commons, saying: 'He has gone
from Flash Gordon to Crash Gordon.'[219]

In the reshuffle that accompanied Brown's ascension, Harriet
Harman, who had become Labour's deputy leader, was also made
Leader of the House, resulting in weekly tussles between two of
the most senior women in each of the main political parties. The
parliamentary sketchwriters relished the spectacle. In her maiden
session, Harman suggested they call an 'armistice', to avoid the
bouts becoming a 'handbagging'. But while May had once postu-
lated that debate between women parliamentarians could be more
civilised than that of their male counterparts, she would go on to

express disappointment with Harman's approach. 'Women's natural debating style is different,' she said.

> That's not to say women aren't able to do the sort of 'attack' debate, as we saw when Harriet Harman took Prime Minister's Questions, but I think women's natural way of debating is, I won't use the word softer because I think that gives the wrong impression, because it's as effective as the more aggressive form of debating, but I think it's willing to be more consensual and ... not just to score party political points. I think we should be above that.[220]

In January 2009, Cameron reshuffled his pack in preparation for the election that would be held by the following spring, promoting May to the post of shadow Work and Pensions (while she also retained the Women and Equalities role). The position was a couple of notches up the shadow Cabinet ranking, but far from the great offices of state shadowing the Home Office, Foreign Office or Treasury. William Hague confirms that, at this stage, May was still regarded by most in the party as a kind of middle-order batter – a proficient and steady all-rounder who could be trusted to deliver, but lacking the flair of the star players. He says:

> Successive leaders all had confidence in her to do major jobs in oppositions, for the same reasons I'd given her first job in opposition, and that continued all through Iain Duncan Smith, Michael Howard and David Cameron's leaderships. Notice they always gave her the quite middle-ranking jobs that needed hard work and application, that needed someone who could master detail. None of them gave her the very top opposition jobs ... but they all entrusted her with quite complex briefs.

Like many, Shaya Raymond believes it was only later, when May moved to a more prominent position, that her abilities were fully appreciated. He says:

She didn't play the political field so I don't think her talents were widely seen by people. Unless you worked with her directly, I don't think you would know her talents that well – unless she was put in a prominent position where she was actually challenged, like in the Home Office.

Asked if May's talents were appreciated by successive leaders of the opposition, Eric Pickles says: 'No, of course not. Including [by] the magnificent William [Hague]. You really need to get to know her and she's not easy to get to know and appreciate.' Nor was May being spoken about as a future leader at this point. Shailesh Vara says: 'Nobody really talked about the leadership then. You had other people doing that. Although he'd lost to David Cameron, David [Davis] was still there in the background, and you had others. Theresa's name was not mentioned often.'

The press response to May's appointment to the Work and Pensions brief was not positive. David Hughes in the *Telegraph* slammed Cameron for giving the 'lacklustre' May the post, adding: 'The idea that Mrs May is going to lead the charge against state welfarism is absurd,' before concluding: 'Surely she could have been side-shuffled to something a little less taxing, something that did not send out the signal that the Tories have given up on welfare reform before even starting.'[221]

Undeterred, May put in the hours to master her new brief, an area in which she had no previous experience, but the response in the press remained far from positive, and her team also got the impression that she found it less suited to her talents. Shaya Raymond says: 'I don't think she enjoyed the Work and Pensions brief. I know that the people who worked for her found it quite tough.' As the recession hit, leading to rising unemployment, and all the parties began to consider such issues as increasing the retirement age and automatic pension enrolment, May found herself under the media spotlight more than she had been, a not entirely welcome experience.

Despite her private misgivings about the Work and Pensions post, May never let those around her, particularly in Cameron's circle or her new team of ministers, sense her discomfort. Mark Harper began working for her as Disabilities Minister. He says:

> I got on well with her in opposition and I thought she handled the brief very well. I have read reports in newspapers that she doesn't delegate. That certainly wasn't my experience. I always found her very supportive. Obviously there were areas she focused on and I focused on, but we worked those out between us. I thought it worked very well.

Cheryl Gillan adds: 'I always thought her contributions were sensible and thoughtful. I grew more and more impressed with her as time passed.'

The minister May was now shadowing, James Purnell, was a courtlier figure than Harman and Straw, and the tone of their debates was less knockabout and more high-minded. Purnell was firmly on the right of his party, and clearly uncomfortable under Brown's leadership, so early on May took the decision to hug him close, applauding the welfare crackdown he had launched while suggesting many of his ideas had been stolen from the Tories. She began her own major review of the welfare system, impressing the shadow Cabinet with her proposals, some of which would be taken on by Iain Duncan Smith once he became the Secretary of State after the election. Hague says: 'I remember major presentations from her about how we could reform welfare.'

A month after May's appointment, Sir David Freud, a Labour adviser who had written an influential report on welfare reform, defected to the Tories, joining her team as a shadow minister sitting in the House of Lords (a role he retains today in her government). Freud came to have a high regard for May, feedback he would pass on to Cameron and Osborne. His suggestion that she was under-valued and under-utilised – he is said to have described her as an 'impressive and thorough operator'[222] – would prove decisive in persuading Osborne to give May a shot at a bigger job after the

election. By the spring of 2009, Cameron was describing her as one
of his 'most effective colleagues'.

A few days after Cameron's praise, on 8 May 2009, a whirlwind
hit in the form of the MPs' expenses scandal. May's own expenses record is unusual. Her personal claims were unimpeachable.
Utterly uninterested in personal enrichment, a natural rule follower
with a cautious, frugal outlook, there was never any question of her
falling into the trap so many of her colleagues of all parties found
too tempting, of abusing the notoriously lax system. Her claims for
the flat in Pimlico where she and Philip stayed when there were late
votes were sometimes zero and never reached above £6,000 a year,
at a time when the maximum allowed was £24,000. The *Telegraph*
would name May an 'expenses saint',[223] and, unlike most of the
shadow Cabinet, she was not required to repay any money.

However, along with her Labour counterparts Jack Straw and
Harriet Harman, during her time as shadow leader, May had served
on the House of Commons Commission, the body headed by the
Speaker, Michael Martin, which had been tasked with addressing
the problem of expenses when the Commons was first subject to a
Freedom of Information request asking for MPs' claims. Unable
to countenance forcing MPs to share details of their private lives
with their constituents, Martin was to some extent responsible for
the fiasco, and was soon forced out of office. May, Straw, Harman
and the other members of the commission bore their share of the
blame for failing to persuade Martin to take a more robust response.
Minutes of meetings running up to the unauthorised release of
the claims show that May agreed that some details at least should
remain private.[224] However, amid the extraordinary fallout from the
scandal, with lurid headlines exposing claims for moats and duck
houses, faked mortgages and bumper decorating bills, with MPs
standing down and even facing prosecution, Cabinet ministers re-
signing, suicide threats and marriage breakdowns, with constituents
baying for blood and the entire political system in crisis, May's role
in failing to prevent the debacle was largely overlooked.

The expenses scandal dominated the run-up to the 2010 general election. In a sign of the growing regard in which she was held by the leadership, May was asked to take charge of the Conservatives' campaign in Norwich North, where the sitting Labour MP had stood down over his expenses, triggering a by-election. The Tory candidate was Chloe Smith, a young management consultant who had been helped in her selection eighteen months earlier by Women2Win. As usual, May proved an indefatigable campaigner. Smith says:

> I was proud to be standing … in a Norfolk seat but expecting a tough ask as it was held by popular Labour MP Ian Gibson, and I was excited to gain the national focus and resources that accompany a by-election. At that time, politics was intense, with the expenses scandal and the prospect of the Conservatives winning the 2010 election … so I was also pleased to be able to work with a serious and capable figure like Theresa. She was an effective campaigner … hands-on and practical as well as strategic. Theresa was extremely supportive to me as the candidate and I thoroughly enjoyed working with her in every way.

On 23 July 2009, Smith was elected MP for Norwich North, the first Conservative to represent the seat since 1997, in a constituency which had stood at only number 162 on the party's target list. Her victory gave many Tories real confidence that they could now go on to win the general election. May's work on the campaign, particularly her innovation of putting leaflets through doors offering a 'contract with voters', was seen as crucial to Smith's success. The contract was adopted for the national campaign a few months later, and May's estimation rose further in the eyes of Cameron and his team. Smith says: 'Our success in 2009 generated momentum towards winning the general election. Some of our campaigning innovations were then widely used by other candidates at the general election.'

But while the Cameroons may by now have held May in high regard in private, so instinctive was it for the leader to surround

himself with his inner circle at times of crisis that when the election
proper began in the new year, he reverted to type. May attended the launch of the Tories' manifesto at Battersea Power Station
on 12 April, wearing a shiny, wide-collared blue jacket mockingly
described as 'straight out of *Star Trek*',[225] and 'a bit sci-fi',[226] to the
general mirth of the commentariat, but she was all but absent from
the national campaign trail – as, indeed, were female politicians
generally.

But if the 2010 general election would prove to be a low-key one
for May, it would be notable for one event – the arrival in her team
of Fiona Hill (known at the time as Fiona Cunningham before she
reverted to her maiden name after getting divorced), who would
become one of her closest advisers and friends. Born in Greenock
in Scotland, Hill is a former journalist who started out covering
football at *The Scotsman*, where she was allegedly barred from one
club after the manager complained she had subjected him to too
fierce a grilling. She then served time on the paper's features desk,
where former colleagues suggest she showed little interest in politics.
It was only after Hill joined the Sky News team in Westminster that
she seems to have developed an enthusiasm for the cut and thrust of
politics. Following a stint in the Conservative Party press office, Hill
worked briefly for the British Chambers of Commerce, returning to
take up posts with Chris Grayling and Andrew Lansley. She gained
a reputation among journalists as a straight-talker, inclined to give
forthright, knowledgeable briefings, often off the record and not
unusually from the pub. Outgoing, friendly and fun, she soon got
a reputation as a 'street fighter' with a line in 'coarse jokes'.[227] Hill
had herself tried and failed to win selection to fight a parliamentary
seat, an experience May would have sympathised with.

In government, like Nick Timothy, Hill gained a reputation as
being brilliant but formidable. One unnamed 'senior official' has
described how a common sight at the Home Office would be Hill,
stockinged feet on her desk and dressed for a night out, giving 'an
absolute rollicking' to a civil servant.[228] But all those who have
worked with her agree she is highly talented. Norman Baker, the

Liberal Democrat who clashed badly with both advisers and May herself during his time as a Home Office minister, has nonetheless described Hill as a 'class act'.[229] He is less complimentary about Timothy. While Hill took on more media work than her colleague, Jonny Oates, who was Nick Clegg's chief of staff, has said it would be a mistake to underestimate Hill's influence, or dismiss her as a press officer. 'She's a very serious and practical policy-maker,' he has said.[230] As interested as her boss in fashion and clothes, Hill can switch from advising May on an imminent terror attack to the most appropriate outfit to wear to a Conservative ball; an invaluable asset. She also shares May's love of food, cooking and recipes. According to one anecdote, when May was Home Secretary, during a trip to the United States, Hill persuaded her to attempt an American accent to say the street phrase 'Oh no you didn't!' May 'gamely' did her best but could not master it. It is a testament both to Hill's sense of fun and to the level to which May could relax in her company that she even tried.[231]

Timothy and Hill would go on to become May's joint chiefs of staff in Downing Street when she became Prime Minister in the summer of 2016. Back in 2010, as the election campaign drew to a close, they would start to form the powerful inner circle that would surround May over the coming years. With few friends and no real allies in Parliament, May would instead draw to her a more personal support team. Along with Philip May, Timothy and Hill would swiftly grow to become the three corners of a triumvirate who on a political and practical level would sustain, protect and inspire May over the following six years in one of the toughest jobs in the country: Home Secretary. Ultimately, the little group that first gathered around May in the spring of 2010 would prove triumphant over the gilded circle that preceded them at No. 10, vanquishing the Notting Hill set from Downing Street, perhaps for ever.

CHAPTER XII

HOME SECRETARY

On the early afternoon of Thursday 6 May 2010, four men and a woman, all in their late thirties or early forties, gathered in a comfortable living room in Oxfordshire, less than twenty-five miles from the village in which Theresa May had spent her formative years, and took a decision which would directly lead to her appointment as Prime Minister. Only one of them had ever been elected to any public office. He was George Osborne. One of May's first acts upon entering No. 10 a little over six years later would be to brutally sack him from the government.

It was the day of the 2010 general election, widely expected to be the closest for a generation. Political parties do not, by tradition, campaign on election day and, in the lull before the polls closed, Osborne, in his unofficial capacity as David Cameron's chief adviser, had gathered the leading players in the close-knit Tory team around him. They met at the home of Steve Hilton, Cameron's director of strategy, and his wife Rachel Whetstone, Michael Howard's former adviser. Their farmhouse, in the pretty village of Asthall Leigh, was considered more private than Cameron's constituency home of Dean Farm, around seven miles away, which was already surrounded by journalists. Osborne wanted peace and quiet for the important discussions which would now take place. As Cameron slept off a marathon 36-hour helicopter tour which had taken him the length and breadth of the country in the days before the polls opened, Osborne began drawing up the government he hoped his close friend and ally would head.[232]

Around the country, MPs and candidates did their best to relax, aware that the coming night would be a long one. The Mays cast their votes early at a polling booth near their home in Sonning. The Camerons' attempt to do the same was delayed for four hours when protesters scaled the roof of Spelsbury Memorial Hall in his Witney constituency, blocking their way. The Tory leader cheerfully went off to buy eggs from a nearby farm and settled down to a cooked breakfast at Dean Farm. With little to do all day but vote, the mood among most politicians as they awaited their fate was tense. By contrast, the atmosphere in Hilton's living room was relaxed. Joining Hilton, a friend of Cameron's from Oxford, and Osborne on the sofas were Ed Llewellyn, Cameron's chief of staff, two years ahead of him at Eton and Oxford; Llewellyn's deputy, Kate Fall, another Oxford friend of Cameron's; and Andy Coulson, director of communications and the only non-public school, non-Oxford member of the team. In the beating heart of what would soon become known as the Chipping Norton set, the group of five settled on a plan that would ultimately elevate a decidedly non-patrician, middle-aged, former grammar school girl to the premiership, by giving her a jumping-off point in one of the great offices of state.

The idea to appoint May to the key position of Home Secretary had first been floated by Osborne a few months earlier, in one of the preliminary discussions held by Cameron about the makeup of the government he hoped to lead. No final decisions had been taken and no word of the scheme was breathed to May herself. The promotion was not an obvious one. In the years running up to the 2010 general election, May had been viewed as a safe pair of hands, but as no more than a middle-ranking player, certainly not someone destined for one of the most testing and influential jobs in government. By the end of Labour's last term in government, the Home Office had become a basket case, viewed as virtually unmanageable and perhaps the most challenging department in the entire government. It had seen off four Labour Home Secretaries in the preceding five years, as it lurched from one crisis to the next. Even Michael Howard, the last Conservative Home Secretary who had managed four years at the helm until the 1997 election, had struggled to get a grip on the vast, sprawling empire officially known as the Home Department. The idea that a politician such as May, whose career many viewed as on the wane, should be given responsibility for this notorious elephant trap had not occurred to anyone outside Cameron's inner circle. It seemed most likely that Chris Grayling, who had shadowed the Home Office since the previous year and who had a reputation as a political bruiser, would stay in the post.

But while May had not been promoted by Cameron in opposition (the move from shadow Leader of the House to shadow Work and Pensions being a sideways move), he had begun to feel her talents had not been fully utilised. Both Cameron and Osborne were also acutely aware of the lack of a female presence at their top table, and felt pressure to allocate a senior post to a woman. This was not the only, or even the most important, consideration, however, in their growing feeling that May should be elevated. In the latter years of opposition, both men had been won over by May's work ethic, loyalty and ability. And as the 2010 election approached, the team had come increasingly to rely on her as a sensible, normal-sounding voice of Middle England. The Home Office would be her (somewhat mixed) reward.

One of those in on the discussions says:

George drove it. He felt that at the Home Office they needed, perhaps more than in any other department, a safe pair of hands. We needed someone very straight but competent, and she had proven herself time and time again. There was no discussion [with May] in advance. It's not the way these things are done, and, anyway, you don't want to jinx it. So, as often happens, the final decision was made on that long election day when there wasn't much else to do. But it was certainly something that George had raised some time earlier.

Andy Coulson has said:

> In 2007, when I first started working for the Tories, the
> general view in the party was that her career had reached its
> peak. The media considered her to be aloof and old fashioned
> and, although in the shadow cabinet, she was only occasionally
> in the central strategic team. Respected, certainly, but rarely fully
> included. David Cameron soon came, however, to rely heavily on
> Theresa – particularly in times of difficulty. Crisis reveals char-
> acter and she never once … shied away from doing battle for her
> boss. Theresa became, for me as communications director, the
> ultimate safe pair of hands who also didn't play the ego-driven
> briefing game behind my back, as others did.[233]

Osborne's tentative view that May should perhaps be made Home
Secretary grew firmer on the eve of the election campaign, when
Chris Grayling unexpectedly stumbled. In March of that year, speaking at an event organised by the Centre for Policy Studies, Grayling
had expressed sympathy for two Christian hotel owners who were
being sued after denying a room to a homosexual couple. *The Observer*
obtained a recording of Grayling's remarks, in which he declared: 'I
took the view that if it's a question of somebody who's doing a B&B
in their own home, that individual should have the right to decide
who does and who doesn't come into their own home.'[234] The resulting story was published on 3 April, nine days before the official
start of the election campaign. Gay rights activists immediately declared Grayling's words offensive. More importantly, in Cameron's
and Osborne's eyes, the shadow Home Secretary's pronouncement
was seen as highly damaging politically, given the party's long programme of detoxification. Ben Summerskill, head of the Stonewall
pressure group, described it as 'very alarming to a lot of gay people
who may have been thinking of voting Conservative'. Most alarmingly, a poll for the gay news site Pink News on 5 April found that
support for the Conservatives among homosexual and lesbian voters
had dropped dramatically. Cameron was livid at the prospect that
months if not years of careful repositioning had been undone by a
few careless words, and took his anger out on Grayling. The shadow

Home Secretary apologised fulsomely for his remarks, but kept such a low profile during the campaign proper that commentators questioned whether he had been deliberately hidden away.

By the afternoon of election day, the team in Hilton's living room was clear that a new Home Affairs spokesman would need to be found. Osborne again put forward May's name, to general assent. Cameron, who now joined them, agreed to the plan, as did Patrick McLoughlin, the party's Chief Whip, arriving as Osborne was leaving for his Tatton constituency.[235] In any case, the thinking went, even if May made a complete hash of the job, Home Secretaries were not expected to serve for more than a year or two. She could always be sacked, or, more likely, an unforeseen calamity might force her to resign. No one sitting in Hilton's farmhouse that day anticipated that May would go on to survive more than six years in the notoriously challenging post, becoming the longest-serving Home Secretary in modern times and leaving the Home Office only to walk through the doors of No. 10.

Back in 2010, however, the firm plan to make May Home Secretary (which she herself still knew nothing about) came close to being aborted before take-off when, within a few hours of settling on it, Osborne started to change his mind. After spending the remainder of the day with local party workers in Tatton, Osborne went home to watch the results of the general election unfold on television. The 10 p.m. announcements of the broadcasters' exit polls on election nights have become one of the set-pieces of modern British politics. They are also among the most thrilling. Released in the seconds after polling stations close, the 2010 exit poll did not just represent a moment of high drama; it would also prove of huge constitutional importance for the course of British politics. As befitting her growing status as a colleague Cameron and Osborne could rely on, May had been entrusted to deliver the Conservatives' response to the poll on the flagship BBC election night show. As Big Ben struck the hour, the BBC's veteran election night host David Dimbleby began:

Ten o'clock. And this is what we're saying: it's going to be a hung

parliament with the Conservatives as the largest party. And the
figures: the Conservatives on 307, short by nineteen of the 326
they'd need for an overall majority, Labour on 255, the Liberal
Democrats on fifty-nine and others on twenty-nine.

The exit poll prediction would prove remarkably close to the eventual election outcome, in which the Conservatives would go on
to win 306 seats to 258 for Labour and fifty-seven for the Liberal
Democrats. It was also broadly reflective of the opinion polls in
the run-up to the election, which, while generally overstating the
strength of the Lib Dems' standing, had been forecasting a hung
parliament for months. Such was the grip, however, of Britain's
two-party system and its series of post-war majority governments
that, despite all the indications that a hung parliament was almost
inevitable, analysts, politicians and voters alike seemed psychologi-
cally unprepared for the event. The exit poll hit the political classes
like a shock wave. It was clear to all those watching that the country
was on course for either an unstable minority government or the
first true coalition since the wartime administration of 1940–45.
How each of the parties responded in the following minutes, hours
and days would prove crucial.

In the BBC studio, May was up against a formidable opponent
in the form of Lord Mandelson, the architect of New Labour who
had recently, and somewhat unexpectedly, become both Business
Secretary under Gordon Brown, and the Labour Prime Minister's
closest ally. With the poll indicating that Labour had fallen short of
the Tories by more than fifty seats, Mandelson now spun into action,
declaring that the Conservatives had 'lost' the election, and that as
the sitting Prime Minister it was Brown's prerogative to be given the
first chance to seek to form a stable government with the support
of the smaller parties. Watching at home in Tatton, Osborne knew
it was crucial that the idea not be allowed to take hold in voters'
minds that Labour had the right to form a government. Mandelson
needed to be challenged. But, to Osborne's frustration, May, sitting alongside the peer in the BBC studio, proved less than robust,

failing to establish the Conservatives as the party on the front foot. When presenter Jeremy Paxman asked both her and Mandelson who had 'won' the election, the Business Secretary declared 'the public', while May, to Osborne's dismay, suggested 'change', rather than the more obvious 'the Conservatives'.

As May left the BBC studio and headed off to her count at the Magnet Leisure Centre in Maidenhead, Osborne grumbled briefly to his aides about the need to find a bigger hitter than May to take on the likes of Mandelson, but soon busied himself organising the response to the likelihood of coalition. He would have no time to give the matter of May's future any further thought until the Conservatives' right to form a government, in conjunction with the Liberal Democrats, was secured.

Over the ensuing five extraordinary days, the country held its breath as the politicians immersed themselves in a series of negotiations to see who would end up with the keys to No. 10. Ultimately, the electoral arithmetic of the Tories' superior tally of seats would prove inexorable. By the evening of Tuesday 11 May, David Cameron had been appointed Prime Minister by the Queen, at the head of a coalition government between the Conservatives and Liberal Democrats. And when he and Osborne were finally able to turn their minds to the Cabinet, the pendulum had swung back in May's favour. Once the division of Cabinet portfolios had been agreed between the parties, along with an understanding that the leaders would be responsible for appointing their own people to those posts, Cameron, Osborne and the Tory negotiators, who included Ed Llewellyn as well as William Hague and Oliver Letwin, Cameron's policy adviser and mentor, settled down afresh to draw up a list of Cabinet ministers.

During the course of the coalition talks, it had become painfully apparent, and the subject of much criticism, that neither the Conservative nor the Liberal Democrat negotiating teams had contained a single woman. The Tory group agreed that a woman – most likely May as the most senior female member of the shadow Cabinet – should be given one of the top jobs. And there

THERESA MAY

was another consideration: Cameron had become concerned that the inclusion of Liberal Democrats in the government, inescapable due to the need to form a coalition, would nonetheless be resisted by right-wing Tory backbenchers, many of whose hopes of becoming ministers would now be disappointed. In order to rebalance the Cabinet, it was proposed that a leading backbencher from the right of the party be appointed to the government. The group settled on Iain Duncan Smith, whose work on welfare reform many admired. Putting him in at Work and Pensions was the obvious move – and that left May, who had been shadowing the post, without a portfolio. With Grayling persona non grata in Cameron's eyes, the logic of appointing May as Home Secretary was clear.

William Hague says:

> When a coalition came along, it … became really important to have a senior woman in a senior position. The shadow Home Secretary had been Chris Grayling. He was at that time not flavour of the month with David Cameron and was set for a demotion. The coalition was being formed and we wanted to bring Iain Duncan Smith into the Cabinet to strengthen it … If there were going to be Liberals in the Cabinet, we wanted people associated more with the right of the Tory Party to be there, and this was the logical position to give to him. That meant we moved the position she had had in opposition, and the fact … she'd handled so many things for so many years so competently meant, there we are: Home Secretary.

Cheryl Gillan agrees that May's unexpected appointment as Home Secretary was partly due to window dressing. 'Not to take away from her skills, but Cameron was looking for a Cabinet that had plenty of women in.'

One of those close to the discussions to appoint May as Home Secretary suggests it disproves the notion that the Cameroons undervalued her. This source says:

> There is this characterisation that David and George had this star

of the future that they were hiding away, but it did not seem that way at the time. She was very involved all the way through the opposition years. In that sense, David and George were in fact ahead of the game in spotting her potential by making her Home Secretary – which came as a huge surprise to everyone.

On the morning of Wednesday 12 May 2010, as a light drizzle fell and a hundred camera lenses snapped, May walked into Downing Street beside Andrew Lansley, the man she had entered Parliament with in 1997 and joined Hague's shadow Cabinet with two years later. To her astonishment, when it was her turn to enter the Cabinet Room, where the new Prime Minister was forming his government, Cameron invited her to become Her Majesty's Principal Secretary of State for the Home Department, only the second woman Home Secretary in history and the first female Conservative. For once, May's cool and calm demeanour deserted her. Andy Coulson, waiting outside, has described her face as she emerged from the room as 'something to behold'. As Coulson congratulated her, the usually inscrutable May stuttered: 'I can't quite believe it.'[236]

May did not have long to savour her appointment before the scale of the challenge she was facing was made clear. She has said:

> When I was first in No. 10 Downing Street and David Cameron had asked me to take on the role of Home Secretary and I walked out of the Cabinet Room … virtually the first thing that somebody said to me was 'Your protection team is waiting for you.' And I hadn't thought about that at all. I haven't driven a car since I became Home Secretary.[237]

The remit of May's new department was huge, with primary responsibility for three of the most pressing challenges facing the government: immigration, security, and law and order. Even though, as some commentators were quick to point out, responsibility for a number of Home Office functions, including the courts and prison services and some constitutional matters, had passed to the Ministry of Justice in 2007, during May's tenure the demands on the Home Secretary if anything increased, as the threat from international terrorism ramped up and concern over rising immigration began to dominate the political agenda. The Home Office brief covers everything from drugs to violence against women, child exploitation to extradition. Under Labour, it had become a mess; 'not fit for purpose', in the memorable words of one of May's predecessors, John Reid. Few had confidence that May would fare any better than those who had gone before her.

The press response to May's appointment was largely unenthusiastic, and, as the first day of the new government passed with no more women being named as Cabinet ministers, largely focused on her gender. The accepted wisdom was that the assignment had been made primarily to attempt to assuage the poor impression given by the lack of women at the top of the new government. The *Standard* described her promotion thus: 'The biggest surprise of David Cameron's first Cabinet is the appointment of Theresa May as Home Secretary. The move was seen as crucial to avoid charges of the line-up being purely men-in-suits but it still came as a shock.'[238] Less charitably, in the *Telegraph*, David Hughes wrote:

> Now how do you tackle the gender balance problem when there is a dearth of top-notch women on both the Tory and Lib Dem front benches? Well, you take one of the great offices of state … and give it to Theresa May … How well qualified is Mrs May to take it on? Not at all, as it happens.[239]

His colleague Gerald Warner fulminated: 'May is a one-woman disaster area, a ticking time-bomb of incompetence waiting to detonate in one of the more sensitive departments of state.'[240] Bookmaker William Hill offered odds of 7/4 that May would be gone by the time of the next election. There were few takers. Those sour notes aside, the formation of the new government had brought so many unexpected eventualities, not least the very existence of the first coalition administration since the war, that the reaction to

May's appointment was more muted than it might have been had it happened in isolation. Busy writing about the love-in between Cameron and Nick Clegg in the Downing Street Rose Garden, few journalists paid May much attention.

But if the appointment as Home Secretary, traditionally the fourth most important job in government after the Prime Minister, Chancellor and Foreign Secretary, was a shock to the media and May herself, it also came as a surprise to those around her. Mark Harper, who had been a member of her team in opposition, confirms that she had assumed she was on course to become Work and Pensions Secretary. 'It was all our expectation, including hers, that that's the job she would have done in government. We had obviously gone through the process with the permanent secretary at the DWP [Department for Work and Pensions], all those meetings you have in preparation for government.' Michael Howard, himself a former Home Secretary, says:

> It was a slight surprise because she hadn't been shadow Home Secretary. The fact you've been shadowing something doesn't entitle you to be given the job when your party comes into government, but there's kind of a vague presumption that if you're shadow, you're going to be given the job.

Nor was there a great deal of confidence, even among May's friends and allies, that she would necessarily make a better job of the Home Office than her predecessors. Andrew Griffiths, May's former chief of staff who had been elected MP for Burton a few days earlier, says:

> I have to say I was massively surprised by David's decision to make her Home Secretary. I was not expecting that and I don't think anyone in the parliamentary party was expecting it. I'm sure that it came as a surprise to her. It is an incredibly difficult job, and I don't think anybody would have predicted either that she would last as long as she did, or that she would have the

nerve and the steel and the determination to drive through the things that she did. But actually it gave her the opportunity to demonstrate what she could do. Theresa was perfectly suited to government. All too often in opposition it's about tell not show. So in opposition it's the peacocks, it's the people who can put on the greatest speech, can make the audience laugh [who thrive]. But government isn't about that. It's about putting in the hard yards, it's about putting in the effort, it's about doing the detail. And that's why Theresa's reputation changed dramatically when she became Home Secretary.

As well as becoming Home Secretary, Cameron made May Equalities Minister, to the disquiet of some. When a couple of press reports referenced her somewhat questionable voting record on gay rights, social media sprang to life, with hostile posts circulating on Twitter in the hours after her promotion, and a petition launched on Facebook calling for Cameron to change his mind. Within a few days it had gained nearly 70,000 signatures. May had indeed voted the 'wrong' way on a number of equalities issues in her early years in Parliament. As shadow Education Secretary in 2000, she had opposed the repeal of Section 28, the controversial Conservative legislation which banned the 'promotion' of homosexuality in schools, saying: 'Parents want the comfort of knowing homosexuality cannot be promoted in schools at public expense and that their children are protected.' She had also voted against same-sex adoption and opposed the equalising of the age of consent. But, as the years had passed, May's thinking had evolved. Eight months earlier, she had voted in favour of civil partnerships for same-sex couples. As her detractors would discover, she would go on to become perhaps the most progressive Home Secretary on gay rights since Labour's Roy Jenkins urged government MPs to back the Private Member's Bill that led to the decriminalisation of homosexual acts in 1967.

The importance with which Cameron viewed the post of Home Secretary was made clear on May's first full day in the job, Wednesday 13 May, when, after holding the first Cabinet of the coalition, he went to the Home Office to meet staff. Addressing a gathering of around 500 civil servants in the central atrium at the modern building at 2 Marsham Street, he told them: 'My reason for coming to this department ... is to point out how important I feel the agenda is in terms of combating crime, keeping us safe, reforming immigration, combating terrorism – these are hugely important tasks.'

The line-up of the men and women who would be aiding May as Home Office ministers was then announced. Her old university friend Damian Green was made Immigration Minister, Nick Herbert became Policing Minister and Baroness Neville-Jones, the former head of the Joint Intelligence Committee, was named Security Minister. For the Liberal Democrats, Lynne Featherstone was appointed the following day, and given the somewhat cumbersome title of Minister for Criminal Information and Equalities. Perhaps of far greater importance to May personally was the official confirmation of Nick Timothy and Fiona Hill as her government special advisers.

Having waved goodbye to Cameron, May then set off for her first appointment as Home Secretary, to visit a neighbourhood police team on the Winstanley Estate in Clapham Junction, south London. The press coverage concentrated largely, as usual, on her shoes; it was noted that she had changed out of the black pumps she had worn to Cabinet and into a leopard skin pair for the short journey. But her words were worth paying attention to. Although May was abiding by tradition by meeting the police in her first official visit as Home Secretary, she made clear they should not expect an easy ride. 'As a new government, one of our commitments is to enable police to get out more on the streets and do the job they want to be doing and the public want to see them do,' she said. 'To do that we want to slash bureaucracy.' Refusing to guarantee that police numbers would not fall, May added that she would begin work immediately on establishing elected police commissioners – a move opposed by many senior officers. She ended by saying that she was 'very keen to get on with it'.[241]

The scale of what May would be 'getting on with' was starting to become apparent. She now received her first briefings with the security services, and began to get her mind round the task of running one of the most complex, multi-dimensional departments in government, a post she had never shadowed in opposition. Over the next few days she would be forced to tackle the intricacies of a complicated immigration legal case, respond to a gun massacre (the Derrick Bird shootings in Cumbria), draw up legislation relating to civil liberties, and deliver a speech to a police conference. As the months and years passed, her challenges would only increase: terrorist plots and atrocities at home and abroad; child sex abuse scandals; the refugee crisis and the camp at Calais; dramas involving royal protection; Olympic security; legislation relating to violence against women and stalking; police reform; gay rights; anti-extremism measures; inquiries into Hillsborough and the murder of Stephen Lawrence; reviews of stop and search, alcohol pricing and the detention of mentally ill people; high-profile extradition cases including those of Gary McKinnon and Abu Hamza; the deportation of Abu Qatada; investigations into the disappearance of Madeleine McCann and murder of Alexander Litvinenko; the 2011 riots; drug policy, cyber crime and sexual exploitation; people-trafficking; passport delays; an undercover policing scandal; anti-Semitic attacks; phone hacking; the 'Snooper's Charter'. And immigration. Always immigration. The list of issues May would have to deal with in her six years at the Home Office was diverse, fascinating, impossible – endless.

The hours May put in at the Home Office were, by necessity, lengthy. She began a habit of working at her red boxes until late into the night, imposing on herself a nightly curfew to stop work of 1 a.m., a target she often did not meet. Lynne Featherstone confirms that the pace at the Home Office was relentless. 'She was incredibly diligent,' she says of May. 'We had ministers' meetings three times a week, and there was always a disaster. It was "Oh God, what's on the front page today?"' Often, the information May received about the threats facing the country would have been enough to render her brief nights at home sleepless. Eric Pickles says:

I often think [about the fact that] her and the Prime Minister are the ones that all the really horrible intelligence is laid on. They know what is out there in a way that you and I don't. She knows the things that would keep you and I awake at night. I think she's coped with that remarkably well.

Mark Harper, who joined the Home Office as a minister in 2012, agrees:

I was always very conscious that on a daily basis she's looking at all the threats to the country, she's talking to those that protect us every day, and that rather concentrates the mind and focuses you on the important things, and you never […] forget […] that you can't take your eye off the ball. The consequences of you not doing your job properly could be quite serious. And she was very, very professional and took her job quite seriously.

At times it must have been difficult for May to focus on anything outside her work, but she refused to let herself be consumed by it, insisting that the many cares she had to bear did not weigh heavily on her. 'One of the aspects of being Home Secretary, of course, is you tend to see some of the most difficult aspects of life,' she has said. 'Fortunately I'm somebody who does sleep pretty well, although I don't get as many hours as I might like. You're probably talking about five or six hours. But there's a lot of work to do.' [242]

Despite the punishing schedule, May did not let go of her hinterland. Even when she was at her busiest, she and Philip were able to enjoy quality time together. They were often spotted by theatre critics at first nights, and continued to attend the opera, cricket matches and horse racing meets. The couple clearly both relish their relationship. May insists that:

Red boxes are very much banned from the bed and indeed the bedroom. I just send Philip up without me if I have lots to do. But he is terribly thoughtful with the little touches that matter, so he might bring me an unexpected cup of tea. He's also very good about flowers, which is nice.[243]

The couple continued to take their annual walking holiday in Switzerland, and enjoyed weekends away at British beauty spots, once surprising fellow guests by frugally picking a £34-a-night Premier Inn for a pre-Christmas break in Bodmin, Cornwall (accompanied by two police minders). The constituency was not allowed to feel neglected either, with May preferring to stay overnight in Sonning whenever possible, particularly at weekends, spending most Saturdays pounding the streets campaigning door to door. And she never let go of her enjoyment of fashion, occasionally attending shows put on by favourite designers. Shoes remained her guilty pleasure. She began to declare discount cards with two of her favourite shops, L. K. Bennett and Russell & Bromley, in the annual Register of Members' Interests. Nor did May abandon Women2Win, continuing to attend events on behalf of the group, and becoming the patron of a women's networking group, the Pink Shoe Club. As Home Secretary, she would host drinks receptions for female journalists in the parliamentary lobby.

Back on their first day at the Home Office, May's new ministerial team was also now settling in. It was a slightly stilted start. Lynne Featherstone says: 'We had a "hello meeting", in which none of us said anything.' Journalists summoned to the department for May's first interviews and briefings in her new post also found the Home Secretary hard work. The BBC's Danny Shaw was among a group of home affairs correspondents invited to Marsham Street to meet May. He later recalled: 'It was an awkward affair. We stood around Mrs May in a semi-circle, gently questioning her about her intentions at the Home Office, but she was guarded and gave little away.'[244] Submitting to her first print interview since becoming Home Secretary, she 'gave so little away' to two journalists from the Conservative-friendly *Telegraph* that the duo were in despair. During the interview, as they listened doubtfully, she boasted somewhat lamely: 'I think I am tough and willing to be tough when necessary.

I'm down to earth and that's important. What I hope, in terms of me, is that people will be able to say she was tough but fair.'[245]

May's attitude towards journalists, even the most senior, would change little in her first years at the Home Office. The BBC's former political editor Nick Robinson has said:

> I have a terrible confession. When I was the BBC's political editor I once turned down lunch with the Home Secretary, complaining to her officials that it was frankly a waste of her time and mine, since she said nothing that couldn't be read on a Tory Central Office press release.[246]

At the end of May 2010, Downing Street put out an official list of Cabinet seniority, showing that Nick Clegg as Deputy Prime Minister and Ken Clarke as Justice Secretary had bumped the Home Secretary down the traditional pecking order to sixth place. By the close of May's first year in the job, no one would seriously accept that ranking for her. And so May's first weeks in government drew to a close. Now the real battles could commence.

CHAPTER XIII

A BLOODY DIFFICULT WOMAN

For someone whose image is defined both in public and in private by politeness and restraint, Theresa May has picked an incredible number of bruising and sometimes rather unseemly fights. In opposition, as a middle-ranking politician with little real power, she was forced to bite her lip when crossed. Once in government, installed in one of the most important ministries in Whitehall, she was under no such constraint. As the Whips' Office could confirm, May had always shown a streak of impatience with those she felt were lazy or not up to the job. From 2010, when she was put in charge of a major department employing thousands of civil servants, plus a team of ministers and advisers, working in conjunction with other members of the government, this tendency was sharply magnified.

But the real focus of May's ire was reserved for those who disrespected her, or were rude in some way. Once crossed, she would always seek revenge. Her grudges could last years. A victim might find themselves frozen out or treated with cool disdain until a right moment could be found for more savage retribution. The description repeatedly applied to the way May spoke to or about those she feuded with was 'icy'. While May likes to boast that she doesn't do gossip or give secret briefings to the media, her special advisers (spads), Fiona Hill and Nick Timothy, were more than happy to get their hands dirty on her behalf. Eric Pickles says:

If you don't treat her with respect, that's about the worst thing you can do. If you are disrespectful and you make the mistake of speaking to a journalist and putting a story out about her, she's got two of the cleverest spads I've ever dealt with, they are top class, they are well-clued in, so [with] even the most anonymous briefing, they will be able to finger someone within a very short time.

Over the six years she served as Home Secretary, May became embroiled in serious feuds with a staggering number of fellow ministers, MPs, officials, organisations and individuals who crossed her path. She would almost always emerge triumphant – in the end. For some, the final defenestration would arrive only once she became Prime Minister, her first act at No. 10 to deposit the bloodied corpses of the Notting Hill set outside the gates of Downing Street. For, if she had been suspicious of David Cameron and his gilded circle in opposition, this tendency only grew in government. David Laws, a former Liberal Democrat Cabinet minister who had an eyewitness seat during the coalition years, has said:

> Theresa May clearly stood apart from the 'inner circle' of the Conservative team. She was not 'one of the boys', and wasn't treated as such. Indeed, there was a distinct frostiness between the Home Secretary on the one hand and David Cameron, George Osborne, Michael Gove and their inner circle on the other, which I never once saw melt away.[247]

In her six years as Home Secretary, those May feuded with included her Conservative colleagues Cameron, Osborne, Gove and Kenneth Clarke – who memorably described her as 'a bloody difficult woman' during the 2016 leadership campaign – as well as the Liberal Democrats Nick Clegg, Vince Cable and Chris Huhne. She also clashed publicly with one of the three Liberal Democrat ministers assigned to her department, Norman Baker, and a Conservative, Baroness Neville-Jones. Brodie Clark, the head of the UK Border Force, and the entire senior management of the Police Federation were also put to the sword following perceived wrongs. It dawned on any number of MPs and former ministers that they had, at some point, been guilty of a perceived slight or insult against May, Hill or Timothy only when they found themselves unceremoniously dumped from her government when she entered No. 10 in 2016.

In her first weeks in government, in May 2010, May marked her colleagues' cards that she was not going to be a pushover. One of the first major acts the coalition would have to tackle was the passing of a Budget, one which, they had agreed, would include £6 billion of spending cuts. With the departments of Health and International Development 'ring-fenced', others, including the Home Office, would have to take on a larger share of the burden. David Laws, who had become Chief Secretary to the Treasury, has described how he gave each of his Cabinet colleagues a deadline of midnight on 21 May to agree their settlement. Those who fell into line quickly he labelled 'good boys' (apparently not recognising any 'good girls'), while late settlers were dubbed 'the awkward squad'. May was very much in the latter camp. Laws has written:

> To my surprise Theresa May insisted on coming to see me in my department. We fenced over the figures … It struck me that Theresa May was the most senior Cabinet minister to come and see me, and she was the last to settle … She looked nervous, and glanced down frequently at her notes … Eventually, the Home Office was forced to accept my minimum offer at 11 p.m. on Friday 21 May – one hour before my midnight deadline.[248]

Successive spending rounds would often come down to the wire, with May fighting tooth and nail against Laws's successor, Danny Alexander, and sometimes Osborne, the Chancellor. Laws says both he and Alexander came to admire her, however. '[She] was a tough negotiator and fought her own corner with some determination. But she was a straightforward person to deal with, and Danny Alexander came to like and respect her: "She is tough, but she will listen and respond," was the Chief Secretary's view.'

Another Lib Dem May picked a fight with, days after entering the Home Office, would also become, unexpectedly, one of her admirers. As the new team settled in at Marsham Street, Lynne Featherstone was summoned by her private secretary and told the Home Secretary wanted to see her. 'We sat down in armchairs – it was a bit like going into the headmistress's office – and she said: "Lynne, Lynne: I don't think we can blog anymore."' It had come to May's attention that on her regular blog, Featherstone had criticised Iain Duncan Smith, the new Work and Pensions Secretary, for retaining a controversial firm to assess sick benefit claimants. Featherstone goes on:

> She said 'It's not appropriate, it's against the ministerial code, to comment on other portfolios.' I was immediately offended. I left Theresa's office in quite high dudgeon at being told what to do by a Conservative, went and Googled my article, and found it had gone worldwide, in every media outlet there was 'coalition split, division' etc. And it dawned on me then that when you're a minister, [things are different]. So after my high dudgeon I could concede that she had a very good point. It was a very early sign of what Theresa was like. And a very good lesson was: 'Theresa was right.'

Featherstone went on to form an excellent working relationship with May, the pair introducing ground-breaking legislation to legalise gay marriage, but, like all those who worked with her, she soon learned their interactions would not be particularly warm. 'We were never going to be girly friends,' she says. 'But … I hugely admire her.' Featherstone believes that May became embroiled in so many high-profile spats, including with a number of senior figures in her own party, because men often found her difficult to deal with, and didn't understand that the best way to get her to do what they wanted was to be persuasive rather than aggressive. 'I think the boys couldn't handle her,' she says. 'I always thought, all the men who found Theresa difficult to deal with, including David Cameron, just weren't used to someone who stood their ground the way that she did. I never really thought there was anything wrong with her arguing, it was just that she argued.'

In her early days at Marsham Street, however, there were signs that May might prove to be someone her colleagues, including her new Liberal Democrat coalition partners, could work with. On 27 May, two weeks after becoming Home Secretary, May confirmed that Labour's widely unpopular plan to introduce a compulsory identity card scheme would be scrapped within the government's first 100 days in office. It would be the coalition's inaugural legislation. Announcing the move, May said: 'This bill is the first step of many that this government is taking to reduce the control of the state over decent, law-abiding people and hand power back to them ... [We] aim to consign identity cards and the intrusive ID card scheme to history.'[249] Two months later, Tony Blair's flagship policy of tackling anti-social behaviour with civil penalties known as 'Asbos' joined ID cards in May's dustbin, as she declared them 'gimmicky, criminalising and coercive'. Civil liberties campaigners – and the Lib Dems – rejoiced. Sean Kemp, an adviser to Nick Clegg, says: 'It was almost on the first day of the coalition, the scrapping of ID cards. Obviously we were so happy.'

The indications that May might prove to be a more liberal Home Secretary than some had anticipated continued when, a week into the job, she made a startling admission on the BBC's *Question Time* show. May was challenged about her voting record on gay issues, which had led many within the community to oppose her appointment as Equalities Minister. She said bluntly: 'I've changed my mind', adding that on gay adoption she now believed that having loving parents was more important to a child than their sexuality. She added that, if given the chance again, she would vote differently. The response to her change of heart was overwhelmingly positive, in the press at least. Cristina Odone in the *Telegraph* wrote: 'It takes a big politician to admit that they've changed their mind. But on last night's *Question Time*, Theresa May carried it off brilliantly.' She concluded: 'In this new era of politics, everything is possible, but one thing is sure: Theresa May is a star.'[250]

Watching at home, Featherstone was also encouraged. Since her appointment to the Home Office, she had been musing over whether she should attempt to take forward her pet project, as a long-time equalities campaigner, of securing equal marriage rights for gay and lesbian couples. As she watched her new boss's remarks on *Question Time*, she realised she might well have a chance. Featherstone says: 'In front of the nation, she had said, "I made a mistake. I'm really sorry, I now understand that two loving parents is far more important than their sexuality." Very brave.' Featherstone asked her private secretary how she should go about getting same-sex marriage onto the statute books. He advised she take the traditional route of drawing up a form of words which could be circulated first to the Home Secretary, and then the entire Cabinet, under a process known as the 'write-round'. Featherstone says:

> My private secretary sends it to her private office to present to her in her [red] box. She came back and said, 'Yes.' And, good as her word, she put it in the write-round ... and all but two of the Cabinet ministers agreed to it. [Iain] Duncan Smith and Philip Hammond didn't, not totally surprising, and, anyway, Cameron overruled them.

The legislation that emerged from Featherstone and May's bold decision to tackle the issue of gay marriage, which had not featured in the Conservative manifesto or the coalition agreement, was hugely controversial at the outset. Many religious leaders and Conservative members were highly critical of the plan at the time, but it has since been claimed by many Tories as one of the major successes of the coalition government. Featherstone says that May never wavered, even in the face of obstacles in the form of Church groups wary of being forced to marry homosexual couples in religious buildings, and despite the objections of many of her advisers and a number of Tory MPs. The vicar's daughter must have found the objections of the Anglican Church difficult to bear. But, Featherstone says, she did not flinch. 'She was absolutely resolute throughout. She went into bat for it. A lot of the bishops were very upset, in fact lots of people were upset. She always would go and meet with them or talk with people who were worried about it. She backed it to the hilt.'

In a 2012 article written to reassure people of faith about the gay marriage proposal, May said:

I don't usually talk about my own faith. In British politics we tend to feel uncomfortable about that sort of thing. But as an Anglican who attends church each Sunday and whose father was a vicar, I understand the Church of England. That's why I want to emphasise that this has nothing to do with telling the Church – or any religious group – what to do.

She concluded: 'Marriage is one of the most important institutions we have. It binds us together, brings stability and makes us stronger. So I don't believe that the State should stop people getting married unless there are very good reasons – and being gay isn't one of them.'[251]

In October 2011, at the Conservative Party conference, David Cameron gave his personal backing to the legalisation of gay marriage. Following a lengthy debate in Parliament, and despite more than half of Tory MPs voting against, the Same Sex Marriage Bill passed through the Commons in July 2013 with the support of Labour and the Liberal Democrats, by 400 votes to 175, becoming law the following spring. Dozens of gay and lesbian couples made their vows at midnight on 29 March 2014. By October 2015 (the most recent figures available from the Office for National Statistics), more than 15,000 same-sex marriages had taken place, and the legislation is hailed as among the most important reforms of the coalition government.

Over the next few years, the relationship between May and Featherstone would grow to be productive, even unusually warm given their different political outlooks and the former's reputation for being unfriendly. The Liberal Democrat says now:

My party is horrified that I like Theresa quite as much as I do.

We've always just really liked each other. I disagreed with her
vehemently on many, many occasions, but I thought she was a
principled person who had good judgement, who really wasn't
swayed by the stupid political game.

May's relationship with the third female Home Office minister
would prove to be less fruitful, however. Around the time that
Featherstone was beginning to see May as a potential ally, Baroness
Neville-Jones, the Tory Minister of State for Security and Counter-
Terrorism, was moving in the opposite direction. There had been
tension in the appointment of the former director of the Joint
Intelligence Committee from the start. As a career diplomat and
specialist in intelligence matters, Neville-Jones saw her role not as
a junior minister answering to May, but as the person responsible
for security on behalf of the entire government. A few months into
her time as Home Secretary, May summoned Neville-Jones to her
office and asked to see the raw intelligence relating to a plot she
had been warned about by officials, a potential terrorist atrocity on
British soil similar to the 2008 Mumbai attacks. According to the
ensuing media briefing (provided, almost certainly, by one of May's
attack-dog spads), Neville-Jones refused to discuss the matter, saying:
'I'm sorry, Home Secretary, but I'm afraid I can't talk to you about
that, because you don't have the security clearance.' A stunned May
is reported to have said nothing, but treated Neville-Jones to one of
her soon-to-be-trademark icy stares, before obtaining the relevant
information directly from MI5.[252] May would later deny the story,
insisting the pair had a 'good working relationship',[253] but the atmosphere between the two women remained frosty.

Finding herself increasingly side-lined at the Home Office,
Neville-Jones is next said to have appealed to David Cameron to
give her the title of 'national security adviser', a request he turned
down. May was clear in her mind that Neville-Jones was one of
her ministers and as such reported to her. The baroness continued
to view her role differently. Within a year, she was gone. Her resignation letter dispensed with the usual courtesy of thanking May as

Home Secretary, and was addressed solely to the Prime Minister. She was not replaced, and, for the next year or so, the ministerial team at Marsham Street would be a harmonious one. None of the remaining members of the team were in any doubt who was in charge.

There was less harmony at Cabinet, however, as May headed into another clash about her departmental budget ahead of the comprehensive spending review in the autumn of 2010. The cuts were brutal, amounting to 25 per cent of her £10.2 billion budget. The police alone saw their funding slashed by 20 per cent. May fought hard to keep the reduction to 17 per cent, but Osborne would not budge – the cuts would have to be found. As part of her savings plan, May began a review of police pay, with a particular focus on cutting the massive overtime bill, which stood at £450 million. The police response would lead to one of the biggest battles – and triumphs – of May's time at the Home Office.

During her first months as Home Secretary, May enjoyed a lengthy honeymoon period, picking up unusually warm plaudits in the press and earning the respect of her fellow MPs, who, for the first time, began to speak of her as a possible successor to Cameron. Watching one appearance at Home Office Questions, the *Daily Mail* sketchwriter Quentin Letts said: 'Tough but unhysterical, she has attained a sense of lofty karma without drifting too far from common sense.'[254] The same paper's Ephraim Hardcastle column said of her: 'Long mocked for her fancy footwear and Thunderbirds jackets, some colleagues groaned when Theresa May MP was chosen as Home Secretary. Critics now admit her performance has exceeded expectations.'[255]

A few weeks after her first Conservative conference as Home Secretary, at the end of October 2010, May faced her first true test in the post when, following a tip-off, packages disguised as ink cartridges but actually containing massive amounts of plastic explosives were uncovered on two cargo planes travelling from Yemen to the United States, while on a routine stopover at East Midlands Airport. It would be the first time that May would chair 'Cobra'

– the top-level gathering of intelligence chiefs, police, civil servants and ministers named for Cabinet Office Briefing Room A, the
secret room in Whitehall where they met. She passed the test with
flying colours. One unnamed civil servant later claimed that the
Home Secretary's coolness under pressure was in marked contrast
to the 'panicky' No. 10 staffers at the meeting. 'Her officials were
impressed with her calm, considered management of the situation
and she was unfazed by the daunting mechanics of the government's crisis committee, Cobra,' the civil servant wrote. 'This was
in stark contrast to the Prime Minister's advisers who flapped and
panicked…'[256]

May, who had hitherto broadly agreed with her Liberal Democrat colleagues about the need for the new government to distance
itself from some of the previous Labour regime's more draconian
counter-terrorism measures, including the use of control orders to
limit suspects' liberty without court proceedings, came away from
her first experience of terrorism on British soil with a new resolve
to do everything in her power to keep the country safe. Her instincts
were reinforced through her first year in office as she was given
sight of security briefings not available to the Tories in opposition,
and which she felt justified the use of more severe measures than
the party had anticipated before coming to office. Her view would
prove a major point of division with Nick Clegg and his team.
David Cameron, who described the collision between the two views
as a 'fucking car crash',[257] attempted to persuade the Deputy Prime
Minister to come round to May's way of thinking on control orders,
but Clegg, having been forced to give way on the thorny issue of
student tuition fees,[258] insisted his party could not be seen to compromise on civil liberties. Eventually, following a three-way meeting,
Clegg, May and Cameron agreed to replace control orders with
new 'terrorism prevention and investigation measures', known as
'T-Pims', which reduced the length of curfews and allowed suspects
access to mobile phones and computers. The relationship between
Clegg and May entered the deep freeze.

May started 2011 by losing a familiar face and gaining a new opponent. The two events were linked. The Home Secretary had grown to like her police close protection officer, Paul Rice, but he was removed from his duties after it emerged that he had entered into an affair with the wife of her Labour predecessor, Alan Johnson, whom he had also guarded. Following the election of Ed Miliband in September 2010, Johnson had become shadow Chancellor and Ed Balls shadow Home Secretary. When Johnson stood down in the wake of his marital difficulties, Balls replaced him, and Balls's wife Yvette Cooper took on the task of shadowing May, a role she would occupy for the next five years.

Cooper would grow to have a grudging regard for May. 'She's a grown-up, sometimes surrounded by people who play childish games, and she wants to be serious about things, and I respect her style in Parliament, where she can be authoritative,' Cooper has said. 'The problem is she tends to be cautious and controlling, doesn't share with other people and doesn't delegate and can often end up really taking a long time to take decisions even when there are crises.'[259] Cooper was herself one of Labour's most highly respected performers and, as they had with May's bouts with Harriet Harman during her time as shadow Leader of the House, Westminster watchers were soon drawn to observe the two women's clashes at Home Office Questions.

In March 2011, following the review she had ordered, May set out the details of her proposed crackdown on police pay and overtime, to howls of outrage from the Police Federation, the effective trade union of the rank and file, which threatened to march through London in the run-up to the royal wedding of Prince William and Kate Middleton on 29 April (the march was eventually held a year later). This was the backdrop to May's second appearance at the Police Federation annual conference, in May. Attending the conference had been one of her first acts as Home Secretary the year before, and the usually testy audience had given her speech, which included a promise to restore to police the power to charge suspects, a respectful hearing. This year would be very different.

Harry Fletcher was attending the conference in Bournemouth in his capacity as assistant secretary of Napo, the probation officers' union. He says:

> I came across Theresa that year in the green room. It was just me and her in it. She was due to speak and she wasn't happy. She was apprehensive. I wandered out into the auditorium and it was packed, there were between 1,200 and 1,500 cops filling it up. They all had copies of the current Police Federation magazine. In the middle of it was an A3 poster which said 'Cuts are criminal'. There was a stage backdrop which also included this 'Cuts are criminal' slogan.

Fletcher watched as, during the lunchtime break, a member of May's staff attempted to remove the offensive banner. 'I wandered over and she was saying: "You can't have the Home Secretary sitting underneath a huge great banner saying 'Cuts are criminal',"' he recalls. 'The Police Fed people told her it was too late.' By the time the afternoon session began, the banner was still in place.

May was now forced to take to the stage and listen as Paul Mc-Keever, the Federation's general secretary, gave a speech in which he accused the government of being 'simply wrong' about police cuts. To May's visible discomfort, a video link had been set up to Northumbria, where PC David Rathband, an officer who had been blinded by a crazed gunman the preceding summer, was waiting to speak. He abruptly asked May if she thought his £35,000 salary was too high. 'How do you sleep at night?' McKeever demanded of May as she squirmed beside him on the stage. Her own speech was then greeted with utter silence. Fletcher says:

> Theresa got up to speak and the police started to hold up the A3 posters saying 'Cuts are criminal'. She gave a kind of 'we're all in it together' speech and then she returned to the green room. There was a break so I went to the green room too – and she was absolutely furious, really incandescent with rage. She felt that there had been an attempt to publicly humiliate her. And

I knew – I knew – I could just tell, that she was going to get her own back.

May did indeed get her revenge – but she bided her time. Her speech to the 2014 Police Federation annual conference three years later has been described as one of the greatest in modern British politics. In it, she vowed to break the power of the police union, directly challenging those who had humiliated her by threatening to deploy the full might of Parliament unless the Federation tackled its questionable financial practices. She accused officers of letting down black people through the overuse of stop and search powers, and women by failing to take domestic violence seriously. As the audience listened, stunned, she reminded them of recent scandals and, in damning words, accused the force of complacency, saying the trouble amounted to more than a few 'bad apples'. 'The problem might lie with a minority of officers, but it is still a significant problem, and a problem that needs to be addressed,' she went on.

> It is an attitude that betrays contempt for the public these officers are supposed to serve – and every police officer in the land, every single police leader, and everybody in the Police Federation should confront it and expunge it from the ranks. If there is anybody in this hall who doubts that our model of policing is at risk, if there is anybody who underestimates the damage recent events and revelations have done to the relationship between the public and the police, if anybody here questions the need for the police to change, I am here to tell you that it's time to face up to reality.

Demanding the union approve a raft of reforms which she put before them, she concluded: 'The Federation was created by an act of Parliament and it can be reformed by an act of Parliament. If you do not change of your own accord, we will impose change on you.'[260]

Harry Fletcher was again at the conference, and saw the glitter in May's eye. For once, the Home Secretary did not attempt to hide her triumphalism at having vanquished this most uncivil foe. Fletcher says: 'She just tore into them, she really tore into them, and again I met her in the green room afterwards and she was much more buoyant.' A few hours later, shell-shocked delegates dutifully voted to accept all thirty-six of the reforms May had demanded of them. The response to May's speech was overwhelmingly positive. The commentator Dan Hodges described it as 'one of the most incredible speeches delivered by a British politician in peacetime'.[261] The *Telegraph*'s leader column was also generous in its praise: 'Her remarkable speech may be a defining moment in both the history of the police force and her own political career.'[262]

May was as good as her word, transforming the police during her six years as Home Secretary. As a first step, the Police Federation was stripped of all public funding. Despite the dire warnings, crime fell even as police numbers were cut. By the time of her speech, it had dropped by 20 per cent in the four years since the general election, to the lowest level for more than three decades. Along with cost-saving measures such as scrapping outdated pay structures and tackling overtime, May was responsible for more positive reforms, including the fast-tracking of young talent and the creation of a new College of Policing. Stop and search was reined back in a bid to halt the disproportionate effect on the black community, and far greater emphasis placed on tackling violence against women. She reinforced protection for whistle-blowers and toughened up the inspections regime. Reviews were ordered into past scandals involving the police, including the suggestion that the family of the murdered black teenager Stephen Lawrence had been spied on, allegations of inappropriate relationships between undercover police officers and activists they were monitoring, and the murder of Daniel Morgan, a private investigator who had taken an interest in police corruption. By the time of her speech, elected police commissioners had become a fixture. The first elections, in November 2012, were, however, characterised by markedly low turnouts, of between 10 per cent and 20 per cent; one of May's rare missteps at the Home Office.

On the whole, though, May's reform of the police service wins uniform praise. Charlie Elphicke, who became the Home Office whip a year after the Police Federation speech, says: 'She was absolutely right to be robust with the police. The police were obviously upset about that. But it's very important that the police understand that they too are subject to the rule of law.' Michael Howard adds: 'She was very brave to speak out as she did.' Harry Fletcher believes the Police Federation was ripe for reform – and that its leaders made a tactical error in antagonising May.

> My personal feelings were that the Police Federation got it wrong in 2011 and it was a strategic mistake for them to have put up those banners, put up those placards, and to have been somewhat disrespectful, given the power that the Home Secretary has. The police were seen extremely favourably by successive Conservative administrations, so they were not expecting the ferocity of the attack on their finances and structures. As a Tory, she was brave to decide to take the police on. I think she saw it as one of the last unreformed trade unions.

Back in 2011, however, May soon found she needed the support of the police very badly. That summer, policing in the capital was in crisis. The phone hacking scandal, which had been rumbling on for some years amid claims that the *News of the World* newspaper had accessed the personal voicemail messages of celebrities and members of the royal family, flared into life. Allegations emerged suggesting the paper had tapped into a phone belonging to the murdered schoolgirl Milly Dowler. Senior members of the Metropolitan Police were accused of cultivating inappropriately close ties with the media, and both Commissioner Paul Stephenson and Assistant Commissioner John Yates resigned, to the frustration of a 'very cross' May, who tried to persuade Stephenson to stay on.[263]

The Met was still without a full-time Commissioner two weeks later when, on 4 August 2011, a 29-year-old black father of four called Mark Duggan was shot and killed by police in Tottenham as they attempted to arrest him. Two nights later, Duggan's family and friends began what was intended as a series of peaceful protests with a march on Tottenham Police Station. Within a few hours, the demonstration had spiralled into a full-scale riot, leaving twenty-six officers and an unknown number of protesters with injuries. Over the following days and nights, disorder spread first around London and then to cities further afield. This was an apparently spontaneous outbreak of violence, looting and affray, the causes and motivations of which sociologists and politicians continue to pore over. May would condemn many of those caught up in the later riots in particular, which were often characterised by the looting of shops selling sporting goods and electrical items, as being motivated by lawlessness and greed, rather than any genuine sense of outrage against the police. She would also become embroiled in a long-running dispute with a number of major social media outlets, including Facebook and Twitter, which she suggested had allowed their services to be used by rioters to spread the disorder. For now, however, the Home Secretary was focused on putting a swift end to the crisis.

It took many of May's colleagues a strikingly long time to respond to the drama that now unfolded across London. Falling as they did on a weekend at the height of the summer, Whitehall, including Marsham Street, was virtually deserted when the riots broke out, with Cameron, Osborne and May herself all on holiday, and Nick Clegg nominally in charge of running the country. Boris Johnson, the Mayor of London, was also away. Lynne Featherstone, the duty minister at the Home Office, failed to respond publicly to the riots until 12.30 p.m. on Sunday 7 August, a full sixteen hours after they broke out, reading a prepared statement which did little to dispel the sense that the country was lacking leadership amid the lawlessness. The next day, after a second night of violence in which the riots spread to Brixton, Walthamstow and Oxford Circus, with shops, cars and restaurants vandalised, May cut short her annual Swiss break and flew back to London to take charge.

Cameron did not return from his own vacation – in Tuscany

– until the following day, by which time the violence had reached Birmingham, while Johnson, on learning that both the Prime Minister and the Home Secretary had returned to the UK, made plans to fly in from the United States, where his family were holidaying. As she awaited the arrival of her colleagues, and the Cobra meeting which Cameron would chair, May gave a televised statement in which she sought to assure the public that the government was in control, and dismissed the riots as 'thuggery'. Revealing that more than 200 people had been arrested, she went on:

> This is sheer criminality and let's make no bones about it. That's why I say that these people will be brought to justice, they will be made to face the consequences of their actions and I call on all members of local communities to work with the police constructively to help them bring these criminals to justice.[264]

Her words seemed to have an immediate effect. The riots continued for a number of days, spreading to Greater Manchester and the West Midlands, but the sense that the government had lost control of the situation was over. May cancelled all police leave and flooded London with 16,000 officers, while giving orders to police chiefs to ramp up the number of arrests. The deployment of both water cannon and plastic bullets was discussed, but the Home Secretary herself opposed their use and, in any case, the chaos had ended by the close of the week. Once order was restored, politicians and citizens alike were left scratching their heads and wondering what had happened, and how the crisis could have spiralled out of control so quickly. In all, more than 3,000 arrests were made, with over 1,000 people charged. Worse, five people lost their lives in incidents directly connected to the disorder, and an estimated £200 million of damage was caused to shops and other businesses.

As a postscript to the riots, May would go on to have one of her now almost routine clashes with a colleague, in this case Boris Johnson, over the Mayor's proposal to purchase water cannon to keep on standby in the event of any further trouble. As Home

Secretary, May had to give permission before water cannon could be deployed on the streets of England and Wales, a legal nicety she dragged her feet over for years. In the spring of 2014, with her decision not yet made, Johnson went ahead and purchased three second-hand water cannon from Germany. 'This was a crude attempt to bounce the Home Secretary, whose decision it was as to whether they could be deployed on the UK mainland,' Norman Baker, then serving as a Home Office minister, has said.[265] Despite Cameron giving their use his personal backing, May continued to spin her decision out, not finally pronouncing until June 2015. To the Mayor's mortification, she turned the request down. As Johnson watched glumly from the government benches, having been told by May of her decision by telephone only twenty minutes earlier, she told the House the water cannon he had bought were not fit for purpose. 'They are twenty-five years old and would have required significant alterations and repairs to meet the necessary standards,' she said sorrowfully. May let slip the pleasure she must have taken in humiliating Johnson over the water cannon saga nearly a year later, during the leadership contest, when, summarising her rival's negotiating skills, she said scathingly: 'Last time he did a deal with the Germans he came back with three nearly new water cannon.'

Back in 2011, May would now clash with yet another Conservative big beast, her veteran Cabinet colleague Kenneth Clarke, the Justice Secretary. The pair had sparred since the start of the coalition, disagreeing on such issues as mandatory life sentences for murderers and compulsory jail time for those convicted of carrying knives, with the Home Secretary invariably more authoritarian than the relatively liberal Clarke. The Justice Secretary had also written to admonish May – and made the note public – after she criticised a judge for ruling that human rights legislation meant criminals could apply to have their names removed from the sex offender register. While, in opposition, May's reputation as a moderniser meant she was usually categorised as being on the liberal wing of the Tory Party, eighteen months in the Home Office had altered that perception dramatically. As her views on security, immigration and civil liberties hardened, her philosophical differences with Clarke would escalate into major rows.

In the run-up to the 2011 conference season, May had provoked pro-Europeans in the Cabinet, particularly Clegg and Clarke, by telling a newspaper she wanted the Human Rights Act scrapped, arguing that the legislation was hampering Britain's attempts to deport foreign criminals and terrorists. Her conference speech infuriated them still further. In it, May said:

> We all know the stories about the Human Rights Act: the violent drug dealer who cannot be sent home because his daughter – for whom he pays no maintenance – lives here; the robber who cannot be removed because he has a girlfriend … The illegal immigrant who cannot be deported because – and I am not making this up – he had a pet cat.

A few minutes after her speech had wrapped up, Clarke, speaking at a newspaper fringe meeting, was asked about the feline claim. 'I cannot believe that anyone has had deportation refused on the basis of owning a cat,' he responded. 'I will have a small bet with her that no one has ever been refused deportation on the grounds of ownership of a cat.'[266] In an interview with his local paper a few days later, Clarke doubled down, describing May's use of the case of the asylum seeker and his pet cat – now revealed to go by the name of 'Maya' – as 'child-like and laughable'.[267]

Clarke has described the furore that followed: 'This was manna from heaven for the bored journalists hanging around the conference centre. They turned the whole episode into a huge media scrum, the main lasting result of which were some rather fine cartoons of my Hush Puppies and Theresa's kitten heels attacking each other.'[268]

Matters became yet more farcical when the Liberal Democrat Energy Secretary, Chris Huhne, was forced to apologise for accidentally sending a public message via Twitter to a *Guardian* journalist comparing May's speech to one given by the UKIP leader Nigel Farage.

Clarke's tone had been jolly – and No. 10 gave May its clear backing – but the Home Secretary was not amused. As well as detracting
from coverage of her big day at conference, May's reputation for
sure-footedness was put in doubt, and her hard work in building her
reputation with the press, public and party membership had been
undermined. Going into the conference, she had been named as
the fourth most popular choice to succeed Cameron among party
members, a meteoric rise for someone who had languished near
the bottom of the polls during the opposition years, and particularly striking given her role running the notoriously difficult Home
Office. Clarke's off-the-cuff remarks had put that in jeopardy, and
she would face a difficult series of interviews in the days that followed, in which she was pressed about the details of the case of the
cat-loving asylum-seeker. She never conceded the point.

May's relationship with Clarke never truly recovered. A number of
disagreements would flare up over the following years, including an
extraordinary ten-minute heated exchange in the Commons Chamber while sitting side by side at PMQs, observed by a number of their
fellow MPs. There would be serious clashes over May's attempts to
allow intelligence officers to give evidence in court in secret, a move
which in Clarke's view was anathema to open justice. He has said:

Theresa and I were not able to reach an agreement because
MI5 inspired her to take a very strong line. This was not, in fact,
an example of the public perception that she and I represented
right-wing versus left-wing Conservatism. Rather, while I have no
doubt that both our positions were based on our sincere appraisal
of the public interest, I took a more legalistic view and she took a
more authoritarian one.[269]

Generally, Clarke has sought to play down their differences, however, writing:

When she was Home Secretary and I was at the Ministry
of Justice, we in fact agreed far more than the parody of our

relationship, and our respective brands of Conservatism, suggested … I used to joke with her on these occasions that I was not as left-wing as I was believed to be, and she was not as right-wing as she pretended to be. Her own joke, when asked how she got on with me, was to say: 'I lock them up, and he lets them out.'[270]

Clarke inadvertently revealed his true feelings about May during the 2016 leadership contest. Caught on an open microphone chatting to fellow grandee Sir Malcolm Rifkind following an interview with Sky News, he made critical remarks about a number of the candidates, before saying of May: 'Theresa is a bloody difficult woman, but you and I worked with Margaret Thatcher … I get on all right with her … and she is good.' Clarke later wrote:

When Sky television released this candid chat a few hours later, I returned to the House of Commons to be greeted by MP after MP laughing as they approached me and saying how much they had enjoyed the whole performance. Three-quarters of the Conservatives who came up to congratulate me also politely said they had agreed with every word I had said.[271]

By then, Clarke had been gone from the Cabinet for two years, and May was one of the favourites to secure the leadership he had long craved and never won. She could afford to be magnanimous, even embracing the 'bloody difficult woman' description. Two days after Clarke's gaffe, at a leadership hustings for Tory MPs, May said, to laughter: 'Ken Clarke says I am a bloody difficult woman. The next man to find that out will be Jean-Claude Juncker [the President of the European Commission].'

The next serious clash with a fellow Tory that May would have as Home Secretary would not end so jovially, however.

CHAPTER XIV

IMMIGRATION

George Osborne looked across the Cabinet table with a sneer on his face. For some time, the Chancellor had been seeking to address the country's flat-lining economy by drumming up business in the Far East, particularly China. His Chinese counterparts had complained for months that they were finding it difficult to obtain visas to travel to the UK. Now, Osborne told his Cabinet colleagues, he had a true 'horror story' to share. At least one wealthy Chinese businessman, with millions of pounds to splurge on British products, had been stopped at Heathrow Airport and forced to submit to hours of interrogation including a full strip search. The businessman had returned to China on the next flight and was now telling his friends to avoid the UK at all costs. Who, the Chancellor demanded to know as he stared around the table, was responsible for the debacle? Theresa May, the Home Secretary, whose department oversaw both visas and the Border Agency, refused to meet his eye and said nothing. What followed, according to several of those seated around the Cabinet table that day in 2012, was the worst 'rollicking' any of them had ever seen dealt out by one minister to another. May would never forgive Osborne for it.

It is no coincidence that the May–Osborne bust-up blew up over the issue of immigration. In fact, immigration would become the biggest flashpoint between May and many of her colleagues during the coalition years, drawing in both Liberal Democrats and a number of her fellow Tories. The challenge of controlling immigration would also become her most intractable problem, and, by her own standard, the one she failed to overcome. In hindsight, the target she was set was probably always unachievable. Long after others had given up, she continued to strive to meet it. As Prime Minister, she still does.

The tension within Cabinet over immigration was centred on the pledge, not included in the coalition agreement but referred to in the Conservative manifesto, to lower immigration levels to the 'tens of thousands'. It was a target that, it became clear as the years passed, was probably never attainable given Britain's membership of the European Union, which guaranteed freedom of movement for EU nationals. During the coalition years, as greater than anticipated numbers of EU citizens began to arrive, the only scope to keep the numbers down lay in targeting non-EU migration. Caught up in the frequent drives May's Home Office launched to tackle this group were the very wealthy students and business people whom her colleagues in the financial ministries, such as Osborne and Vince Cable, the Business Secretary, as well as Michael Gove at Education, were eager to court. David Cameron, who would often complain privately to his aides that May was the only senior minister truly committed to the 'tens of thousands' goal, is said to have seen the promise to control immigration as a touchstone by which the electorate would judge him, the consequences of failing to meet the target particularly hazardous given the apparent rise of the anti-immigration UK Independence Party.

May's aides are said to claim privately that the 'tens of thousands' pledge was arrived at by accident.[272] While the Conservative manifesto had described returning 'net migration back to the levels of the 1990s – tens of thousands a year, not hundreds of thousands', following the formation of the coalition, and with Liberal Democrats taking a far more lenient approach to mass migration, the exact status of the policy remained unclear. No minister put a figure on the desired level of future migration until November 2010, when Damian Green, May's long-time friend and now the Immigration Minister working for her at the Home Office, under pressure in an interview on the BBC's *Newsnight*, blurted out that a proposed immigration cap May had announced was 'just one of the ways we will reduce net immigration to the tens of thousands'. The mention of the figure apparently took both Cameron and May by surprise, but they were reluctant to publicly row back from it, meaning it stuck, despite many within the government, on both sides of the party divide, considering it both unobtainable and undesirable.

Michael Howard, who had made cutting immigration a major part of his pitch to voters as party leader five years earlier, says it was always a forlorn hope to return immigration to 1990s levels while Britain remained in the EU. 'I don't know whose idea the original promise was, but I rather doubt that it was hers [May's],' he says.

> Obviously, we couldn't get to that level without leaving the EU. She did get the non-EU numbers down, not nearly far enough but ... she got them moving in the right direction. But we could never get them down to the tens of thousands while we stayed in the EU.

Norman Baker has said of the 'tens of thousands' pledge: 'It was like setting a target for the maximum number of days each year it should rain ... The Home Secretary and the Prime Minister could not resist tinkering around endlessly with the immigration rules and regulations, like continually picking at a spot.'[273]

The first clash over immigration came within a month of the coalition's formation, when a serious row in the Home Affairs Cabinet committee, chaired by Nick Clegg, was taken to full Cabinet. Both Michael Gove, as Education Secretary, and David Willetts, who as Universities Minister worked under Vince Cable at the Department for Business, warned that a proposed cap on non-EU immigration would have a damaging effect on economic growth, with City firms and universities in particular losing out by being blocked from recruiting talented overseas students and workers.

The row would become interminable, the first of many over the years, and, unusually, one which set the Prime Minister against his close friend the Chancellor. Cameron and May lined up on one side, pushing for lower immigration, against Clegg, Gove, Cable and Osborne on the other, arguing that the measures used to tackle the problem were damaging the economy.

Cameron and May pushed on, announcing an interim immigration cap for non-EU nationals of 24,400 by the end of the 2010/11 financial year. In an interview with *The Sun* on 28 June 2010, May said: 'People know controlling immigration makes sense. They see the pressure on housing, schools and hospitals. They know it can't go on … Immigration has been good for us. Uncontrolled immigration isn't.'[274] But if May thought the question of the immigration cap had been settled in her favour, she soon discovered that the row had not been put to bed. A few weeks later, at the end of July, while accompanying Cameron and a contingent of business leaders on a trip to India, Cable, in his capacity as Business Secretary, sought to reopen the negotiations in public. In doing so, he was speaking with the latitude he believed he enjoyed to criticise government policy as a Liberal Democrat within the coalition, and with the knowledge that many Tory colleagues, including Osborne and his own deputy, Willetts, concurred with his view that the cap was damaging Britain's ability to attract talent from places like India. 'It's no great secret that in my department and me personally, we want to see an open economy, and as liberal an immigration policy as it's possible to have,' Cable declared soon after landing on Indian soil. 'We are arguing, within government, about how we create the most flexible regime we can possibly have, but in a way that reassures the British public.'[275]

May was furious at the public declaration of war, and her spads retaliated by rubbishing Cable's remarks, an intervention that gave him and Cameron a diplomatic headache, given that they were in the middle of a charm offensive in India. Cable says now:

> Theresa launched the first big crackdown on overseas students
> within months of being in government, and that was when we

had our first clashes. It had an immediate negative impact in India, because large numbers of Indians stopped sending their kids here because they thought we were rejecting them, and they went to Australia and America instead. She just shut her ears to the whole problem. We knew that Osborne and Hague were pleading, and saying: "This is silly and damaging our interests." The fortress Home Office just dug in.

One No. 10 insider at the time says: 'That might have been the first-time demonstration of her ability to be as tough as everyone now knows her to be.'

On his return to the UK, Cable says, the briefing against him continued. He is clear, however, that it was the special advisers, rather than May personally, who treated him with discourtesy, adding that he always found her personally polite and civil. 'Most of this [arguing] was done at second and third hand by special advisers and civil servants,' Cable says. 'I always rather liked her, even though we were approaching the problem from opposite directions. But we both had a job to do. Her job was keeping people out and my job was getting them in. So it was as simple as that.'

Sometimes, May was prepared to reprimand Cable herself – always with icy politeness. He says:

> I remember early on I made some fairly aggressive remarks about how much damage was being done on overseas students, and I got a call on my mobile telephone at about eleven o'clock at night. I was walking home from Twickenham Station, and it was Theresa on the phone taking some exception to that. This wasn't common. The very fact that episode stands out, she must have been really irked by what I'd said. It was very much: 'Vincent, I'm very disappointed.' That was one of her phrases: 'I'm very disappointed.'

On another occasion, May is said to have given Cable a 'dressing-down' in front of officials, accusing him of trying to sabotage a crackdown on overseas students attending bogus colleges, by leaking it to the media. 'Vince, your conduct is most disappointing, don't do it again,' she is said to have admonished him, as the Business Secretary stared at his shoes.[276] Cable does not bear a grudge, and says the pair were able to maintain a civil relationship. 'She's not like Mrs Thatcher, kind of abrasively angry. She was always cool and I always thought rather charming and rather feminine in her way of dealing with people. We all respected her in a strange way.'

While May generally (but not always) had the backing of a sympathetic Cameron in her clashes with colleagues over immigration, the Tory with whom May had the greatest disagreement was George Osborne. David Laws has said:

> Some of the most robust clashes at the Cabinet were not between Liberal Democrats and Conservatives, but between Theresa May and George Osborne over her department's rigid attitude to economic immigration, and it was clear that there was no love lost between the two. The Prime Minister may have been worrying about tabloid newspapers and the rise of UKIP, but around the Cabinet table most of the discussions about immigration – particularly early on in the parliament – were dominated by Cabinet ministers attacking the Home Secretary, Theresa May, over her department's restrictive immigration and visa rules.[277]

By the early months of 2012, with net immigration having risen to 250,000, May was growing increasingly exasperated at what she saw as her colleagues' lack of commitment to the tens of thousands figure. Osborne, Cable, Gove and a number of other Cabinet ministers were equally frustrated that, at a time when the recession was biting hard, their ability to attract investment from overseas was being hampered by the ever greater restrictions imposed by the Home Office. During one clash between the two sides, Osborne and Cable remonstrated with May on behalf of Jeremy Hunt, the Culture Secretary, who complained that the tourism industry was struggling to attract wealthy Chinese visitors with cash to spend on

British products, due to the difficulty they were having obtaining visas. Rather than respond, May simply said nothing. Mark Harper, who became Immigration Minister in 2012, says of the 'tens of thousands' target: 'It was a clear manifesto commitment. What happens though … is you get lots of pressures. Other ministers, whilst being committed to the overall position, argue for their bit of the brief. To some extent you expect them to.'

The Liberal Democrats who served in the coalition government insist that May was unreceptive to their attempts to help her hit the 'tens of thousands' target with less aggressive measures. One suggestion, that students be excluded from the net migration figures, on the grounds that they were expected to leave the UK once their courses had finished (a path adopted by many other countries although not in line with OECD (Organisation for Economic Cooperation and Development) practice), was dismissed out of hand. While this might have made the task of hitting the 'tens of thousands' target easier, May was implacably opposed, telling colleagues the public would view the move as 'fiddling the figures'. Cable says his feeling was that it was easier for the Home Office to launch a series of crackdowns on bogus colleges, which May once described as 'diploma factories',[278] and to ramp up the rhetoric against non-EU students who over-stayed after their degrees had finished than to accept that the 'tens of thousands' figure was unattainable due to EU freedom of movement rules. He adds: 'The Home Office propaganda, which she promoted, fed on itself. It meant she was very locked into a very hard-line position which she couldn't retreat from even if she wanted to.'

The trigger for what most onlookers describe as the worst Cabinet bust-up of the coalition era was the briefing Osborne had received about the trouble a group of Chinese businessmen had experienced on arriving at Heathrow. Cable says:

Osborne … was very keen on having Chinese coming here and investing, and they had endless problems … We had occasions where top Chinese people were turned away at Heathrow. [May] was adamant that she wasn't going to relax the regime. It was the stubbornness, the refusal to bend. The person she antagonised the most over all that was Osborne.

Eric Pickles adds:

> She had disagreements with George in terms of immigration, particularly with regard to numbers, particularly with regard to Chinese numbers. A lot of pressure was placed on her with regard to Chinese passports and visas in Cabinet. She had a firm view about what should be done ... and she was also quite skilful in not quite delivering what they wanted without being overtly obstructive.

Laws has described the incident as 'the worst bollocking I can ever remember any senior minister receiving at a Cabinet meeting ... George Osborne berated her for an incident in which a Chinese billionaire had been strip-searched at Heathrow, and the Home Secretary sat sulkily but unrepentant.'[279]

The Cabinet dressing-down planted in May a burning resentment against Osborne which would continue for the next four years. One fellow minister who remains in the Cabinet under May, and who observed the 2012 row, confirms: 'She couldn't stand him after that.' Andrew Lansley, who served in the Cabinet until 2014, says that during these years, while May and Cameron were on reasonably good terms, she and Osborne became increasingly estranged. As Health Secretary, Lansley sat to the left of May around the Cabinet table, while Osborne was on her right. Invariably, in the chit-chat which preceded and ended meetings as ministers gathered to arrive and later departed, Lansley says she engaged him in small talk but would not usually converse with the Chancellor. 'Theresa and I were much more likely to have a cheerful conversation about life than they were,' he says. 'When she got to deal with David Cameron in person, she probably got on fine with him. I suspect that it was with George Osborne that the difficulties emerged.'

Osborne, however, is understood to have seen their exchanges, including the Chinese visa row, as part of the of the usual cut and thrust of political debate, with each fighting on behalf of their department, and was blind-sided when it emerged, after May became Prime Minister, that she had viewed him with hostility. One ally says the former Chancellor does not recognise the characterisation, put about after he was left out of her first government, that theirs was a 'difficult' relationship. 'Theresa isn't close to anyone, but everyone respected her,' the ally says. 'I think that's how George saw her. The relationship was cordial, if not warm. No one got on with her. But there were definitely people around the Cabinet table who had a worse relationship with Theresa than George – and who George had a worse relationship with.'

Eric Pickles says that Cameron too was unaware that May felt resentful at the high-handed way she had been treated by Osborne, and did not take steps to smooth her ruffled feathers. 'Cameron wasn't a very good manager of people,' he says. 'If you were in the room with him, there was no one more important. I don't think he noticed [she was upset].' One of those who observed Osborne and May up close suggests the reason the then Chancellor took their disagreements less seriously than she did was down to a fundamental difference of approach. The onlooker says:

> The style is very different. She clearly felt about George that perhaps it was a game to him, and she hated that. She definitely felt that perception of politics as being a game where you plant traps for the opposition to try and catch them out was not for her.

William Hague agrees that May found it more difficult to put conflicts aside than her more light-hearted colleagues, such as Michael Gove, whom she clashed with over both immigration and counterterrorism. 'As is well-known, she had a lot of disagreements with some members of the Cabinet,' he says.

> They were usually over some policy area. And since she has this approach of taking time to decide what to do but then really

sticking to it, that sticking to it can lead to some friction with other people who wanted a different approach. She would not give ground – and I'm not saying she should have given ground – but that meant there were instances with Michael Gove or with some Liberal members of the coalition, where there were some long-running disagreements going on. And she would stand her ground and sit the disagreement out. And that's different from some politicians who would say, 'We can't go on like this, let's go for a drink and sort it all out.' Maybe that's a man's way, a strength and weakness of male politicians sometimes. But her approach is: 'No, no, I'm right, I'm sticking to my ground and you have to back down.' She generally came off best from these things.

A few months before the dressing-down from Osborne at Cabinet, in November 2011, it had been May who had dealt out an angry and very public rebuke, after it emerged that the UK Border Agency had relaxed checks on overseas visitors without her permission. The scandal became highly charged when May suspended Brodie Clark, the director of the agency, who quit a few days later claiming constructive dismissal. May is said to have responded with 'incredulity and fury' [280] after learning that the force, which had been overstretched at the time, had extended an instruction to down-play checks on EU citizens to cover non-Europeans, without her consent. At one point, May came under pressure to resign, when Clark accusing her of seeking to save her career by sacrificing his. Having stored up enough goodwill through strong performances over the preceding eighteen months in office, and enjoying the full backing of No. 10, May weathered the storm easily enough. In a debate on her role in the scandal called by Yvette Cooper for Labour, she was protected by a series of helpful interventions from friendly Tory backbenchers, in a display of support organised by the Whips' Office. Brodie Clark later settled with the Home Office for an undisclosed sum of money, without either side admitting liability. Just over a year later, May abolished the agency, bringing its functions back under the direct control of the Home Office.

May's third year in office, from the spring of 2012, marked a turning point in her fortunes. She had come through the early years relatively unscathed, even earning a reputation as a safe pair of hands, a triumph in itself given the series of crises her predecessors had lurched between. Now, her star would begin to rise, her stewardship of the Home Office coming to be seen as one of the big successes of the coalition government. A pivotal moment came with May's adept handling of what could have been a catastrophic series of events leading up to the 2012 London Olympics. A problem with lengthy delays at Heathrow Airport on the eve of the Games, which left athletes and visitors queuing for hours, was dwarfed by another looming disaster: the reluctant and alarmingly tardy revelation by the security firm hired to protect Olympic venues that it was seriously behind schedule in its plans to recruit and train 10,000 guards.

The admission by the firm, G4S, came just sixteen days before the Games began, plunging the preparations into chaos. May calmly took control of the situation, ordering the Army to take over guard duties and eventually recouping £88 million from G4S. She would hold daily Cobra meetings to ensure that the Games passed off safely and smoothly. And they did. The 2012 London Olympics proved to be a triumph, providing a moment of fellow-feeling in a troubled world, as Londoners and visitors to the capital alike basked in a collective mood of goodwill. In the anxious days before the start of the Olympics, while millions of Britons held their breath and prayed that the G4S crisis would be resolved in time for the Opening Ceremony on 27 July, May was in the firing line for what she had known and when. One opinion poll found that more than half of voters felt she should resign.[281] By the time she visited the Olympic Stadium (wearing special Union Jack pumps) on what became known as 'Super Saturday', 4 August, where she was among the crowd which thrilled to see three British athletes win gold in the space of forty-four minutes, she was inundated with spectators thanking her for 'rescuing' the Games.

The tensions within government continued, however, as May

became embroiled in a series of public arguments with Nick Clegg.
Their disagreements over the immigration cap, May's antipathy towards the Human Rights Act and EU freedom of movement, and
her plans for what the Lib Dems called a 'Snooper's Charter' were
all aired in public. Sean Kemp, who was in charge of Clegg's press
operation at the time, says:

> I don't think it was an easy relationship, certainly. They weren't
> throwing crockery at each other … but if you compare it to the
> [far warmer] Nick–Cameron one … there was a real frostiness
> about that relationship [with May], which was reflective of per-
> sonality and the differences there on the big issues.

Sometimes, it helped both Clegg and May to be seen by their
respective party memberships to be at odds. Kemp says: 'It was
crowd pleasing for her, it was crowd pleasing for us. Both sides were
appealing to our party bases. But also there were clear ideological
differences.'

Vince Cable is more blunt:

> She didn't get on well with Clegg. I don't think they could
> stand each other. I obviously talked to Clegg quite a lot, and
> his eyes would go up whenever her name was mentioned. I
> got the impression that his was such an utterly different world
> view that there was just no meeting of minds at all. Part of it
> was that Clegg had this system where he would bargain with
> Cameron over issues … whereas … Theresa … was never up
> for that. She had a position, she would never compromise it, and
> she just wasn't willing to engage in that kind of bartering. I had
> a certain respect for her, for that reason. I found it infuriating but
> you couldn't help respecting her.

Like Lynne Featherstone, William Hague feels that rather than attacking May in public, as Clegg tended to do, it was more fruitful
to treat her with kid gloves. It was an approach he took during one

of the greatest tests of their generally warm working relationship when, in October 2012, the Home Secretary ruled on a controversial extradition case involving Gary McKinnon, a 46-year-old Scottish computer systems expert. Ten years earlier, McKinnon had been accused by the US Justice authorities of 'the biggest military computer hack of all time'.[282] He was facing a sentence of up to seventy years in prison for tapping into Pentagon computers (McKinnon claimed he had been searching for evidence of UFOs). His extradition had been held up following legal arguments over his claim to be suffering from Asperger syndrome, a form of autism, which, his doctors argued, meant dispatching him to the US would put him at risk of unreasonable stress or even suicide. On 12 October 2012, May cancelled the extradition order. The Americans were furious.

May's move to halt the McKinnon extradition is perhaps the quintessential example of her decision-making process. The timing was agonisingly slow; having first been asked by her civil servants to rule on McKinnon's extradition within days of coming to office, May took her time, as she prefers to do with all the most challenging decisions she faces, not giving her final ruling for another two and a half years. She is said to have ultimately made up her mind not in her office surrounded by civil servants, but late at night, at home, with her husband.[283] Fiona Hill later described the moment May told her of her decision: 'The call came at about quarter to six in the morning. Theresa simply said, "I'm not going to extradite him," and I leapt out of bed with excitement.'[284]

May's decision was both extraordinary and bold. In unilaterally defying Britain's closest ally, the last remaining superpower, she risked upsetting not only the Americans but her Prime Minister and the Foreign Secretary, who now faced a huge diplomatic headache with potentially long-term repercussions for the security, both military and economic, of the nation. Despite her reputation for caution, May had certainly not taken the easy option and her decision was utterly unexpected; all of her Labour predecessors had been clear that McKinnon would have to be sent to America. It also showed total independence. In ruling on McKinnon's fate, May was acting in her quasi-judicial role as Home Secretary, a function she took seriously. Where others might have given in to the temptation of chatting through the thorny case with colleagues, May kept her counsel – to the bafflement of many. Eric Pickles says: 'There was some surprise that she wasn't taking it to the Prime Minister, she wasn't taking it to Cabinet, [but] that wasn't her being precious, it was being precise and constitutional.'

Characteristically, May was unswayed by the many pressures on her, deciding on the facts of the case alone, and informing Cameron and Clegg of her ruling only a few hours before she announced it to MPs in the House of Commons. It was the first the American government heard of the news. Hill has said: 'I think she is a massive risk-taker – huge. When she decided not to extradite Gary McKinnon, she knew the wrath from the States [would follow] and by God, you know, the tornado that came out of Washington was immense.'[285] The UK press greeted May's decision with surprise and overwhelming approval, some even describing the Home Secretary's decision as her *Love Actually* moment, a reference to the 2003 film in which a British Prime Minister played by Hugh Grant stands up to a bullying US President. The Obama administration was far from charmed, however. Such a slap in the face from a long-term ally was virtually unprecedented. Eric Holder, the US Attorney General, wrote what was described as a 'strongly worded' letter to the Home Secretary complaining about her action. US officials briefed that the relationship between May and Obama was 'finished' and that Holder personally felt he had been 'screwed over'.[286]

A few weeks later, Hague found himself on his way to Washington, DC, for a meeting in which he fully expected the Americans to vent their rage. He was, however, philosophical. When the complaint came, as he knew it would, along with an appeal to persuade May to change her mind, he shrugged his shoulders. 'You go and talk to her,' Hague said helplessly, adding: 'Good luck!' His opposite number stared for a moment before being forced to concede defeat.

'They would look knowingly and say, "We're never going to change her decision,"' Hague says now.

> She made her decision independently, and was meant to do so, was not meant to discuss it with the Foreign Secretary, so we all have to live with that. That's how I explained it to the Americans. It did complicate relations with America [but] I did not press her to do anything different. That would not have been proper.

Hague respected May's rather formal, controlled approach, but also observed how many of his colleagues struggled with it.

> She's a difficult person to negotiate with. Once she has decided what the right thing is to do, she's very hard to budge from it. Even by the standards of ministers negotiating with each other, often who are friends together, or they're a mixture of friends and rivals … she's right up there near the top of the scale of colleagues who are definitely not unpleasant in any way, but tough to negotiate with. That is why she is described sometimes as a difficult colleague. She's not difficult in terms of personal relations.

The McKinnon decision came at a time when May was already being lauded over another extradition request she had ruled on just eleven days earlier. Abu Hamza, an Egyptian-born radical Islamist cleric who had been convicted of a number of terrorist offences in the UK, had been sought by the US authorities since 2004 on similar charges. His extradition had been blocked by the European Court of Human Rights in July 2010, two months after May came to office, on the grounds that he could be subject to inhumane treatment in the harsh US prison system. May's frustration at the court's ability to block her desire to dispatch Hamza to the US was one of the motivations behind her increasing antipathy towards the Human Rights Act. Having fought the case all the way through the courts, when May finally secured Hamza's deportation, it was seen as a personal vindication of her persistence. Eighteen months later, he was found guilty of all charges in a New York court and sentenced to life in prison. Coming so soon after the Abu Hamza case and her adept handling of the Olympics, the McKinnon decision was seen as another triumph for an increasingly assured and confident Home Secretary. May began to be spoken of seriously as a likely successor to Cameron.

A few weeks before the Hamza ruling, Cameron had carried out the first reshuffle of his government. There had been suggestions that May would be moved from the Home Office, but in fact, in a sign that Downing Street backed her in the tiff over the asylum-seeking cat, it was Kenneth Clarke who was demoted from the Department of Justice, becoming a lowly Minister without Portfolio. Clegg took the opportunity to reshuffle his pack too, moving the 'Orange Booker' Jeremy Browne (so named for his contribution to a 2004 collection of right-leaning essays by leading Liberals, bound in an orange book jacket), into the Home Office. May was sorry to see Lynne Featherstone go, but, according to Sean Kemp, she and her team soon came to see Browne as their 'dream Liberal Democrat minister'. Although socially liberal, Browne was more pragmatic than most Lib Dems on civil liberties, and shared May's concerns about security and spiralling immigration.

During the following months, as Clegg continued his series of running battles with May over net migration, the Human Rights Act and freedom of movement, the Deputy Prime Minister felt, increasingly, that he needed more ballast in the department than Browne was providing. The final provocation came in July 2013, when it emerged that the Home Office had ordered advertising vans to tour six London boroughs known to contain high levels of illegal immigrants displaying posters declaring 'Go Home'. When the news broke, there was outrage. Mark Harper, who was Immigration Minister at the time, says the vans were part of a pilot scheme.

> We trialled a range of measures, and they were one … in areas where there were a lot of people living illegally. It did create a lot of interest. We weren't rolling out a new policy, we were testing

out some operational things. I don't think we thought it would get
quite so much attention.

Amid general outrage, a Labour peer, Lord Lipsey, complained to
the advertising standards authority, arguing that the vans were racist.
It was a view Clegg shared. He was also concerned that Browne had
either not been consulted about the plans to trial the 'Go Home'
vans, as they became known, which would have given him a chance
to raise the matter with Clegg, who would have battled to block
them, or that he had tacitly given his approval. Harper says: 'It did
cause some tension. There was a very boring argument about what
things have to get collective agreement and what things do not.'
Lynne Featherstone adds: 'I haven't spoken to Jeremy, but I can't
believe he knew about the "Go Home" vans. If Nick had got wind
of that, it would have been stopped. I can't even believe Theresa
knew about them. It was just such a crass thing to do.'

As the Cabinet minister responsible for the entire Home Office,
May has never publicly disclosed whether or not she was aware of
Harper's trial before the row blew up.

In October 2013, Clegg reacted by moving Browne out of the
department and installing instead Norman Baker, who took a far
more liberal line on both civil liberties and immigration. The new
Lib Dem minister was also a free-thinker, who six years earlier
had suggested that MI5, which falls under the brief of the Home
Office, had covered up what he alleged was the murder of Dr
David Kelly, the government scientist who had leaked information
suggesting the Blair government had misled the public ahead of the
Iraq War. May was enraged, both by the choice of Baker and by
what she saw as Clegg's incivility in shuffling her ministerial team
without consulting her. May confronted Cameron about the matter
personally. David Laws has said: 'The next day's Cabinet meeting
started a most unusual five minutes late, because the Home Secretary was in the Prime Minister's office complaining about her new
minister. "How could you agree to Nick putting this man into my
department? Norman Baker, for goodness sake."'[287]

Cameron was sympathetic, but under the terms of the coalition agreement, he could do nothing; Clegg was free to appoint who he wanted to ministerial posts allocated to the Lib Dems. Sean Kemp says:

> With Norman, I think they [May's team] felt it was deliberate provocation. I don't think it was quite that, but it was clearly someone who was being put there as a 'This is going to cause difficulty for you, this is going to obstruct things that you want to do'. That was partly why he was sent there – not to obstruct but to be a more forceful Lib Dem presence in one of the big departments. I can see why they would have regarded it as an 'up yours'. From our point of view, the 'up yours' had also been the other way for the previous few years.

May's response was to strike back, hard. Baker has described the chilling reception he received as he moved across the street from the Department for Transport (DfT), where he had enjoyed three happy years as a Transport minister, to the 'dry and oppressive' Home Office.

> I met the Home Secretary briefly on the day of my appointment for a short five- or ten-minute introductory chat in her office. Her office was quite barren and looked like it could be evacuated of all traces of its occupant within a matter of minutes … She bore the icy smile of a snow queen.[288]

Worse was to follow. 'I learnt the next morning that my transfer had generated a welcome present from the Home Secretary's special advisers in the form of the hatchet job in the press,' Baker later wrote of the next day's headlines, which included descriptions of him as 'bonkers', a 'green-ink crank' and a 'conspiracy theorist' because of his David Kelly book. 'I had moved from the sunny beach to the snake pit,' Baker went on.

> My first proper meeting with the Home Secretary came that day

and it was a tense one. I told her I did not expect to be briefed against by her special advisers. I did not want to have this confrontation in our first substantive meeting, but I sensed that if I did not put down a firm marker in response to this head-on challenge then I would be sunk. She said she did not think her spads were behind the press stories. I told her bluntly that I had been told they were by two different sources. She said she would investigate.

Baker would never feel at home in his new department, becoming embroiled in frequent clashes with Fiona Hill and Nick Timothy. He would not be the only person to feel the heat from, in Lynne Featherstone's almost-but-not-quite-joking description, the 'evil Tory spads'.

May's Sisyphean drive to get immigration down would continue for the rest of her time at the Home Office. There has been much debate over the question of whether she was philosophically committed to lowering immigration, or if she viewed hitting the 'tens of thousands' target as a kind of grown-up homework, a commitment which was in the Conservative manifesto and so to be considered an unbreakable bond. Sean Kemp says:

> I remember having a drink with Fiona [Hill] in a pub, and her saying to me: 'You do know we are going to hit the "tens of thousands" target? We are going to hit it.' I always think of it as their tuition fees. It is a promise made for many, many good political reasons, possibly ideological reasons, but it's undeliverable, and when you get down to it, it doesn't actually make much sense. The difference is that they haven't gone back. Even as it became more and more irrational, they would stick to it. Now, to what extent is it because they are true believers, or is it because, certainly for Cameron, 'I don't want to go back on a promise I've made?' For the May team, I don't know.

Vince Cable agrees that the tuition fees comparison is valid.

A lot of it had to do with the Conservatives' reaction to student tuition fees, because they saw a public pledge broken and they saw the terrible damage it did. I think Cameron resolved that he wasn't going to go back on any of their public pledges, no matter how much damage it did.

Vince Cable doubts that May came into the Home Office as a fervent believer in tight immigration control, but suggests that the manifesto promise and the institutional beliefs of the department shaped her thinking. 'Most Tory ministers accepted that the immigration cap [on non-EU migration] was utterly and completely ridiculous and did immense harm, but they felt trapped by their own pledge and unable to go back on it,' he says.

Theresa May, who probably did not invent the promise, I suspect she was given it and was told it was her job, was just the industrious minister trying to do what she was told rather than necessarily from complete conviction. Obviously, when you've done this for five years you start believing your own propaganda, and the Home Office is deeply entrenched with this way of thinking. No one else in government believed it. They all thought it was insane.

Eric Pickles, however, believes that May's commitment to immigration control was real, and that by focusing on net migration, May was far more in touch with public sentiment than most of her Cabinet colleagues. He says: 'In a way, I think [she] understood the importance of immigration before a lot of us did. She got it, she kind of understood what was necessary, and if we're being really blunt she got it before Cameron did.'

May's determination to tackle the one aspect of the immigration figures that she could control – migration by non-EU nationals – meant that, however blunt her methods, within four years she had forced the numbers down to their lowest levels since the start of the first Blair government in 1997. However, with immigration from EU nations increasing to a record 550 a day, the net effect was an inexorable rise. When the Conservatives faced significant losses to UKIP at the 2014 European elections, May overtly blamed the Liberal Democrats for her failure to hit the 'tens of thousands' target, and vowed that a majority Tory government would end freedom of movement within the EU. She declared: 'It is no surprise to anybody that there have been long-standing, possibly heated at times, discussions among the coalition on some these issues on immigration.'[289] By the time of the 2015 general election, net immigration stood at just under 300,000, three times higher than the Conservatives' target. It was a rare failure for May. As Prime Minister, as recently as October 2016, she re-avowed her commitment to the 100,000 figure, although she would not give a timescale for when the goal would be achieved.[290]

CHAPTER XV

EVIL TORY SPADS

On the afternoon of 22 May 2013, a 25-year-old off-duty soldier and father of one, Fusilier Lee Rigby, was strolling just outside his barracks in Woolwich, south London, when a car careered into him. Originally from Middleton in Greater Manchester, Rigby had previously served in Afghanistan, but was in London to carry out ceremonial duties at the Tower of London. Although he was not in uniform, he was wearing a Help for Heroes hooded sweatshirt, showing his support for the charity, which raises money for wounded veterans, and his presence on a road leading to the Royal Artillery Barracks would have been a strong indication that he was a soldier. As Rigby lay prone in the street, two men got out of the Vauxhall Astra that had hit him, and set about attacking him with knives and a cleaver. To the horror of onlookers, the pair attempted to behead the fallen soldier.

The murder of Lee Rigby would bring out both the strengths and the weaknesses of Theresa May's stewardship of the Home Office. Her calmness under pressure, decisiveness and mettle were viewed with gratitude and relief by her colleagues, officials, the police and the wider community in the hours and days that followed the attack. In the longer term, the atrocity confirmed May's view that, as Home Secretary, her primary responsibility was to the security of the nation. She would become ever stauncher in her determination to give the police and security services the tools she felt they needed to keep the country safe. This latter strength would also be viewed as a weakness by some of her colleagues, particularly her coalition partners, the Liberal Democrats, who saw her drive to bolster security legislation as veering into authoritarianism. More immediately, some opponents regarded the way she and her team reacted to the crisis of Lee Rigby's murder as opportunistic.

David Cameron had been meeting French President François Hollande in Paris when word of the attack came through. In his absence, it fell to May as Home Secretary to summon and chair Cobra. Eric Pickles, the Communities Secretary, was among those who attended the meeting. He says:

> I was in London; nice sunny day. Everyone was out of the country. I got this message there'd been a killing, there was going to be a Cobra, could I come. So I turned up, she's there [May], and I think the only other Cabinet minister there was [Baroness] Sayeeda Warsi. We didn't know what was going to happen next – was it the first of a series? It was bad enough as it was. There were a lot of nervous people around the table, and there were a lot of nervous people in uniform around the table. She [May] just took command in a very nice, very business-like, very straightforward way. And I remember looking round the table, and you could tell a lot of the people there, including the folks in uniform, it was like: 'They're back, their mojo's back, someone's taking charge here, we can get through this.' I thought 'bloody hell'. It was fascinating; the dynamism was there. And I thought that was pretty impressive.

Sean Kemp was working in the Office of the Deputy Prime Minister when the breaking news about Rigby's death came through on television. As he watched the developments with horror, another thought occurred to him. He says:

> The day Lee Rigby was murdered, this is a horrible insight into the cynicism of politics, I remember watching that and thinking: 'There's going to be a briefing about us.' And there was.

Obviously your first reaction is, 'Oh my God,' but then I remember thinking, 'I guarantee I'm going to open a paper, I'm going to get a phone call in the next couple of days, and it'll be that.' And that's exactly what happened.

A few weeks before the attack, Clegg had effectively scrapped May's planned Data and Communications Bill, nicknamed the 'Snooper's Charter', by abruptly announcing that the Liberal Democrats would not back the legislation in the Commons, on the grounds that they considered it overly intrusive. Clegg told May of his plan to veto the bill during a private meeting described by David Laws as 'difficult'. Laws quotes Clegg as telling him afterwards:

> I've grown to rather like Theresa May. She is a bit of an Ice Maiden, and has no small talk whatsoever – none. She is instinctively secretive and very rigid, but you can be tough with her and she'll go away and think it all through again. But I had to tell her the existing Bill wouldn't get through the Commons, let alone the Lords … I've told her she's got to go away and look at it all again.[291]

Now, in the wake of the Lee Rigby attack, May went on an all-out campaign to restore the bill in its original form, saying on *The Andrew Marr Show*: 'I have made my view very clear … The law enforcement agencies, the intelligence agencies need access to communications data, and that is essential to them doing their job.'[292] In the days after Rigby's death, she also urged broadcasters not to air interviews with radical Islamist preachers, launched a new drive against extremism on university campuses – and refused to make more than cursory changes to the Data and Communications Bill. When Clegg again threatened to veto it, as Laws has described, 'the reaction from the Home Office was immediate and unpleasant: a briefing to various newspapers saying that "Nick Clegg is a friend and protector of paedophiles and terrorists". It was hardly calculated to win over the Deputy Prime Minister.'[293]

Lynne Featherstone says the row over the 'Snooper's Charter' was almost inevitable:

> There are such fundamental differences around issues such as the 'Snooper's Charter'. People are passionate about it, and if they can't get the other person to see their way to a compromise, they're left in a really difficult position. I suppose Nick or David Cameron or any of them would have said [May] is just very intransigent. But she was standing up for what she believed in.

Charlie Elphicke, who later served as a Home Office whip, agrees: 'It was a massive source of frustration to her because she cares very much about catching terrorists and paedophiles.'

By the end of 2013, Clegg and May were no longer on speaking terms, sometimes sitting through lengthy meetings together without exchanging a word. During the 2014 conference season, in perhaps the most unseemly row of the entire coalition period, one of May's spads was quoted in newspapers as describing Clegg as a 'wanker'[294] after he accused her of 'peddling false and outrageous slurs'[295] for suggesting in her speech to delegates that the 'outrageously irresponsible' Liberal Democrats had put children at risk of sexual exploitation by blocking the legislation. Ultimately, it would take the election of a majority Conservative government in 2015 for the bill, renamed and with a few adjustments but still referred to by critics as the 'Snooper's Charter', to be put before Parliament. It became law in November 2016.

The type of negative briefing dealt out to Clegg was something all the Liberal Democrats who came into contact with the Home Office grew used to, as, indeed, did some Conservatives. The suspects were almost always Fiona Hill and Nick Timothy, who guarded May with a ferocity remarkable even given the fierce loyalty which is the hallmark of the spad species. Some of those who found themselves briefed against were philosophical, viewing it as part of the territory of coalition. Lynne Featherstone describes May's advisers almost admiringly: 'Nick Timothy and Fiona, the "evil Tory spads", as I call them, they're evil, and they would not hesitate to give horrible things about me to the *Daily Mail* whenever possible, but that's the political battle. I don't think they were bad people. I liked them enormously.'

Others, not so forgiving, were infuriated by the spads' briefings, however. Norman Baker has written: 'Her spads were very different from the friendly pair I had been used to at the DfT. They were ruthless in pursuit of their party goals and took no prisoners. Coalition for them was an unwelcome necessity to be tolerated…' Baker also claims that Timothy, Hill and the third Home Office special adviser, Stephen Parkinson, kept an iron grip over the civil servants in the department, particularly those working in the press office, whom they ordered to clear every line issued by ministers. Baker kicked against this 'rather central, Soviet way',[296] resulting in some spectacular rows with the advisers and May herself. Baker has claimed:

> What was in place, at least as far as senior officials were concerned, was close to a thinly veiled reign of terror. The tramlines were laid down by Theresa's spads, and woe betide any civil servant who went outside them. Officials who did not please found themselves shunted out to cul-de-sac postings elsewhere.[297]

In time, however, Baker came to have a grudging regard for Hill, if not for Timothy. He said: 'She was the one most likely to see the need for a sensible working relationship. I did not myself dislike her. I just thought she was doing her job.'[298]

There is little consensus over the extent to which May, who has repeatedly insisted she does not gossip to journalists or backbite about her colleagues, condones such behaviour in those who do so on her behalf. Sean Kemp says: 'They all say that, [but] they're aware. They know the personality of the people they hire. All ministers like having someone they think fights their corner. I'm sure she loved seeing her people briefing "Michael Gove is an idiot", or "Nick Clegg is putting things at risk".' Norman Baker has said:

'During my time at the Home Office, I concluded that while Theresa May did not initiate such behaviour herself, she gave her spads
considerable latitude coupled with a general steer, and did not look
too closely at exactly what they were doing, which as a consequence
gave her deniability.'[299]

Others disagree. Eric Pickles says: 'I'm not sure I can imagine
her saying [that kind of] stuff. I think it's more likely they're good
people and they protect her. It's the nature of things. Spads are
very partisan, it's like a member of the family.' William Hague also
shrugs off the spads' bullishness in May's defence as part of the cut
and thrust of the Westminster Village. 'We all have had over the
years advisers who get more zealous and enthusiastic about promoting their leader than their leader,' he says.

As the Rigby murder showed, security had become an increasing
problem through the coalition years, and, as a result, May worked
ever more closely with Hague during his time as Foreign Secretary.
They appear to have formed a far more cordial relationship than
May had with many other colleagues: 'As Home Secretary, on in-
ternal intelligence things, she's always been at the tough end ...
even if it got us into trouble with foreign countries,' he says.

> I don't recall any course of action we fell out about at any stage.
> Through all those points of contact and personal meetings, we
> actually always made sure that we never cut across each other in
> front of other ministers, that really the Foreign and Home Secre-
> taries were always very closely aligned and didn't have rows in the
> Cabinet. That also made her a colleague who was good to work
> with ... She would stand by something, she would agree with you.
> Not all ministers were like that.

Hague's good working relationship with May helped her secure one
of her greatest triumphs as Home Secretary: the deportation to
Jordan of the radical cleric Abu Qatada, in July 2013, following a
long-running legal battle. The principal impediment to Qatada's
extradition on terrorism charges related to claims by his lawyers

that he risked being tried on the basis of evidence obtained by tor-
ture. During a complex series of negotiations, May personally made
a number of trips to the Arab nation to obtain assurances from
the Jordanians, which needed to be strong enough to convince the
courts that no such material would be used. Hague praises May's
tenacity over the Qatada case – and laughs as he describes how she
was perceived by the Jordanian leadership.

> The Jordanians would look at [me], and I would say to the Jor-
> danians: 'Theresa May's coming out again to Jordan.' There
> would be this look of 'Oh right, we'd better get ready for a serious
> discussion.' She doesn't go to waste her time. When she visits a
> foreign country, there's going to be an outcome … Her visits …
> were really helpful, they were crucial. Lesser Home Secretaries
> would have given up on that whole business.

In a rare interview, Nick Timothy once used May's handling of the
Qatada case to defy suggestions that she was 'risk-averse', saying:
'She went out on a limb on Abu Qatada and never relented, despite
various setbacks.'[300]

The long-running saga of Qatada's extradition would indeed
have defeated a weaker character than May. As she had with the
extradition of Abu Hamza a year earlier, she was determined to see
the process through. At one point, in April 2012, she was humiliated when, in an astonishingly ham-fisted bungle, she announced to
MPs that a deadline for Qatada's lawyers to appeal to the European
Court had passed, and that deportation proceedings would begin
shortly, only for it to emerge that Home Office officials had got their
dates wrong and an appeal had been lodged after all. While the
mistake was that of her civil servants, as the minister in charge, May
was responsible – and faced full-scale ridicule in the media. To make
matters worse, it emerged that during the key hours in question,
when the Home Office assumed the deadline had passed but Qatada's lawyers were in fact preparing to fax his eleventh-hour appeal
to the court in Strasbourg, she had been at what was described as a

'glittering fiftieth birthday party of Jonathan Shalit, a celebrity agent, at the Victoria and Albert museum in west London'.[301] 'Theresa May "partied with *X Factor* judges" while Abu Qatada appealed',[302] read one headline, while another newspaper revealed that, during the hours Qatada's appeal was being submitted, 'wearing a typically showy pair of gold-coloured shoes, a beaming May was pictured with the TV presenter Lorraine Kelly and rubbed shoulders with the model Kelly Brook and the *X Factor* judge Tulisa Contostavlos'.[303]

But May's persistence won through; Qatada was finally deported in July 2013. She had been the sixth Home Secretary to attempt to return the cleric to Jordan, but the first to bother to fly to Amman to personally negotiate a deal. The entire eight-year saga had cost the British taxpayer nearly £2 million. Announcing his departure, a gleeful Home Secretary said:

> This dangerous man has now been removed from our shores to face the courts in his own country. I am glad that this govern-ment's determination to see him on a plane has been vindicated and that we have at last achieved what previous governments, Parliament and the British public have long called for.[304]

She went on to promise to reform human rights legislation, to ensure the courts were no longer tied up in lengthy appeals.

Newspapers and politicians of all parties were united in their praise. In a leader column, the *Daily Mail* noted the importance May placed on keeping her word:

> For a politician to make a promise and deliver on it is a rarity these days. But even more impressive was Mrs May's determina-tion not to dwell on Qatada's departure. Immediately, she made it clear there remains an urgent need to reform human rights laws which are a charter for countless other foreign killers, rapists and terrorists.[305]

Under the headline 'A goddess stands tall in her kitten heels after laying low the enemy', *Telegraph* sketchwriter Michael Deacon described the scene in the Commons, as MPs hailed:

> the divine Theresa, Protector of the Realm, Saviour of Immigration Control, Mother of Elected Police and Crime Commissioners, Queen of the Kitten Heel – and now Victorious Slayer of Abu Qatada … Worshippers prostrated themselves before the holy vision, and gave praise for the just and righteous vanquishing of the wicked Qatada.[306]

Suddenly, May had become a big player. From now on she would be a fixture in the speculation that always accompanies the question of the leadership succession. At various times, the babble around the identity of David Cameron's successor would be louder or quieter. May's name would always be mentioned. In the immediate aftermath of the Qatada case, the bookmaker Ladbrokes made May the 4–1 favourite to become the next Prime Minister. As Cameron departed for his annual summer holiday in Portugal, leaving May officially in charge of the country while George Osborne and Nick Clegg were also away, an opinion poll by ComRes found she was viewed more favourably by voters than anyone else in government, and second only to Boris Johnson, who, as London Mayor, had not yet returned to the Commons.[307]

Four months later, May was awarded the *Spectator*'s Politician of the Year award. Such was the growing interest in, and approval for, the Home Secretary – and her colourful fashion sense – that, on the morning of the prize-giving, the *Daily Mail* ran a double-page spread asking: 'Is Theresa May turning into Cara Delevingne?'[308] As she picked up the award, May said dryly: 'For those of you who don't know, [Delevingne] is twenty-one, a supermodel and one of the most beautiful women in the world. So I think we can safely say that … is a question to which the answer is no.'[309] Amid all the adulation, May even managed to brush aside an embarrassing incident the day after the awards, when a terrorist suspect held under a T-Pim and due to appear at the Old Bailey, Mohammed

Ahmed Mohamed, was able escape surveillance by donning a burka and disappearing. It was an episode which might well have brought down a weaker Home Secretary. But, by January 2014, ConservativeHome's poll of party members found she had narrowly overtaken Boris Johnson in the popularity stakes. Six months later, the gap had widened to sixteen points.

Among her Cabinet peers, respect for May had been growing since their entry into government in 2010. Like William Hague, Liam Fox, who served as Defence Secretary until 2011, found her productive to work with – and pleasant company:

> We worked very closely when I was Defence Secretary, and we started going out for lunches then just to keep in touch with what was going on. We tended to have a very similar view – we tended to see everything from the primary perspective of security. Security isn't something that just happens, it has to be made to happen. Because we tended to think the same way, we've always had a very, very good working relationship.

George Osborne, observing May's lunches with Fox with suspicion, is said to have nicknamed them 'the Securocrats'.

Fox adds that when he was forced to resign after breaking the ministerial code by inviting an unofficial adviser into meetings, May was one of the few Cabinet ministers who stuck by him, even attending a function in his North Somerset constituency. He says: 'It was not that long after I left office, and it was a time when a lot of those who had been colleagues were not answering the phones, and Theresa came down in person and did an event. These things you remember.' Former Welsh Secretary Cheryl Gillan, who, along with her friend Caroline Spelman, the Environment Secretary, was sacked by Cameron in his September 2012 reshuffle, tells a similar story.

> She was the only Cabinet member who bothered to keep up with Caroline Spelman and I when we left. It was very hurtful to both

Caroline and me that we went. She came to my constituency
a couple of times, we had dinner together. She's quite a good
listener. Most other colleagues – when you're out, you're out.

May had less friendly dealings with the next Cabinet colleague to
quit the government, Andrew Mitchell, who was forced to resign a
few weeks after the reshuffle over the 'Plebgate' scandal, in which
he was accused by police officers guarding Downing Street of calling them 'plebs' and swearing in anger when they refused to let
him ride his bicycle through the main gates. To Mitchell's dismay,
May, who as Home Secretary was responsible for the police, sided
with the officers rather than her Conservative colleague. Asked by
reporters about the growing scandal, May did not defend Mitchell,
and instead made clear her displeasure. 'I have had a conversation with Andrew Mitchell,' she was reported as saying 'icily'. 'I do
not intend to reveal the contents of that conversation … I was not
happy.'[310] In fact, May had told Mitchell he should stand down.

Mitchell denied the allegations ferociously, but the furore eventually became so heated that he had little choice but to resign. When
it later emerged that one of the officers involved had lied about the
incident, the MP received an apology from Met Police Commissioner Bernard Hogan-Howe. Friends who briefed newspapers on
his behalf made clear his continuing resentment at May, claiming
she was responsible for his departure. The veteran Conservative
MP Keith Simpson says of May's attitude to Mitchell: 'I think she
saw Mitchell as a so-called wealthy toff, a member of the chumocracy, an absolute Vicar of Bray … She would just decide he was
unacceptable.'

By now, within Cabinet, May's voice was usually listened to with
respect. While she mainly kept to her own brief, both in Cabinet
and the Conservative-only Political Cabinet which preceded it,
when she did stray her contributions were taken seriously. She made
a habit of listening politely to colleagues and sizing up what they
had said before sharing her own view, a practice she has continued
as Prime Minister. Her interventions were not overly verbose, and

they were intelligent – traits welcomed by some around the table.
Eric Pickles says: 'Cabinet is not exactly the *Brains Trust*, it's not
exactly the sparkiest thing you're ever likely to attend. There's nothing more tedious than when you realise that everyone wants to say
something at each item.' Vince Cable adds:

> She was a very active participant because so many issues involved
> her. Together with Osborne and [Michael] Gove, she was proba-
> bly the most prolific contributor to Cabinet discussions. She was
> always very polite and very well-prepared. She was very, very
> good in that context. Didn't talk too long like some of them.

William Hague agrees:

> She would be very active in Political Cabinet, the sort of person
> who largely listens to the discussion and then intervenes in the
> discussion, rather than kicks it all off from the beginning. I think
> that's generally her style … that's her way of influencing the
> course of events. I wouldn't want to give the impression that she's
> shy about it – not at all. She would always give as good as she
> got. You could see her sometimes rolling her eyes and fuming
> quietly at something that somebody else had said. She does not
> conceal that she disagrees with something. And then ten minutes
> later she'll be giving them both barrels. I would sit across from
> her in Cabinet and it would be – sigh, puff – and then you get
> Theresa's view.

Liam Fox defends May against claims by some of her colleagues
that she was both indecisive and 'difficult': 'When people say that
Theresa was difficult, I think what they're misunderstanding is that
she liked due process to be followed before decisions were arrived
at, and would be frustrated at shortcuts taken.'

Like Fox, Hague began to socialise more with May during their
time together in government, sometimes at the Foreign Secretary's
official residence of Chevening. He says:

I've known her for quite a long time, not as close friends, but obviously I've known her since 1997. She went out of her way to maintain a personal friendship when she was Home Secretary, which is not really the image that people have of her among her colleagues. At her initiative, she and I would go out to dinner to have political and personal discussions, and she and her husband came to Chevening to have dinner with [his wife] Ffion and me alone. I found she was a convivial colleague, pleasant to work with. Such evenings were always pleasant, enjoyable, plenty of things to talk about, personal as well as political things. I think she can be a friendlier colleague than the impressions people have of her.

Hague adds that he believes May saw her increasingly warm friendship with him as a means of maintaining a conduit to the charmed inner circle of the Cameroons, at a time when her relationships first with Osborne and Clegg and later with Cameron himself were beginning to break down. 'She probably did feel outside of that [inner circle], but she had her own way of coping with that, in the way that she conducted relations with people like me,' Hague says. 'I was a daily visitor to No. 10, when I wasn't travelling abroad, and went to all the morning meetings, so … she had her bridges into No. 10.'

Other relationships were less friendly. Following the departure of Andy Coulson in 2011, Craig Oliver, a former BBC journalist, joined the No. 10 team as David Cameron's director of communications. Within a few months, he found himself at odds with May's special advisers, clashing particularly with Fiona Hill. Within a short time, both Hill and Nick Timothy stopped attending the weekly spads meeting at No. 10, at which all Cabinet ministers' advisers were supposed to gather under Oliver's leadership, to coordinate the government's message to the public. Exasperated by Oliver's style – he had a reputation for 'testosterone-fuelled speechifying', to quote another spad who did attend – Hill and Timothy made themselves absent. Nor would they abide by Oliver's requirement that they run major policy announcements, speeches and media appearances past him, so they could be included on the fabled Downing Street 'grid' that ensures ministers do not cut across each other.

One former spad to a senior Cabinet minister at the time says: 'Craig Oliver couldn't stand Fiona. They didn't speak.' Another ex-adviser adds: 'Anything that would involve Craig Oliver saying, "You're doing this, you're doing that," they didn't want to know.' Sean Kemp says: 'Fi and Craig hated each other. [She and Timothy] didn't come to the Friday meeting, or Spad School, as we would call it. I don't think they ever went.' In the months and years that followed, the mistrust that built up between Oliver and Hill began to infect the wider relationship between No. 10 and the Home Office, and, ultimately, the Prime Minister and Home Secretary themselves. Norman Baker has said: 'No. 10 was always wary of the Home Secretary, who it was assumed was interested in the top job … Her spads were not well liked at No. 10 and so did not have the influence they might have had.'[311]

But despite the difficulties they caused, her spads were invaluable to May at the Home Office, as personal support and in helping her on a practical level with the heavy burden she faced as Home Secretary. Both Hill and Timothy were encouraged to pursue their own policy interests. It was Timothy who prompted May to take a tough stance over the 1989 Hillsborough disaster, in which ninety-six people lost their lives. Responding to a powerful campaign organised by the victims' families and the Labour frontbencher Andy Burnham, May agreed that the original inquest verdicts should be set aside and a new hearing ordered. In April 2016, the coroner ruled that the victims had been unlawfully killed. May was instrumental in securing a public apology from David Cameron for the ordeal the Hillsborough families had been put through, and was clear that police officers and others responsible for the tragedy should not be immune from criminal prosecution. Her uncompromising words for the police and the sympathy with which she treated the relatives earned warm public praise from Burnham. A number of MPs wept when a visibly emotional May delivered a speech to the

House of Commons following the new inquest verdicts, as she said: 'No one should have to fight year after year, decade after decade, in search of the truth. I hope that for the families and survivors who have been through such difficult times, yesterday's determinations will bring them closer to the peace they have been so long denied.'

Timothy also took a special interest in mental health, and oversaw a review of police detention for those suffering from psychological problems. In particular, he sought to end the use of police cells to detain children with mental health issues. Timothy also took a close interest in the review of the police stop and search powers, which concluded they had a detrimental effect on the relationship between the police and black communities. May made a number of speeches publicly calling on the police to curtail the practice, a notable departure from the era of Michael Howard, who had extended the use of stop and search as Home Secretary and defended it as party leader a decade later.

Fiona Hill's greatest contribution to the Home Office agenda came in the passage of the 2015 Modern Slavery Act, a piece of legislation she was instrumental in creating. Hill took a deep interest in the issue of sex trafficking, and persuaded May and the rest of government to take far greater steps to stamp it out. Under Hill's guidance, May made a number of powerful speeches on the subject. In an article in the *Sunday Times* in the summer of 2013, she wrote: 'For too long modern slavery has been seen as someone else's problem ... Let me tell you what I believe it to be. It is a horrendous crime, it has got to stop and it is everyone's problem.'[312] May ordered the new National Crime Agency, which came into being in October 2013, to prioritise sex trafficking, saying she wanted 'every police force in England and Wales to do the same'. Caroline Haughey, a lawyer who worked with the Home Office in crafting the Modern Slavery Act, says that Hill's input was key. She has said of the spad: 'I have to say she was clearly a very dynamic woman, she clearly read up on the portfolio and brief, and was actually asking questions about empathy: how could we make it better for the victims, how could we prevent this happening in this country?'[313]

May's action on sex trafficking was part of a wider body of work she undertook both as Equalities Minister and in her role as Home Secretary, dedicated to protecting women and children from violence and intimidation. Victims' charities are full of praise for measures such as the Domestic Violence Disclosure Scheme, which gives members of the public a 'right to ask' if an individual has a history of domestic violence. Nicknamed 'Clare's Law', after Clare Wood, a young woman from Yorkshire who was murdered by her ex-boyfriend in 2009, the scheme is designed to help women discover if a potential or current partner has a criminal record for violence during past relationships. May also spoke out about sexual grooming in the wake of the Rotherham abuse scandal, highlighted the use by teenage gang members of rape as a weapon, encouraged the police to take cyber-stalking and trolling more seriously, campaigned against forced marriage and female genital mutilation, and introduced ground-breaking legislation to criminalise psychological abuse within relationships. Lynne Featherstone, who worked on equalities issues with May at the Home Office, says: 'She was very, very good on violence against women, continually attacked by Labour on the women issue, but, really, wrongly.'

Harry Fletcher, who is a director of the campaigning group Victims' Voices, describes May's interest in victims' issues as 'very unusual' for a senior politician on the right. He says:

> I made approaches to her about the need for stalking law reform and she was extremely receptive and said, 'You're pushing at an open door.' We had a couple of meetings with her and then meetings with her advisers. I found her, as a Conservative Home Secretary, to be extremely approachable on issues of protecting vulnerable women. Unlike many of her colleagues, she immediately grasped the issues, and the importance. There are many, many commentators who've described her as cold and serious and lacking a sense of humour. But I didn't find that in either the encounter with the Police Federation or when lobbying on critical issues of stalking and coercive control. I found her easy to get on

with, she was accessible, understood the arguments, was decisive and effective.

By the time the Modern Slavery Act became law in 2015, Fiona Hill had been forced out of the Home Office. The cause was a bitter row which erupted between May and Michael Gove, the Education Secretary, in June 2014. The pair had long had a testy relationship, with Gove on the opposite side of the immigration battle line from May in Cabinet. Their colleagues say the Home Secretary generally found his manner obnoxious. As a member of the Notting Hill set and, like George Osborne, perhaps open to the accusation that he saw politics as a game, Gove had a reputation for being startlingly forthright and outspoken in Cabinet and its related committees, to the extent that he often rubbed the more controlled Home Secretary up the wrong way. For his part, as May's popularity grew through 2012 and 2013 following her assured handling of the London Olympics and the cases involving Abu Hamza, Gary McKinnon and Abu Qatada, and she began to be talked of as a future successor to Cameron, Gove, who at this time was heavily backing Osborne for the job, became increasingly suspicious of her motives. In March 2013, he slapped May down in Political Cabinet when she gave a speech which he considered a far too obvious ploy to set out her stall in the event of a leadership contest.

During another meeting, after May delivered a carefully prepared paper to which Gove responded with some 'slightly provocative and not terribly well considered remarks', she is said to have 'erupted' with fury.[314] One witness is quoted as saying: 'What she could have done is just brush them aside but she leapt on it. She went off the handle. David Cameron just stared.'[315] David Laws has detailed another awkward moment between the two, at a Cabinet away day in 2013, when the Education Secretary launched into one of his now infamous rants about an area of government policy, in this case a Gang Task Force that May had created at Gove's own suggestion. Laws wrote: 'Theresa May stared icily down at her papers. She had, as Michael had suggested, set up the Gang Task Force and was often, unsuccessfully, seeking to engage him in cross-departmental work.'[316]

One of the long-running flashpoints between May and Gove was counter-terrorism, and particularly how it applied to measures to stop the radicalisation of young Muslims, which fell under the remit of both. As far back as June 2011, a proposed government counter-terrorism strategy had been held up for a number of weeks, with Gove arguing that the work, which largely emanated from the Home Office, did not go far enough. The disagreement was philosophical. Eric Pickles, who took May's side in the dispute, says:

> This was serious high stuff … There was more than a whiff of neo-con about what [they] wanted to do, not necessarily David [Cameron], but others around. The neo-cons' view of what was happening [was that] you could actually deal with militant Islam in the same way as you dealt with Lenin and the whole [Soviet] thing. She always had a more sensible, grounded view in terms of what society really is like. She kind of understood that … for some people religion is a dominant part of their life. That doesn't necessarily make them a dangerous person, but it does mean that if you're going to try and pull people across, then you're going to have to do it with a degree of subtlety. The Home Office under her did some really clever stuff in terms of reaching out to Muslim women, young people, did some really sensible things … which I think actually has been quite effective. So I don't think it was just a sense of style, it was also a pragmatic thing of what would work.

By June 2014, the question of how best to prevent radicalisation and home-grown terror was again high on the agenda amid reports that groups of Islamic fundamentalists were seeking to take over some schools in Birmingham, as part of a 'Trojan horse' strategy to recruit young people to their cause. Gove, a former comment editor at *The Times*, had been invited to a lunch at his old newspaper where, on being asked about the Birmingham situation, he could not resist speaking in disparaging terms about the Home Office. He singled out the head of the Office for Security and Counter Terrorism, Charles Farr, for particular criticism, claiming that both he and May were more concerned about targeting individual suspects than in tackling the deeper problems that allowed radicalisation to thrive. Farr, a former intelligence officer, worked out of the Home Office and reported directly to May. He was also in a relationship at the time with Fiona Hill. The resulting front-page story ran under the headline 'Cabinet at war over extremists in schools'. In it, a source – later revealed to be Gove – blamed:

> a reluctance within Whitehall, especially in the Home Office, to confront extremism unless it develops into terrorism … Charles Farr always believed if extremists become violent we should deal with it. It has been characterised by others in government as just beating back the crocodiles that come close to the boat rather than draining the swamp.[317]

When *The Times* contacted Hill for a response to the story on behalf of the Home Office, she launched a ferocious counter-attack in defence of her boss and her lover. Providing quotes as an official Home Office spokesman, she hit back at Gove directly, accusing the Department for Education (DfE) of failing to act on warnings about infiltration for years. 'Why is the DfE wanting to blame other people for information they had in 2010?' she said. 'Lord knows what more they have overlooked on the subject of the protection of kids in state schools? It scares me.'[318]

Hill probably would have got away with it had she stopped there. But, rampaging around the Home Office in a furious rage, she now crossed a line, drawing the *Times* reporters' attention to a letter May had sent Gove that day and circulated around other members of the Cabinet committee overseeing extremism, which had been set up following the murder of Lee Rigby. 'Is it true that the Department for Education was warned in 2010?' May had written to Gove bluntly. 'If so, why did nobody act? … It is clear to me that we will need to take clear action to improve the quality of staffing and

governance if we are to prevent extremism in schools.'[319] Hill spent
the evening on the phone briefing journalists who called to follow
up on the *Times* story. She made no attempt to hide her anger at
Gove. The BBC's Chris Mason later said: 'She was clearly furious
at the front page of *The Times*, furious with Mr Gove. Miss [Hill]
was talking about a fellow Conservative. She was really putting the
boot in.'[320] At 12.42 a.m., Hill tweeted out a link to the letter, which
had been posted on the Home Office website, from the department's official account.

The letter was later taken down, but the damage had been
done. Both Gove and Hill had committed serious breaches of
the convention of collective Cabinet responsibility by airing their
disagreements so publicly. Westminster observers were stunned at
the scrap. Benedict Brogan, the *Telegraph*'s deputy editor, wrote:

> One of Mrs May's many qualities is that she does not normally
> brief against colleagues. It would surprise me if she has done
> on this occasion. Whatever the source, we now know that she is
> angry about the way Mr Gove has tried to blame her for what she
> evidently believes is a failure on his watch. Really angry.[321]

In Downing Street, David Cameron was also really angry. The row
had overshadowed the Queen's Speech, in which the government
sets out its legislative programme for the coming parliament, which
took place on the day the initial *Times* story ran. As he set off for
a G7 meeting in Brussels, he ordered the Cabinet Secretary, Sir
Jeremy Heywood, to speak to those involved and produce a full
report of how the unseemly row had become so public.

Unfortunately for Hill, the debacle handed Craig Oliver, Cameron's director of communications whom she had treated with disdain for the previous three years, just the ammunition he needed to
target his personal bête noire. For months, Oliver had been complaining that Hill treated him with no respect and would not return
his calls, while she openly described him as an 'idiot'.[322] Norman
Baker has said:

With some goodwill, she might have got away with it, but there was precious little goodwill between Downing Street and Theresa's spads. Here was also a chance for No. 10 to clip Theresa's wings. Fiona needed a lifebelt but Craig Oliver at No. 10 threw her a block of concrete instead.[323]

As Sir Jeremy began his investigation, BBC political editor Nick Robinson brought Hill's relationship with Farr into the debate for the first time, describing it on the *Today* programme as a 'complicating factor' in the drama. In the past, May's team had suspected Oliver of using Robinson to brief against them, after the reporter had revealed that Cameron had described both the Home Secretary and Hill as 'grotesquely naive' to have allowed her to be talked up as a future successor. They detected Oliver's fingerprints at work again. The *Today* story served to escalate the scandal still further, with colourful accounts of Hill and her relationship with Farr dominating the coverage. Under the headline 'Theresa's leggy aide, an ex-spy and the affair that fanned the flames', the *Daily Mail* devoted 1,276 words to the saga, illustrating the piece with photographs of both Hill and Farr and including a number of juicy personal details about the couple's lives.[324] Conservative MPs began calling for Hill's head. Cameron went from Brussels to France, where he attended commemorations to mark the seventieth anniversary of the Normandy landings. On his return, he read Sir Jeremy's report, which concluded that while Gove had been unwisely indiscreet, Hill had breached the ministerial code by briefing against him. Her fate was sealed. Reluctantly, May asked for her resignation.

Gove was forced by Cameron to make a formal apology to both May and Farr for his briefing to *The Times*, a humiliating act for a senior politician. But it was May – who, all agree, had no advance knowledge of Hill's actions – who had come off worst. She was devastated at the loss of her spad. For once making little attempt to hide her dismay, she was widely reported as being 'angry and upset'.[325] Two days later, May was summoned to the House of Commons to explain the extraordinary events of the previous week.

She was described by *Times* sketchwriter Ann Treneman as being in 'Ice Queen mode, one stare freezing critics in their tracks', while Gove, who dutifully turned up to watch her statement, 'seemed to have developed an almost puppy-doggish devotion to Mrs May. He nodded at everything she said, his head going up and down like a water pump handle, until I feared for his neck muscles.'[326] As the session finished, 'Mr Gove reached over ... to pat Mrs May on her forearm. She did not react, at least visibly, and I am sure that not even one molecule of her melted.'[327]

May was not ready to forgive Gove – and never would be. But while her distress was clear to everyone, she never shared it with her colleagues. William Hague says:

> For a senior Secretary of State, [if] your adviser gets dismissed from underneath you, she would be pretty cross about that. She's very loyal to people working with her. But that's an assumption. She didn't say to me, or anyone else as far as I know, 'I'm furious about that', she just bit her lip and got on with it.

Others were also sad to see Hill go. Norman Baker has said: 'Cameron wanted her head and she had to resign. I was actually sorry about what had happened ... Fiona and I had actually got to a stage where we had a sensible working relationship. I had even come to quite like her.'

In the long run, it is Gove who has come off worst from the row with Hill. Even in the short term, he would suffer when, in a cooler frame of mind, Cameron came to appreciate that he bore more responsibility for the scandal than May. Within a month, Gove was moved out of the Education brief he loved and demoted to the post of Chief Whip. (A move he, however, claimed he sought.) May, who was widely described as 'unsackable', not only survived the reshuffle but on the same day became the longest-serving Home Secretary for fifty years, second only to Rab Butler. Asked by Keith Vaz, the Labour chairman of the Home Affairs Select Committee, if she would be celebrating with a glass of champagne, she said, 'icily': 'I don't celebrate these things.'[328]

Perhaps it was only later, when she became Prime Minister, that May allowed herself an icy glass of champagne. Revenge would indeed be a dish served cold to Gove, as he was unceremoniously sacked from the government when she announced her first Cabinet. Before then, however, May would suffer the indignity of losing her second adored spad, Nick Timothy, at the behest of No. 10.

CHAPTER XVI

AMBITION

As the grandstanding chairman of the powerful Home Affairs Select Committee, the self-important Keith Vaz liked to keep his many Twitter followers entertained with a steady stream of posts about life in the Commons. Keeping a beady eye on Theresa May, the Home Secretary, as his role required him to do, he was certain he had a plum nugget to share one day in February 2013. 'A bit worried about Home Secretary she is looking a bit thin these days. A new diet or pressure of work?' he tweeted. In fact, Vaz had not been the first to spot May's rather dramatic weight loss. Several newspapers had already drawn their readers' attention to her increasingly svelte figure. But it was Vaz's rather facetious observation which gained traction, with May's supporters, of whom there were a growing number, labelling it and him 'sexist'. Caroline Nokes, who had been helped by May and Women2Win to capture the seat of Romsey and Southampton North, took to the *Today* programme to describe the remark as 'silly' and 'patronising'.

May herself was deeply irritated by Vaz's tweet, later describing herself as 'not best pleased'.[329] Asked by journalists to respond at the time, she snapped: 'All I would say is I'm not going around tweeting about male MPs and I'm not sure there are many female MPs going around tweeting about male MPs.'[330] It was a sign of the growing regard in which May was held by friends and enemies alike in Westminster that discussion of her newly trim figure soon segued into a received wisdom that she was slimming down in order to make herself more appealing to voters in the event of a leadership contest. By the time May emphatically scotched those rumours by revealing, six months after Vaz's tweet, in July 2013, that her dramatic weight loss was in fact the result of Type 1 diabetes contracted only recently, the manner in which she did so was seen by David Cameron and his team at No. 10 as an open declaration of war.

The roots of the increasingly poor relationship between the Prime Minister and the woman who would replace him lay a few years earlier. Cameron was generally a relaxed Prime Minister, less susceptible to paranoia than many of those who have occupied No. 10 over the centuries. But the team around him did not share his insouciance. As May's eye-catching successes racked up in the middle years of the coalition – the Olympics, Abu Hamza, Gary McKinnon, the Police Federation, Abu Qatada, gay marriage – the fact that the Home Secretary was openly spoken of in the media as a potential future Prime Minister and regularly topped opinion polls of both voters and Tory members began to set warning lights flashing inside No. 10. The Cameroons' wariness was compounded by both the refusal of May's spads to cooperate with Craig Oliver and the rest of the Downing Street operation, and her long-standing reaction to her status outside the inner circle, which increasingly came to be seen as a refusal to operate as a team player. William Hague says:

> You can see how advisers would have a difficult relationship when you have a minister … who No. 10 can't really boss around [and] who stands her own grounds on things … You can see how advisers would start having a testy relationship about that without that spoiling her relationship with David Cameron. But underneath there was a great deal of tension.

Sensing that tension, Labour began to make merry. In March 2013, in one particularly awkward exchange during Prime Minister's Questions, Ed Miliband, the party's leader, noticed May's apparent disapproval as he accused Cameron of failing to answer a question. 'The Home Secretary shakes her head,' Miliband declared. 'I'm looking forward to facing her when they are in opposition.' While MPs on both sides of the Commons collapsed in laughter, May sat stony-faced and Cameron smiled sheepishly. He may not have been given to paranoia, but it was clear that the warnings from those around him that the team at the Home Office was agitating for a change of regime were beginning to sink in.

Hague absolves May herself of actively plotting. But he says it was very obvious to all those around the Cabinet table – including the Prime Minister – that if Cameron fell under the proverbial bus, she would be waiting. He says:

> I don't think she was making clear she wanted to take over, I think she was putting herself in a position where she could take over. Leaders know that other people are getting ready to take over from them eventually. I think she has always been interested, for many years, in being leader of the party. But she's not obviously [been] manoeuvring.

Hague says that although he was one of the closest ministers to May at this time, she never discussed the leadership issue with him.

One source who was close to Cameron agrees that he was aware that May's strategy was to keep her options open, and says it was obvious that her advisers were keen to help her get to the top. However, the source adds:

> Her people are very bright, very good at their jobs and very effective. They probably were having conversations with her about running for No. 10. But those conversations probably lasted for about ten seconds every six months. The demands of a job like hers are just so strong that it would have been impossible to spend hours and days sitting around in a room war gaming what was going to pan out. And, even if they had, they never could have predicted what actually transpired.

Whether or not she was actively plotting to topple Cameron, the relationship between May and the Home Office on one side, and Cameron and his No. 10 team on the other, began to deteriorate through the end of 2013 and into 2014. They might have had no plans to seek to topple Cameron, but May and the close-knit group around her never again wanted to find themselves in the position they had faced in 2005, when she had found that her lack of position and low profile had scotched her ambition to stand for the leadership. The team launched a subtle series of moves to enhance her standing with her fellow MPs. Under Timothy's tutelage, the 'Tea Room Surgeries' were revived, with May forced to submit to the weekly ordeal of making small talk with her colleagues after PMQs.

Perhaps as importantly, given that any future contest would ultimately be decided by party members, she also stepped up her activities on the 'rubber chicken' circuit. As a legacy of her and Philip's days in Merton, May had always been assiduous in accepting requests to speak at functions on behalf of the local party. Now the couple spent their precious evenings touring the country, making sure May established a personal connection with tens of thousands of Conservative activists. The days when Chairman May had been despised by the grassroots for her 'nasty party' speech were by now a distant memory. Eric Pickles says:

> She's actually always been diligent at attending party functions. That's why I thought that if she had gone to the country [rather than being elected leader unopposed] she would have romped home. Because in most places, there would have been someone in that association, probably two or three, who had actually met her. She sat as a councillor, she's actually been involved in the party from the bottom up. It gives you a kind of understanding of the party, a kind of liking of the party.

Liam Fox makes the same point: 'She knows and likes the Conservative Party,' he says.

But while the positioning may have been subtle to most, for those watching from No. 10, it was screamingly obvious, particularly once the media picked up on it. Newspapers began reporting briefings from May's 'friends' that she was the most likely 'Stop Boris' candidate, with one suggesting that, while she understood that Cameron was 'not going anywhere' for the time being, the Home Secretary viewed Boris Johnson as 'a faintly ridiculous figure', and fully intended to give him a run for his money when the time was right.[331]

But if there was no overt plotting against Cameron by May and her team, the distinction between agitating for the Prime Minister's removal and placing herself in a position to take over once the time came was lost on many at No. 10. Sean Kemp, watching from the Deputy Prime Minister's Office, says:

> For a very long time, there was always speculation about Cameron. There were plenty of backbenchers saying he should quit. Any Secretary of State who is quite clearly having their eyes on the prize, you're going to be sensitive to. Could they be oversensitive at times? Yes. But do remember what it felt like at the time. Not that they thought that May was going to launch a coup, but it was quite obvious that Theresa May and her team thought that if they lost [the 2015 election], Cameron's out, then they're going to run for it. How does that feel if you're surrounding a party leader and you know that other people you work with are waiting for you to be nationally humiliated and retired? You always get that sensitivity.

William Hague insists that any 'sensitivity' in Downing Street was down to irritation at the lack of cooperation from the Home Office. He says:

> Sometimes there would be tension between No. 10 and the Home Office, not over 'Does Theresa May want to be Prime Minister' but over – 'The Home Office is sticking to its plan even though someone in No. 10 wants to change the argument … they're doing what Theresa May says', and that would really cause frustration and tension.

Fiona Hill has herself insisted of May's attitude: 'In my time as a special adviser, I never heard her criticise David Cameron.'[332] Eric Pickles is clear about the genesis of the growing gulf between the two sides. 'It was more paranoia than preparation [by May],' he says. 'Not actively doing anything but not ruling it out.'

In mid-March 2013, the worst fears of the most suspicious operatives in No. 10 appeared to be confirmed when May gave what was euphemistically described as a 'wide-ranging' address to party activists attending an event organised by ConservativeHome called 'Victory 2015', in which she strayed wildly from her Home Affairs brief. Those in the hall, journalists and May's colleagues were left in no doubt that this was the speech of a would-be leader, a clear introduction to the type of 'One Nation' Prime Minister she hoped one day to become. The thinking of Nick Timothy on social justice and the need to target communities who felt left behind was overt in passages sprinkled all the way through. In particular, a hint that the Conservatives may not have done enough to tackle 'vested interests' and 'take power from elites'[333] was seen as throwing down a gauntlet to the Cameroons and the privileged, gilded regime they had installed in No. 10.

While she began her speech by praising Cameron, May's next words made everyone at No. 10, and No. 11, where George Osborne still actively nursed ambitions to succeed his friend as Prime Minister, sit up and take notice. 'We have a good record and we have the right team,' May said.

> But those advantages alone will not be enough. We have to become the party that is tireless in confronting vested interests. The party that takes power from the elites and gives it to the people. The party not just of those who have already made it, but the home of those who want to work hard and get on in life.[334]

May went on to set out the policies she thought the party should introduce – and, by logical extension, that she would bring in were she leader. To cheers from delegates, she vowed to scrap the

Human Rights Act, ensure companies paid their share of taxes, allow private firms and charities to run public services and, to the astonishment and approval of her Liberal Democrat Cabinet colleague Vince Cable, carve out a greater role for the state in the economy with a planned industrial strategy.

The speech, immediately dubbed May's 'Vision for Britain', was greeted with delight by activists in the room, some of whom began tweeting their approval under the hashtag #TM4PM. Many MPs were also pleased at her revitalisation of the concept of One Nation Toryism. Indeed, Keith Simpson feels that the 'Vision' speech was a rare example of May allowing her exasperation with what she saw as Cameron's benign but somewhat elitist paternalism to show in public. He says: 'Apart from suppressing a deep frustration and anger about the way she was patronised, I think increasingly, [and] although she kept this very much to herself you got hints of this, she thought [she knew how] the country wanted to be governed, and it was in a different way.'

The response from the Cameroons was less sanguine. Coming as it did at a time when opinion polls were predicting that Miliband's Labour Party would easily win a majority at the 2015 general election, and with Cameron facing a hopeless but nonetheless unsettling leadership challenge from the obscure backbencher Adam Afriyie, her unscripted entry into the debate around the party's future was an unwelcome distraction. At the monthly meeting of the parliamentary party two days after the speech, one loyalist MP urged Cameron to 'control his Cabinet'.[335]

Generally, however, the speech was greeted positively, including by MPs. May and her team were able to bask in the warm aftermath for only a short period before the Cameroons hit back – hard. Three days after the speech, at Political Cabinet, Michael Gove, a staunch supporter of Osborne, accused unnamed fellow ministers of 'disloyalty' by seeking to burnish their 'leadership credentials',[336] adding that he had been 'shocked to see some around the table had been participating in this leadership speculation'.[337] He did not name May or address her directly, but everyone present knew who he was referring to. The briefing and counter-briefing from each side stepped up, with reports of both the parliamentary party meeting and Political Cabinet making their way into the papers. In retaliation, May's team made clear that (unusually) they had sent the speech to No. 10 for approval. A few days later, Boris Johnson, seen as the other main challenger for the throne, stirred the hornets' nest with an interview which, again without naming her, he clearly intended as a rebuke to May. 'If ministers are setting out their stall now, it strikes me as being very odd,' the Mayor said. 'They should save their breath and cool their porridge. Put a sock in it and get on and back the Prime Minister.'[338]

The Home Secretary herself was stunned by the response to her speech, and bitterly upset that she had been portrayed as disloyal. She made clear to her spads, and instructed them to brief the media to the effect, that she was taking a self-denying ordinance and would never again as Home Secretary stray beyond her brief. It was a vow she largely stuck to – occasionally to the irritation of No. 10 when, as during the 2016 EU referendum campaign, her presence in some of the more difficult debates would have been welcomed.

May's 'Vision' speech and Gove's furious reaction to it marked the backdrop to their clash over Islamic extremism, which led to the departure of Fiona Hill. It was fuelled by Gove's determination to see George Osborne, whom he viewed as Cameron's natural successor, inherit the post largely unchallenged (a desire Cameron shared). Ironically, Osborne himself was far more relaxed about May's alleged manoeuvrings, seeing his greatest rival as Boris Johnson. One member of his inner circle at the time says:

> George saw Boris as the bigger threat. Although everyone knew Theresa had ambitions, or certainly her team did, it wasn't as if she had a great following among MPs. There wasn't any sense of a great Theresa May leadership campaign ready to go, or that she had a great number of people waiting to support her. It was quite hard to see how Theresa ended up in the final two [in a

leadership contest as the choice of MPs to go into a final run-off decided by members]. Whereas George had an extraordinary amount of people [backing him]. He was like the proverbial octopus; the tentacles were everywhere.

One lasting effect of the 'Vision' speech was that interest in the desperately shy Home Secretary grew. She was the subject of a number of newspaper profiles during the spring and early summer of 2013, virtually all of which referenced both her by now quite dramatic weight loss, as well as an interview she had given to the *Daily Telegraph* a few months earlier in which, for the first time, she had discussed her childlessness in detail.[339] She also now began to be compared to both Margaret Thatcher and Angela Merkel, the German Chancellor. By June 2013, May's aspirations for the top job were so taken for granted that they were openly discussed on the floor of the House. During one exchange, Labour's John Spellar asked the Business Minister Michael Fallon: 'Will he talk to the Home Secretary and get her to back British industry? It might even help her leadership ambitions.' To which Fallon replied: 'They may not need that much help.' It was open confirmation from a fellow Conservative minister that May aimed one day to reach No. 10 – and was seen as likely to succeed.

But while Westminster seemed obsessed with May's future political aspirations, the Home Secretary had a rather more tangible problem to grapple with: her health. The first eagle-eyed journalist to spot that May had shed a few pounds was Simon Walters of the *Mail on Sunday*, who, in a piece nine months earlier about a somewhat risqué outfit she had worn to address the 2012 Conservative Party conference, had written:

> Cabinet fashion icon Theresa May has lost nearly two stone, thanks to a summer regime of salads and walks … She has shed the pounds over the summer by cutting back from three main meals a day to two, drinking black tea, eating salads, ditching processed foods and lots of walking with banker husband Philip.[340]

By December, in the *Telegraph* interview about her childlessness, May was blaming the fact she was 'almost too thin' on 'pressure of work, a flu bug that lasted two months, thrice weekly visits to the gym'.[341]

In fact, in between the two articles, and three months before Keith Vaz sent his tweet, May had learned that her weight loss was not connected to either her fitness regime or the flu. In November 2012, struggling to shake off a cold, she had been seen by a doctor and discovered that she had high levels of blood sugar, suggesting she had developed diabetes. To begin with, despite her impressive fitness levels, it was assumed, largely because of her age, that she was suffering from Type 2 diabetes, a condition usually associated with being overweight, in which the body fails to respond properly to insulin. She was prescribed tablets, but as the months passed, her weight continued to fall. By the time she returned to her doctor, she had lost two stone in a year, and had dropped to a size ten, having been a size fourteen when she entered Parliament. In May 2013, further tests revealed that, highly unusually for a woman in her mid-fifties, her diabetes was in fact Type 1, also known as 'childhood diabetes' due to its common onset in early life, in which the pancreas fails to produce enough insulin.

Type 1 diabetes is a chronic, sometimes dangerous condition, carrying a risk of heart disease and stroke, and it would require May to make substantial lifestyle changes, including injecting herself with insulin four times a day. To her regret, given her love of baking and appreciation for the BBC's *Great British Bake Off*, cake was now off the menu, including her favourite sticky toffee pudding. She would have to take care too with the timing of her meals, not an easy task for a busy politician accustomed to travelling the country and flying around the world. At times, she had to be ingenious, once telling the Diabetes UK charity's magazine *Balance*:

> There was one occasion when I had been expecting to go into the Chamber later, but the way the debates were drawn up meant I had to go in at 11 a.m. and I knew I wasn't coming out till about

five. I had a bag of nuts in my handbag and one of my colleagues would lean forward every now and then so that I could eat some nuts without being seen by the Speaker.[342]

May has been determined not to allow her diabetes to slow her down or overly affect her life – aims she has overwhelmingly succeeded at. As with so many challenges in her life, her response to her condition was to 'just get on and deal with it, get on and do the job'.[343] Her decision to speak out about her condition in the summer of 2013 would establish her as a role model for many young diabetes sufferers and their parents, showing that a diagnosis of diabetes need not impair their lives – or even stop them becoming Prime Minister should they wish to.

The interview was conducted with Liz Sanderson, a feature-writer on the *Mail on Sunday*, who wrote: 'Her decision to talk candidly stems partly from cruel Westminster gossip.'[344] May made clear her irritation with the rumours about her weight, saying: 'This was not some great Machiavellian plan – there is no leadership bid.' Describing her reaction on being told the news that she had Type 1 diabetes, May said:

It was a real shock and, yes, it took me a while to come to terms with it. The diabetes doesn't affect how I do the job or what I do. It's just part of life … It doesn't and will not affect my ability to do my work. I'm a little more careful about what I eat and there's obviously the injections but this is something millions of people have…

If May had hoped to dampen down speculation about the leadership with her interview, she was to be disappointed. If anything, her adept handling of the whole issue of her diabetes, including the way she had used it to turn the tables on those who had raised questions about her weight, further fuelled the chatter about her ambitions. However, the response was warm, with May's standing in the opinion polls rising still higher, and her image in the media and among her colleagues increasingly positive. In No. 10, however, the Cameroons grew yet more suspicious. Like Talleyrand, who is said to have pondered on the death of an enemy 'I wonder what he means by that', the Downing Street response to May's diabetes interview and the resulting attention she received was to question her motives.

There would be another lasting repercussion of the *Mail on Sunday* article. May had clearly developed a rapport with Liz Sanderson, the feature-writer who had produced the warmly written piece. Eleven months later, when Fiona Hill, her trusted media adviser, was forced to walk the plank over her row with Michael Gove, May turned to Sanderson, asking her to join her team of Home Office spads. At the Home Office, Sanderson gained a reputation for being friendly and less abrasive than Hill, and while she would not quite pack the punch or be as powerful a figure in government as her predecessor, she was someone whom the Home Secretary came to trust. When May became Prime Minister, Sanderson went with her to No. 10 to join her press operation.

The months between the diabetes interview and Hill's departure in June 2014 saw May at the height of her powers at the Home Office. She used her 2013 speech to Conservative conference in October to renew her attack on the Human Rights Act, which she promised a majority Tory government would scrap. Recounting the story of the deportation of Abu Qatada, she revealed that the cleric had referred to her as 'Crazy May'.

'I admit I was crazy – crazy with the European Court of Human Rights – and I know I wasn't the only one,' she said.

> Here was a foreign terror suspect, wanted for the most serious crimes in his home country, and we were told time and again – thanks to human rights law – we couldn't deport him. It's ridiculous that the British government should have to go to such lengths to get rid of dangerous foreigners.

Her words again put May at odds with colleagues on both sides of the coalition, frustrating the likes of Dominic Grieve, the Conservative Attorney General. Two months later, Lord Judge, the former Chief Justice, made an outspoken attack on May over her speech, saying he was 'astounded' by her criticism of the judiciary.[345]

With May riding high, some noted that an autocratic air had begun to creep into the Home Office, as the team took an increasingly high-handed approach with their rivals in No. 10 and across Whitehall. There were whispers that May could be overbearing and overly prescriptive to ministers and officials. Dame Neville-Jones had stormed out of the Home Office in 2011 after just a year in post. Dame Helen Ghosh, the department's Permanent Secretary, lasted only twenty months before she too abandoned ship, making clear that she found May difficult to work with.

Mark Harper disagrees with the characterisation of May as overly controlling, however. He says:

> She was very clearly the boss, and you expect the boss to take an interest in things. Certainly at the Home Office you have to, because ultimately it's the Home Secretary whose job is on the line if things go wrong. So you expect her to pay attention, but it wasn't my experience that she did that in an inappropriate way. She wasn't a minister who felt she had to do everything herself. She was secure enough in her own position to let people in her department do the things they were responsible for.

Nick Timothy has said of May's management style: 'She wants to know what's going on and wants to have a handle on things.'[346]

In October 2013, the minister who would find it more difficult than any other to get on with May joined the Home Office. Norman Baker, whose appointment by Nick Clegg May viewed as an imposition, never settled, and his tenure was an unhappy one. While he came to respect May, and even learned to get along with Fiona Hill, he never developed a working relationship with Nick Timothy, and felt generally that both the Home Secretary and her special advisers had no interest in including him in the day-to-day

running of the Home Office. Baker believed they profoundly misunderstood the realities of operating within what was a coalition
government. In his book *Against the Grain*, he claims that he was
continually excluded from the decision-making process and denied
the documents and briefings he felt he was entitled to. Sean Kemp
believes Baker's frustration was understandable:

It was a difficult brief. It's not natural home-run territory for Lib
Dems. In fact, the only successes you're going to get are when
you are picking a fight. And you're talking about an incredibly
impressive Secretary of State, two incredibly impressive special
advisers who are controlling everything, so it was not a fun job for
the Lib Dem minister to be in.

Baker summed up his attitude to May as follows:

I never felt any animosity towards Theresa May. Indeed, I respected and even admired her … The problem was that I did
not like the way she ran the department. She would argue that
without this vice-like grip at the centre, she would not have lasted
so many years in post, and perhaps that is true. But the price of
that was a climate of fear in officials, a gloomy air of drudgery
around the department, and the stifling of ideas and innovation.
We could all see the stick, but where was the carrot?[347]

May herself has effectively confirmed reports that she can be tough
on her officials. Asked about a story that she banged her head on
the table while listening to what she felt to be an inadequate briefing from one mandarin, she laughed and said: 'I didn't quite bang
my head on the desk, it was sort of in despair that I leant forward
on to the desk.'[348] In a survey of Home Office civil servants carried
out in 2015, one in six, amounting to 2,500 people, complained of
having been bullied or harassed at work.[349]

Baker's time at the Home Office wasn't all bad, however. He
describes one pleasant if slightly awkward Christmas meal at a

restaurant opposite the department on Marsham Street, which was
followed by an unlikely postscript.

> There was some light relief when we all – the ministerial team,
> the Permanent Secretary and the spads – were invited by Theresa
> to Christmas lunch, even if this did not finally happen until early
> January. We duly assembled one lunchtime in the basement of
> Osteria Dell'Angelo ... I arrived a few minutes late and took in
> the room and its atmosphere of slightly forced jollity ... A few
> days later, each of the ministers received a bill from Theresa for
> £58.74.[350]

After a series of rows, Baker eventually quit the Home Office in
a temper at the end of November 2014, after he felt he had been
side-lined over a review of drugs policy. The fundamental cause of
his departure, however, was his antipathy towards the Home Office
regime, and the lack of freedom he was allowed. On leaving, Baker
gave a series of highly critical interviews, one of which included
the memorable phrase that his experience of working at the Home
Office had been like 'walking through mud'.[351] Lynne Featherstone,
who was drafted in by Nick Clegg to replace Baker for the final
months of the coalition government, was, however, pleased to be
re-joining May and the Home Office team, even though it meant
leaving a job she had been enjoying at the Department for International Development (DfID). She is critical of Baker for acting in the
way he did. 'He flounced out,' she says.

> He said he couldn't work with Theresa because [he said] it was
> like walking through mud, which really pissed me off ... When
> she heard I was coming back to the Home Office ... I was walk-
> ing through the lobbies one night to vote and she just held out her
> arms and we had a hug.

Another criticism that Baker flagged up in his angry farewell interviews was the suggestion that May was too in thrall to her special

advisers. It is a view that Featherstone also fears may have some
truth to it. 'Nick and Fiona are obviously incredibly close to her,'
she says.

> And I think if there's one thing she needs to be careful of [as
> Prime Minister], it's that she makes all the decisions. I know she
> trusts them with her life, and she is so busy, and you do come
> totally to rely on people who you trust because they know how
> you think.

Soon after May became Prime Minister, taking both Fiona Hill
and Nick Timothy into Downing Street with her, one anonymous
source told *The Guardian* that her relationship with her spads was
comparable to that between Gordon Brown and his adviser (and
later fellow Cabinet minister) Ed Balls. Claiming that May wouldn't
come to a firm view in front of officials, the source said she 'goes
away for an hour with Nick and Fiona and – boing! – a decision is
made. Which is exactly like Gordon Brown. He'd go away, and we
all assumed Ed [Balls] then told him what to do.'

The loss of Fiona Hill was excruciating for May, and it also
marked something of a downturn in her relationship with the
public and press. More fundamentally, whereas the bad feeling between Downing Street and the Home Office had hitherto generally
been at the adviser level, she now, perhaps understandably, felt an-
tagonistic to David Cameron as well. While she was still invariably
referred to as 'unsackable', she began to experience some of the
hiccups that in the past might have led to previous Home Secretaries' resignation and which, even for May, resulted in a series of
embarrassing headlines.

The first came along with unseemly haste less than two weeks
after Hill's departure, when it emerged that delays at the Passport
Office had led to a backlog of nearly 550,000 applications. While the
problem seemed on the surface to be at the less serious end of
the scale, compared to the Home Secretary's usual diet of terrorism, immigration and crime, in fact the function of passports as

an everyday but crucial necessity made them unexpectedly toxic. The timing, mid-June, was also terrible given that many thousands of families looking forward to their annual summer break risked having their holidays ruined. The fact that those families were scattered around the country meant each MP in the House of Commons was 'inundated by constituents in panic and distress'.[352] They all wanted answers from May. The crisis was resolved quickly enough, but it is a sign of the seriousness with which she took it that a few months later, in September 2014, May announced that, as with the Border Agency, she was taking the Passport Office back under the auspices of the Home Office. Once again, she would not tolerate being forced to take responsibility for an agency she did not directly control.

May's next missteps would have long-running consequences. In July 2014, in response to what felt like a tsunami of revelations, rumours and complaints of child molestation at all levels of British life, in some cases going back decades and with many alleged incidents involving politicians and celebrities, the Home Secretary announced that she was ordering a major inquiry into the historic sex abuse of children. May's desire to set in place a robust inquiry which could fully investigate what had rapidly become a national scandal was clear. She has since spoken often of how moved she had been by the experience of meeting abuse survivors. But the inquiry would be dogged by a series of blunders and ill-advised appointments, to the extent that by the time May was Prime Minister it had descended into farce. The day after announcing the inquiry, May named Baroness Butler-Sloss, a cross-bench peer and former president of the Family Division of the High Court, as its chair. There were immediate misgivings. Sloss's brother, Lord Havers, had served as both Attorney General and Lord Chancellor in the 1980s alongside the late Leon Brittan, who as Home Secretary was alleged to have been given a dossier naming a number of MPs as paedophiles. The file had since gone missing. At the time of Sloss's appointment, Brittan was himself facing child abuse allegations. When he died in January 2015, he and the wider public were still unaware that the police had already concluded he had no case to answer. Sloss's appointment six months earlier, however, came while the investigation into Brittan was still active, and the reaction to her role on the panel was highly negative. Within a week she had resigned.

In September, May named her next choice, Fiona Woolf, a solicitor and the Lord Mayor of London. She lasted only a few weeks longer than her predecessor, when it emerged that she too had a number of professional and personal links to Brittan, and had entertained the peer and his wife at her home on the north London street where they all lived. After victims' groups threatened to launch a judicial review of her appointment, Woolf too stood down.

But it was May's third choice of chair for the panel that would prove the most damaging. With the inquiry now seriously behind schedule, and fearing it would be impossible to find a chairman without links to the establishment within the UK, Home Office officials launched what has been described as a 'frantic search'[353] for a replacement for Woolf. At some point, it was decided to extend the hunt to the Commonwealth, presumably due to the similar legal systems in place in former colonies, and Dame Sian Elias, the Chief Justice of New Zealand, was contacted and asked for her advice. She recommended a New Zealand High Court judge called Dame Lowell Goddard, whom she had gone to school with and trained alongside. A Skype call was set up to New Zealand for May and Liz Sanderson to interview her. Goddard performed well and seemed to tick all the boxes. Her appointment was duly announced.

If the rash choices of Butler-Sloss and Woolf had perhaps been thoughtless, that of Goddard was downright disastrous. It was only after May had left the Home Office that the full dysfunction of the inquiry under Goddard's stewardship became clear when she abruptly resigned, giving little explanation for doing so other than that she was homesick for New Zealand. Two months later, in October 2016, a front-page story in *The Times* revealed more of the backdrop to her departure, publishing claims that Goddard's 'aggressive and abusive conduct at times reduced the inquiry's operation to "near paralysis"'.[354] The judge was alleged to have spent extensive amounts of time at home in New Zealand, to have flown into frequent rages, and to have made a series of racist remarks. Goddard has emphatically denied the claims, which remain the subject of a parliamentary investigation. The issue of the wisdom of her appointment continued to dog May months into her premiership, particularly after she admitted during a session of PMQs that she had been told of 'stories' about Goddard while she was still Home Secretary, but had felt it inappropriate to intervene on the basis of 'suspicion, rumour or hearsay'. Questions remain today over whether the inquiry is, as May once promised the victims it would be, 'fit for purpose'.

It was while May was still hunting for a replacement for Woolf that the train of events began that would result in her losing the second of her treasured special advisers. The ejection of Fiona Hill from the Home Office had not improved the relationship between her team and the Cameroons at No. 10. The Home Affairs department continued to operate on a broadly arm's-length basis, and May's advisers still refused to kowtow to Craig Oliver. On one occasion, in September 2014, Oliver is said to have 'gone shouty-crackers' at May,[355] demanding she show him more respect. Two months later, Nick Timothy, who, along with Hill and Philip May formed the holy trinity of May's personal inner circle, put himself beyond the pale in the eyes of No. 10.

It is a long-established Westminster convention that special advisers brief the media anonymously, usually under the guise of a 'source close to' or 'spokesman for' their minister, largely to give the person on whose behalf they speak a degree of deniability. Timothy now smashed the convention to pieces, giving an interview to the *Spectator Life* magazine for a wide-ranging profile of May, in which he allowed himself to be named. Timothy's on-the-record quotes were devoted to praising May's 'vision [for] what the future should be about and what politics and the party should be about'.[356] Westminster-watchers were stunned. In the *Telegraph*, James Kirkup spluttered:

> In the last decade or so, I can't remember a special adviser being quoted by name in this way. I don't think Mr Timothy is

freelancing here. It is unthinkable that he spoke on the record without his minister's knowledge. So we can infer that Theresa May has licensed her staff to talk up her 'vision' for the future of Britain and the Conservative Party. This all tells us a lot about Mrs May's ambition and the state of her relations with No. 10.[357]

Timothy's on-the-record quotes were juxtaposed with a series of highly inflammatory remarks given by an unnamed source about how May now viewed David Cameron, raising the Downing Street hackles still further. The 'friend', who may or may not have been Timothy, was quoted as saying: 'She doesn't rate Cameron any more. She did, but not any more. There was a time early on when she would want to please David, but slowly she has seen just how incompetent that operation is. She's given up on him.'[358] Still more provokingly, the *Spectator Life* interview was published as part of what was described as a 'three-day media blitz'[359] by the Home Secretary, which included appearances on the BBC's *Desert Island Discs* and *Andrew Marr Show*, a major speech on the threat from Islamic State, and the acceptance of the Politician of the Year award from the Political Studies Association. Many observers, including No. 10, were convinced that with her 'media blitz' May was overtly positioning herself for a leadership battle she believed could come within six months if, as the polls suggested, Cameron again failed to secure a Conservative majority at the general election.

During her spot on *Desert Island Discs*, May attempted to play down speculation about her ambitions, saying she had wanted to take part in the show not in order to set out her wares, but in recognition of the honour of being invited to participate in what had become an 'integral part of British life'.[360] She insisted: 'David Cameron is a first-class leader of the party and a first-class Prime Minister and I hope he is going to be doing that for a very long time.'[361] Few believed her. Her choice of records for the show, in which famous people are invited to select eight tracks, usually musical, to take with them in the event of being stranded on the proverbial desert island, was pored over by Westminster Kremlinologists. Much was made of May's selection of the Frankie Valli and the Four Seasons song 'Walk Like a Man' from the West End show *Jersey Boys*, which she said she had seen with her husband Philip, and which reminded her of evenings spent with friends in Pearson Hall, the village hall in her constituency. Explaining the choice, she said she had long ago decided she did not need to be 'clubbable' or attempt to break into the old boys' network to succeed, adding: 'I'm very clear that women in politics, in business, in whatever field they are in, should be able to do the jobs as themselves and not feel they've got to "walk like a man".'[362]

The *Desert Island Discs* appearance was an irritant to the Cameroons, as was an end-of-year ConservativeHome leadership poll which showed that May had extended her lead over Boris Johnson to eleven points, sixteen ahead of George Osborne. But it was Timothy's overt cooperation with the *Spectator Life* profile that sealed his fate, taken as it was as an open declaration of war. David Cameron was said to have been shown the article during his 4 p.m. daily strategy meeting inside No. 10 with George Osborne, at which Grant Shapps, the party chairman, was also in attendance. The trio are said to have agreed that the piece amounted to 'treachery'.[363] Downing Street would enact its revenge within three weeks.

Timothy had long entertained aspirations to become an MP, an ambition in which he was fully supported by May. But in December 2014, less than five months before the general election, he was suddenly told by Conservative Central Office that he was barred from standing for the safe West Midlands seat of Aldridge-Brownhills. A second May adviser, Stephen Parkinson, was also taken off the candidates' list, on which would-be Tory MPs must secure a place to be eligible to enter a selection battle. In (anonymous) briefings given by No. 10, the media were told that the pair were being disciplined for failing to campaign in a recent by-election. When it emerged five days before Christmas that Cameron himself had approved their removal from the list,[364] it was clear that Downing Street's long irritation with the Home Office special advisers had finally erupted into open warfare. Timothy and Parkinson argued that, as members of the government payroll, they were barred by the special advisers' code of conduct from campaigning in elections, and had decided not to take part in the Rochester by-election after failing several times to receive assurance from the Cabinet Office that to do so would not be in breach of the code. May intervened personally, pleading with Shapps to restore the pair to the list. He refused.

On the eve of the general election campaign, Timothy and Parkinson were exonerated when the Commons Public Administration Committee ruled that CCO had been wrong to ask them, as government employees, to campaign. But by then it was too late. The pair had failed to be selected in time to fight seats at the 2015 general election. Furious at the treatment he had received, Timothy walked out of government six months later, and into a job at the New Schools Network, which champions free schools. Over the next year, he soothed his bruised feelings by writing a series of unflattering articles about Cameron and Osborne for ConservativeHome. For May, the loss of a second member of her inner circle in the space of twelve months, both times at the instigation of No. 10, was almost too much to bear. Andrew Lansley says:

> Quite clearly, the events that most stung would have been the row with Gove and the way No. 10 treated her and Fiona, and [subsequently] Nick Timothy. They had an animus against her advisers, which must have offended her considerably, not least because she is loyal to her people. She would never have wanted them to have got in the middle. It would have been hard for her to see them tossed out by No. 10 and trashed.

With the 2015 general election approaching rapidly, May was clear that if the moment arose and Cameron stumbled, it would be she, not Boris Johnson, not George Osborne, and certainly not Michael Gove, who would become the next Leader of the Conservative Party.

CHAPTER XVII

EUROPE

Fiona Hill and Nick Timothy were not entirely happy. It was the morning of Friday 8 May 2015 and the Conservatives had just unexpectedly won their first majority at a general election for twenty-three years. It was a personal triumph for David Cameron, the Prime Minister who had steered his party through the rocky years of coalition to defy his critics by forming a majority Conservative administration. As the sun rose, jubilant Tory supporters the length and breadth of the country were celebrating. For Hill and Timothy, however, the satisfaction they undoubtedly took in the surprise victory was not undiluted. One insider who bumped into Hill early that morning says:

> It was clear that she was not a happy bunny. I expected her to be on great form, but she was really quite down. It dawned on me that she had assumed the election would go another way, and that she had hoped Cameron would be forced to stand down and that Theresa May would be in with a shot of replacing him.

The evidence is that both Hill and Timothy had hoped to be reunited with May at No. 10 – or, at the very least, in the office of the Leader of the Opposition – after the election. Following her departure from the Home Office a year earlier, Hill had been working at the Centre for Social Justice, a respected right-wing think tank, where she had recently produced a major report on modern slavery. With the general election predicted to result in another hung parliament, there was a high likelihood that if Cameron failed to secure a majority for a second time, he would be forced to stand down as Tory leader. May was among the favourites to replace him. But if the result of the 2010 exit poll had shocked the entire political establishment despite the fact that it had been widely expected, the 2015 poll was a bombshell precisely because it had not. In the run-up to election day, most opinion polls had put the two main parties in a virtual tie. All the indications were that Britain was on course for another coalition; indeed, the main thrust of the Tory attack had been that Labour would be forced to do deals with the Scottish Nationalists if they were in a position to form a government. The strategy worked brilliantly. Far from predicting another hung parliament, as the exit poll was released at 10 p.m. those watching were stunned to see it forecast a clear victory for the Conservatives.

Once again, as a respected senior voice for her party, May was in the BBC studio on election night as the exit poll was announced. With Liberal Democrat support collapsing in the wake of the broken student tuition fees pledge, the exit poll predicted that Nick Clegg's party would win only ten seats (in fact, the eventual tally would be just eight), with 239 for Labour and the Tories on 316. This was ten short of an overall majority, but with the Irish Republican party Sinn Féin refusing to take up their five seats, it would probably be enough to govern. In fact, the poll slightly underestimated the strength of the Conservatives' standing. By end of the night, it was clear that David Cameron would be able to form the first majority Conservative government since 1992. If she shared the mixed emotions of her loyal advisers at the election's surprising outcome, May did not let it show. But her words betrayed her. When the BBC's David Dimbleby asked what the result meant for her own leadership ambitions, she stuttered confusingly: 'I have only one eye on one thing in politics.'[365] The emphatic tone of her response, if not its literal interpretation, conveyed the message that she was getting on with the job in hand.

By the end of the following day, May's spads, past and present, had also got a grip on their emotions. But their next actions would speak louder than words. The source who saw Hill on the morning after the election goes on:

I saw a month or so afterwards that she had gone to work for a lobbying company. I always felt that if I was Fiona, and thought my boss was going to become party leader, I'd do what she did when she left the Home Office: go to work somewhere very non-controversial, doing something I really believed in, and bide my time. When Cameron won the election, there was no point hanging around in politics, so she just cashed in her chips and went off to work for a lobbying firm.

Hill began a new job, with the public affairs company Lexington Communications, a few weeks after the general election. She would later be criticised for having done so without reporting the move to civil servants, as required under Whitehall rules, an error which was attributed to forgetfulness.[366] Following the election, Timothy too saw no point in remaining in politics, given the way he had been treated by Cameron and No. 10 over his own political aspirations. He left his post less than a month after polling day.

There was still, however, a glimmer of hope that May could yet be installed in Downing Street, albeit later than Hill and Timothy had hoped. In March 2015, at the outset of the general election campaign, Cameron had given an almost casual interview in which he revealed that he would not seek to remain leader for a third term. Interviewed in his kitchen in Witney, Cameron had named May as one of his potential successors, saying:

There definitely comes a time where a fresh pair of eyes and fresh leadership would be good, and the Conservative Party has got some great people coming up – the Theresa Mays, and the George Osbornes, and the Boris Johnsons. I've said I'll stand for a full second term, but I think after that it will be time for new leadership. Terms are like Shredded Wheat – two are wonderful but three might just be too many.[367]

In his relaxed way, Cameron may have considered that he was simply giving a straight answer to a question posed by the BBC's James Lansdale about his future intentions. But there is a reason why, by convention, Prime Ministers seek to avoid speculation about retirement dates. Cameron's words would prove fatally unsettling, helping to undermine his authority by ensuring that speculation about his successor would begin at once. While he had suggested he would serve a full five years, it rapidly became common currency that Cameron would stand aside by late 2018 or early 2019 at the latest, to give his successor plenty of time to bed in before the 2020 general election. In effect, the Prime Minister had triggered a leadership contest at least three years before he was likely to retire.

On election night 2015, as the news broke that the Tories had achieved an outright majority, it was still assumed that Cameron's departure would be some years away. The Prime Minister watched the exit poll at home in Witney, and celebrated with his wife over beef pie, salad and broccoli, before making plans to return to No. 10 to draw up the first Tory majority government for a generation. Within fourteen months, he would be out of office. Like so many Conservative leaders before him, Cameron would come to grief thanks to the perennial tinder box that is Britain's relationship with Europe. Having effectively called time on his own leadership by disclosing that he intended to stand down, Cameron foreshortened it even further, compounding his initial folly by calling a referendum on membership of the EU. The mistakes he and his closest ally, George Osborne, would make during the referendum campaign would bring a brutally swift end to the gilded reign of the Notting Hill set. Unlike some of her Cabinet colleagues, in the months that followed, May held back from firing rockets into the sinking ship. But, given the increasingly hostile relationship between No. 10 and the Home Office in the run-up to the general election, and particularly following the departure of her two prized special advisers, it is perhaps of little surprise that she did not throw Cameron a life belt either.

From the moment Cameron made clear that he would be standing down, the potential candidates to replace him were obsessively assessed for their strengths and weaknesses. A few days after Cameron's BBC interview, in March 2015, a YouGov poll found that Boris Johnson was favourite among voters to succeed his former Eton schoolmate, with May in second place and George Osborne third. For the next fifteen months, the three would repeatedly swap places in what would become an avalanche of opinion polls about the Tory leadership, with Michael Gove and Sajid Javid, the Business Secretary, occasionally joining them as likely contenders. Conservative MPs too now began to weigh up the options. Margot James says: 'We all knew there would be a vacancy, because Cameron had said he wouldn't serve another term, so we all knew come 2018 there would be a [leadership] election. It was at the back of the mind, but it was there.' The question of the succession was now firmly implanted at the back of May's mind too – sometimes moving up to the front. Despite being from a different party, when the time came for Lynne Featherstone to leave the Home Office following the end of the coalition, she urged May over goodbye drinks to grab the opportunity: 'We had a good conversation when I left, and I said to her: "You know, Theresa, I think you should go for the leadership of your party." She smiled. Knowingly.'

By the end of 2015, just six months into the new government, many of the prospective leadership challengers had begun hosting regular social events for backbench Tory MPs, in an overt attempt to butter them up ahead of the coming contest. Boris Johnson's pre-Christmas champagne reception at Mark's Club in Mayfair was said to be particularly lavish, while attendees at George Osborne's festive bash at 11 Downing Street complained that only wine of the non-sparkling variety was on offer. Monday nights became something of a social whirl, as MPs corralled in Westminster to take part in late-night votes were given a choice of soirées to attend. Johnson, who had returned to the Commons at the 2015 election and been made Minister without Portfolio, attending Political but not full Cabinet, issued invitations to nearby curry houses, while Osborne entertained in his flat in No. 11. At least eight other ministers, including Priti Patel, the Employment Minister, and Nicky Morgan, the Education Secretary, were said to be entertaining colleagues in the hope of enhancing their standing in the contest to come.[368]

Tory MPs enjoying the free hospitality remarked that of all the likely contenders for the crown, only May was not hosting social events for potential supporters.[369] If, as before, her advisers were encouraging her to spend more time with her colleagues, the Home Secretary wasn't listening. Eric Pickles says: 'Everyone says that to her [to socialise]. And actually, sitting having a drink with her, she's really good company. But I can kind of understand [why she didn't mix with fellow MPs in Westminster], because it can be very gossipy, it can be very backbiting.'

Some MPs were prepared to make up their minds about the future of the leadership on somewhat weightier grounds than who served the best champagne, however. Margot James says that while she had always assumed she would vote for Osborne in the event of a leadership contest, she became less impressed with the Chancellor over his last year in office. Her mind kept returning to May's speech to the 2014 Tory conference. 'It was the speech where she talked about how unfair it was that black people were four or five times more likely to be searched on the street,' James says. 'It was a wonderful speech and it really inspired me. And I thought, "Gosh, she could be leader, she could be Prime Minister," and it had never occurred to me before.' In the wake of Cameron's interview, James was not alone in deciding that, when the time came, they would be backing May for the leadership. Before then, and despite the jockeying that began as soon as Cameron was safely installed back in No. 10, there was the matter of the EU referendum to get through.

Ahead of the reshuffle that followed the 2015 general election, there was speculation once more that May might be elevated to the theoretically more senior post of Foreign Secretary, but again Cameron decided to leave her where she was. If she was disappointed, she, as usual, did not show it. Instead, freed from the shackles of coalition, May plunged straight into a drive to push through legislation the Liberal Democrats had blocked, including the 'Snooper's Charter' and tougher measures to tackle immigration. Two days after the election, May gave an interview in which she said of the Investigatory Powers Bill, as the 'Charter' was now officially known:

> We were prevented from bringing in that legislation into the last government because of the coalition with the Liberal Democrats and we are determined to bring that through, because we believe that is necessary to maintain the capabilities for our law enforcement agencies such that they can continue to do the excellent job, day in and day out, of keeping us safe and secure.[370]

May also reaffirmed the government's commitment to the target to reduce net migration to the tens of thousands, and promised a new Immigration Bill containing a series of far tougher measures than the Lib Dems would have stomached, including the creation of a new offence of employing illegal immigrants, and the denial of services such as bank accounts to those with no right to be in the UK.

Both Home Office bills were included in the first Queen's Speech of the new majority Conservative government on 27 May, along with perhaps the most controversial – and consequential – piece of legislation for a generation: the formal bill to trigger a referendum on Britain's membership of the European Union. The referendum had been a Conservative manifesto commitment, and followed a promise made by David Cameron in January 2013 to let the British people 'have their say' over continuing membership of the grouping the UK had first joined in 1973 when it was still largely an economic union known as the European Economic Community (EEC). In a speech described as 'heartfelt',[371] the Prime Minister proposed to enter a process of negotiation which he pledged would recalibrate Britain's relationship with the EU. He would put the deal he won to a public plebiscite, which he proposed holding by the end of 2017 at the latest. 'It is time to settle this European question in British politics,' Cameron said in his speech. 'I say to the British people: this will be your decision.'

No referendum on Britain's membership had been held since 1975, and the clamour for one had grown since the 1992 Maastricht Treaty, which had transformed the EEC into a new body called the European Union. The issue of Europe had contributed to the downfall of Margaret Thatcher in 1990 and dogged John Major throughout his seven years in office, as he fought a running battle with his own backbenchers to get the treaty through the Commons. Cameron was determined not to suffer the same fate as his two most recent predecessors as Conservative Prime Ministers. Yet somehow he now contrived to do just that. Pressure for what was called an 'in/out' referendum on Britain's membership of the EU had increased on the Tory benches through the coalition years. Partly this was a result of persistent Euro-scepticism which had never gone away. On returning to government in May 2015, many of those Eurosceptic Conservative MPs, particularly on the back benches, felt freer to give voice to their desire for a public poll. The pressure was also fuelled by the rise of UKIP, with its raison d'être of quitting the EU. With UKIP polling ever higher – reaching a peak of 21 per cent in mid-2013 – and polls showing that more than half of voters wanted a referendum, the Prime Minister believed that, despite the reservations of many in his inner circle, including George Osborne, by giving way he could 'lance the boil'[372] of Euroscepticism for a generation.

It was a gamble. William Hague, who as leader had faced his own problems with the Eurosceptics, had been among those urging Cameron on towards a referendum, saying: 'I got killed by Europe. A Tory leader needs to nail this once and for all.'[373] On the other side, Osborne is said to have 'implored' Cameron not to hold the referendum, arguing it would 'split the Conservative Party down the middle'.[374] His analysis would be proved right. Instead of lancing the boil, almost by accident, Cameron would bring the Tories to the cusp of civil war, while at the same time triggering Britain's withdrawal from the EU. Along the way, he would destroy

Osborne's ambitions to succeed him, and bring his own term in office to a shuddering halt.

May's attitude towards the European Union and the decisions and actions she would take during the run-up to the referendum were somewhat opaque. Having entered Parliament in 1997, just after the furious ructions within the Conservative Party over Maastricht, she had seen at close hand the damage that the Tories' obsession with Europe could do. For more than a decade, she largely avoided the debate, preferring to focus on domestic issues. But on becoming Home Secretary in 2010, May found herself drawn into the EU remit. There were summits of fellow Interior Ministers, joint legislation on matters such as arrest warrants, and cooperation, or a lack thereof, over immigration and the growing refugee crisis. And, of course, the influence of European human rights legislation on British law. In many of her encounters with Europe, May was left feeling frustrated. In particular, her inability to hit the 'tens of thousands' net migration target as a direct result of Europe's freedom of movement rules, and the inhibiting effect of the European Court on such matters as the Abu Qatada case, were viewed by May as intolerable. As the Referendum Bill began its progress through Parliament, she decided to bide her time before making up her mind which side to back.

But the issue would not go away. During the late spring of 2015, the steady trickle of migrants fleeing poverty and war in the Middle East and Africa by crossing the Mediterranean into Europe grew to a torrent, as unscrupulous people-smugglers took advantage of better weather to launch often unseaworthy vessels crammed with desperate migrants. Within a week of the general election, it became apparent that the rapidly escalating migrant crisis would form one of the greatest challenges for the new government – and would require the cooperation of all the countries of the EU. May now made clear her tough approach to the problem. With thousands risking their lives to cross the Med, she rejected plans drawn up in Brussels for an EU-wide quota for accepting migrants, saying that allowing those seeking refuge to enter the EU by such dangerous means would act as a 'pull factor' to encourage more to follow. Her words were condemned by Labour and refugee groups as lacking compassion, and her obstinate refusal to bend frustrated her fellow EU ministers. It was the start of an increasingly testy relationship between May and many senior figures within the EU.

This formed part of the background to David Cameron's attempt to recalibrate Britain's place within the European Union. At the outset, it had been assumed that the deal would focus on three aspects: establishment of the principle of sovereignty for the Westminster Parliament, maintenance of access to the single market and the economic benefits this brought the UK, and increased control of Britain's borders in order to lower net migration. Within a short period of time, however, the third aspect came to dominate the other tranches of the debate, with the negotiating process with Cameron's fellow EU leaders soon inextricably linked in the minds of the public, the media and many Tory MPs to immigration. May herself played a role in ensuring that immigration was at the centre of the renegotiation. In August 2015, in an article in the *Sunday Times*, she made clear she expected any deal to include an agreement that EU nationals would be barred from entering Britain without a job. 'When it was first enshrined, free movement meant the freedom to move to a job, not the freedom to cross borders to look for work or claim benefits,' she wrote. 'If we want to control immigration – and bring it down to the tens of thousands – we must take some big decisions, face down powerful interests and reinstate the original principle underlying free movement within the EU.'[375]

At the Conservative Party conference five weeks later, May ramped up the rhetoric, with an address which earned unfortunate comparisons to Enoch Powell's infamous 'Rivers of Blood' speech.[376] 'We must have an immigration system that allows us to control who comes to our country,' she said. 'When immigration is too high, when the pace of change is too fast, it's impossible to build a cohesive society … There's no case, in the national interest, for immigration of the scale we have experienced over the past decade.' The speech sharply divided those who heard it. Simon

Walker, director-general of the Institute of Directors, said: 'We are astonished by the irresponsible rhetoric and pandering to anti-immigration sentiment,' while Maurice Wren, chief executive of the Refugee Council, described it as 'chilling'.[377] The *Daily Mail*, however, called May 'magnificent', in a glowing leader column which said: 'This was perhaps the bravest attempt by a mainstream politician to confront the issue – ranked voters' number one concern – since the bien-pensant Left pulled down the curtain on open debate decades ago.'[378] Even some of May's supporters were shocked at the stridency of the speech. Her Lib Dem friend Lynne Featherstone says: 'She gave a terrible conference speech. It was just really ill-judged, and I don't know what happened. I was disappointed in her for that. I think Theresa's better than that.'

Downing Street was also taken aback by the harsh tone, which, it was felt, heaped further pressure on David Cameron in his EU negotiations. Pointedly, the Prime Minister used his own speech to conference to praise both George Osborne and Boris Johnson at length, but mentioned May only in a list of ministers he said were keeping the country safe 'at home and abroad', an omission described as a 'snub'.[379] Whatever Cameron's feelings, May's speech clearly struck a positive note among voters. At the end of October, a new poll by Survation showed her as the favourite politician with voters to lead the Leave campaign, ahead of both Boris Johnson and the UKIP leader Nigel Farage. Appearing on *The Andrew Marr Show* the day after the poll was published, May appeared to hold out the possibility that she could indeed campaign in favour of quitting the EU. Asked outright whether she could lead the Out campaign, May said:

> There are some people who say you should be in at all costs, there are people who say you should be out at all costs. Actually, I say let's do this renegotiation, let's see what reform we can bring about as a result of that renegotiation and then put it to the British people.[380]

In Brussels, however, the negotiations were not going well. Gripped by the migrant crisis and still grappling with the fallout from the

2008 economic turmoil, which had brought countries including Greece, Spain, Ireland and Portugal to their knees, most of Europe's leaders entered the process with somewhat less zeal than the British Prime Minister. Cameron floated the prospect first of limiting European migration by imposing an annual cap on national insurance numbers for low-skilled workers, then, when this was rejected by fellow EU leaders, proposed an 'emergency brake', to be triggered when migration by European nationals reached unsustainable levels. The brake would deny benefits to EU nationals and was designed to ease the pressure on public services. Both ideas contravened the sacrosanct, in EU terms, principle of freedom of movement. Angela Merkel, the German Chancellor, made clear they would not fly.

In November 2015, Cameron prepared to deliver a major speech at the headquarters of the construction firm JCB, outlining his final demands for Britain's continued membership of the EU. These were to be the red lines over which, should his fellow leaders fail to deliver, he would pledge to recommend quitting the Union. Having been told on the eve of the speech by Merkel that she would not compromise on the 'emergency brake', Cameron was considering calling her bluff and including it in the speech anyway, the reasoning being that when it came to the crunch the German Chancellor and her fellow EU heads of state would not allow Britain to walk away from the Union. As the final draft of the speech was still being finalised, Cameron summoned Philip Hammond, the Foreign Secretary, and May to an 8.30 a.m. meeting at Downing Street to discuss the proposed gamble. In his book, *All Out War: The Full Story of How Brexit Sank Britain's Political Class*, journalist Tim Shipman quotes a Downing Street source as saying:

> The PM told them what the Germans had said, and asked for their view on whether we should go ahead and announce in any case. Hammond spoke first, and argued that we just couldn't announce something that would receive an immediate raspberry in Europe … Theresa simply said that we just couldn't go against Merkel.[381]

As a direct consequence of the discussion with Hammond and May, it is claimed, Cameron scrapped the reference to the 'emergency brake' from his speech – to the fury of Leave campaigners such as Iain Duncan Smith who had been briefed that it would be included. Afterwards, Cameron is alleged to have described May and Hammond's lack of support over the 'emergency brake' as torpedoing his renegotiation strategy, which now focused exclusively on attempts to limit benefits to EU migrants. 'Look, we tried, but I can't do it without their support,' he is said to have told an official. 'If it wasn't for my lily-livered Cabinet colleagues…'[382]

In December 2015, Cameron brought months of speculation to an end by revealing that he expected the referendum to be held the following June, far sooner than most observers had expected, and long before his own cut-off date of December 2017. It was a risk, given that the package of reforms he had secured in Europe was somewhat underwhelming following the abandonment of the 'emergency brake'. Attention now turned to which way the Cabinet would vote in the referendum, with Chris Grayling, Iain Duncan Smith and Michael Gove all identified as likely to back the 'No' campaign (as the Leave camp was still called at this stage) amid speculation over whether or not Cameron would suspend collective Cabinet responsibility and allow a free vote. Asked soon after Cameron's JCB speech which way she planned to vote, May refused to be drawn.

A few weeks later, Grayling, the Leader of the House and a passionate Eurosceptic, asked to see Cameron, and respectfully enquired if he would be suspending collective Cabinet responsibility, which would allow ministers to campaign and vote in the referendum according to their own views rather than being forced to follow the lead of the Prime Minister. Grayling made no threats, saying only that he needed 'certainty' from Cameron,[383] but it was clear that if collective Cabinet responsibility was not suspended, he would resign. Grayling's visit was followed within hours by a phone call from Northern Ireland Secretary Theresa Villiers, who delivered a similar message. Other senior ministers were likely to follow suit. Alarmed at the prospect of losing two or more Cabinet ministers, Cameron now took another step that would help to hasten his departure.

Without first informing the Cabinet, some of whom learned of his move via the media, on 5 January 2016, Cameron announced that he was suspending collective Cabinet responsibility and granting his MPs the free vote many had been demanding, saying he was unwilling to 'strong-arm' his colleagues into backing a position they did not support. We may never know how many ministers, including Boris Johnson, who were on the fence over the EU would have ended up backing Remain had collective responsibility remained in place. By suspending it, Cameron gave free rein to his entire team of ministers, his friends and allies included, to campaign against their Prime Minister. In a number of cases, those friendships and alliances would not survive what would turn out to be a bitter war of attrition. As soon as the free vote was announced, there were suggestions that as many as 150 Tory MPs, just under half the parliamentary party, would vote against their leader.

It was now increasingly obvious that May too would have to make her position clear. The longer she held out, the more speculation mounted that she would campaign against Britain's continuing membership. To win the Home Secretary to their cause would have been a major coup for the Leave camp. Excitement grew that she might do just that when Stephen Parkinson, one of her closest advisers following the departures of Fiona Hill and Nick Timothy, quit the Home Office to work for the Vote Leave campaign. Along with Michael Gove and Boris Johnson, May now came under sustained pressure to reveal her hand. In a leader column on 15 January, *The Sun* urged her to 'come off the fence' and campaign for Leave. At the next day's Cabinet meeting, which Cameron used to plead with his ministers to maintain an air of civility through the campaign, her colleagues waited for some hint of which way she would jump. None came. The Home Secretary sat, according to one attendee, 'magnificently silent'.[384]

Speculation mounted still further a few days later when May

was spotted having lunch with her friend Liam Fox, a vehement Eurosceptic and leading member of the Leave campaign, at the popular Westminster Italian restaurant Quirinale, a stone's throw from Parliament. Their meeting was interpreted as a sign that she was being recruited to the Brexit cause. Fox himself laughs off the suggestion: 'There were all these stories before the referendum of us having secret lunches,' he says. 'As if anyone would go to Quirinale for a secret lunch.' In Downing Street, the Cameroons were not amused. The Prime Minister had become increasingly irritated by May's failure to 'come off the fence', as he too put it. He was also frustrated by an anonymous briefing which appeared in the press a few days after the Fox lunch, casting doubt on his success in tackling abuses surrounding the entry into the UK of non-EU migrants via other states within the Union.[385] In a note written at the time, Craig Oliver said:

> On a train to Chippenham for a speech, DC is visibly wound up by the report. Suddenly he picks up his mobile and calls May, asking her to make clear we have been victorious in our plan to crackdown on 'swindlers and fiddlers' attempting to come into the UK. When he hangs up he seems to think he's made an impact.[386]

In response, finally, and to Cameron's great relief, the following day, 2 February, May discreetly, if somewhat unenthusiastically, nailed her colours to the Remain mast. That day, Donald Tusk, the President of the EU Council, had unveiled the terms of the package of measures that Cameron had secured. They amounted to a watered-down version of the 'emergency brake' on in-work benefits, the paying of child benefit at the rate set by a national's home state, rather than the UK level, a 'red card' system for the vetoing of EU legislation (but only if approved by 55 per cent of votes on the Council), an end to British bailouts of the Eurozone, and a halt to 'ever-closer union' for the UK. As a package it was underwhelming, and Cameron would be pilloried in the next day's newspapers; *The*

Sun's front page portrayed him as Captain Mainwaring from the wartime comedy *Dad's Army*, under the headline 'Who do EU think you are kidding Mr Cameron?' But it was apparently just enough for May. Later that day, she issued a statement declaring the measures as 'a basis for a deal'. The hopes of the Leave campaign that May would come over to their cause were dashed.

So how close did May come to backing the Leave side? Even Liam Fox is not sure. 'I think only Theresa could ever answer that question for you,' he says. 'As with everything else, she could see both sides of the ledger. She was certainly never an enthusiastic Europhile, that's for sure.' Since the referendum, May has been accused of political calculation; assuming, as most did, that Remain would prevail, she wanted to make sure she was on the winning side. In his book *Unleashing Demons*, Craig Oliver has claimed that, with May still refusing to reveal her hand, Cameron (who had just announced publicly that he would remain in office should he lose the referendum) told him at the end of January: 'Well, it may work for her. She could be PM in six months' time.'[387] She would beat the timescale by two weeks. Calculation is a charge that Eric Pickles absolves May of, however. 'Unless I've misunderstood her, I don't think she's calculating, I don't think she'd do something to be politically popular,' he says. 'I'm not saying she's a saint or an angel, but by and large she would do what she would think was right.'

The end of the referendum phony war came on 20 February, when Cameron stood on the steps of No. 10 and announced the date of the referendum: 23 June. He then called an emergency Cabinet meeting, the first to be held on a Saturday since the Falklands War, which ended amid furious recriminations. Michael Gove, now officially backing the Leave campaign, upbraided the Prime Minister for suggesting during his announcement that quitting the EU would be a 'threat to national security'. The Prime Minister was defended by both George Osborne and May. As the bad-tempered meeting broke up, a car waiting at Downing Street's back door took the five Cabinet Brexiteers – Gove, John Whittingdale, Theresa Villiers, Chris Grayling and Iain Duncan Smith – and Priti Patel (who attended Cabinet without being a full member) to the headquarters of the Leave campaign. The starting gun had been fired.

If May had found it hard to make up her mind which side to back, Boris Johnson's decision-making process was excruciating. Even more than her, he would later be accused of taking his decision on the basis of how best it would help his personal ambitions. It has since emerged that Johnson spent the hours after the emergency Cabinet meeting 'agonising' over what path to take, before sitting down to write two separate articles, setting out the benefits of each side.[388] The next day, 21 February, he stunned Cameron by delivering a statement to journalists outside his house in which he described the EU as 'a political project that has been going on for decades, and is now in real danger of getting out of proper democratic control'. He had told the Prime Minister of his decision to campaign for Leave just nine minutes earlier, with a text message in which he nevertheless predicted that the cause of Brexit would be 'crushed'.[389] Cameron later told Craig Oliver that Johnson was a 'confused Inner'. Four hours before declaring for Leave, he had sent the Prime Minister a text message suggesting he was moving towards Remain.

A week after Johnson's somewhat chaotic press conference, a YouGov poll showed he was the overwhelming favourite among voters to take over from Cameron, leading his closest rival, George Osborne, by 21 per cent. May, who barely figured in the poll, must have wondered if she had backed the wrong horse. But, amid bubbling speculation that, despite his protestations, Cameron would be forced to step down should he lose the referendum vote, and the virtual anointing of Johnson as his successor, some of May's supporters retained confidence in her prospects of capturing the leadership. Margot James says:

> I remember encountering her in the House of Commons car park, the forecourt where the ministerial cars go, in the middle of the referendum campaign ... and she was on her own, which was very unusual. So I went over and had a brief chat with her ...

and then just as an afterthought I said, 'Oh, by the way, just want you to know that whatever comes over the coming months and years you have my support.' And she was very happy to hear that.

On 16 March, George Osborne delivered a much-criticised Budget, which prompted Iain Duncan Smith to storm out of the Cabinet in disgust at proposed cuts to disability benefits. Even before Duncan Smith's dramatic departure, the Budget had been somewhat overshadowed in some sections of the press by May's decision to wear a cleavage-exposing dress as she sat alongside Osborne to hear what would be his last Budget statement. A few days later, a poll by ORB found that May had overtaken the Chancellor in the leadership stakes; both, however, trailed Johnson by double digits.

While speculation over the leadership would not go away, for now the more immediate consideration was the referendum. Johnson's unexpected backing for the Leave cause gave the campaign the big beast they had hoped to attract in May. While the likes of Nigel Farage and some of the Tory Eurosceptics, perhaps even including Gove, could be characterised as either eccentric or peripheral, Johnson could not be dismissed so easily. From looking like an unfair battle at the outside, with the might of the political establishment united in support for the EU, as winter turned to spring it was clear that Cameron and the Remainers faced a tough fight. All hands were needed on deck. And yet, through March and April, the Home Secretary seemed to have vanished.

Craig Oliver has described how the exasperated team at No. 10 nicknamed the Home Secretary 'Submarine May'.[390] He claimed Cameron asked his Home Secretary to take a higher-profile role in the Remain campaign no fewer than thirteen times, only to be let down on each occasion. At one point, in April 2016, as May vaguely promised to deliver a speech 'after Easter', Oliver wrote a diary entry reading: 'In terms of pure politics you have to hand it to her, she is playing it well. She is on the right side making clear she is "In", but not looking overly enthusiastic. It's making life uncomfortable for us.'[391]

But while May's behaviour was irritating to No. 10, it made sense in context. On balance, she had eventually backed remaining in the EU, but she had never been a passionate Europhile. And although she was conscious of the loyalty any Prime Minister deserved from his Home Secretary, the animosity that had grown up between her and Cameron meant she did not see that she was required to do much more than confirm she would be voting Remain. The Cameroons, however, saw this as overt disloyalty. George Osborne in particular was furious at May's disappearing act – and made it widely known that her lack of support could result in demotion (a threat Cameron was eager to distance himself from). Eric Pickles says: 'We had that ridiculous thing where Osborne was going to have her sacked because she wasn't doing enough. [But] I can understand why she was not involved heavily. By God, she put him in his place [after she became Prime Minister].'

One source close to the Conservative Remain team at the time makes clear the suspicion in which the Home Secretary was held in both Downing Street and the Treasury:

> There was definitely friction that she had done the bare minimum. She was obviously not keeping a low profile in order to stand for the leadership after the referendum, because like everyone else she thought Remain would win, but she did seem to be playing a longer game. She maybe thought it would do her no harm to keep her head down. And there was frustration in the Cameron camp about that.

On the rare occasions when May did surface, the Cameroons complained that she would veer off-piste, expressing criticism of human rights legislation and freedom of movement. In the speech she finally agreed to deliver at the end of April, May told her audience she would not 'insult people's intelligence by claiming that everything about the EU is perfect, that membership of the EU is wholly good'. In contrast to Osborne's 'Project Fear' strategy of delivering dire warnings about the economic risks involved in leaving the Union,

May even admitted the UK 'could cope' outside the EU, and was 'big enough and strong enough to be a success story in or out of the EU'. She somewhat tepidly concluded that 'right now, and looking ahead to the challenges facing Britain and Europe in the future – on security, trade and the economy – I believe it is clearly in our national interest to remain members of the EU'.[392] After the speech, Will Straw, director general of the Remain campaign, texted Craig Oliver to ask, only half-jokingly: 'Are we sure May's not an agent for the other side!?'[393] The Tory Remain source says: 'When she did speak, she was definitely off message. You could argue she was more in tune with the public by talking about immigration but … she was definitely seen in No. 10 as not abiding by the script.'

Ameet Gill, Cameron's former adviser, believes that May's low-key approach to the referendum campaign was understandable. 'I think it's no secret that Theresa was sceptical of some of the tactics employed by No. 10, and the Remain campaign, in terms of our messaging. She wasn't a convinced and totally wholehearted convicted Remainer, she was a sceptical, Tory Remainer.'[394]

May herself has defended her low profile during the referendum, saying: 'I did do campaigning. But just as the campaign was running I had some pretty serious business … going on in the House of Commons which demanded my attention.'[395] Ultimately, her instincts about the country's feelings on Europe would prove to be far more attuned than George Osborne's. His warning, a week before referendum day, that Brexit would force him as Chancellor to produce an emergency Budget complete with sweeping tax increases is widely seen as one of the turning points that lost the campaign for Remain. The public did not believe the dire warnings about the economic impact on their daily lives – and were irritated by the perceived threat from Osborne.

For a country almost acclimatised to political shocks following two highly unexpected general election results in the previous six years, the thunderbolt that was the Brexit vote on the night of 23 June 2016 was on a scale like no other. Even the most ardent of Leave supporters, including the campaign's leaders, Nigel Farage, Boris

Johnson and Michael Gove, had no realistic expectation that the result would go their way. On the evening of the vote, the Cameroons gathered at No. 10 to await the result, dining on the decidedly European dishes of moussaka and lasagne, washed down with wine and elderflower cordial. Cameron and Osborne were confident that, while it was clear that the contest had been uncomfortably close, when it came to it, the British people would accept the advice of virtually the entire political establishment and vote to remain in the EU. To reinforce their confidence, the final opinion poll of the campaign, by YouGov, gave Remain a four-point lead.

As she had during the entire referendum campaign, Theresa May kept a low profile, watching the results on television at home with her husband. Johnson, who had flown back from his daughter's graduation in Scotland just in time to vote, also stayed home. Gove took his mind off what he assumed would be a valiant defeat by inviting some close friends over to his house in Ladbroke Grove, west London, for a boozy supper. None of the actors in the drama that would now unfold had any idea of how the events of the next few hours would change all their lives for ever.

At 10.30 p.m., Gove bid goodnight to his friends, leaving them to continue socialising while he went to bed, assuming the fight was lost. In the living room of No. 10, meanwhile, Cameron, with his sleeping daughter on his knee, was joined by Osborne and the team of close advisers who had formed his tight circle of Cameroons for the past eleven years. As the polls closed and even before the first results had been announced, Nigel Farage appeared to concede defeat on behalf of the Leave campaign, saying: 'It's been an extraordinary referendum campaign, turnout looks to be exceptionally high, and it looks like Remain will edge it.' But within the hour, as the early results trickled in, Osborne noticed something strange: where Remain was winning, as in Newcastle, the margins were too small; losses, such as an overwhelming vote to leave in Sunderland, were far greater than expected. As the hours passed, it became increasingly clear that the battle was lost. After more than forty years, Britain was on its way out of the European Union.

By 3 a.m., the gathering in the Downing Street living room had broken up, with Cameron reconvening in the No. 10 kitchen with his very closest inner circle, Osborne, Kate Fall and Ed Llewellyn. Having staked his premiership on the outcome of the referendum, and despite the entreaties of his friends, at least one of whom was in tears, he was clear that he could no longer remain as Prime Minister. Woken by an adviser an hour after Cameron's kitchen conclave with the news that Leave had achieved the unexpected and actually clinched the referendum, Gove suddenly and starkly realised he had no real plan for what to do next. Forty minutes later, at 4.39 a.m., the BBC formally declared that Britain had voted to leave the European Union. Outside Boris Johnson's home in Islington, journalists began pounding on the door, imploring him to come out and provide some response to the astonishing events of the preceding hours. Unsure what to do, he declined. Within minutes of the markets opening, the pound had dropped to its lowest level since 1985. Then, at 8 a.m., looking all but broken and with a weeping Samantha beside him on the steps of No. 10, David Cameron announced his resignation.

In the early hours of Friday 24 June, therefore, the new realities that had suddenly and most unexpectedly hit the leaders of the two sides of the Brexit debate had converged to create the perfect conditions for someone new to take over. A safe pair of hands, a grown-up, was needed, to take control of what had suddenly become a country in chaos. Theresa May now had a glorious opportunity to fulfil the hopes that had been dashed by Cameron's surprise election victory just over a year earlier. It was time for the 'submarine' to rise from the deep.

CHAPTER XVIII

LAST WOMAN STANDING

No one was surprised when Theresa May announced she would be running for the leadership of the Conservative Party following the resignation of David Cameron as Prime Minister on 24 June 2016. What came as a total shock was the speed with which, one by one, her rivals fell away in a chaotic bloodbath of recrimination, backbiting and betrayal. For sixteen days in June and July 2016, it seemed as if only May kept her head as first her party and then the entire political establishment fell apart, the ensuing leadership vacuum sending the financial markets into freefall. The stunning result of the European referendum on 23 June had, overnight, knocked the Cameroons, including Cameron's presumed heir George Osborne, out of the game. By 11 July, when May was formally anointed Leader of the Conservative Party and Prime Minister-elect, all of the leading Tory representatives of the Leave campaign, the victorious Brexiteers Boris Johnson, Michael Gove and Andrea Leadsom, had seen their leadership ambitions come crashing down as well. Meanwhile, across the aisle, Jeremy Corbyn, the Labour leader, was facing a leadership challenge of his own following the mass resignations of most of his front bench. Nigel Farage, the UKIP leader, had announced his departure, triggering a contest to replace him which would result in farcical scenes and his temporary return as leader. Only May came through the bloodletting unscathed; a grown-up in a world of petulant toddlers.

By their final years in government, it had been assumed that the

battle to succeed David Cameron would come down to a three-way
fight between George Osborne, Boris Johnson and May. Following his success in masterminding the Tories' unexpected outright
majority in the 2015 general election, for more than a year it had
seemed as if the next change of leader would prove to be a smooth
transition from Cameron to Osborne, the Prime Minister's closest friend in politics, a move next door so apparently natural that
the public would barely notice any difference. All that went out of
the window with the referendum. Far from being the automatic
favourite to replace the outgoing Cameron, his Chancellor was
the first of the rivals to fall by the wayside. From the moment the
early results came in on referendum night, Osborne as much as
Cameron knew he would be for ever associated with the defeat.
His eve-of-poll threat to hold an emergency Budget to raise taxes in
the event of a vote to Leave had backfired spectacularly, attracting
widespread derision among his MP peers, meaning he stood little
chance of making it onto the ballot in the contest now triggered by
Cameron's departure. In any case, so associated was he with the
previous regime that he was aware his colleagues – and the public
– would agree there was little point replacing one deeply wounded
Cameroon with another.

On 28 June, four days after Cameron's resignation, Osborne
formally ruled himself out of the contest to replace him, saying:
'I am not the person to provide the unity my party needs at this
time.' Soon afterwards, he telephoned May, offering his support. A
Treasury insider says:

> George supported Theresa from the very beginning. He was so
> closely associated with the Remain campaign, he decided quite
> early on that he wouldn't stand, and from that moment he believed
> Theresa was the right person. He didn't go public at that point, but
> he certainly told her he was supporting her. Temperamentally he
> thought she was absolutely the right person to take it on.

If the politically astute Chancellor believed that his privately expressed support would be enough to save his seat in a May Cabinet, he would be proved wrong.

As ever in British politics, particularly with the ruthlessly effective Conservative Party, the mourning period for the fallen leader was brief. The contest to replace Cameron began, informally at least, within hours of his departure. At the outset, with Osborne out of the picture, it appeared that Boris Johnson was a virtual shoo-in to inherit the referendum spoils. Having long enjoyed a celebrity status and connection with the public that other politicians of his generation could only envy, Johnson had, despite the heavy weather he made of choosing which side to back in the referendum campaign, eventually picked the winner. It seemed obvious that it should fall to a Leave politician to see Britain through the process of actually quitting the European Union. And what better person to do that than the most popular politician of his era?

The third long-anticipated candidate was Theresa May. For some years she had been accused by many of the team inside No. 10 of overtly plotting to replace David Cameron. In fact, while May and her closest advisers had always been keen to maintain her position as a likely candidate, and were clear that when a vacancy arose she would be among the contenders, no concrete plans had ever been made to institute a leadership campaign. May – and virtually everyone else in politics – had taken Cameron at his word when he had insisted he would stay on as Prime Minister regardless of the outcome of the referendum, and, in any case, she had not anticipated that the Leave campaign would actually win.

In the hours after Cameron's resignation, as the country waited for someone to display leadership, May's supporters scrambled into action. First Fiona Hill and Nick Timothy and soon Katie Perrior and Stephen Parkinson were among the trusted lieutenants swiftly recalled from their jobs outside Westminster, the political equivalent of getting the old band back together. With her closest advisers from the past dozen years at her side, May must have felt energised. George Pascoe-Watson, a PR executive and former political editor of *The Sun*, has said:

As soon as David Cameron resigned after the referendum, the leadership race for the Conservative Party was underway, effectively, and of course no one had a leadership team up and running. So Fi and Nick dropped whatever they were doing and the two of them went in to run a campaign operation for the first four or five days before they could recruit anyone else. Phenomenal piece of work.

The leadership election would be staged in two phases: first, in a series of ballots, MPs would cast their votes, the bottom-placed candidate in each round being eliminated until the race was whittled down to two. The second stage would see the remaining candidates take part in a series of hustings and events around the country, before Conservative members voted for their favourite. While it was therefore necessary to finish only in second place in order to make it into the final round, the received wisdom was that it was better for candidates to get on to the front foot and establish a clear narrative as a winner by emerging as the top choice of MPs. The contest was set to conclude on 9 September. May's team now discussed how best to woo MPs to their cause. Her famous lack of 'clubbability' was once again a potential issue. Eric Pickles, who first backed Boris Johnson but within a few days changed his mind and came over to May's side, says: 'We had a kind of a discussion about it, but it was too late. If she started appearing in the tea rooms now, we [really] would think the party [had] a problem.' Philip May was deputed to hit the telephones on his wife's behalf to encourage her fellow MPs to back her.

Contrary to the perception held by the Cameroons that May had a fully-fledged leadership campaign ready to go, no work had been put into establishing a 'ground war' at a constituency level either. Pickles, who had deep roots into the local party from his days as party chairman, says: 'There wasn't really an organisation there. I'd agreed to take on part of the war when we got to the constituenc[y phase of the contest] so I was getting started on that, and it was pretty clear that not much had been planned.' What May did have, however, was a long history of taking the time and trouble to travel to far-flung local Tory associations to speak to members. Liam Fox says: 'She's one of those politicians who will go to parts of the country where we don't necessarily have huge majorities or huge party associations. People do remember that. It may not register in the Westminster bubble, but it registers out there in the country, where it matters.'

On Sunday 27 June, May attended church in Sonning as usual with Philip. This time there were cameras there to greet her. Earlier that morning, the first opinion poll of the campaign had been published. It came as a shock to supporters of Boris Johnson, but not to those who understood the hard work May had put in over the years meeting tens of thousands of Conservative activists. The poll, by Survation for the *Mail on Sunday*, showed that while Johnson was the clear favourite of all the likely candidates with both the public and Conservative members, when the choice was whittled down to two, putting him head to head against May, she was predicted to win by 53 per cent to 47 per cent.[396] Two days later, a YouGov poll for *The Times* gave May an even clearer lead, with 31 per cent of Conservative members backing her, compared to just 24 per cent for Johnson.[397]

By the next day, Johnson's camp was claiming he had the support of more than 100 MPs, raising the prospect that the former Mayor of London could 'do a Ken Clarke' by winning the vote among his parliamentary colleagues only to lose out to May in the final round when the membership was polled. Sensing a problem, Johnson's team now made May an offer: back him, and he would reward her with the post of Chancellor. On the day of the YouGov poll, a secret meeting was arranged at the Cabinet Office, away from prying camera crews, for Johnson and May to thrash out a deal. Johnson waited for forty minutes before it became apparent that she was not going to turn up. Later that night, Gavin Williamson, until then David Cameron's parliamentary aide, having previously carried out the same duties for May and now working on her leadership campaign, met with Johnson's campaign manager,

Ben Wallace, a Northern Ireland minister, to relay a message: 'No deal.'[398] It would later be claimed that May was one of three people to whom Johnson offered the keys to the Treasury during his short leadership bid.

One early Johnson supporter was not convinced by the way his campaign was operating, finding it chaotic and lacking a clear message for what the candidate wanted to do in power. Eric Pickles says:

> I was very unhappy with the campaign. My instincts would have been to go with Boris because I thought he truly understood the nature of what the country was like … But I think he was negligent about some of the things that happened. I had a meeting with him because I didn't want to come out for [May] without telling him, and I kind of expected it to be dreadful, but he was awfully understanding. But in terms of me deciding, it was nothing compared to what was going to happen later in the week.

Pickles's defection was indeed only the start of Johnson's problems. 30 June 2016 will go down in history as one of the most extraordinary days in modern British politics. The deadline for candidates to submit their nomination forms to the 1922 Committee, which, as usual, would be overseeing the contest, was set for noon. In any circumstances, it would have been a day filled with drama. As it was, over the course of twenty-four hours, the entire race was turned upside down, as Michael Gove, Boris Johnson's brother-in-arms during the EU referendum campaign, turned on him with a ruthlessness rarely seen even in the brutal world of Westminster.

In government, Gove had always insisted he had no interest in standing for the leadership of his party, saying he was aware he was temperamentally unsuited to the task of being Prime Minister. As a close ally of Boris Johnson, it was naturally assumed that Gove would play a leading role in the former Mayor's leadership campaign, probably ending up with a senior post – either Chancellor or

Foreign Secretary – in a Johnson-headed administration. Yet on the morning of 30 June, completely out of the blue as far as Johnson was concerned, Gove turned on his long-time friend, launching a leadership campaign of his own. Gove gave Johnson just seven minutes' notice of his move, and did not have the courtesy to deliver the news in person, instead phoning campaign manager Sir Lynton Crosby. He then twisted the knife, declaring publicly that he had decided to stand against his best instincts because, he said bluntly, he had come to see that his friend was not up to the job.

In a statement issued to journalists at 9 a.m., Gove explained his decision to turn on the man who had been expecting to stand alongside him to launch his own leadership bid two hours hence:

> I have repeatedly said that I do not want to be Prime Minister. That has always been my view. But events since last Thursday [the day of the referendum] have weighed heavily with me … I wanted to help build a team behind Boris Johnson so that a politician who argued for leaving the European Union could lead us to a better future. But I have come, reluctantly, to the conclusion that Boris cannot provide the leadership or build the team for the task ahead. I have, therefore, decided to put my name forward for the leadership.

Even for the Conservative Party, with its long tradition of political assassinations ranging from Michael Heseltine to Michael Portillo, Gove's destruction of his hitherto friend and ally was mercilessly savage. By the end of the day, Johnson's leadership ambitions were dead. It would take a few days before Gove's deaf ear picked up what all those around him instantly realised: that in killing off Johnson in such a brutal manner he had so disgusted his electorate of fellow MPs that his own chances of winning the highest office were also now virtually zero.

A few minutes after Gove's astonishing intervention, at 9.13 a.m., Andrea Leadsom, the Energy Minister who had played a leading role in the Leave campaign, announced her intention to enter the

race, with a tweet which said: 'Delighted to say I'm running for
the @Conservatives Leadership. Let's make the most of the Brexit
opportunities!' It later emerged that Leadsom had been offered a
deal by Boris Johnson's team not to stand, in return for one of the
top jobs in his government. Amid farcical scenes, Johnson was said
to have forgotten to bring a letter confirming the offer along with
him to the Conservatives' summer ball at the Hurlingham Club in
west London, where he was supposed to hand it over to Leadsom.
It read: 'Dear Andrea, Delighted that you're in our top 3, Yours
Boris.'[399] By the time the note was retrieved, Leadsom had left the
party assuming the deal was off. Thus the inexperienced Leadsom,
who had never held a seat in Cabinet, became the race's fourth
candidate, Stephen Crabb, the Work and Pensions Secretary, and
Liam Fox, the former Defence Secretary, having announced their
intentions to stand the day before.

Seventeen minutes after Leadsom's tweet, at 9.30 a.m., May
became the fifth candidate to enter the contest, with a formal
campaign launch at a Westminster club. Wearing a smart Vivi-
enne Westwood tartan trouser suit, she was positioned in front of a
handsome wall of bookcases, and gave a speech designed both to
reassure a public utterly discombobulated by the melodrama of the
past week and to inspire them with her prescription for the future.
Setting out her vision as a One Nation Tory, she vowed to unite the
country and stick up for those she felt had been left behind under
David Cameron's leadership: the poor, ethnic minorities, women,
the mentally ill, young people who could not get a foot on the housing ladder and all those handicapped by the lack of an expensive
education. In a direct attack on what she portrayed as the elitism
and gamesmanship of both Cameron and Boris Johnson, she said:

> If you're from an ordinary, working-class family, life is just much
> harder than many people in politics realise. You have a job, but you
> don't always have job security. You have your own home, but
> you worry about mortgage rates going up. You can just about
> manage, but you worry about the cost of living and the quality of

the local school, because there's no other choice for you. Frankly, not everybody in Westminster understands what it's like to live like this. And some need to be told that what the government does isn't a game, it's a serious business that has real consequences for people's lives.

In touching references to her father, Hubert, and grandfather, Tom Brasier, May went on to explain the roots of her dedication to public service, while giving an astute assessment of her own, non-flashy brand of politics:

I know some politicians seek high office because they're driven by ideological fervour. And I know others seek it for reasons of ambition or glory. But my reasons are much simpler ... Public service has been a part of who I am for as long as I can remember. I know I'm not a showy politician. I don't tour the television studios. I don't gossip about people over lunch. I don't go drinking in Parliament's bars. I don't often wear my heart on my sleeve. I just get on with the job in front of me.

She concluded: 'My pitch is simple: I'm Theresa May and I think I'm the best person to lead this country.'

May's launch seemed to represent a moment of sanity in a political world in chaos. As Johnson licked his wounds following Gove's brutal knifing, MPs and the wider country sat up and paid attention to the calm, reasoned woman presenting her rational and compelling case. Youthful exuberance and excitement may once have been in vogue, when both David Cameron and before him Tony Blair were running for office, but in a post-referendum age of uncertainty, May seemed to represent what the public craved: order and stability; a safe pair of hands. The optics alone of May's launch left one former Tory spin doctor impressed:

Fiona [Hill] and Nick [Timothy] did an amazing job, with no notice, no time to plan, of presenting Theresa May to the public as a future Prime Minister. In the chaos after Brexit, she stood there in that press conference in front of those library shelves with all those books and everyone just sighed with relief that someone was in charge.

Andrew Griffiths says that over the course of seventy-two hours, it suddenly seemed inevitable May that would become the next Prime Minister:

It's interesting in those few days after the referendum how quickly colleagues went from many people thinking, 'Well, it's an inevitability that Boris can be leader' to 'Theresa can do this' to 'Theresa is going to do this'. Politics is all about timing … The implosion of Boris and the destruction of Michael Gove, the fears over what Brexit meant for the economy and the view that we needed a safe pair of the hands on the tiller, the lack of any other credible candidates that emerged from the papal conclave, so to speak, all of those things; the planets aligned to allow it to happen.

Liam Fox adds: 'Theresa's election is a victory of substance over style. That's not to say that there's no style, of course, but it is a victory for experience, for intelligence, for conscientiousness; just all the things, I'm sure, her father would have instilled in her as being the most important.'

Meanwhile, the effect on Boris Johnson of Michael Gove's devastating remarks was catastrophic. Almost immediately, he decided that the character assassination from the man he had viewed as his closest ally meant he could not continue in the race. Johnson's leadership launch had been due to take place at the St Ermin's Hotel an hour after May's. His supporters gathered at the event as planned, wondering how he would address Gove's remarks. To the astonishment of all those present, including his own brother, Jo, the MP for Orpington, instead of setting out his stall for the leadership, Johnson began by saying that Brexit presented opportunities for the next Prime Minister to think globally, before going on to add:

'Having consulted colleagues, and in view of the circumstances in Parliament, I have concluded that person cannot be me.'

The audience in the hotel was visibly shocked, their emotion shared by all those watching on television. Johnson is an attractive, popular figure, and many of his supporters were distraught at the turn of events. Most were also very clear where the blame lay for Johnson's sudden decision to quit the race. A few minutes later, Jake Berry, the MP for Rossendale and Darwen, tweeted: 'There is a very deep pit reserved in Hell for such as he', adding the hashtag '#Gove'. Johnson's father, Stanley, a former Conservative MEP, said: '"Et tu Brute" is my comment.'[400] Amid the bitter recriminations, many Johnson supporters ran to what now seemed a haven amid the storm: Theresa May. Having witnessed the morning's extraordinary events, a number of previously unaligned MPs also announced they would be backing May. More than one MP expressed disgust at what appeared an only slightly grown-up version of the skulduggery that had gone on a few decades earlier in the battles for the presidency of the Oxford Union. Kwasi Kwarteng, the MP for Spelthorne who had previously been a Johnson supporter, said: 'I'm backing Theresa. I want a grown-up. This is student politics.'[401] The Health Secretary Jeremy Hunt and Business Minister Anna Soubry also now opted for May, the latter saying: 'Perhaps we've had enough of these boys messing about.'[402] At midday, as the nominations closed, Graham Brady, chairman of the 1922 Committee, formally announced that the contest would take place between five candidates: Michael Gove, Stephen Crabb, Liam Fox, Andrea Leadsom – and Theresa May. The first round of MP ballots was due to take place on 5 July.

Charlie Elphicke, who served as Home Office whip and was now a member of May's campaign team, began to woo Johnson supporters. He says: 'The mood of anger towards Gove, not obviously from the Theresa May camp because it didn't affect us, but the mood of anger from the supporters of Boris, was palpable. Gove, considering what he did, it was very clear he was going to struggle.' May, who had had a somewhat difficult relationship with Johnson over the years, was nonetheless among those appalled at the way he had been treated. That night she sent him a text message sympathising over what had happened.

The day after the Gove and Johnson bloodbath, the *Daily Mail* printed an enthusiastic and lengthy editorial endorsing May's candidacy, under the headline 'A Party in Flames and Why It Must Be Theresa for Leader'. As a stamp of approval from Middle England, it could not have been clearer. After an excoriating assessment of the two leading Brexiteers, the paper which had endorsed the Leave side in the referendum campaign and employed Gove's wife Sarah Vine as a columnist said:

> In normal circumstances, this paper would hesitate to declare its hand before the closing stages of such a contest. But whatever these times may be, they are anything but normal. And among the five candidates vying to succeed David Cameron, the *Mail* believes only Mrs May has the right qualities, the stature and experience to unite both her party and the country – and possibly usher in a new, cleaner, more honest kind of politics.[403]

Charlie Elphicke says that, unlike her previous attempt to run for the leadership, in 2005, the time was now right for May.

> What changed was simply the dynamic of the leadership contest … The circumstances meant that there needed to be a strong, proven, experienced, tested leader of the party who had the skills to take us out of the European Union and deliver what the British people had voted for. I think many people [thought] that it would end up being a contest between Theresa May and Boris Johnson. No one expected quite the intervention Michael Gove came up with.

The day after Johnson's departure from the race, and with the May camp claiming nearly 100 MP supporters including the Cabinet ministers Amber Rudd, Justine Greening, Michael Fallon and

Patrick McLoughlin, her rivals Michael Gove and Andrea Leadsom both deployed their trump card against her: the fact that she had sided with the losing Remain campaign in the referendum. It was May's weak spot, but in the rush to support her amid the rubble of Johnson's campaign, it appeared to gain little traction. By 3 July, 60 per cent of Tory members polled by ICM for the *Sun on Sunday* said they were backing her, more than were supporting all her four rivals put together.[404] That day, the *Mail on Sunday* followed its daily sister paper in endorsing May. Boris Johnson, however, now announced that he was backing Andrea Leadsom. In a statement on his Facebook page, he suggested his fellow Brexiteer had 'the zap, the drive, and the determination essential for the next leader of the country'.

The first hustings of the campaign were held on 5 July, in an event behind closed doors for Tory MPs. It was Leadsom who made headlines, of the negative kind. She was said to have left her colleagues baffled by discussing at length the narrow topic of early years education, part of her self-described agenda of 'bankers, Brussels and babies'. By the end of the day, May had picked up the public endorsement of 122 MPs, guaranteeing she would make it into the contest's final round (barring any unexpected calamities). The question was who would join her; the man whom one MP had dubbed Judas Iscariot, or the woman whose pitch to MPs had been described as 'a cup of cold sick'.[405]

When the first ballot was held the next day, 6 July, it appeared the answer was that Tory MPs preferred incoherence to treachery. While May easily topped the poll, winning exactly half of MPs' votes, 165, an impressive victory in a five-horse race, it was Leadsom rather than Gove who came second, with sixty-six votes to his forty-eight. Liam Fox was the contest's loser, and was automatically disqualified. Stephen Crabb, who came fourth with thirty-four votes, decided to drop out of the race. He endorsed May.

Fox, too, was swift to throw his support behind May. He says:

People said: 'Oh, you're a Leaver, how could you support Theresa who's a Remainer?' It's simply because I [thought] she was the

THERESA MAY

best and most rounded candidate to be Prime Minister. It's not like you're choosing a leader in opposition, where you've got time to learn and play yourself into the job, nor could it be about just Leaving and Remaining; that question had been solved … I deliberately went into the leadership contest to get to the hustings to make the point that you've got to have someone with experience. So when I pulled out of the contest, the most natural thing in the world for me was to now go with the most experienced candidate who was there. I didn't see it as a left/right question, I didn't see it as a Remain/Leave question, I saw it as purely 'Who's the most qualified person to do the job?'

With May way out in front, the battle between Gove and Leadsom to finish second and win passage through to the next round began in earnest. While Gove struggled to shake the stench of betrayal that clung to him over the Boris Johnson affair, Leadsom found herself under the kind of scrutiny she had not experienced before, having never served in Cabinet. She was accused of exaggerating her CV about her work at a major investment firm, leading to a series of excruciating interviews as she attempted to explain her role. Gove's team began a final push to take Leadsom out of the race. His campaign manager Nick Boles sent a text message to May's supporters urging them to vote tactically and support Gove in the next ballot, arguing that it would be dangerous to allow the untested Leadsom into the membership phase of the contest.[406] It was a desperate eleventh-hour gamble that went nowhere. In the final MPs' vote on 7 July, Gove received just forty-six votes, two fewer than in the previous round. With May polling 199 and Leadsom eighty-four, Gove was comprehensively knocked out of the competition. For the first time in history, the final contest for the right to become Britain's Prime Minister would come down to two women: Andrea Leadsom and Theresa May.

While May's margin of victory had been impressive, her team was still concerned about the unpredictable nature of a two-month-long contest. Charlie Elphicke says:

You never want to count your chickens in politics. There still were a strong number of people who thought that the party ought to be led by a Leaver. There was a view that if it couldn't be Michael Gove because of the way he had behaved, then Andrea Leadsom had been a Leaver.

Andrew Griffiths, who was also working on May's campaign, adds: 'Theresa … never takes anything for granted, she never gets over-cocky. In political campaigns it's quite easy to run away with yourself. Theresa is always a level head. So she wasn't confident until she got the call to say: "You're leader of the Conservative Party."'

Eric Pickles says: 'The party was in a weird mood … At no time did I think she had it in the bag … If she did, she's too much of a pro to have shown it. She was very calm and very relaxed.' Pickles now swooped into action, laying down preparations for a ground war at constituency level. They were plans he never had to implement. He says: 'I said I would do it [organise in constituencies] on the Friday, spent the weekend getting things together, was going to meet with Stephen [Parkinson] to talk it through properly, and it wasn't necessary. Blink of an eye and it was over.' What brought Pickles's plans – and the leadership campaign – to a juddering halt was an own goal by May's opponent that rivalled even Gove's knifing of Boris Johnson.

Andrea Leadsom had been enjoying the leadership campaign. Just six months earlier, she had been a relatively obscure minister of middling rank, serving in the unglamorous Department of Energy and Climate Change. Having entered Parliament at the 2010 general election (ahead of which she had been helped by Women2Win and mentored by Theresa May), she had long felt disgruntled that other members of her intake, including Nicky Morgan, Amber Rudd and Sajid Javid, had overtaken her in getting to the Cabinet. She blamed George Osborne for her lack of promotion to the highest level, having embarrassed the Chancellor while serving on the Treasury Select Committee soon after she entered Parliament by suggesting he owed his Labour opposite number, Ed Balls, an apology for blaming him for a financial scandal.

The 2016 EU referendum had given Leadsom a taste of the limelight she craved. A fervent Eurosceptic, she played an active role in the campaign, representing the Leave side during one of the set-piece televised debates. She was seen as having performed well, and emerged from the victorious campaign with her star in the ascendant. The unexpected mutually assured destruction of the two senior Tory Brexiteers, Michael Gove and Boris Johnson, had given Leadsom an opportunity to rise further still. Suddenly, amid the whirlwind and drama of the days following the referendum, she had emerged as one of the two remaining candidates in the Conservative leadership contest. And while May was the clear favourite going into the final round, there were eight long weeks remaining to persuade the Tory membership of the wisdom of electing someone from the Leave side to steer the country through the difficult process of Brexit.

So it was a happy Andrea Leadsom who sat down with *The Times*'s Rachel Sylvester on Friday 8 July for what would be one of her first ever in-depth personal interviews. The softly spoken Sylvester is known as one of the best in the business at interviewing politicians, a master at creating an atmosphere relaxed enough to entice her subjects into spilling their secrets. As Leadsom would soon find out, there was a reason Theresa May had so long been wary of these kinds of apparently friendly yet deeply loaded encounters. In the face of the blunder that Leadsom would now be lulled into by Sylvester's seemingly innocuous questioning, May's tendency to roll out her 'safe' topics for discussion – shoes, cookbooks and walking holidays – suddenly seemed rather brilliant.

The Times hit the newsstands just after 10 p.m. on Friday evening. Its front page focused on one key passage from the Leadsom interview. Under the headline 'Being a mother gives me edge on May', Leadsom was quoted as saying that she would make a better Prime Minister because, unlike her rival, as a mother she had a 'stake' in the future of the country. In the most damaging words of all, she appeared to express pity for May, saying: 'I am sure Theresa will be really sad she doesn't have children.'[407] Inside, the full interview set out her remarks in more detail:

I don't want this to be 'Andrea has children, Theresa hasn't' because I think that would be really horrible, but genuinely I feel
that being a mum means you have a very real stake in the future
of our country, a tangible stake. She possibly has nieces, nephews,
lots of people, but I have children who are going to have children
who will directly be a part of what happens next.

Leadsom went on to suggest that mothers were imbued with a
greater empathy than those who do not have offspring, because:
'you are thinking about the issues that other people have: you
worry about your kids' exam results, what direction their careers
are taking, what we are going to eat on Sunday'.[408]

As the immediate reaction to Leadsom's words would prove, the
world had changed from the days when May's childlessness could
have been viewed as a negative; the suggestion that it was a factor in
her fitness for office brought a shower of opprobrium down on her
opponent's head. When Leadsom saw with horror the response on
social media to her interview, she backtracked furiously, first claiming she had been misquoted and then that her remarks had been
taken out of context. When Sylvester released the transcript of the
interview, showing that the write-up was a faithful representation of
what had been said, it was clear Leadsom was in trouble.

The response from senior Tories MPs as much as from the
public was immediate and angry. Alan Duncan, May's friend from
Oxford, tweeted: 'I'm gay and in a civil partnership. No children,
but ten nieces and nephews. Do I not have a stake in the future of
the country? Vile.' In another tweet, Anna Soubry said: 'Today's
@thetimes interview shows #AndreaLeadsom is not PM material.
She should do us all a favour including herself and step aside…' Ruth
Davidson, the leader of the Scottish Tories, said: 'I am childless. I
have nieces and nephews. I believe I – like everybody else – have a
very real stake in our country.' While May maintained a dignified silence, Eric Pickles was among those prepared to call out Leadsom on
her behalf. He says: 'I did one or two things on telly because I just saw
the red mist form. I quite like Andrea but it was … beyond the pale.'

Coming on top of the attention she had received over her CV, Leadsom found the negative coverage unnerving and unpleasant. On Saturday morning, she texted May to apologise, then got on the phone to another journalist to make her contrition known more widely. 'Having children has no bearing on the ability to be PM. I deeply regret that anyone has got the impression that I think otherwise,' she said. Her voice betraying that she had been weeping, Leadsom added that she felt 'under attack, under enormous pressure', saying: 'It has been shattering.'[409] With May so far in the lead and her own campaign apparently dead in the water, Leadsom spent the rest of the weekend discussing with her family whether she should withdraw from the contest. By Sunday night, her mind was made up.

After her family and campaign team, the first person Leadsom informed that she was withdrawing from the contest, on the morning of Monday 11 July 2016, was Theresa May. Britain's second female Prime Minister therefore found out that she was on the brink of becoming leader of her party and country while waiting in a green room at a wedding venue and conference centre in Birmingham, where she was due to launch her campaign. Her friend Liam Fox takes up the story:

> I was with Theresa when Andrea Leadsom put in her call to say that she was pulling out. There were only three of us there: myself and Philip and Theresa. I'd agreed to do what was going to be the first of a number of campaign stops where I was going to do the warm-up for Theresa's [speeches]. This was the first one. I think it was Fiona [Hill] who came in and said, 'Andrea Leadsom would like to speak to you on the phone.' [I] sort of glanced around the room, and Philip and I looked at each other, and Theresa said: 'Would you mind if I take the phone?' So Philip and I waited outside. And, naturally, there was only one reason why she would call – and that's because she was going to pull out.
>
> So we went back into the room. Theresa, unblinking, says nothing. [We] go on with [working on] the speech. Of course,

by this time she knows Andrea's pulling out. We go on and do the [event], I do the warm-up, she delivers her speech, as though there's still a contest going on. Because she had promised Andrea she wouldn't say [anything] to anybody until she had made her announcement at twelve o'clock. And Theresa's speech was at eleven o'clock. And she went through with it, not even blinking. Of course, we guessed. And afterwards, when Andrea made her announcement, Theresa said, 'I'm really sorry, but I promised her that I wouldn't mention it to anybody at all until she'd made her announcement.'

Having given her word to Andrea Leadsom, Theresa May had kept the secret of her imminent appointment as Prime Minister even from her husband. They must have been the longest ninety minutes she had ever lived through. Liam Fox goes on:

The most important moment of her whole life, she was still willing to put the assurance she'd given about confidentiality before absolutely anything else. I thought, 'How instructive was that?' And I also thought, 'What a performance.' Because she was taking [questions] from the press about 'If you become Prime Minister…' knowing that the next day she *was* going to be Prime Minister. For me, that spoke volumes about integrity. If you can be that controlled, if you can maintain that confidentiality, at a time when, goodness knows, your first reaction would be to say, 'Oh my God, I've done it' … to [instead] say, 'No, I've given my word and I'll stick to it', it was a very interesting moment.

When the news finally broke at around 11.30 a.m., with rumours of what Leadsom would say at the press conference she had called for noon beginning to circulate on Twitter, May still did not see it as a time for celebration. Fox says:

She was calm. I gave her a big hug and said how pleased I was for her. She was going to say something [to the waiting media]

and I said, 'I think you should go back to London. What you say
… next, will probably be the most important thing you've ever
said, and you need to think about the words that you say.' The
next time I saw Theresa was when she was appointing me to
the Cabinet.

The events of the next few hours passed with breathtaking speed.
Driving back to London from Birmingham, May must have been
glad of the opportunity to pause and consider what she wanted to
say as she entered a new phase of her life; one which would catapult
her onto the global stage, fulfilling all the ambitions she had had for
herself as a young girl. In rapid succession, the other actors in the
drama now played out their final scenes. Andrea Leadsom gave a
press conference confirming her withdrawal from the race, saying it
was in the 'best interests' of the country for May to become Prime
Minister immediately, rather than dragging the contest out. For
some members of May's campaign team, it was the first they heard
of the news. Charlie Elphicke was in the team's headquarters, close
to the House of Commons in Greycoat Street, when Leadsom's
press conference was broadcast live on television. He says: 'There
was a level of astonishment. I don't think anyone expected this to
turn out like that. I knew it was a historic moment. There [May]
is in Birmingham, then Andrea Leadsom withdraws from the race
and she's Prime Minister-designate.'

Graham Brady, chairman of the 1922 Committee, announced
that May would formally be anointed leader. The markets immediately jumped from their post-referendum slump. On her return to
Westminster, May met briefly with David Cameron to discuss the
timetable for their handover. Now that the contest had been cut
well short of its original end date of 9 September, they agreed he
would hold one last Cabinet meeting the next day before going to
see the Queen to renounce the offices of state. On Wednesday 13
July, Cameron came out of No. 10 to tell the waiting world of the
plan. As he went back inside Downing Street, the still-live microphone on his lapel caught him humming a little tune to himself.

At 5 p.m., May met with MPs at the 1922 Committee, where she was formally declared Leader of the Conservative Party. Having watched so many leadership contests from the side-lines in her long years in Parliament, her victory must have been sweet. At 5.35 p.m. she made her way outside, standing in front of St Stephen's Entrance to the House of Commons to deliver her first address as Tory leader and Prime Minister-in-waiting. Under the white clouds of a typically chilly British summer, while a crowd of more than 100 enthusiastic Tory MPs jostled for position as they attempted to get into the television shots on the evening news and appear in the newspaper images which would become history, May said she was 'honoured and humbled' by her new role, before restating that she would deliver on the country's demand for Brexit. She and Philip next went to Greycoat Street, where a small celebration was held. May gave a speech expressing her gratitude to all those who had worked on her short campaign. Some of those present noted, how-ever, that the new leader omitted to thank them personally for their work. As the party drew to a close, May resisted the temptation to keep the celebrations going. Instead, with the characteristic commitment to duty which the vicar's daughter has displayed throughout her life, the Prime Minister-elect returned to the House of Commons to take part in a series of late-night votes.

Her team was left to reflect on the extraordinary series of events of the previous sixteen days. Andrew Griffiths says: 'It was a re-markable period of time. I don't think we'll live through a time of such turbulence again … The Conservative Party, within two weeks, was able to go through all those machinations whilst the Labour Party [was] still ripping [itself] apart.' Liam Fox was confi-dent that the right person had come through the brief and brutal contest. He says:

What's interesting is that, in an era where everything is obsessive about image, looks, celebrity, the person who got to No. 10 was the oldest candidate, who was the one with the experience, the non-flashy, hard-working achiever, and not the ones who were getting coaching about how they should stand during conference speeches.

The world's newspapers made satisfying reading for May the next morning as she prepared for her last Cabinet meeting as Home Secretary. Her fellow world leaders greeted the prospect of a Prime Minister May with warmth. US President Barack Obama said the US–UK relationship could 'advance' under her leadership, while Russian President Vladimir Putin said he looked forward to a 'constructive dialogue' with May. Many of the foreign newspapers, as their British counterparts had been accustomed to do in the past, focused on the new leader's shoes. Spain's *El Mundo* highlighted her 'high heels, firm step, absolute control, total loyalty', Italy's *Corriere della Sera* remarked on May's 'stiletto heels', while Germany's *Bild* also referenced her famous leopard prints. At Cabinet, David Cameron was said to be close to tears, his farewell address interrupted four times by his ministers banging on the table as he said goodbye and wished them well for the future. Leading the tributes, May told him he was viewed with 'warmth and respect' by all those present.

May has said that it was only when she met the Queen to be confirmed as the new Prime Minister of Great Britain and Northern Ireland on 13 July 2016 that the full magnitude of her position fully sunk in. The transition between one ruler and the next is always a carefully choreographed affair. That between David Cameron and Theresa May was no different, as, accompanied by his young family, the outgoing leader was driven to Buckingham Palace to formally resign and advise the monarch to invite May to form a new administration. After his private meeting with the Queen, Cameron's wife, Samantha, and three children, Nancy, Elwen and Florence, were invited into the room to say their farewells. They were ushered out of Buckingham Palace at 5.25 p.m. A few minutes later, Theresa and Philip May entered the Palace.

Photographs of the historic meeting between the monarch and the new Conservative leader show both women beaming as, shortly before 5.30 p.m., the Queen formally invited May to become the thirteenth Prime Minister to serve her, only the second woman to occupy the role. What else was said between the two remains secret. As they spoke, Buckingham Palace issued a statement: 'The Queen received in audience the Right Honourable Theresa May MP this evening and requested her to form a new administration. The Right Honourable Theresa May accepted Her Majesty's offer and kissed hands upon her appointment as Prime Minister and First Lord of the Treasury.' (In reality, the 'kissing hands' referred to in the statement was likely to have amounted to a handshake.) After thirty-four minutes, Philip May was invited to join the pair for a brief chat, before the couple returned by car to Downing Street.

There, on the steps of No. 10, wearing a navy dress by Amanda Wakeley and matching coat with a striking yellow band – and, of course, those leopard print kitten heels – Theresa May addressed the country for the first time as Prime Minister. She said: 'The government I lead will be driven not by the interests of the privileged few but by yours. We will do everything we can to give you more control over your lives. When we take the big calls, we will think not of the powerful, but you.' It was a pledge to serve from a woman who learned a devotion to duty from birth.

CHAPTER XIX

PRIME MINISTER

The first items that caught Theresa and Philip May's eyes as they entered the private flat above 10 Downing Street to survey their new home on the evening she became Prime Minister were two expensive bottles of wine left by David Cameron and his wife Samantha, and a colourful banner reading 'Welcome', drawn by the couple's children. The gifts were a reminder of the golden family who were being turfed out as a result of the change of regime (although in fact the speed with which the Tory leadership contest had taken place meant the Mays were ultimately forced to give their predecessors another ten days to fully move out). Despite the cordiality, from her first minutes inside No. 10, May made clear her determination to put as much distance as possible between her new administration and the old one dominated by Cameron's gilded circle. It is an approach she has continued through her early premiership, breaking with her predecessor's personnel, policies and ethos to such an extent that within two months an appalled Cameron had quit Parliament in disgust. Just after 6 p.m. on Wednesday 13 July 2016, May sat down at her new desk inside Downing Street and began the process of driving out all traces of the Cameroons from No. 10. First on her list was appointing a Cabinet in her name. And she began her purge with her old foe George Osborne.

Returning downstairs, still less than half an hour after entering Downing Street for the first time as Prime Minister, May sent for the Chancellor. Osborne made his way through the passageway connecting Nos 10 and 11 Downing Street. It was a stroll he had taken thousands of times in the past, having made a habit of popping in and out of Cameron's office during their six years in power. He had never before been so unsure of the reception he would receive at the other end. While Osborne was of course aware of the disagreements between himself and the then Home Secretary over the six years they had served together in government, the most recent arising over what he felt had been her low profile during the referendum campaign, in his view their clashes were not personal, and he had little sense of the strong antipathy she bore him. While he was taking nothing for granted, as he walked through the passageway from No. 11 he was optimistic that May was about to offer him a senior role in her new government. One Osborne ally says:

> Going into the conversation, he knew she might or she might not offer him a job. He definitely was angling to stay on. He wanted the Foreign Office. There was some speculation that he could even stay on at the Treasury. He would have done that. He did feel some responsibility to help out given the way things had turned out. Contrary to speculation, there had been contingency planning, and he would have liked to have made sure it worked. So he definitely would have stayed on.

Instead, in a conversation which lasted no more than ten minutes, May made clear there would be no room for Osborne around her Cabinet table. The exact nature of what was said between the two is disputed. Osborne has told friends that the tone of the conversation was 'cordial', and has confirmed that he did not resign but was dismissed, but beyond that he does not recognise the briefing put out – almost certainly by May's advisers – that he was subjected to a severe dressing-down. The other version of events is far more colourful. May is said to have told Osborne that he had overpromised and under-delivered on the economy. She even gave him a little advice should he wish to seek the highest office at some time in the – distant – future: to show more humility. Whatever took place between May and Osborne, the fact that the new Prime Minister allowed such stories to gain widespread currency is testament to the resentment she had felt towards him for many years. Over the next few months, May would set about undoing many of Osborne's prized policies, such as the concept of a 'Northern Powerhouse' of development and even his fiscal target of achieving a surplus by the end of the parliament in 2020. It was an overt rejection of the man who, perhaps more than anyone else in government, had made her feel excluded from the inner circle.

With Osborne sent packing, May now made her first formal appointment to her new Cabinet, naming her friend Philip Hammond as her Chancellor at 6.58 p.m. It was a move which had widely been anticipated; May's next step was far more unexpected. Just after 7 p.m., a familiar tousle-headed blond figure wandered sheepishly up Downing Street, to the delight of the waiting television cameras. Johnson's arrival so early in the reshuffle process, when the most senior appointments are usually made, was a surprise. Following the knifing he had suffered at the hands of Michael Gove two weeks earlier, Johnson had become a somewhat diminished figure, and he and May had never been close; he had not been anticipating a promotion – and nor had anyone else. When he entered the Cabinet Room and found out what May had in store for him, he was astounded.

May now informed Johnson that she was appointing him as her Foreign Secretary, one of the most prestigious jobs in government. Having long enjoyed national treasure status, Johnson's occasional lapses into clownishness made him a strange fit for a role marked by its dignity. No. 10 made clear, however, that May considered Johnson's showman status a positive virtue in the task of selling Brexit to the world. To help him in this enormous undertaking, May told Johnson, she was creating two new senior Cabinet positions: a Secretary of State for Brexit, which she gave to the former shadow Home Secretary David Davis, and a Secretary of State for International Trade, the first holder of which would be her friend Liam Fox. Davis's Brexit ministry was established at the heart of government, 9 Downing Street, while Fox moved into the Foreign Office alongside Johnson. Fox says of the new arrangements:

> Theresa's judgement on this has been terrific. I actually had wanted to have a department of foreign trade affairs, like they have in a lot of other countries. But Theresa took a judgement that we should separate it out so there was a very distinct trade department, and actually I think she made the right call on that.

By appointing a triumvirate of Brexiteers to oversee Britain's departure from the European Union, May had protected herself against accusations that, as a former Remain campaigner, she would not be wholehearted in overseeing withdrawal. As commentators were quick to point out, she also had some insurance in case the process went badly; those responsible for securing a Leave vote in the referendum were now charged with clearing up the mess. More immediately, by giving three of the leading Conservative Brexiteers senior jobs in her Cabinet, there was no need to find space for the fourth: Michael Gove. The next scalp May claimed would perhaps be the one she enjoyed most, but she would have to wait. Having begun the process of drawing up her new government, she was forced to break off for the evening to attend a function in honour of the police, her first as Prime Minister and perhaps an ironic one given the verbal battery she had dealt out to the Police Federation two years earlier.

The ruthlessness with which May dispatched foes and appointed friends to her Cabinet has been compared to Harold Macmillan's 'night of the long knives'. In fact, it was even more brutal than the dramatic events of 1962. Of the twenty-two Cabinet ministers who assembled for David Cameron's final meeting as Prime Minister on 12 July 2016, only thirteen remained at May's first a week later. Nine were sacked or stood down voluntarily, with most of those in the latter category doing so because they were offered demotions (in contrast, Macmillan got rid of only seven Cabinet ministers). Just four ministers remained in the posts they had held under Cameron.

It was a stunningly ruthless display of prime ministerial power on May's first full day in the job.

After George Osborne, Michael Gove, the Justice Secretary, was the next to be given his marching orders. Unlike Osborne, he was not hopeful of being given a job in the new government. Gove was waiting at the Ministry of Justice when he received the call from No. 10 at 9.50 a.m. on Thursday 14 July asking him to go to May's new office in the House of Commons. Their meeting lasted only two minutes. 'There is not going to be room for you,' May is said to have informed Gove, making clear to him that his sacking was a direct consequence of the way he had treated Boris Johnson. 'I have been talking to colleagues and the importance of loyalty is something on people's minds. I'm not saying there is no way back or that you'll never serve in my government, but it would perhaps help if you could demonstrate that loyalty from the back benches.'[410] May did not mention Gove's role in the departure of Fiona Hill two years previously, nor the many times he had embarrassed her at Cabinet, but they must have been uppermost in her mind. Gove did not argue. 'Thank you very much, Prime Minister,' he said simply.[411] Having arrived at the Commons in his ministerial Jaguar, Gove was forced to hire a private car to travel to Buckingham Palace; as Lord Chancellor (a role which often accompanies that of Justice Secretary), he had been Keeper of the Great Seal, the stamp attached to state documents indicating that the monarch has given her consent. Now the Great Seal had to be returned.

By lunchtime, May had also dispatched John Whittingdale as Culture Secretary, Oliver Letwin, the Cabinet Office Minister, and Nicky Morgan, Education Secretary, the latter two almost certainly because of their association with David Cameron and George Osborne. On leaving May's Commons office, Whittingdale headed off with his former aides to find a pub. 'We are going to get drunk,' he declared.[412] Morgan has said that while she 'knew it was coming', when it came to deliver the blow, the new Prime Minister struggled: 'I had to help her utter the phrase – so you'd like to "let me go"?'[413] Morgan would become a leading critic of May's government, but would come to regret her remarks about the new Prime Minister's leather trousers, in November 2016, which led to accusations of sexism. An infuriated Fiona Hill retaliated by barring Morgan from No. 10.

Stephen Crabb, the Work and Pensions Secretary who had run against May for the leadership, was the next to depart the Cabinet. He was offered another post on the condition that he think hard whether he wanted it in the wake of newspaper revelations that the married father of two had exchanged messages of a sexual nature with a young woman. On reflection, Crabb decided he would be wiser to spend more time with his wife and children. Ed Vaizey, the Culture Minister and a close friend of David Cameron, was sacked by telephone as he drove to his constituency, having served in the post for six years. Theresa Villiers, the Northern Ireland Secretary, was offered a role outside the Cabinet and declined.

Many MPs were shocked at May's merciless treatment of her former colleagues, particularly that of George Osborne. Keith Simpson says:

> It was disrespectful. Whatever George had done to her, I'd like to think that what I would have done is said: 'I'm sorry, George, you did a very good job and who knows about the future.' And I would have put that out in a statement. I am told that another minister, a Cameroon, was sacked in a forty-second telephone call.

Andrew Lansley feels more sympathy for May's less high-profile victims:

> In the circumstances when she took over, and she thought Gove had behaved badly with her and now had behaved badly again, it is not surprising she left him out of her government. I was surprised, though, at how brutal her gutting was. Osborne was less of a surprise, but some people, like Nicky Morgan or Ed Vaizey, was rather brutal.

William Hague is diplomatic about May's ruthless reshuffle, however, saying: 'It's up to the Prime Minister. She was obviously determined to show that a new start was being made, that it was basically a new government. And that requires quite a big change, so that's understandable, I think.'

The hiring and firing continued over the next few days. Perhaps of as much importance to May as many of her Cabinet appointees, her new line-up of No. 10 advisers was confirmed, with Nick Timothy and Fiona Hill appointed joint chiefs of staff and Katie Perrior made head of communications. Former Home Office advisers Joanna Penn, Stephen Parkinson, Chris Wilkins and Alex Dawson also joined the team. Then it was back to the ministerial appointments. Amber Rudd was given May's old job of Home Secretary, while two of May's favoured ministers from her own time at the Home Office, Karen Bradley and James Brokenshire, were rewarded with Cabinet posts at the Department for Culture and the Northern Ireland Office respectively. Other newcomers included the prominent Brexiteer Priti Patel as International Development Secretary and Gavin Williamson, whose reward for running May's leadership campaign was the post of Chief Whip. In a rare sign of magnanimity, Andrea Leadsom was invited to become Environment Secretary.

The new Cabinet contained the greatest number of state school-educated members since the Second World War, and eight women, amounting to 30 per cent of the total, equalling the record set by Tony Blair's final Cabinet in 2007. All the women in the Cabinet bar May and Baroness Evans, the new Leader of the Lords, had been helped to enter Parliament by Women2Win. Andrew Griffiths says of the radical changes May made in appointing her top team: 'What is clear from her first Cabinet is she sat around the Cabinet table for a long time sizing up her colleagues and working out who she thought were good and who she would not give house room to.' William Hague agrees: 'I think the dismissal of a lot of ministers when she came to office is truth of her style. "I've got my own view about X, Mr A, Mrs B, this is for me to sort this out, nobody else is making this decision." That's what she's like.'

Others believe May could have stored up trouble for herself, as the Cultural Revolution taking place inside No. 10 continued beyond the Cabinet. Ministers who were expecting to remain in post or even receive promotion found instead that their heads were for the chop. Among the departures in the following two days were Anna Soubry, the Business Minister; Dominic Raab, an ally of Michael Gove; and James Duddridge, a Foreign Office minister. After departing his post, another Foreign Office minister, Hugo Swire, sent a tweet reading: 'Not a good time to be a Cameroon. The tumbrils are rolling again!' – a reference to the carts that carried condemned aristocrats to the guillotine during the French Revolution.

Several ambitious MPs who had served time as parliamentary aides or volunteered to help on May's leadership campaign were among those disgusted to find themselves overlooked. So angry was one group of parliamentary private secretaries (the most junior rung on the ministerial ladder) at being passed over for promotion that they were said to have 'flung' their government passes at the whip who broke the news.[414] May was forced to invite the group to tea at No. 10 to smooth their ruffled feathers. Some have blamed May's advisers, Nick Timothy and Fiona Hill, or, alternatively, Gavin Williamson for the resentment May's appointments to the middle and lower orders of her government created. As Chief Whip, Williamson was left to fill many of the more junior roles, a task some suggest he made a hash of. Charlie Elphicke confirms that he was one of those who received the bad news in a phone call from Williamson, rather than May herself. 'When she decided to return me to the back benches, Gavin Williamson was the one who called me up,' he says.

Timothy and Hill are also suspected by some of using the reshuffle to wreak petty revenges.

In the whirlwind of becoming Prime Minister, May also forgot to send MPs who worked on her campaign thank-you letters, a simple and customary courtesy. One of those disappointed by the omission says: 'Politicians all have massive egos, we are all neurotic, and emotional – and very human. It is easy to keep people sweet by the little gestures – the thank-yous, the phone calls, the notes. If you fail to do that then people can get offended very easily.'

A number of Tory MPs have raised concerns that the sheer number of former ministers who were dispatched to the back benches in May's reshuffle could come back to haunt her. She was, after all, a Prime Minister presiding over a government majority of just sixteen. Within months, the number would fall to fourteen, as Zac Goldsmith, the unsuccessful Conservative mayoral candidate, fought and lost a by-election over his opposition to the expansion of Heathrow Airport. Keith Simpson says: 'She's sacked so many people, I laughingly said: "There are more ex-ministers as back-benchers than genuine backbenchers."' Another MP adds:

> There are some big players on the back benches now, the likes of Gove and Osborne. They're not going to bother to turn up to every vote. With a majority of sixteen [*sic*], that will cause prob-lems. At the moment the Labour Party is in chaos, but there are issues where they will agree on, and will organise to vote against us. May won because of a perfect storm of a leadership election. There is no base, there is no 'May faction' in the way Osborne or Boris have a following. When things get difficult, there will not be enough loyalists to protect her.

As the disaffected MP points out, however, May's precarious posi-tion is masked by the near-implosion of both the Labour Party and UKIP (the Liberal Democrats having already been reduced to mar-ginal status at the general election of 2015). Two months after May became Prime Minister, Jeremy Corbyn was re-elected as Labour leader in the face of opposition from most of his parliamentary party. Nigel Farage, meanwhile, returned temporarily to the leader-ship of UKIP when his successor, Diane James, quit after only eighteen days in the job in October. A second contest descended into farce, with the favourite, Steven Woolfe, getting into a violent altercation with a fellow UKIP MEP at the European Parliament in Brussels, apparently over admiration he had expressed for Theresa

May. It remains to be seen whether the new leader, Paul Nuttall, who was finally elected at the end of November 2016, will prove able to move the party forward.

For now, with no real opposition either inside or outside her party, May's honeymoon has proved a lengthy one. In the first poll after she became leader, produced for *The Sun* by YouGov on 20 July, the Tory lead over Labour was put at eleven points. After her first six months in office, in January 2017, YouGov put the party's lead at seventeen, with the government enjoying the Conservatives' longest 'honeymoon' since the 1950s. May's lead over Corbyn as the leader voters most want as Prime Minister is even more impressive.

May's bumper opinion poll ratings in office have led many of her Tory supporters to urge her to call an early general election. They point out that despite the substantial challenges she has faced, particularly the government's apparent failure to coherently identify how Britain's departure from the EU will play out, none of her difficulties have shaken her personal popularity. The public appears to like Prime Minister May, and seems content to leave her in place. It is characteristic of May, however, that, having pledged at the outset of her leadership not to hold an election before the end of the current term in 2020, she is determined to keep her promise. Many believe her implacable opposition flies in the face of her own self-interest. If she did call an early election, she would undoubtedly win by a landslide. But, to the frustration of many in her party, she sees the prospect of an election as a distraction from the task at hand – primarily Brexit. It is a move which in her eyes might be good for the Conservative Party but would not necessarily benefit the country.

So instead of planning an early election in her first days after becoming Prime Minister, May, as usual, got on with the job. In the hours after appointing her Cabinet on 14 July, her next step was to telephone the European partners who, during the course of her premiership, she intended would no longer be so. The first world leader she spoke to was German Chancellor Angela Merkel, followed by French President François Hollande and Irish Taoiseach

Enda Kenny. She made clear to all three that she would need time to prepare for Brexit, prompting a now familiar call from Europe, and soon Westminster, for more clarity about both the timing and the manner of Britain's departure from the EU.

The next day, 15 July, May made her first prime ministerial visit, to Scotland, to meet First Minister Nicola Sturgeon of the Scottish Nationalist Party. During her time as Home Secretary, in the years running up to and following the 2014 referendum on Scottish independence, May had made a number of speeches expressing her belief that Scotland's security depended on remaining part of the UK. It was a point she reiterated in her Downing Street address on becoming Prime Minister. But, unlike most of the rest of Britain, Scotland had voted to remain part of the EU. Now May was confronted with calls from Sturgeon and others for Scotland's dissenting Remain vote to be recognised. Within months, the SNP would be arguing that Scotland should either be allowed to retain separate membership of the EU or be granted a second independence vote. But for now the visit was cordial. After their meeting, Sturgeon tweeted a photograph of herself with May, saying: 'Politics aside – I hope girls everywhere look at this photograph and believe nothing should be off limits for them.'

Later that night, May was forced to call her first Cobra meeting as Prime Minister, to be briefed on the Bastille Day terrorist attack in Nice, France, in which eighty-nine people were killed by an Islamic extremist driving a truck. The following day, the extent to which foreign affairs would occupy her time as premier was underlined as she was again required to break off from her work to respond to an international emergency, this time a failed coup d'état in Turkey. Away from the high drama unfolding overseas, it must have been with some relief that the Mays returned to Sonning that weekend, where, on Sunday 17 July, they attended church services as usual at St Andrew's Church.

May's first Cabinet meeting as Prime Minister was held on Tuesday 19 July. With Britain experiencing a mini-heatwave, she invited the men present to remove their jackets. In words which had become almost a personal mantra, she told her new team to 'get to it and get on with the job', adding that 'politics is not a game'. She vowed that her government would not be defined by Brexit, insisting that as well as posing a challenge, leaving the EU presented a 'huge opportunity'. In this first meeting, those of her team who had previously sat around Cameron's Cabinet table noticed a big difference from what had gone before.

Liam Fox says:

> She's got a very steady but light touch. There's quite a good flow of ideas back and forth. It's becoming clear we're going to have a lot of meetings, because Theresa likes to thrash out everything and it then gets fleshed out in a very logical way. Her way of working means that discussions run until the discussion's finished, rather than, 'I've got an appointment in forty-five minutes.' That's such a refreshing way of doing business because there will be a genuine debate. She's not one who says: 'Well, this is what I think first. Does anyone dare to disagree with me?' Which is how Margaret Thatcher used to do things. It's very much: 'Here's the problem, what do we think?' And then she will sum up at the end.

During her short time leading a Cabinet as 'first among equals', May has had to face some big personalities and serious arguments. Often these have involved a fundamental clash of view between, on one side, Chancellor Philip Hammond and Greg Clark, the Business Secretary, who see their responsibility as protecting the economy, and, on the other, the 'three Brexiteers' of Boris Johnson, David Davis and Liam Fox, who are focused on ensuring the demands of those who voted to leave the EU are met. It is a circle that May has struggled to square. Her own instincts lie in the middle: she is a realist and a pragmatist, and alive to the warnings given by Hammond and the Treasury about the potential risk to the British economy of a 'hard' Brexit, which would involve Britain's withdrawal from the European single market. But perhaps more than any of the Remainers in government, before and since the referendum, she is also aware of the importance of delivering on the very clear instructions of the British public, delivered in an emphatic if narrow referendum result, to quit the EU. In this she remains true to her principle of keeping her word and serving the people's will. The test of her leadership will be how May manages to protect the economy while taking back control of Britain's borders and sovereignty. It is a problem that presents her greatest challenge.

But despite the in-built tension within her Cabinet, on the whole May's approach to dealing with ministers has been praised. While some have chafed at what they describe as the new team in No. 10's tendency to seek to control the entirety of government output, particularly when it comes to the media – at one point ministers were told they were required to clear all speeches and interviews in advance – her personal handling of Cabinet wins approval.

Cheryl Gillan compares May favourably to the Prime Minister she served under, David Cameron:

> She's going to have proper Cabinet government, whereas I always felt with her predecessor that it had all been decided elsewhere, possibly in the kitchen over a lasagne. That's not healthy. She's had the opportunity of sitting in Cabinet for many years and seeing a completely different style, which was basically dominated by two people in the front deck and several people in the row at the back. I think she will bring in everybody.

On Wednesday 20 July, May faced one of the biggest tests for any incoming premier: her first session of Prime Minister's Questions. She prepared in her Commons office with a small team of advisers, including Philip May, who then watched her first outing from the public gallery. As an experienced parliamentarian, May was well-used to the Commons Chamber, but those who have taken part in it say there is nothing to compare to the gladiatorial nature of PMQs. May was judged afterwards to have put in a solid performance against a wounded Jeremy Corbyn, at the time still facing a leadership challenge. She wished him well in the contest, saying she hoped to enjoy their exchanges for many years to come, a barbed compliment, implying as it did that Corbyn's unpopularity was a help to the Tories. The former Labour spin doctor Ayesha Hazarika described May's performance as 'brutally brilliant'.[415] After it was all over, May looked up at the ceiling and sighed with relief.

PMQs out of the way, May now set off for her first overseas visits as Prime Minister, to Germany and France. Alongside Angela Merkel, she joked with German reporters about football, before concluding of her new relationship with the Chancellor: 'We are two women who get on with the job.' In her press conference with François Hollande, she spoke serviceable French, before offering her condolences over the Nice attack. When it was his turn to speak, Hollande seemed to marvel at the speed of what had taken place in politics across the Channel, saying: 'A few weeks ago I was with David Cameron...' Behind closed doors, the serious talk in both Berlin and Paris was of Brexit.

The Scottish, German and French visits were the start of an exhausting timetable in which May clocked up 7,000 air miles in just two weeks, making seven official visits, meeting six foreign leaders and the three heads of the UK's devolved governments. The countries she visited included Poland, Italy and Slovakia. Before the end of the year, she would add China and India to the list.

But while much of her international travel in the months after she became Prime Minister focused on Brexit, May's time in office was initially characterised by an opacity over the government's plan – and, indeed, questions over whether there even was one – for Britain's departure from the EU, leading to frustration both at home and abroad. Although May consistently stated that Britain was on course to trigger Article 50 of the EU Treaty in March 2017, beginning a formal two-year process for the UK to leave the Union, in her early months she frequently came under fire for failing to set out whether she was seeking a 'hard' or 'soft' Brexit by defining whether or not she was proposing that Britain remain part of the single market.

In December 2016, with her favoured phrase of 'Brexit means

Brexit' beginning to attract derision, May suggested she was seeking a bespoke 'red, white and blue Brexit', tailored to Britain's particular position as a former member of the EU with a desire to continue a favourable trading relationship while retaining control of immigration. By the New Year, with a number of EU leaders expressing unwillingness to allow the UK to remain in the single market without permitting freedom of movement, May conceded that Britain could not expect to retain 'bits' of EU membership. In a major speech at Lancaster House in mid-January 2017 designed to answer the growing calls for clarity, she made explicit that Britain was on course for a 'hard' Brexit, warning that she was prepared to walk away from the negotiations altogether unless a positive outcome could be achieved.

'Let me be clear, what I am proposing cannot mean remaining in the single market,' she said. 'We seek a new and equal partnership – between an independent, self-governing, global Britain and our friends and allies in the EU. Not partial membership of the European Union, associate membership of the European Union, or anything that leaves us half in, half out.'

In her Lancaster House speech, May also suggested, for the first time, that Parliament would be given a vote on the Brexit deal, following months of arguing over her initial plan to use executive powers to trigger Article 50. In early November 2016, the government had lost a case at the High Court over its refusal to hold such a vote. The executives of both Scotland and Northern Ireland, which voted to remain in the EU, have also sought to join in the legal challenge, arguing that they too should be given a vote over Brexit.

Quitting the EU particularly complicates the position of Northern Ireland, remaining as it will a part of the United Kingdom while sharing a contiguous land border with the Republic of Ireland, which will continue to be a member of the EU. May and her new Northern Ireland Secretary, James Brokenshire, have yet to explain how such issues as customs controls and free movement will be handled in a region which has no desire to return to the checkpoints of its troubled past. The Prime Minister made her first visit to Belfast in her new role on 25 July 2016, where she met First Minister Arlene Foster, and Martin McGuinness, then Deputy First Minister. In January 2017, the Northern Ireland Assembly collapsed over a scandal in which Foster was accused of wasting money on an epic scale by mishandling an energy scheme, presenting yet another challenge for Brokenshire and May.

Back in mid-August 2016, the Mays returned to the Swiss Alps as usual, leaving Philip Hammond in charge of the country. With one poll now showing that an estimated 2.5 million voters who had supported Labour in the general election just over a year before pre-ferred May to Jeremy Corbyn as Prime Minister, she could afford to relax. Photographs released of the couple in their walking gear of Airtex T-shirts and comfortable slacks highlight how much images from prime ministerial vacations have come to serve as a metaphor for their entire style of rule. Tony Blair holidayed in flashy exotic sun traps, rubbing shoulders with millionaires and celebrities; Gordon Brown was so paranoid he could barely bring himself to take a break, his careful choices of staycation holiday cottages clearly picked by his spin doctors. David Cameron's chillaxed family breaks, whether in Cornwall or trendy European destinations such as Ibiza or the Algarve, spoke of a man who relished his down time.

May, in contrast, was all business even while ostensibly relaxing. Her energetic, unfashionable walking holiday with Philip saw her return to the same hotels she has visited for decades. Later in the month, she and Philip took a day off from work to watch England play Pakistan in the cricket at Lord's. There is no lying on a sun lounger for May; she likes her recreation time to have a purpose, even if it is just watching England racking up the runs. May's friend Anne Jenkin believes that the image she projects as a dependable work-aholic is an attractive one given the uncertain times: 'What people say they want is a conscientious, hard-working, sensible, diligent person. All the things that we know she is. Do we want an MP who's had a wild social life? We could have had Boris [Johnson], who's had a wild social life. She's a totally dedicated public servant.'

On her return to Westminster after the summer break, May

gathered her Cabinet at Chequers, the Prime Minister's official country retreat, to tell them of her determination to make a success of Brexit. 'That means there's no second referendum; no attempts to sort of stay in the EU by the back door; that we're actually going to deliver on this,' she said in a statement which was made public. It was by now clear that making a success of Brexit would – and will – largely depend on how successfully the government could negotiate new trade deals both with its former European partners and with those further afield. With that in mind, May headed off to her next major international challenge: her first meeting of the G20 group of industrialised nations, in Hangzhou, China. Journalists travelling with her on the ten-hour flight were struck by the figure she cut as she emerged from the plane. The *Telegraph*'s Stephen Swinford says:

> She wore red in China – we were very impressed. We'd all slept on the plane, were in the same clothes and looked terrible. She looked amazing. She came down the steps, and there everyone was waiting for her, and it was quite a moment, her first big foreign trip as Prime Minister. She looked at us all, and suddenly just threw up her hands and said: 'Well, I've never been to China before!' And it was just so refreshing and human. That was her response and she was just saying exactly what she felt at that moment.

Some of May's fellow leaders were less impressed by her, however. Her hosts, the Chinese, had particular cause to be wary. As one of her first acts on becoming Prime Minister in July, May had called a temporary halt to plans by a joint French and Chinese consortium to fund an £18 billion investment project in UK nuclear energy at the Hinkley Point nuclear power plant in Somerset. Many saw the hand of Nick Timothy in the pause; he had written in the past about the potential security risks in placing national infrastructure in the hands of overseas powers, including potential rivals such as the Chinese. Others suggested the delay was a feature of the caution with which May approaches all major decisions; she will not be rushed. William Hague says:

> I had to have a knowing smile when the Hinkley Point thing was postponed ... because she was like that as Home Secretary. The civil service might have decided there was a schedule for deciding something, but she would say: 'Well, no, I haven't decided yet, I need more information' ... She would remain in command of her own timetable.

Liam Fox suggests both Hinkley Point and the decision to build a third runway at Heathrow, which May put on hold for a few weeks before giving the go-ahead in late October, are examples of thoroughness rather than indecision. 'People will say she's indecisive; that's not true. She will not come to a snap decision. She likes to know the background and all the details.'

While the Hinkley Point project was eventually given the green light later in September, at the time of the G20 summit it was still very much up in the air, leading to diplomatic tensions between May and her hosts in Hangzhou. She also found her bid to tee up negotiations for new trade deals by portraying the UK as a global leader in a post-Brexit world somewhat problematic. Barack Obama, the US President, said bluntly in a press conference that a trade deal with the UK would not be a priority for America. Japan's Shinzo Abe delivered a similar message, going so far as to present May with a fifteen-page analysis of the – as Tokyo saw it – largely negative consequences of Brexit, with the threat that a number of major Japanese companies might now seek to quit the UK. (In mid-October, the Japanese car company Nissan announced its commitment to its giant manufacturing plant in Sunderland, after its bosses received assurances from May personally about the firm's future following Brexit. The good news was overshadowed by the government's refusal to elaborate on the nature of the promises made to Nissan, or whether other overseas firms would similarly benefit.) Other nations expressed more warmth towards May's attempts to forge trade relationships. Both Malcolm Turnbull, the Australian Prime Minister and her old friend from Oxford, and India's Narendra Modi left the door open to new trade deals. The summit also saw May's first meeting with Russian President Vladimir Putin; she urged him to do more to cease the bombing in Syria, but it was a message he chose to ignore.

Through the autumn of 2016, difficulties mounted on the home front as well as abroad, including a strike by junior doctors and turmoil surrounding the resignation of Dame Lowell Goddard as chairman of the inquiry into child sexual abuse. Yet still the Conservatives' substantial lead in the polls over Labour held up, and May's personal popularity over Jeremy Corbyn stretched even further. At the start of September, her rating according to Survation stood at +34 compared to –31 for the Labour leader, a gap of 65 points.[416]

The new government now decided to pick a fight of its own. In the first week of September, a civil servant fell victim to the oldest trick in the photographers' handbook when he was photographed in Downing Street clutching a memo on his way into a Cabinet meeting. Duly photographed and enlarged, the memo, signed by the most senior official at the Department for Education, suggested that Justine Greening, the new Education Secretary, was preparing to launch a consultation into the expansion of grammar schools. It swiftly became apparent that the memo was both genuine and reflected the Prime Minister's own wishes. May had almost certainly planned to put the grammar school consultation at the heart of her first Conservative conference as leader the following month. Creating more grammars had been a dream for many years, a fantasy that had seemed impossible under successive Tory leaders keen to prove their egalitarian outlook. It was a vision shared by Nick Timothy, one of her closest advisers. Now they were both in No. 10, the two former grammar school kids could begin to make it a reality.

But the suggestion that grammar school provision could be expanded proved fiercely controversial, not least on the government benches. Nicky Morgan, who had been sacked as Education Secretary six weeks earlier, led the charge against the proposal, posting a statement on Facebook declaring: 'I believe that an increase in pupil segregation on the basis of academic selection would be at best a distraction from crucial reforms to raise standards and narrow the attainment gap, and at worse risks actively undermining six years of progressive education reform.' Lord Willetts, the former Universities Minister, added that school places 'tend to be captured by the better-informed, more affluent parents' rather than poorer pupils.[417] Responding, May gave a speech at the British Academy in which she insisted that her proposed education reforms were based on the principle of expanding choice for parents. 'Politicians – many of whom benefited from the very kind of education they now seek to deny to others – have for years put their own dogma and ideology before the interests and concerns of ordinary people,' she said. 'There is nothing meritocratic about standing in the way of giving our most academically gifted children the specialist and tailored support that can enable them to fulfil their potential.' The consultation went ahead.

Almost immediately, David Cameron announced his departure from the Commons, overturning an earlier promise to remain as an MP until the election. Making clear his disenchantment with many of the decisions May had made, particularly over grammar schools, and the tone she had struck in repeatedly calling out the socially divided nature of the country he had presided over, Cameron did not have the appetite to remain any longer. 'The realities of modern politics make it very difficult to continue on the back benches without the risk of becoming a diversion,' he said. It was the death knell for the Notting Hill set.

With grammar schools out in the open and Cameron on his way out, May could concentrate on preparations for her first conference as leader. It was to be held in Birmingham, and began the day after her sixtieth birthday on 1 October. Her speech was designed to form the centrepiece of conference week. Nearly thirty years earlier, Margaret Thatcher had declared: 'There is no such thing as society.' May used her speech to utterly reject the philosophy of her only female predecessor, making clear that she saw great potential for an active, interventionist state. 'There is more to life than individualism and self-interest,' she said. She also announced a 'Great Repeal Bill' to untangle British law from EEC and EU legislation introduced since the 1972 European Communities Act.

In the most controversial passages of her speech, she accused the political classes of ignoring what she described as voters' understandable concerns about the impact of immigration on the jobs market and public services.

Not for the first or last time, May also used her speech to poke fun at Boris Johnson. She began by setting out the questions facing the new government: 'Do we have a plan for Brexit? We do. Are we ready for the effort it will take to see it through? We are.' With a dramatic pause for effect, she went on: 'Can Boris Johnson stay on message for a full four days? Just about.' May was crueller still in a speech made as she collected *The Spectator*'s Politician of the Year award a month later. When Johnson, accepting an award for the comeback of the year, joked that he felt like Lord Heseltine's dog – who, somewhat bizarrely, the peer had that week been forced to deny choking to death – May responded: 'Boris, the dog was put down – when its master decided it wasn't needed any more.' There were further digs at the expense of George Osborne, who was hosting the event, and the newly knighted Craig Oliver, the former Downing Street spin doctor whose clashes with Fiona Hill two years earlier had ended in the departure of May's devoted aide. Referring to a passage in Oliver's book in which he described 'retching' in the street after Britain voted to leave the EU, May said: 'Most of us experienced it too. When we saw his name on the resignation honours list.' The reversal in fortune in the months since the referendum was stark.

Less than a week after the *Spectator* awards, May was presented with her greatest foreign policy challenge after Brexit, with the unexpected election of Donald Trump as President of the United States on 8 November. Like the rest of the political establishment in both the UK and the US – none of whom seemed to have learned the lessons of the Brexit vote – May had trusted the opinion polls and assumed his Democratic rival Hillary Clinton would come through. She and her spads had been somewhat less than circumspect in their criticism of Trump during the long US election cycle. Nonetheless, it still came as a shock when, in the aftermath of his victory, it took forty-eight hours for the two leaders to speak by phone, by which time Trump had held discussions with representatives from Egypt, Ireland, Mexico, Israel, Turkey, India, Japan, Australia and South Korea. Compounding the poor start to the relationship, Nigel Farage, the outgoing UKIP leader, was able to make contact with the President-elect with ease, visiting Trump on at least three occasions. Downing Street was not amused when, in a major breach of diplomatic protocol, Trump used Twitter to urge May to appoint Farage as US ambassador.

Like the rest of the world, May and No. 10 have struggled to come to terms with the new orthodoxies of the Trump era. But bridges were made over the holiday period in December 2016, when Nick Timothy and Fiona Hill travelled to the US to meet with key members of the Trump transition team. The trip appears to have reaped rewards. While May continued to condemn lewd remarks about women made by Trump, describing his suggestion that he had 'grab[bed] them by the pussy' as 'unacceptable',[418] Trump appears not to have held it against her. The President-elect has affirmed his commitment to the 'special relationship' and even suggested, in contrast to his predecessor Barack Obama, that he would swiftly agree to a favourable new trade deal with the UK. He also extended an invitation to the White House.

'I love the UK,' Trump told Michael Gove in an interview for *The Times* in mid-January.

We're gonna work very hard to get it [a trade agreement] done quickly and done properly. Good for both sides. I will be meeting with [Mrs May]. She's requesting a meeting and we'll have a meeting right after I get into the White House … I think we're gonna get something done very quickly.

At the time of writing, the White House trip was imminent – an intriguing prospect given the almost comical contrast between the characters of the new leaders of Britain and the United States.

* * *

Theresa May has come a long way in her first six months in office. While the challenges facing the country appear greater than ever, the public seems to respond to her determined insistence that everything is in hand. She enters her second half-year in a stronger position than ever. Her friends are not without their worries, however. Anne Jenkin fears for her health. 'I think we're incredibly lucky that she came along at the right time. Somebody, somewhere, was watching us,' she says.

> But she's got a long way to go, and she's got an incredibly difficult job. There is a limit to how long people can last at the top without their health being damaged or their sanity being damaged. I think she just needs to be careful of her health. Because working at that pace is unsustainable.

Others, including Cheryl Gillan, worry about the state of the party: 'I really do hope the parliamentary party settles down, because she needs backing. We have a big lead at the moment and we have really no opposition so we have the potential to tear ourselves apart. We seem to think we have the luxury.'

Eric Pickles is more sanguine.

> I don't doubt for one moment that we've got the best person by a country mile to get us out of this Brexit, to steer us through. If there is a route, she can find it … Forget about Jeremy Corbyn, it's about delivering Brexit in a reasoned way that keeps the party together, keeps the country together. The party bloody loves her. I think there's a kind of feeling that she's well into her honeymoon period and there's no suggestion of it ending any time soon.

Despite his past differences with May, Michael Howard agrees:

> I'm enthused by her. I admire what she's doing and I wish her very well. Time will tell, [but] I think she has the potential to be a great Prime Minister. She's got some very formidable challenges to face,

obviously Brexit, but she doesn't, as things look at the moment, have any serious opposition, not only from the Labour Party but also as things stand I think from within the Conservative Party.

The challenges facing Prime Minister Theresa May are indeed formidable. Even if she did not have to grapple with the most complex task of the modern political era, negotiating Britain's exit from the European Union and establishing a new place on the world stage, the problems facing her would appear overwhelming. The National Health Service is at breaking point; immigration remains high on the list of voters' concerns, with no sign of how the new government will meet the 'tens of thousands' figure it is still pledged to; the election of Donald Trump as US President and growing confidence of Vladimir Putin present an unexpected and unknowable international scene; divisions among the public remain high following the bitter referendum campaign, with a substantial increase in hate crime; the prison system is on the cusp of meltdown; the inquiry into child sex abuse becomes more dysfunctional by the week; the economy remains in flux – these are just some of the legion of challenges facing May and her Cabinet.

Yet through it all, with no real opposition to worry about, one thing is clear: the vicar's daughter remains in control.

PARADISE LOST

Theresa May is not a fearful woman, but on the evening of 8 June 2017, the tension was too much for her to bear. Seven weeks earlier, she had gambled by calling an early general election, and the exit poll which would be a guide to the final result was now moments away. Would her boldness in bringing the election forward by three years be rewarded? Anything less than a healthy increase in her party's tally of 331 seats would be viewed as failure – a personal humiliation for the Prime Minister. She couldn't bring herself to watch.

As Philip May switched the television on in the couple's home in Sonning in her Maidenhead constituency, she remained out of earshot in another room. That morning's opinion polls had varied wildly in their predictions, but despite what had turned out to be a far more challenging campaign than they had expected, May and her closest advisers remained confident that, if not the landslide they had expected at the outset, they were still on course for a credible result. The minutes following the striking of 10 p.m., when the exit poll would be released, must have seemed like an eternity to May as she waited while her husband watched. When Philip finally came in to bring her the news, it was worse than either could have imagined. The poll suggested that the Conservatives would lose more than a dozen seats, resulting in a hung parliament. May had not only failed to increase her majority, she had thrown it away altogether. What had appeared the safest of gambles was turning out to be the epitome of hubris; a spectacular act of self-harm. As she took in what her husband was saying, the Prime Minister of Great Britain and Northern Ireland began to weep.

* * *

There can be few politicians in modern history who have suffered such a dramatic reversal of fortune as Theresa May. Her dizzyingly swift journey from a Prime Minister in total command of the political terrain to one labelled a lame duck is almost Shakespearean in its pathos. With hindsight, it is clear that, like all Shakespeare's tragic heroes, the seeds of May's undoing were there all along, lying dormant until the moment when, at 11 a.m. on Tuesday 18 April 2017, she stood in front of a phalanx of cameras outside 10 Downing Street and announced she was going to the country less than half way through her government's fixed five-year term in office in order to end the 'political game playing' of those opposed to Brexit. By the time the election was held she had lost not just her parliamentary majority but her much vaunted reputation for strength and stability.

But if the clues to May's downfall were there all along, it is fair to say that few commentators, lay or expert, foresaw the shock result of the general election of 8 June 2017 when May called it seven weeks earlier (the first of the Tories' many errors would be to hold such an unnecessarily lengthy, fifty-day campaign). In the immediate prelapsarian period when the action of the hardback edition of this book ended in January 2017, May was still master of all she surveyed, so dominant in her own party that she had attained the premiership unchallenged six months earlier, and commanding twenty-point opinion poll leads over her Labour rival, Jeremy Corbyn. Sure, there was the thorny task of Brexit ahead, but with no sign of May's honeymoon with party or public ending in the immediate future, even the process of achieving a smooth departure from the European Union did not seem insurmountable. As the hardback concluded: the Vicar's daughter appeared utterly in control. And then the Vicar's daughter drove the purring Bentley of her leadership off a cliff edge.

So who or what is to blame for the crisis May finds herself in as her second year in office gets underway? In the shell-shocked aftermath of the general election, attention has focused on the role played by the 'evil Tory spads', to use Lynne Featherstone's memorable phrase: Fiona Hill and Nick Timothy. It is now obvious that May's joint chiefs of staff did indeed create a toxic environment at No. 10, to the extent that after just a few months, a quite startling number of their colleagues had voted with their feet by walking out of their jobs. Many of these former staffers have since sought catharsis by sharing their experiences in print, providing an early sneak peek behind the curtain of May's premiership. What they reveal makes clear that the conditions were there for the spads to self-destruct, taking May's re-election prospects with them, from their first moments in Downing Street. Many believe that May has only herself to blame for what appears to have been an inability or unwillingness to get a grip on what swiftly became a highly dangerous dynamic.

Katie Perrior, May's popular director of communications, resigned the day the election was called in April 2017 when it became clear that Hill would be taking charge of media during the campaign. She has since written extensively about the regime of terror under Hill and Timothy at No. 10, saying:

> I knew their behaviour couldn't last for ever and that they would, at some point, implode … I knew that without these two chiefs of staff, Theresa May would never have become Prime Minister. They were there for her the whole way – as Home Secretary and into No. 10 – but by the very nature of the way they acted, I knew they would also be her downfall. And they very nearly were … She let two people ruin the very thing she always wanted more than anything – to be Prime Minister – and for that she has to take some responsibility.[419]

Joey Jones, a former Sky News reporter who began handling media for May at the Home Office shortly before she became Prime Minister, lasted less than a day at No. 10 before clashing with Hill and walking out. He agrees that May is to blame for failing to rein her spads in:

> Let us not forget, there was never any secret about Nick and Fi's excesses. Everyone in Westminster knew that they could be unacceptably aggressive. Responsibility for the toxic dynamic in Downing Street was not Nick and Fi's alone – it goes without saying that the Prime Minister herself should have stopped the rot and is now the one most damaged by her failure to act...[420]

A third former No. 10 staffer, Alasdair Palmer, has written that May's innate reticence and inability to trust meant she could not divest herself of Hill and Timothy, even when it had become clear to everyone around her that the pair were damaging her.

> Timothy and Hill had two great attributes as far as May was concerned: they seemed to have all the answers on the issues about which she felt uncertain; and they made it clear that they were utterly loyal to her – they would sacrifice themselves for her whenever that was necessary. May does not find it easy to trust people. She often feels there are plots and conspiracies against her. And there often are, because in politics intense rivalry and ambition mean there are plots against every politician of significance. But her reluctance to place her trust in people means that when she finds people she thinks deserve it – such as Timothy and Hill – she places excessive confidence in them and is too willing to allow them to substitute their judgement for her own on too many issues.[421]

It is now apparent that the spads did not discriminate in the hostile treatment they doled out to senior ministers, civil servants, journalists and advisers, with Hill in particular accused of appalling rudeness. Perrior has provided lurid accounts of her behaviour. 'Where are the f***ing hydrangeas?' Hill is said to have shouted when flowers were not provided for a photoshoot with the *Sunday Times* in November 2016.[422]

But there were deeper consequences to Hill and Timothy's horrendous manners than bruised feelings. One of the most negative aspects of May's over-reliance on her spads was that, in their creation of a circle of three and their hostility towards everyone outside it, she was denied sufficient touchstones to bounce ideas and policy off. This would become glaringly apparent during the election campaign, when senior Cabinet ministers were not consulted on the manifesto, but it was a fault that was present from the start of her leadership. Missteps might have been avoided had voices other than Hill or Timothy been encouraged or at least not prevented from speaking up. Nick Timothy has denied that he and Hill formed a 'kitchen Cabinet' around May, although, amid a barrage of accusations about the secrecy at No. 10, he has conceded in retrospect that: 'We probably didn't communicate as well as we could have done, directly with the public and the media, and probably to a certain extent around Whitehall.'[423]

The visit by May to the White House at the end of January 2017 (three months earlier than anticipated) is a case in point. With Brexit on the horizon, it was indisputably in the UK's national interest for the Prime Minister to forge close relations with the Trump administration. But Downing Street left May open to criticism with the optics of her visit, symbolised for many by an extraordinary photograph in which the President and Prime Minister were snapped holding hands as they walked outside the White House. There were angry protests when it emerged that No. 10 had persuaded Buckingham Palace to honour Trump with an invitation for a full state visit, an offer that, at the time of writing, he appears unwilling to avail himself of, almost certainly through fear of further unrest. It is tempting to wonder if the inclusion of a broader range of voices in No. 10's decision-making structure might have sounded an alarm bell which could have resulted in a recalibration of May's approach to the visit, one which paid more heed to the clear antipathy which the British public has for Trump.

The disastrous decision to call an early general election was perhaps another case of the May administration's tin ear to public
sensibility. On this occasion, May did consult beyond the inner
circle – but not very far. Only a handful of people were aware she
was considering an early run, with most of the Cabinet kept in the
dark. Of those in the know, the Brexit Secretary, David Davis, was
a vociferous advocate of going to the country early, in the expectation that it would deliver a valuable mandate as he prepared to go
into the Brexit negotiations. Philip Hammond, the Chancellor, was
also in favour, but for rather more negative reasons: he cautioned
that Brexit was likely to prove so toxic for the economy that the
Conservatives would be likely to lose if they waited until the end
of the fixed term in 2020. Hill and Timothy also encouraged an
early poll, suggesting that by taking advantage of the most benign
political landscape for a generation, with an opinion poll lead of
more than twenty points in March 2017 and Labour led by the
left-wing and (they assumed) electorally poisonous Jeremy Corbyn,
May could secure a three-figure majority for herself. Of the small
group May consulted, only Sir Lynton Crosby, who ran both the
successful 2015 Tory election campaign and the most recent one,
has made it clear that he urged her not to call the election.

Since becoming Prime Minister in July 2016, May had repeatedly promised to serve a full five-year term. Her initial reluctance to
call another election stemmed from an instinctive sense that, following the 2015 general election and referendum of June 2016, voters
were both tired of politicians and they wanted their leaders to get
on with the job of governing and delivering Brexit without the
distraction of yet another campaign. In this she would be proved
entirely correct. But along with the voter-fatigue she had feared,
May seems not to have appreciated the untold damage she would
cause herself by breaking her vow not to hold an early election. It is
tempting to wonder if, had she widened the debate over whether to
call an early election, someone might have made the case that for a
politician such as May, whose appeal was based on straightforward-
ness, plain dealing and honesty, breaking a promise was potentially

more dangerous than if it had been committed by a more flexible character, such as, say, a Boris Johnson or a Tony Blair.

The final decision to hold the early election was taken by May alone while on a walking holiday in Snowdonia, north Wales, with her husband over the Easter break from the House of Commons. There was no discussion in full Cabinet or political Cabinet, and the number of people who knew that she was considering the move remained tiny. On Easter Monday, May attended Buckingham Palace, where she received formal permission from the Queen to call a general election. Under the rules of the Fixed Term Parliament Act, May would also have to seek approval from Parliament, but with Labour having called for an early poll, she was aware this was unlikely to prove an impediment. The following morning, 18 April 2017, with the opinion polls showing the Conservatives in a commanding 24-point lead over Labour, the Downing Street comms team swung into action, briefing journalists that the Prime Minister was preparing to make a 'personal' statement outside No. 10, code for either resignation or the calling of a general election. Sterling plummeted as a frenzy of speculation ensued, but there was not long to wait.

Just after 11 a.m., May stepped out of the famous black door of No. 10, approached the lectern, and began: 'I have just chaired a meeting of the Cabinet, where we agreed that the government should call a general election, to be held on 8 June.' Accusing Labour and the other opposition parties of seeking to block the process of leaving the EU, she continued:

> The country is coming together, but Westminster is not. It was with reluctance that I decided the country needs this election, but it is with strong conviction that I say it is necessary to secure the strong and stable leadership the country needs to see us through Brexit and beyond.

May's insistence that the election was being called for the good of the country during the Brexit negotiations, rather than to further the cause of the Conservative Party, was greeted with a collective hollow laugh from a cynical public. The image she had carefully cultivated, of a grownup without guile marking a refreshing break from the silly games of the public schoolboys she had replaced, was squandered in an instant. May would not recover the high regard the public had held her in prior to her announcement on that April morning. And many more mistakes were to follow in what will go down in history as perhaps the worst ever election campaign fought by the Conservative Party.

With the election called, the political centre of gravity shifted down the road from Westminster to Victoria, where the main political parties set up their headquarters. The dysfunction of No. 10 moved along with its actors. In the finger pointing that followed election night, it has been widely accepted that the Tory campaign suffered from a lack of cohesion at the top. Australian election expert Sir Lynton Crosby and his associates Jim Messina (the Obama administration veteran and US data whiz) and Mark Textor (a respected pollster), were rehired for 2017. The cost to hire Sir Lynton alone was £4 million. These election specialists are now known to have been unhappy at the extent of the influence Hill and Timothy had over the campaign. With far too many cooks stirring the Tory broth, the infighting began immediately.

Right from the start, Nick Timothy has admitted, the tone of the campaign was off. Both he and May herself have suggested that it failed to capture the egalitarian mission they set out so powerfully in her elegiac speech on being appointed Prime Minister nine months earlier. Katie Perrior agrees. 'Mrs May's speech outside No. 10 after becoming Prime Minister last year was everything I believed in, and everything I signed up to be a part of,' she has said. 'I hung it on my wall in my office. I should have known it wasn't going to be that simple.'[424] The campaign did not carry through with the promise of demonstrating, in Timothy's words, that the Tories planned to govern in the interests of 'ordinary working people'. 'The electoral strategy was fundamentally different,' he has said. 'It was a reassurance and continuity campaign rather than a change campaign and, on reflection, I think that was wrong.'[425]

Rather than focusing on helping the 'just about managing', the campaign sought to build on May's strong opinion poll lead over Jeremy Corbyn by stressing the contrast in their leadership qualities. Timothy would later accuse Sir Lynton of going against May's instincts by drawing up a strategy based around her personality rather than the Conservatives' policy platform. Others have insisted the opposite was true – that it was Hill and particularly Timothy who saw May's appeal as the person most trusted to manage Brexit.

Whoever was to blame, the focus on May was unrelenting. Never comfortable in the spotlight, she floundered in the full glare of the campaign. There was no escape: the Tory battle bus was emblazoned with the words 'Theresa May: for Britain', the Conservative logo was so discreet that it could barely be seen. The Cabinet was redubbed 'Theresa's team', while senior ministers were kept off the airwaves. Philip Hammond, who seemed to have attracted Fiona Hill's ire, was briefed against with reports that he would be sacked following the election, meaning that, almost unknown during a campaign, the Chancellor had to be kept away from the broadcast studios. Instead of daily press conferences featuring members of the Cabinet, the Conservatives concentrated their efforts on a roaming prime ministerial tour largely focused in Labour seats, spending little time shoring up marginal Tory-held constituencies. During May's brief campaign appearances, journalists were kept as far out of the way as possible and, more often than not, blocked from asking questions. Nick Timothy has said:

> Theresa, never comfortable hogging the limelight, expected to make more use of her ministerial team. On the advice of the campaign consultants, and following opinion research that showed Theresa to be far more popular than the party or her colleagues, we eschewed our instincts. We were wrong to do so.[426]

Running a presidential-style campaign with a candidate known to be uncomfortable in front of the camera, who found interacting on any kind of personal level a chore, would prove a serious error.

May's nervous discomfort with journalists and voters alike had once seemed engaging – it spoke of a refusal to schmooze or to chase tomorrow's headline at any cost. In the midst of an election campaign, her inability to interact became a millstone. Before long, the leaden answers she gave to the most basic of questions had earned her the nickname 'Maybot', a robot Prime Minister marching stiffly to electoral disaster.

While it is possible to identify any number of mistakes by the Conservatives before and during the 2017 election, if there was a single turning point it was 18 May 2017: the launch of the manifesto. The offending document is perhaps the most striking example of the May leadership's flawed approach to decision-making. Drawn up in tight secrecy by Nick Timothy and Ben Gummer, the young Cabinet Office Secretary who would go on to lose his seat on election night, input from beyond the inner circle was not sought or welcome, meaning there was no one to point out its obvious flaws. Cabinet ministers who would ultimately bear responsibility for implementing the manifesto were not permitted to see the entire document until the day of its launch in Halifax, West Yorkshire, and then only twenty minutes before journalists received their copies.

It is damning evidence of how supine the Cabinet had become under May's premiership that they accepted being reduced to 'Theresa's Team', as the party's branding put it. At the manifesto launch, ministers were effectively silenced. Apart from David Davis, who introduced May onto the stage, none spoke or were even referred to by their leader. In her speech, the Prime Minister said the word 'me' seven times, and 'Conservative' only once. At this stage, with the party's lead in the polls standing at an average of seventeen points, the Tories were still so confident of the result that Jim Messina was predicting they would capture 'well over' 400 seats.[427]

At the Tory manifesto's heart was a plan to transform social care by requiring home owners to use their assets to pay for nursing assistance. Fatally, the proposal included a threshold of £100,000 and no ceiling, meaning an individual with assets such as a house could be forced to forgo tens or even hundreds of thousands of pounds to receive care for conditions such as dementia, while a neighbour with cancer would continue to be treated for free on the NHS. In characteristic fashion, Timothy and Gummer did not consult with either Health Secretary Jeremy Hunt, or Communities Secretary Sajid Javid, who would have responsibility for the scheme in Whitehall were it to be introduced; they were informed of the plan only twenty-four hours before the launch.

Timothy would later deny that he and Gummer performed the Whitehall equivalent of drawing up policy on the back of a fag packet when formulating the social care plan. But the scheme the two thirty-somethings presented in the manifesto made little reference to the work of experts in the field, including the prestigious Dilnot Report into social care, which received cross-party support when it was published in 2011 and which, crucially, proposed a cap on payments of £35,000. Timothy is said to have personally removed the concept of a ceiling which had been in an original version of the plan drafted by Gummer. Soon dubbed the 'dementia tax', the social care section of Conservative manifesto is estimated to have cost the Tories the votes of many thousands of middle-aged and elderly people who, rightly or wrongly, were allowed to gain the impression that they could lose their homes as a result of the reforms. Grant Shapps, the former Conservative Party chairman, later said the Timothy/Gummer social care plan 'literally went down like a bag of sick'.[428]

But it was far from the only flaw in the manifesto. With Labour promising such voter-friendly offerings as an end to student loans and the renationalisation of the railways, many Conservative MPs complained that their own manifesto contained nothing they could advocate for on the doorstep. On top of the hammer blow of social care, the elderly were hit with an end to the pension triple lock and universal benefits. But the pain was not discriminatory. The young were effectively side-lined, with no mention of important issues for the under-thirties, such as housing and inequality. Polls suggesting overwhelming support for the ban on fox-hunting were ignored, with the pledge of a Commons vote on repeal – yet another electoral own goal. On austerity, the party appeared to promise more of the same, with no new money for the overstretched NHS. Families, particularly mothers, were turned off by a short-sighted plan to end free primary school lunches in favour of a cheap breakfast (calculated by experts at 7p per meal).[429] At a time of rising anger over cuts to school budgets, May and Timothy's obsession with grammar schools was seen by many parents as a distraction.

But it wasn't just swing voters who were alienated by the manifesto. With Timothy's fingerprints all over it, many on the right detected too great a whiff of Red Toryism, with a proposed energy price cap reminiscent of former Labour leader Ed Miliband's proposal at the 2015 election. As a result, it was difficult to motivate Tory activists to get behind it. Nor was there anything of substance on Brexit or even immigration, both areas of strength for the Conservatives in the wake of the collapse in support for the UK Independence Party. Somehow, the manifesto's authors had contrived to appeal to not a single group of voters. Rather than robbing Peter to pay Paul, it promised a nation of Peters with no Pauls in sight.

As with Budgets, there is usually a lull following the presentation of a manifesto, as journalists take the necessary time to scrutinise its contents and uncover the landmines. While the social care proposal ticked away, waiting to explode a few hours later, May faced questions in Halifax about the broader tone of her offering. Asked if the manifesto was an example of 'Mayism', she declared: 'There is no "Mayism". There is good, solid Conservatism, which puts the interests of the country and the interests of ordinary working people at the heart of everything we do in government.'

And then the social care bomb went off. If the media was slow to appreciate voter antipathy to the plan, Tory activists were not. Over the weekend of 20–21 May, as Conservative HQ was inundated with phone calls from candidates warning how poorly the policy was going down on the doorstep, Sir Lynton held a series of focus groups that delivered the same message: the plan was a disaster. By the Sunday, the decision had been taken that the social care plan had to go. May now performed what has been described as the first ever U-turn on a manifesto proposal, seeking to limit the damage by announcing that there would, after all, be an – unspecified – ceiling on the amount recipients would be required to contribute to their social care costs.

It could be argued that the decision to reverse course so dramatically, utterly and swiftly was not necessarily a bad one. If a politician is forced to change tack, it is better to do so as soon as possible, in order to minimise the amount of time and energy spent discussing the mistake. But May now reverted to what seemed to have become an unfortunate habit when under pressure, of making a bad situation worse. She announced the about-turn during a press conference in Wrexham, and immediately found herself pressed on the reversal. Clearly in discomfort, May blurted out: 'Nothing has changed. Nothing has changed.' Given that everyone present, and all those watching live on television at home, could see that just about everything had changed on social care, the declaration once again battered her reputation for rectitude and left voters with the unfortunate impression that she took them for fools.

May's tendency to compound mistakes with poor presentation represents another example of a perceived strength – in this case her inability to spin – which had helped her achieve the highest office but which became a weakness when she sought re-election to that office. Neither Tony Blair or David Cameron would ever have made such presentational errors, nor did they lack the necessary deftness to talk their way out of trouble should they find themselves in similar bother.

The social care U-turn throws up a second instance of a strength which became a weakness during the campaign: May's innate pragmatism. Alasdair Palmer has suggested:

Her lack of intellectual confidence can … help explain why May is liable to sudden policy reversals. Her response to the criticism of the manifesto's dementia tax is one example: she immediately said the Tories would drop its most criticised features, a reaction that clearly made many voters wonder why she had adopted them in the first place. I think it is May's lack of intellectual self-confidence, together with her lack of an ideological framework, that explains why she delegated so much power to her advisers.[430]

The flawed manifesto with its unpopular social care pledge, followed by May's insistence that 'nothing has changed', rendered her a figure of fun at a time when Jeremy Corbyn, the Labour leader, was proving an unexpectedly appealing character. While Labour had its own share of disasters on the campaign trail (Diane Abbott's bungled proposal to recruit 100,000 police officers at a cost of £300,000 – an annual salary of £30 – was a particular low),[431] its manifesto appeared popular with voters, and Corbyn was enjoying rapturous receptions at rock star-style rallies similar to those he fronted during his leadership campaigns. Most critics of Labour and its leader felt that the party was at its weakest over the economy – how, precisely, would it fund the many goodies it was offering to voters? But with Chancellor Hammond sidelined by Fiona Hill, the task of attacking Corbyn over his costings fell to May. And this she singularly failed to do. In interview after interview, journalists complained of her cautious, 'Maybot' answers, her inability to engage. She appeared defensive, shifty, even, refusing to answer simple questions and so prone to repeating her campaign slogan of 'strong and stable' that interviews often bordered on comical.

As the campaign entered its final weeks, the Tories made matters worse by foolishly allowing a guessing game to ensue over whether the Prime Minister would take part in the televised debates, which began on 18 May and represented the Conservatives' best chance to challenge Corbyn on Labour's economic record. In the end, Amber Rudd, the Home Secretary, was deputed to stand in for May at the seven-way leaders' debate on 31 May, which Corbyn turned up to at the last minute. Rudd was widely seen to have performed well, but May was further criticised for ducking the bout. The traditional advice for leaders considering whether or not to take part in debates is that the frontrunner in any contest should avoid them as they can only lose ground. In 2017, however, a new truth emerged.

By avoiding the contest, May had allowed her challenger to gain traction, presenting himself as the change candidate in an era of anti-politics. Alasdair Palmer has said:

> The effect of that decision was that Corbyn's claims went unchallenged. To the voting public, it made it seem as if she did not want to argue with him because she could not argue with him: she was not up to it, and she knew it. She was frightened that she would lose.[432]

As the establishment figure, it was now decidedly uncool to support May – or vote Tory. By 5 June when, in answer to a question about the 'naughtiest' thing she had done as a child she mentioned that she used to 'run through fields of wheat', May had become a figure of ridicule, too.[433]

The day after the social care U-turn, the country suffered the first of three devastating human tragedies to take place during and just after the general election. May would be praised for her response to the first, come under some criticism over the second and be roundly condemned for her handling of the third. Even her greatest critics would agree that the strain of responding to two terrorist attacks and the worst fire since the Second World War in the space of twenty-four days, with an estimated combined death toll of more than 100 including children and babies, would have pushed any Prime Minister to the limit at any time, let alone one in the middle of what had become a highly challenging election campaign.

The first of the two terrorist incidents (which followed an earlier attack on tourists and police in Westminster in March) took place at the Manchester Arena on Monday 22 May. Just after 10.30 p.m., a suicide bomber detonated a device as concert-goers, many of them young girls and their parents, were leaving the arena, having seen the singer Ariana Grande perform. The twenty-two dead included an eight-year-old girl attending her first concert, a mother and father from Poland who were picking up their daughters, now orphaned, and two teenage sweethearts. In a statement released at 2.20 a.m. the following morning, May described the attack as 'appalling', adding that her thoughts were with the victims. She convened a meeting of Cobra later that day and made preparations to visit Manchester, where she sat by the hospital beds of some of the gravely injured. Highly unusually, campaigning in the general election was suspended for two days.

But if the politicians were off the campaign trail, the pollsters remained busy. When May returned to business on 25 May, she was forced to confront the fact that the ill-conceived and poorly received manifesto had proved costly. The Conservatives' lead had shrunk to twelve points, and although this was still enough to deliver a decent majority, there were warning signs of further trouble to come. The party appeared to be haemorrhaging voters in London in particular, while young people were switching from 'don't knows' or 'will not vote' to supporting Corbyn. Parents were expressing disquiet over school meals, while reaction from elderly voters to the social care plan showed that the U-turn had not stopped the rot.

The second terrorist attack took place twelve days after Manchester, in the heart of central London on a beautiful June evening. Three men in a hired van drove at high speed over London Bridge, mowed down pedestrians and then, leaping from the vehicle, ran into nearby Borough Market where they began stabbing drinkers and restaurant-goers. Dozens were injured and eight killed. Only the swift response from the police stopped the death toll from being far higher. In an indication of the cosmopolitan nature of the city the terrorists sought to attack, all but one of the dead were from overseas.

Again, campaigning was suspended, and again Cobra convened. But as May steeled herself to deal with the existential threat from Islamic terrorism, the political consensus was breaking down. Labour took the ultimately successful gamble of criticising the government over police cuts, pointing to falling officer numbers at a time when the nation was vulnerable to further attack. As the Home Secretary who had prided herself on streamlining the police, May was directly in the firing line. With the emergency services stretched to the limit and complex investigations underway in the heart of two of the country's primary cities, the row dominated the final days of the campaign.

By the morning of polling day, 8 June, the Conservatives knew the election would not be the walkover they had anticipated. The final opinion polls all gave the Tories a lead over Labour, but they varied wildly. ICM put the gap at twelve points, which would have delivered a triple digit majority, while Survation suggested only a 1 per cent lead, indicating a hung parliament. Nick Timothy has said that he believed the party was on course to win a majority of ninety-two, and claimed that Jim Messina's polling was off (a charge the latter has denied).[434]

May, who spent election day in Maidenhead as usual, was hoping the more favourable of the morning's polls would prove accurate. 'We didn't see the result coming...' she has said. 'I think I realised as the campaign was going on that everything wasn't going perfectly, but throughout the campaign the expectation was still that the result would be a different one, a better one for us.'[435] She would later describe the 'devastating' moment her hopes were dashed:

> When the result came through it was a complete shock. I didn't actually watch the exit poll. I have a little bit of superstition about things like that. My husband watched it for me and came and told me. It took a few minutes for it to sort of sink in what [he] was telling me. My husband gave me a hug. I felt devastated, really. [I had] a little tear at that moment, yes.[436]

Forced to remain in Maidenhead until the result of her own count, May spent much of the next few hours in conference calls with the campaign team at Conservative HQ. The response there to the exit poll had also been visceral. One staffer is said to have 'gagged' on hearing the news.[437]

What followed was a long night of the soul for many of those involved in the campaign, as the predicted landslide failed to materialise, and it became agonisingly clear that the exit poll would prove

broadly accurate (the Conservatives would end the night with
three seats more than the poll forecast, including two where victory was by narrow double digits). Were it not for an unexpectedly
strong showing in Scotland, where the Tories won thirteen seats,
the result would have been even worse (the success of the Scottish
Conservatives would create a new powerbase north of the border
headed by the group's leader Ruth Davidson, posing a potentially
powerful Europhile counterbalance to the Tory right's push for a
hard Brexit). As the new reality of a hung parliament sunk in, 'back
channel' talks with Northern Ireland's Democratic Unionist Party
began. One report suggested Tory chiefs were on the phone to their
DUP counterparts within ninety minutes of the exit poll.[438]

By 3 a.m., when the Maidenhead result was finally in, the full
scale of the electoral disaster was apparent. The Conservatives had
lost twelve seats, including those of eight ministers, among them
Ben Gummer. Crucially, the party had fallen nine short of an overall majority, meaning there was indeed a hung parliament. That
May had been returned in her own constituency with two thirds of
the vote was no consolation. Her voice cracked as she delivered her
acceptance speech, stressing that:

> At this time, more than anything else, this country needs a period
> of stability. And if, as the indications have shown, and this is cor-
> rect, the Conservative Party have won the most seats and proba-
> bly the most votes, it will be incumbent on us to ensure we have
> that period of stability.

Nick Timothy has said he knew he would have to resign as soon as
he heard the result.[439] Did May also consider her position? She says
not. 'No, I didn't consider stepping down, because I felt there was
a responsibility there to ensure that the country still had a government,' she has said.

> I was there as leader of the party and Prime Minister and I had
> a responsibility then, as we went through the night, to determine

what we were going to do the next morning. I called the election,
I led the campaign, and I take responsibility for what happened.
But there's also a responsibility for the future, for the country, and
that was about ensuring that the country had a government.[440]

May and those close to her insist her determination to stay in
office stemmed not from a despotic reluctance to relinquish power,
but her innate sense of duty and a determination to put right the
damage she had done to the party she loves. Whatever her motivation, as dawn broke and she was driven at high speed down the
M4 to London, she was entirely focused on taking what steps were
necessary to establish both that Britain still had a functioning government, and that she was the head of that government.

Her first stop on arriving back in Westminster was Campaign
HQ in Matthew Parker Street, where she thanked staff for their
efforts amid an atmosphere like that of a wake. After a few minutes, she excused herself and gathered her now fatally wounded
consiglieri, Timothy and Hill, in a private room. Timothy offered
to resign immediately; May decided to delay the inevitable. Her
next talks, at Downing Street at 8 a.m., were with Brexit Secretary
David Davis. By now, the country was waking to the news of the
extraordinary election result. May and her advisers were all clear
she needed to act fast to establish her authority as a Prime Minister
who was going nowhere.

Just after noon, having showered and changed into a smart blue
skirt suit, May left Downing Street for Buckingham Palace to ask
permission from the Queen to attempt to form a minority administration. She must have reflected during the short drive on the
difference in her emotions from the last time she had taken that
same journey, just under eleven months earlier. When she returned,
May stood outside No. 10 and addressed an electorate that had all
but rejected her as Prime Minister, and a world uncertain whether
she remained in charge. Her words would constitute yet another
serious misstep.

'What the country needs more than ever is certainty,' she said.

And having secured the largest number of votes and the greatest number of seats in the general election, it is clear that only the Conservative and Unionist Party has the legitimacy and ability to provide that certainty by commanding a majority in the House of Commons. As we do, we will continue to work with our friends and allies in the Democratic Unionist Party in particular. Our two parties have enjoyed a strong relationship over many years, and this gives me the confidence to believe that we will be able to work together in the interests of the whole United Kingdom.

She finished with a flourish: 'Now let's get to work.'

May was a diminished figure compared to the woman who had stood in the same spot seven weeks earlier to announce she was calling an election, yet appeared no humbler. She made no apology to those Conservative MPs who, thanks to her, had lost seats they'd had every expectation of holding for at least another three years. Nor was there any acknowledgement of the message the public had delivered in rejecting her call for a mandate in the Brexit negotiations. In focusing on the need to establish herself as the head of a stable government, with an eye, perhaps, to how events were being viewed overseas, and in Brussels in particular, she had struck a jarring note. Rushing to secure a deal with the socially conservative DUP, she seemed unaware of the queasiness many inside as well as outside the party (including Ruth Davidson) were already expressing at such an arrangement, or the potential strain it would place on the Northern Ireland peace process.

Later, in response to criticism of the tone of her statement, May would explain her thinking on that highly charged morning:

At that point in time what I felt was important was giving people the confidence of knowing that there was going to be a government ... getting down to work and dealing with the day to day issues that they face in their lives and that they want government to help them with.[441]

But as Katie Perrior put it:

> Her speech outside No. 10. ... ignored the fact that millions of people had stuck two fingers up to her and her party. Where was the empathy? Where was the emotional intelligence to say, 'I hear you. I get it. We were not offering enough of what you wanted and I take the responsibility for that'? Instead, we got more of the same.[442]

George Osborne put it more brutally on the front page of the *London Evening Standard*, which he now edited: under a photograph of May delivering her defiant message ran the headline: 'QUEEN OF DENIAL'.[443]

Far from easing the pressure on May, her ill-judged statement had intensified it. As the last election results trickled in through the morning and the reality of the disaster she had presided over became apparent, attention focused on who to blame for the debacle. Culprits were swiftly identified: Nick Timothy and Fiona Hill. During the afternoon, May met with more of her senior ministers. At least three – Boris Johnson, Chris Grayling and Philip Hammond – made the departure of the joint Chiefs of Staff a condition of their remaining in government. All three also insisted on other olive branches, including more money for their departments and, in Hammond's case, an agreement that the Brexit process would seek to avoid damage to the economy. The Chancellor is said to have kept a log of Hill's abusive messages to him, which he threatened to release if he was demoted.[444] In fact, so hobbled was the Prime Minister in this, her weakest hour, that she was unable to move any of her senior ministerial team, bar some minor adjustments to fill the space created at the Cabinet Office by Ben Gummer. One consequence of this minor reshuffle was that May unexpectedly brought her old foe Michael Gove back to the Cabinet, in the unglamorous post of Environment Secretary; a potential trouble-maker squared off or, as US President Lyndon B. Johnson once put it, invited to piss out of the tent rather than in.

Others would also demand Timothy and Hill's heads. Graham Brady, the chairman of the 1922 Committee, met May that same afternoon to pass on the strong sentiment in the parliamentary party that the now infamous pair should be defenestrated. If they remained in place, he suggested, May could face a leadership challenge over the weekend. Made painfully aware by Brady that a show of remorse was needed, May scrambled to deliver a second response to the election, in a clip filmed in Downing Street and sent out to broadcasters. Adopting a markedly different tone, she belatedly apologised to her party: 'I wanted to achieve a larger majority. That was not the result we secured,' she said. 'And I'm sorry for all those candidates and hard-working party workers who weren't successful, but also for those colleagues who were MPs and ministers and contributed so much to our country and who lost their seats and who didn't deserve to lose their seats.'

As she spoke, the reign of terror of the 'evil Tory spads' was drawing to a close. Having offered to resign during the meeting with May earlier in the day, Timothy telephoned her that afternoon to formally quit. Even May could now see that both his and Hill's position had become untenable. When, inexplicably, the announcement of their resignations was delayed into the weekend, the press joined in the clamour. By the next day, Saturday 10 June, the news was out. Both advisers issued statements announcing their resignation and wishing May well. Hill expressed confidence in May remaining Prime Minister while Timothy wrote an article refuting the suggestion he bore primary responsibility for the loss of the election.

The departure of Nick Timothy and Fiona Hill had become necessary and inevitable. But their loss left the battered Prime Minister without two of her three pillars (the third being her husband) at a time when she was at her lowest ebb. As Joey Jones put it at the time: 'I do not think people realise how hard it will be for her to operate without her two lieutenants. Theresa May without Nick and Fi will be a hollowed-out figure.'[445] The personal toll on May of losing 'Nick and Fi' was heavy; exhausted and depressed, she would continue to make serious errors of judgement, ones which would further imperil her shaky premiership.

Politically, May was now in grave danger. On the Sunday following the election, again showing that he too could serve ice-cold revenge, Osborne summed up her situation by declaring: 'Theresa May is a dead woman walking.'[446] Suddenly, May had developed a reverse Midas touch. Far from securing the speedy deal with the DUP she had expected, negotiations dragged on. Representatives for the DUP declared themselves astonished at the ineptitude of those they were dealing with. May's team clearly underestimated the strength of the Northern Irelanders' hand, and their hard-nosed skill – evolved during many years of crisis talks – in making the most of the cards they held. As Sunday night passed into Monday morning, Downing Street first tweeted that a deal had been struck for the smaller party to supply the Conservatives with 'confidence and supply', then was forced to issue a further statement admitting a deal had not yet been agreed. The negotiations would drag on for nineteen long days while the country lacked a majority government. In the end, the price of the DUP's ten votes, which gave May a working majority of thirteen (but only on the great issues of the day: votes of confidence, finance bills, the Queen's Speech and legislation relating to Brexit), was £1 billion – the equivalent of £530 for every man, woman and child in the Province.

It was not until the Monday evening following the general election, nearly four days after her premiership was plunged into crisis, that May recovered her equilibrium enough to take the first steps towards steadying the ship, while appearing before the 1922 Committee. More assured, perhaps, away from the television cameras, a contrite May gave what those present described as an impressive performance. 'I got us into this mess and I'm going to get us out of it,' she was quoted as saying, adding that she would 'serve as long as you want me'. For the moment, her MPs appeared content to give her a chance to fulfil her promise. A leadership challenge was avoided – for now.

But if May hoped her valiant performance before the 1922 Committee would mark a turning point, she was to be disappointed. Matters were to get worse before they got better. With her premiership still in crisis and the deal with the DUP not yet done, a sleep-deprived May was woken in the early hours of Thursday 14 June, exactly a week after the election, to be told of an unfolding catastrophe six miles away from Downing Street in north Kensington, where a twenty-four storey tower block had gone up in flames. Like previous peacetime tragedies such as Aberfan or Hillsborough, the Grenfell Tower disaster will leave an indelible scar on the consciousness of the British public. At the time of writing, it still cannot be confirmed how many people perished in the inferno; the authorities estimate that more than eighty lost their lives, including a high number of infants and children. They met agonising deaths, virtually all suffering unimaginable terror in the hours and minutes before they succumbed to flames and fumes, as they gradually realised no one was coming to their aid and there was no way out. The hundreds of Grenfell residents who escaped the fire were left traumatised and homeless. They deserved the very best in sympathetic care. They didn't receive it. That Theresa May, their Prime Minister, was under heavy strain, preoccupied by the disastrous outcome of the election and rudderless following the loss of her two advisers explains but does not excuse her failure to ensure the response to the Grenfell disaster was adequate. As a human being, the lack of empathy she would show for the victims was widely condemned as downright unacceptable.

May visited the site of the disaster two days after the fire, nine days on from the election. She declined to meet any survivors or victims' families, opting instead for a private tour of the area, where she was introduced to members of the emergency services. As she departed the scene, she was subjected to boos from local residents, along with shouts for her to resign. Her actions contrasted strongly with those of Jeremy Corbyn, who stood below the still-smoking carcass of Grenfell Tower a few hours later and consoled residents, putting an arm around one survivor. It is a sign of how friendless May was in Downing Street by now that no one thought to advise her to make sure she met with the residents. Operating by herself, the Prime Minister made a strategic as well as a human error. In the words of her former colleague Michael Portillo:

> She wanted an entirely controlled situation in which she didn't use her humanity. She met in private with the emergency services, a good thing to do no doubt, but she should have been with the residents, which is what Jeremy Corbyn [did], and he was there being natural with people and hugging them. The Prime Minister would have been shouted at by the residents, but she should have been willing to take that. You have to be prepared to see people's emotions.[447]

Safe at home in Downing Street, May is said to have wept again, both for the Grenfell residents and herself. In the following days and weeks, she found it hard to move on from the shock of the election and the events that followed. Aides and fellow ministers found her distracted and tense. The *Mail on Sunday* reported one 'prominent Conservative' describing her as 'shrivelled'.[448] A few days later, a poll by YouGov showed for the first time that she was less trusted by the public than Corbyn to be Prime Minister. By the end of the month, Labour was six points ahead in the opinion polls.

This, then, was Theresa May as she marked her first year as Prime Minister on 13 July 2016. She had thrown away her majority in an act of political hubris comparable perhaps only to her predecessor David Cameron's misstep in holding the EU referendum. The public viewed her as a figure of fun, an uncomfortable position for a woman with great personal pride. She had lost her authority in Cabinet and been forced to accept the resignations of her two advisers, a man and woman who had become almost family to her over the years. Her standing on the world stage was much diminished. Behind closed doors, she was emotional; in public, she was inhibited to the point of being robotic. Her legislative agenda had effectively been binned – the Queen's Speech, delayed until 21 June while the DUP negotiations continued, was a stripped-down affair including little of substance beyond the necessary preparations for Brexit, and virtually nothing from the manifesto that had been crafted with such confidence by Nick Timothy. And she had been harangued in the street by an understandably angry crowd, having failed to show the most basic of human emotions towards a group of people experiencing unimaginable grief. It was the nadir of her premiership.

* * *

What now for Theresa May? At the time of writing – exactly two months on from Grenfell, in August 2017 – she is still Prime Minister, a fact which in itself seems surprising from the vantage point of two months earlier. The frenzy of the early summer appears to have died down as MPs relax on their sun beds or, in May's case, in her alpine boots as she takes a walking holiday. So how did May cling on, and what are her future prospects for remaining in office? In one sense, she survives because she survives – every day she remains in office makes it more likely that she will not be forced to quit. Having claimed squatters' rights in the days after the election, her grip has tightened with each passing hour as her leadership resumes an aura of permanence. She has regained her lead over Jeremy Corbyn as the person best placed with the public to be Prime Minister, and while Labour is still ahead in the opinion polls, the gap is now just two points.

That is not to say that the jostling to replace May is not underway – the moment the clock struck 10 p.m. on 8 June and the shocking result of the exit poll was announced, the phones began buzzing with challengers and their acolytes plotting against her. But the same failings that disqualified potential rivals a year ago remain in place today. And with the passing of the weeks, as June made way for July, the rivals to succeed May were trotted out one by one and found wanting. In the weeks running up to the parliamentary recess at the end of July, Westminster was swept up by a veritable soap opera, the Cabinet descending into a full-scale war of attrition of briefing and counter-briefing, often, but not exclusively, over Brexit.

By the end of it, all the likely candidates to replace May, including Boris Johnson, David Davis, Philip Hammond and, to a lesser extent, Amber Rudd, were badly damaged (Rudd facing additional impediments to leadership in the form of a now perilously small majority in her Hastings & Rye constituency).

It was almost as if the events of the previous summer were being replayed as comedy. As before, May's place in No. 10 was secured by her rivals' demonstrable unsuitability for the job. This time around, it wasn't that May was clearly the best candidate for the job – rather, the Tory Party had reluctantly decided that, right now at least, she was the least-worst option. For Theresa May, something important has shifted. She is still doing her duty, she is still in service, but she is no longer in control.

What of the future? If May can survive into conference season, there is every chance that her position will become reasonably secure. Given her huge limitations as a candidate, which the 2017 election exposed, there is little chance that the Conservative Party will allow her to fight the next general election (now due in 2022), even if she wanted to. But it appears highly probable that she will be tolerated to remain in place through the Brexit negotiations, not least because none of those vying to replace her have any appetite to take on such a formidable project. The younger, more ambitious ministers in particular see no sense in tarnishing their reputation with this thankless task.

So the likelihood is that Theresa May will serve until the formal process of Brexit is concluded in the spring of 2019, before quietly bowing out soon afterwards, like a work horse returning to the stable. Whether by then she will have fulfilled her promise made in the immediate aftermath of the election to fix her mistake by restoring the Conservatives' electability remains to be seen. Perhaps the bigger question, however, is whether she can turn her premiership around and achieve anything of importance during her time in Downing Street. If not, she will go down in history as the Prime Minister who oversaw Brexit – and whose folly cost her the bright promise of potential greatness.

ACKNOWLEDGEMENTS

This book was due to be published towards the end of 2018 or even in 2019. It arose from a conversation I had with Olivia Beattie, my editor at Biteback Publishing, in early May 2016, around six weeks before the referendum on Britain's membership of the European Union. The general consensus at the time was that, regardless of the outcome of the vote, David Cameron would remain as Prime Minister for at least another two years. Well, that's what the man himself had told us, after all. Olivia and I were pretty sure that Theresa May would be one of the leading candidates to replace Cameron, and felt she would make an interesting subject for a biography. I agreed to begin making notes on the then Home Secretary, and (having written my last book, *Comrade Corbyn*, a biography of the Labour leader who seemingly came to office overnight, in the space of four months) looked forward to a leisurely two or three years of research and writing. Just over a month later, Cameron was gone and Theresa May was Prime Minister. Suddenly, a biography of this most enigmatic of politicians was required yesterday. Oh well, I thought to myself as I prepared to drastically foreshorten my timetable, I guess I'm not the only person in and around politics whose summer plans have been changed dramatically by the shockingly unexpected outcome of the EU referendum.

My thanks must therefore begin with Olivia, for proposing the book in the first place, being an invaluable source of help and support throughout the writing process and in particular for her light-handed, intelligent editing. I am so grateful too to Iain Dale and James Stephens at Biteback for swiftly taking the decision to proceed with the biography in the hours after it became apparent that May was on course for No. 10. Also from Biteback, my thanks go to Victoria Gilder, Isabelle Ralphs and Sam Jones, and I am so grateful as always to my agent, Victoria Hobbs, and her colleagues at AM Heath, Pippa McCarthy and Jo Thompson.

The truncated timetable for writing this book presented challenges for scheduling interviews, so I am incredibly grateful for the large numbers of people who have known Theresa May at various stages of her life who gave up their time at very short notice to share their memories, views and accounts of her. Many of these interview subjects agreed to speak on the record, while others, particularly those still at the heart of government, preferred to feature anonymously. Their generosity was invaluable to the swift production of this book. My great thanks too go to Marilyn Yurdan and Ann Pierce for their help in describing in detail two of the Oxfordshire schools May attended.

Finally, my thanks and love go to my family, in particular my children: the sweet, smart and sensational Ariel, and Baby ?, whose expected publication date falls on the same day as this book's. Above all, I want to thank my husband, Conor Hanna, who read and critiqued every word, and provided invaluable encouragement, advice and ideas.

Rosa Prince
January 2017

ENDNOTES

1   Interview, Theresa May, *Desert Island Discs*, BBC Radio 4, 23 November 2014
2   https://roystockdillgenealogy.com/theresa-may/
3   Ibid.
4   'Revealed: Both Theresa May's Grannies Were Domestic Servants', Geoffrey Levy, *Daily Mail*, 24 February 2015
5   Ibid.
6   Ibid.
7   Ibid.
8   'Revealed: Both Theresa May's Grannies Were Domestic Servants', Levy, op. cit.
9   Ibid.
10 Ibid.
11 Ibid.
12 'Theresa May Still Be the Next Maggie', Simon Walters, *Mail on Sunday*, 2 September 2016
13 'Revealed: Both Theresa May's Grannies Were Domestic Servants', Levy, op. cit.
14 'The Times Diary: Pope to rock Madison Square Garden and Theresa May tells a joke', Patrick Kidd, *The Times*, 17 June 2015
15 Chris Goss, *Luftwaffe Fighter-Bombers Over Britain: The Tip and Run Campaign, 1942–43*, Crecy 2003
16 'Social experiment in churchmanship that led to Downing Street', Allan Mallinson, *The Times*, 23 July 2016
17 'The agony and ecstasy of Saint Theresa, the vicar's daughter', Giles Fraser, *The Guardian*, 14 July 2016
18 'Revealed: Both Theresa May's Grannies Were Domestic Servants', Levy, op. cit.
19 *Desert Island Discs*, op. cit.
20 'Long-standing effect of religion: Faith, Hope and Charity', Genevieve Roberts, *The Independent*, 20 November 2015
21 *Desert Island Discs*, op. cit.
22 'The Interview: Theresa May', Eleanor Mills, *The Times*, 27 November 2016
23 Ibid.
24 'Theresa May interview: "I probably was Goody Two Shoes at school"', Allison Pearson, *Daily Telegraph*, 22 December 2012
25 'Theresa May Still Be the Next Maggie', Walters, op. cit.

26 'Grocer's shop in idyllic Cotswolds village "forged Theresa May" … and her vicar dad inspired her', Oliver Harvey, *The Sun*, 15 July 2016

27 'Yes, we were affected by not having children … but we coped', Simon Walters, *Mail on Sunday*, 3 July 2016

28 Harvey, op. cit.

29 'Grocer's shop in idyllic Cotswolds village "forged Theresa May"', Ibid.

30 Theresa May, essay written for the Pre-Schools Count campaign, Pre-School Learning Alliance, May 2000

31 Ibid.

32 'Where next? – Interview – Theresa May, Conservative Party chairman', Tom Chesshyre, *The Times*, 12 October 2002

33 'I'll give every child a chance', Theresa May, *Mail on Sunday*, 1 September 2016

34 *Desert Island Discs*, op. cit.

35 'Theresa May still be the next Maggie', Walters, op. cit.

36 'Freedom fighter prepares to hit back at bossiness', Anne Perkins, *The Guardian*, 8 June 1998

37 *Desert Island Discs*, op. cit.

38 'Yes, we were affected by not having children … but we coped', Walters, op. cit.

39 Interview, Theresa May, *Today*, BBC Radio 4, 4 October 2016

40 *Desert Island Discs*, op. cit.

41 'The owl unseats the No. 10 pussycat', Tim Shipman, *Sunday Times*, 2 October 2016

42 'Order! Order!: Politicians spend their working lives condemned to the rubber-chicken circuit. But where do they go when they leave the House?' Vincent Graff, *The Observer*, 25 May 2008

43 Interview, Theresa May, Roseanna Greenstreet, *Windsor, Ascot & Maidenhead Magazine*, 2005, reprinted August 2016

44 'Theresa May interview: "I probably was Goody Two Shoes at school"', Pearson, op. cit.

45 *World at One*, BBC Radio 4, 2 October 2016

46 *What Does Theresa Really Think?*, Nick Robinson, BBC Radio 4, 1 October 2016

47 *Desert Island Discs*, op. cit.

48 Interview, Theresa May, Greenstreet, op. cit.

49 'Home Secretary's old school marks 40th anniversary', Liam Sloan, ThisisOxfordshire, 19 July 2011

50 *School Songs and Gymslips, Grammar Schools in the 1950s and 1960s*, Marilyn Yurdan, The History Press, 2012

51 *Desert Island Discs*, op. cit.

52 *The World This Weekend*, BBC Radio 4, 2 October 2016

53 'Theresa May interview: "I probably was Goody Two Shoes at school"', Pearson, op. cit.

54 *What Does Theresa Really Think?*, Robinson, op. cit.

55 'Theresa May went to my school', Martin Robinson, https://martinrobborobinson.wordpress.com/2016/07/17/theresa-may-went-to-my-school/

56 Ibid.

57 'The Interview: Theresa May', Mills, op. cit.

58 'Old classmate Theresa may tear up the rules', Patsy Davies, *The Guardian*, 18 July 2016

59 *What Does Theresa Really Think?*, Robinson, op. cit.

60 *Desert Island Discs*, op. cit.

61 *What Does Theresa Really Think?*, Robinson, op. cit.

62 'Theresa May? I beat "Terri" to role of Prime Minister', Patrick Evans and Francesca Neagle, BBC News Online, 14 July 2016
63 'I beat Theresa May to be PM', Stephanie Linning, MailOnline, 18 July 2016
64 Ibid.
65 *What Does Theresa Really Think?*, Robinson, op. cit.
66 'Oxford contemporaries remember Bhutto's vibrancy and ambition', Graeme Weardon, *The Guardian*, 28 December 2007
67 'Theresa May, the thinking woman's woman', Zoe Brennan, *The Spectator*, 2 August 2016
68 Ibid.
69 *Desert Island Discs*, op. cit.
70 *Desert Island Discs*, op. cit.
71 'A determined woman with a massive social conscience', Dominic Kennedy and Lucy Bannerman, *The Times*, 9 July 2016
72 'How Theresa May's Wirral father-in-law predicted her success', Eleanor Barlow, *Liverpool Echo*, 12 July 2016
73 Ibid.
74 'Theresa May, the thinking woman's woman', Brennan, op. cit.
75 'The highest achiever of all in the starry geography class of '74', Robert Mendick, *Sunday Telegraph*, 17 July 2016
76 'Theresa May, what lies behind the public image?', Elizabeth Day, *The Observer*, 24 July 2015
77 'Theresa May nursed ambition to be Britain's first female PM', Matthew Weaver, *The Guardian*, 12 July 2016
78 Interview, Damian Green, BBC News, 13 July 2016
79 'A determined woman with a massive social conscience', Kennedy and Bannerman, op. cit.
80 'The Oxford romance that has guided Theresa May from tragedy to triumph', Robert Mendick, *Sunday Telegraph*, 9 July 2016
81 Ibid.
82 Ibid.
83 Ibid.
84 'Crick's gaffe loses friends – and influence', *London Evening Standard*, 7 June 2013
85 'The Oxford romance that has guided Theresa May from tragedy to triumph', Mendick, op. cit.
86 *Desert Island Discs*, op. cit.
87 'Theresa, Philip and Oxford Union', Rajiva Wijesinha, *Ceylon Today*, 21 July 2016
88 'Husband's student days reveal passion of devoted rightwinger', Henry Zeffman, *The Times*, 5 October 2016
89 'The Oxford romance that has guided Theresa May from tragedy to triumph', Mendick, op. cit.
90 'The World According To… Theresa May', *The Independent*, 24 May 2004
91 'Theresa, Philip and Oxford Union', Wijesinha, op. cit.
92 Ibid.
93 'A determined woman with a massive social conscience', Kennedy and Bannerman, op. cit.
94 'Husband's student days reveal passion of devoted rightwinger', Zeffman, op. cit.
95 'Husband who'll be Denis to her Maggie (Without the G&Ts)', Geoffrey Levy, *Daily Mail*, 12 July 2016
96 *Desert Island Discs*, op. cit.

97   'The Oxford romance that has guided Theresa May from tragedy to triumph', Mendick, op. cit.

98   'Passenger in car that collided with Theresa May's father reveals shock of discovering victim's identity', Jane Atkinson, *The Sun*, 17 July 2016

99   *Desert Island Discs*, op. cit.

100 'The owl unseats the No. 10 pussycat', Shipman, op. cit.

101 'The Wilson Committee Review of the Functioning of Financial Institutions – Some Statistical Aspects', Peter Moore, *Journal of the Royal Statistical Society*, 1981

102 'Lady in waiting: Deborah Orr meets Theresa May', Deborah Orr, *The Independent*, 14 December 2009

103 'Can we learn any lessons from 30 years ago?', David Smith, *Sunday Times*, 2 October 2011

104 'Philip May: the reserved City fixture and husband happy to take a back seat', Simon Goodley, *The Guardian*, 12 July 2016

105 'My life as a female MP', Theresa May, BBC News, 17 June 2009

106 'Transferring Money Abroad', Jill Papworth, *The Guardian*, 3 April 1993

107 'Bag of tricks', Theresa May, *The Times*, 11 December 2004

108 'Theresa May's "Wimbledon set" usurps David Cameron's "Notting Hill posh boys"', Paul Wright, International Business Times, 20 July 2016

109 Ibid.

110 'Icy cold, she took Cable apart', Andrew Parsons, *Sunday Times*, 17 July 2016

111 'Racing has an ally in Number 10', Mark Scully and John Randall, *Racing Post*, 13 July 2016

112 'Lady in waiting: Deborah Orr meets Theresa May', Orr, op. cit.

113 'Diana Rigg meets Sybil Fawlty in her first newspaper interview as the Conservative chairman', Matthew d'Ancona, *Sunday Telegraph*, 28 July 2002

114 'Interview – We must prove we're not the "nasty party"', Rachel Sylvester, *Daily Telegraph*, 5 October 2002

115 'Theresa May interview: "I probably was Goody Two Shoes at school"', Pearson, op. cit.

116 'Yes, we were affected by not having children… but we coped', Walters, op. cit.

117 *Desert Island Discs*, op. cit.

118 'Diana Rigg meets Sybil Fawlty in her first newspaper interview as the Conservative chairman', d'Ancona, op. cit.

119 'Theresa May's leather skirt was too much for Holborn and St Pancras', Richard Osley, *Camden New Journal*, 13 July 2016

120 'The Home Secretary forgives Holborn', Richard Osley, *Camden New Journal*, 9 June 2011

121 'Theresa May: From North West Durham to No. 10', Chris Lloyd, *Northern Echo*, 11 July 2016

122 'May poll', Anne McElvoy, *London Evening Standard*, 4 April 2013

123 'Theresa May, the 37-year-old Merton councillor and graduate of St Hugh's', *London Evening Standard*, 22 March 1994

124 Ibid.

125 'Theresa May "tried to look like Essex girl" in 1994 Barking by-election', Iain Burns, *Barking and Dagenham Post*, 18 July 2016

126 'Tories launch fight for seat', *Barking and Dagenham Post*, 1 June 1994

127 'Theresa May "tried to look like Essex girl" in 1994 Barking by-election', Burns, op. cit.

128 'Joke Is on Tories as Essex Voters Have the Last Laugh', Tom Leonard, *London Evening Standard*, 10 June 1994

129 'Shortage of women worries as "dames" depart', Michael White, *The Guardian*, 26 October 1995

130 'It's George not Jeremy for Theresa', Robert Hardman, *Daily Mail*, 16 July 2016

131 'Tory woman looking forward to May day – Election 97', Michael Evans, *The Times*, 22 April 1997

132 'Candidate who left ministers trailing', Rebecca Smithers, *The Guardian*, 10 November 1995

133 'Tory woman looking forward to May day – Election 97', Evans, op. cit.

134 'Candidate who left ministers trailing', Smithers, op. cit.

135 Ibid.

136 'Tory woman looking forward to May day – Election 97', Evans, op. cit.

137 *Three Men in a Boat*, Jerome K. Jerome, Penguin Classics New Edition, March 2004

138 'It's George not Jeremy for Theresa', Hardman, op. cit.

139 'The blossoming of Theresa May', Emily Bearn, *Sunday Telegraph*, 2 June 2002

140 *Desert Island Discs*, op. cit.

141 'Remember When: *The Advertiser* interviews new Maidenhead MP Theresa May in 1997', Nicola Hine, *Maidenhead Advertiser*, 11 July 2016

142 'Icy cold, she took Cable apart', Parsons, op. cit.

143 'Unlucky for some', Julia Langdon, *The Guardian*, 15 July 1997

144 'Frantic day in the race for power', *Western Morning News*, 11 June 1997

145 *Desert Island Discs*, op. cit.

146 'It's a fresh start, but a long way to recovery', Andrew Pierce, *The Times*, 31 July 1997

147 'Your questions answered', Charles Arthur, Jeremy Laurance, Glenda Cooper, Cole Moreton, Raymond Whitaker, John Carlin et al., *Independent on Sunday*, 28 December 1997

148 'Unlucky for some', Langdon, op. cit.

149 'Theresa May: My Shocking Illness', Elizabeth Sanderson, *Mail on Sunday*, 28 July 2013

150 'Unlucky for some', Langdon, op. cit.

151 'Tricky questions made simple by the great pretender', Matthew Parris, *The Times*, 9 June 1998

152 'Germans have love covered at G8 summit', Atticus, *Sunday Times*, 20 June 1999

153 'Editorial – Now Mr Portillo must prove that he really is a caring Conservative', *The Independent*, 4 November 1999

154 'Editorial – After a bad week for the Tories, Mr Portillo's return is a mixed blessing', *The Independent*, 27 November 1999

155 'Top post "to buy Portillo's loyalty"', Paul Eastham, *Daily Mail*, 2 November 1999

156 'Hague urged to kick no-hopers into shadows', *Daily Express*, 31 August 2000

157 Ibid.

158 'Mike the Knife', Paul Gilfeather and James Hardy, *Daily Mirror*, 14 June 2001

159 'How the Conservatives guarantee to set our schools free', Theresa May, *Yorkshire Post*, 20 December 1999

160 'Action urged over lack of female Tory MPs', *Evening News*, 2 October 2000

161 'May rekindles row over Carlton Club', Melissa Kite, *The Times*, 24 April 2001

162 'The Nobodies are drifting to their doom', Stewart Steve, *Mail on Sunday*, 25 February 2001

163 'It's got to be Labour', Jonathan Freedland, *The Guardian*, 31 May 2001

164 'May the best man come third', John O'Farrell, *Daily Telegraph*, 30 April 2005

165 'Duncan Smith questions Portillo's ability', Martin Bentham, *Sunday Telegraph*, 17 June 2001

166 'Call for more women candidates', Jason Beattie, *The Scotsman*, 26 July 2001

167 *GMTV*, ITV, 21 October 2001

168 'Labour in a spin – Tories lost the chance of forcing resignation', Nigel Morris, *The Independent*, 27 February 2002

169 'Byers gives May reprieve', *London Evening Standard*, 29 May 2002

170 'Theresa May: I have no role model, I do what I think is right', Alexandra Topping and Jessica Elgot, *The Guardian*, 9 October 2015

171 'A big beast in kitten heels', Harry Cole, *Spectator Life*, 25 November 2014

172 'My life as a female MP', Theresa May, op. cit.

173 'Theresa May lifted her nose like Concorde at take-off', Quentin Letts, *Daily Mail*, 18 July 2000

174 'My week – Theresa May – The first female chairman of the Conservative Party, in conference week', Sean O'Grady, *The Independent*, 12 October 2002

175 'Mayday! Theresa takes Tory chair but MPs slam shake-up', George Pascoe-Watson, *The Sun*, 24 July 2002

176 'Have the Tories learned nothing?', *Daily Mail*, 24 July 2002

177 'Britain: a new look for Tories', Warren Hodge, *New York Times*, 24 July 2002

178 'Diana Rigg meets Sybil Fawlty in her first newspaper interview as the Conservative chairman', d'Ancona, op. cit.

179 'My week – Theresa May – The first female chairman of the Conservative Party, in conference week', Grady, op. cit.

180 'A denial of spin doctors', Matt Chorley, *The Times* Red Box Podcast, March 2016

181 'Tories must ditch "nasty" image, says chairman', Melissa Kite, *The Times*, 8 October 2002

182 'Tories at Bournemouth – Old guard criticises May over "nasty" tag', George Jones, *Daily Telegraph*, 9 October 2002

183 Ibid.

184 '"Nasty" tag rebounds on Duncan Smith', Nicholas Watt, *The Guardian*, 18 October 2002

185 'Backing singer with a lyric for the new Tories – Interview – Theresa May', Jasper Gerard, *Sunday Times*, 16 November 2003

186 'Rift opens again between modernizers, traditionalists in Britain's opposition party', Associated Press, 21 February 2003

187 Ibid.

188 'May tells Duncan Smith to halt secret briefings', Benedict Brogan, *Daily Telegraph*, 21 February 2003

189 'Howard steps into the ring', Patrick O'Flynn, Alison Little and Kirsty Walker, *Daily Express*, 30 October 2003

190 'Howard tells party activists – Don't risk our new unity', Colin Brown, *Sunday Telegraph*, 2 November 2003

191 'Howard warns of hard slog to election victory', *Western Mail*, 7 November 2003

192 'Backing singer with a lyric for the new Tories – Interview – Theresa May', Gerard, op. cit.

193 Ibid.

194 'Howard picks two men to fill Theresa's shoes', Benedict Brogan, *Daily Telegraph*, 10 November 2003

195 'Why do you want us to work longer, and who's your best mate in politics?', *The Independent*, 26 October 2009

196 'Opinion', Jane Moore, *The Sun*, 16 June 2004

197 'Theresa's family values', Tim Walker, *Sunday Telegraph*, 20 June 2004

198 'Senior Conservative issues call to bring in more women to improve party's fortunes', *Liverpool Daily Post*, 16 June 2005

199 'Cameron declares candidature with social cohesion plea. May urges Tory party "to be a little more female"', Tania Branigan, *The Guardian*, 17 June 2005

200 'We must be positive to overcome our nasty past', Helen Rumbelow, *The Times*, 29 June 2005

201 Anne Jenkin speech, Oxford conference, 'Rethinking Right-Wing Women', 29 June 2015

202 Ibid.

203 'May: "Conservatives are male, white … and sexist"', Marie Woolf, *The Independent*, 10 September 2005

204 Ibid.

205 *Newsnight*, BBC2, 4 October 2016

206 'We must change or die, say the modernisers', George Jones, *Daily Telegraph*, 4 October 2005

207 'Tory women get militant in push for female MPs', Andrew Porter, *Sunday Times*, 20 November 2005

208 'May: I helped my rival on her way to Commons', Tim Shipman, *Sunday Times*, 10 July 2016

209 Ibid.

210 'Harriet Harman: Theresa May "is no sister" on women's rights', Anushka Asthana, *The Guardian*, 23 September 2016

211 'May "fights just as hard for women as Labour's equality saint"', Anushka Asthana, *The Times*, 24 December 2011

212 'What does the Conservative Party offer a working-class kid from Brixton, Birmingham, Bolton or Bradford?', Nick Timothy, ConservativeHome, 22 March 2015

213 'Brummie Rasputin', Simon Walters, *Mail on Sunday*, 4 September 2016

214 *What Does Theresa Really Think?*, Robinson, op. cit.

215 'Tories lost in swirl of backbiting Cameron aide's e-mails leaked', Isabel Oakeshott, *Sunday Times*, 9 July 2006

216 'Conference Spy', Jonathan Isaby, *Daily Telegraph*, 2 October 2006

217 Ibid.

218 'Should Michael Martin resign? Have you toned down your shoes?', *The Independent*, 8 December 2008

219 'Parliamentary Quotes of the Day', Press Association, 26 June 2008

220 Women's Parliamentary Radio, April 2008

221 'Theresa May will not reform welfare', David Hughes, Telegraph Online, 19 January 2009

222 'Minister in kitten heels who wants to be tough, not nasty', Andrew Porter and Robert Winnett, *Daily Telegraph*, 15 May 2010

223 'The Frugal Few: Commuters who refused to board gravy train', Gordon Rayner and Rosa Prince, *Daily Telegraph*, 16 May 2009

224 'The MPs who tried to stop you seeing their expenses claims', Ben Leapman and Alastair Jamieson, *Sunday Telegraph*, 18 October 2009

225 'A long time to wait for a Big Society', Anne McElvoy, *London Evening Standard*, 13 April 2010

226 'Cameron's inspiration? Tory manifesto: Anatomy of a photograph – The Conservative launch', Rajeev Syal and Simon Chilvers, *The Guardian*, 14 April 2010

227 'Political tsar with a hankering for old Conservatism', Tim Mongomerie, *The Times*, 16 July 2016

228 'Beware the aides of May! The people who'll really run the new government', Isabel Hardman, *The Spectator*, 16 July 2016

229 'Profile: Fiona Hill and Nick Timothy', BBC Radio 4, 2 October 2016

230 Ibid.

231 'Theresa May, what lies behind the public image?', Day, op. cit.

232 *George Osborne: The Austerity Chancellor*, Janan Ganesh, Biteback Publishing, 2014

233 'Theresa, the safe pair of hands, versus Michael, the wit of Westminster', Andy Coulson, *Daily Telegraph*, 2 July 2016

234 'Secret tape reveals Tory backing for ban on gays', Toby Helm, *The Observer*, 4 April 2010

235 *Hung Together: The 2010 Election and the Coalition Government*, Adam Boulton and Joey Jones, Simon & Schuster, 2012

236 'Theresa, the safe pair of hands, versus Michael, the wit of Westminster', Coulson, op. cit.

237 *Desert Island Discs*, op. cit.

238 'May breaks the mould of new cabinet's men in suits', Paul Waugh, *London Evening Standard*, 12 May 2010

239 'Theresa May strikes the only clunky Cabinet note so far', David Hughes, Telegraph Online, 12 May 2010

240 'Theresa May, Commissar for Wimmin and Equality, gives her first car-crash interview', Gerald Warner, Telegraph Online, 12 May 2010

241 'Theresa May: Police on the beat a priority', Chris Mason, *The Independent*, 13 May 2010

242 *Desert Island Discs*, op. cit.

243 'Theresa May interview: "Red boxes are very much banned from the bedroom"', Judith Woods, *Daily Telegraph*, 9 July 2016

244 'Theresa May: Home Office record-breaker', Danny Shaw, BBC News, 12 July 2016

245 'Step in to tackle yobs: New Home Secretary says more police on beat will give public confidence to intervene', Robert Winnett and Andrew Porter, *Daily Telegraph*, 15 May 2010

246 *What Does Theresa Really Think?*, Robinson, op. cit.

247 *Coalition*, David Laws, Biteback Publishing, 2016

248 Ibid.

249 '£1bn saving as ID card scheme to be scrapped within 100 days: Project to be consigned to history, May declares', Alan Travis, *The Guardian*, 28 May 2010

250 'Theresa May will prove to be the star of the Coalition Government', Cristina Odone, Telegraph Online, 21 May 2010

251 'If marriage is good it should be for everyone', Theresa May, *The Times*, 15 March 2012

252 'Mrs Steady V Lady Spiky: A feud between two powerful Tory women led to the departure of the security minister', Melissa Kite, *Sunday Telegraph*, 15 May 2011

253 Interview, Theresa May, *The Andrew Marr Show*, BBC1, 15 May 2011

254 'Like the Head Girl, she is rarely caught on the hop', Quentin Letts, *Daily Mail*, 27 July 2010

255 Ephraim Hardcastle, *Daily Mail*, 8 September 2010

256 'Seven days: Secret diary of a civil servant: No bunkum in the bunker as terror rises back up the agenda', *The Observer*, 7 November 2010

257 'James Slack on Politics and Power', *Daily Mail*, 8 January 2011

258 The Liberal Democrats' 2010 manifesto included a pledge not to raise tuition fees,

which the party broke once in coalition, with disastrous consequences at the polls in 2015.

259 *What Does Theresa Really Think?*, Robinson, op. cit.

260 'May stuns Police Federation with vow to break its power', Vikram Dodd, *The Guardian*, 22 May 2014

261 Ibid.

262 'A defining moment for Theresa May and the police', *Daily Telegraph*, 23 May 2014

263 'Met police: "We quit, now others should resign at News International"', Vikram Dodd, *The Guardian*, 20 July 2011

264 'May: Riots are sheer criminality', *Metro*, 9 August 2011

265 *Against the Grain*, Norman Baker, Biteback Publishing, 2015

266 'Conservative Party Conference 2011: Ken Clarke and Theresa May fall out in row over pet cat', Christopher Hope and James Kirkup, *Daily Telegraph*, 4 October 2011

267 'Clarke hits out at "childish remarks"', Joe Watts, *Nottingham Evening Post*, 6 October 2011

268 *Kind of Blue: A Political Memoir*, Ken Clarke, Macmillan, 2016

269 Ibid.

270 Ibid.

271 Ibid.

272 'We don't want silly promises on immigration from Theresa May – we just want an honest debate', Fraser Nelson, *Daily Telegraph*, 25 August 2016

273 *Against the Grain*, Baker, op. cit.

274 'We'll reduce immigration and you can judge us on it', Tom Newton Dunn, *The Sun*, 28 June 2010

275 'Coalition at war on immigration', Jason Groves, James Chapman and Daniel Martin, *Daily Mail*, 28 July 2010

276 'Black Dog', *Mail on Sunday*, 15 May 2011

277 *Coalition*, Laws, op. cit.

278 'I'm axing bogus diploma factories: Coalition crackdown on immigration', Theresa May, *The Sun*, 22 March 2011

279 'Second iron lady has no time for small talk', David Laws, *The Times*, 2 July 2016

280 'Border control scandal revealed', Richard Ford, *The Times*, 5 November 2011

281 'Poll: Home Sec should step down', Vincent Moss, *Sunday Mirror*, 22 July 2012

282 'Profile: Gary McKinnon', Clark Boyd, BBC News, 30 July 2008

283 'OK, there's the jazzy shoes, but one of life's thigh-slappers she ain't', Quentin Letts, *Daily Mail*, 13 July 2013

284 'A big beast in kitten heels', Cole, op. cit.

285 Ibid.

286 'Gary McKinnon: Eric Holder formally complains to UK and refuses to take Theresa May's calls', Christopher Hope and Con Coughlin, Telegraph Online, 19 October 2012

287 *Coalition*, Laws, op. cit.

288 *Against the Grain*, Baker, op. cit.

289 'Theresa May waters down Tory migration target', Nicholas Watt, *The Guardian*, 26 May 2014

290 Interview, Theresa May, BBC Radio 5Live, 4 October 2016

291 *Coalition*, Laws, op. cit.

292 Interview, Theresa May, *The Andrew Marr Show*, BBC1, 26 May 2013

293 *Coalition*, Laws, op. cit.

294 'Clegg called a "w*****" by Theresa May's allies', Steve Hawkes, *The Sun*, 2 October 2014

295 'Nick Clegg accuses Theresa May of peddling "false and outrageous" slurs about Lib Dems', Nigel Morris, Independent Online, 2 October 2014

296 *Against the Grain*, Baker, op. cit.

297 Ibid.

298 Ibid.

299 Ibid.

300 'A big beast in kitten heels', Cole, op. cit.

301 'Another day, another bungle', Mark Hookham, *Sunday Times*, 22 April 2012

302 'Theresa May "partied with X Factor judges" while Abu Qatada appealed', Alan Travis, *The Guardian*, 20 April 2012

303 'Another day, another bungle', Hookham, op. cit.

304 'Abu Qatada in Jordan prison after deportation', Richard Ford, Sheer Frenkel and Hani Hazaimeh, *The Times*, 8 July 2013

305 'Comment', *Daily Mail*, 8 July 2013

306 'A goddess stands tall in her kitten heels after laying low the enemy', Michael Deacon, *Daily Telegraph*, 9 July 2013

307 'Special report: Theresa May is on manoeuvres, but she must conquer the Eurosceptics if she is to reach the top', Jane Merrick, *The Independent*, 14 July 2013

308 'As the Home Secretary steps out in boots worthy of a supermodel... Is Theresa May turning into Cara Delevingne?', *Daily Mail*, 7 November 2013

309 'May shows she is model performer', *The Times*, 8 November 2013

310 'May fires warning over migration abuses', Mark Hookham and David Leppard, *Sunday Times*, 7 October 2012

311 *Against the Grain*, Baker, op. cit.

312 'Modern slave drivers, I'll end your evil trade', Theresa May, *Sunday Times*, 25 August 2013

313 'Profile: Fiona Hill and Nick Timothy', op. cit.

314 'She's tough, cool and efficient ... but could she lead the Tories?', Gaby Hinsliff, *The Guardian*, 28 September 2013

315 Ibid.

316 *Coalition*, Laws, op. cit.

317 'Cabinet at war over extremists in schools', Greg Hurst and Francis Elliott, *The Times*, 4 June 2014

318 Ibid.

319 Ibid.

320 'Theresa's leggy aide, an ex-spy and the affair that fanned the flames...', Andrew Pierce, *Daily Mail*, 5 June 2014

321 'Theresa May is angry. Really angry', Benedict Brogan, Telegraph Online, 4 June 2014

322 'Axed aide feud with spin chief', Tom Newton Dunn, *The Sun*, 9 June 2014

323 *Against the Grain*, Baker, op. cit.

324 'Theresa's leggy aide, an ex-spy and the affair that fanned the flames...', Pierce, op. cit.

325 'Axed aide feud with spin chief', Newton Dunn, op. cit.

326 'Ice queen loses her cool in very cold war', Ann Treneman, *The Times*, 10 June 2014

327 Ibid.

328 Ephraim Hardcastle, *Daily Mail*, 15 July 2014

329 'Theresa May: My Shocking Illness', Sanderson, op. cit.

330 'Theresa's tweet nothing', Rowena Mason, *Daily Telegraph*, 16 February 2013

331 'May's stock rising as Tories contemplate life after Cameron', James Chapman, *Daily Mail*, 7 March 2013

332 'A big beast in kitten heels', Cole, op. cit.

333 'Full text of Theresa May's 2013 ConHome speech: We Will Win by Being the Party for All', ConservativeHome, 12 July 2016

334 Ibid.

335 'May's bid for Tory leadership falls flat with the Cabinet', Christopher Hope and James Kirkup, *Daily Telegraph*, 13 March 2013

336 Ibid.

337 'Cameron cleared Theresa May's "leadership" speech say her allies', Joe Murphy, *London Evening Standard*, 13 March 2013

338 'Cool your porridge and put a sock in it: Boris sends message to wannabe May', Tom Newton Dunn, *The Sun*, 15 March 2013

339 'Theresa May interview: "I probably was Goody Two Shoes at school"', Pearson, op. cit.

340 'Theresa's "little slut" conference fashion secret', Simon Walters, *Mail on Sunday*, 14 October 2012

341 'Theresa May interview: "I probably was Goody Two Shoes at school"', Pearson, op. cit.

342 'Diabetic May defies food ban in Commons', Chris Smyth, *The Times*, 7 November 2014

343 *Desert Island Discs*, op. cit.

344 'Theresa May: My Shocking Illness', Sanderson, op. cit.

345 'Strasbourg not superior to British courts, says former senior judge', David Barrett, Telegraph Online, 4 December 2013

346 'A big beast in kitten heels', Cole, op. cit.

347 *Against the Grain*, Baker, op. cit.

348 *Desert Island Discs*, op. cit.

349 'One in six Home Office staff bullied at work', Craig Woodhouse, *The Sun*, 4 January 2016

350 *Against the Grain*, Baker, op. cit.

351 'Lib Dem Baker quits as minister', Joe Churcher, Press Association, 3 November 2014

352 'Sketch: May loses her passport to Tory leadership', Esther Addley, *The Guardian*, 13 June 2014

353 'How she landed the job over Skype', *Mail on Sunday*, 16 October 2016

354 'Abuse judge's "racism was covered up"', Andrew Norfolk, *The Times*, 14 October 2016

355 'Simon not going to "Ed off to join UKIP"', Guido Fawkes, *The Sun*, 7 September 2014

356 'A big beast in kitten heels', Cole, op. cit.

357 'Has Theresa May just declared war on Downing Street?', James Kirkup, Telegraph Online, 25 November 2014

358 'A big beast in kitten heels', Cole, op. cit.

359 'Theresa's three-day media blitz', *Daily Mail*, 25 November 2014

360 *Desert Island Discs*, op. cit.

361 Ibid.

362 Ibid.

363 'Bitter squabble designed to punish Theresa', Andrew Pierce, *Daily Mail*, 20 December 2014

364 'Cameron approved removal of May's aides from candidate list', Francis Elliott, *The Times*, 20 December 2014

365 'Mandy backhands Mili while Paxo puns and zombies fill the Commons', Michael Deacon, *Daily Telegraph*, 8 May 2015

366 'Prime Minister's top aide broke rules on lobbying', Oliver Wright, *The Times*, 1 August 2016

367 Interview, David Cameron, James Lansdale, BBC News, 24 March 2016

368 'Wine flows as Tory hopefuls court support', Sam Coates, *The Times*, 14 January 2016

369 Ibid.

370 'Theresa May to revive her "snooper's charter" now Lib Dem brakes are off', Damien Gayle, *The Guardian*, 9 May 2015

371 'Cameron speaks', *The Spectator*, 26 January 2013

372 *All Out War: The Full Story of How Brexit Sank Britain's Political Class*, Tim Shipman, William Collins, 2016

373 Ibid.

374 Ibid.

375 'A borderless EU harms everyone but the gangs that sell false dreams', Theresa May, *Sunday Times*, 30 August 2015

376 'David Cameron is the new leader of the British Left', Dan Hodges, Telegraph Online, 8 October 2015

377 'May under fire after urging migrant curb', Michael Savage and Richard Ford, *The Times*, 7 October 2015

378 'Magnificent Mrs May shows PM the way', *Daily Mail*, 7 October 2015

379 'David Cameron snubs Theresa May and lavishes praise on George Osborne and Boris Johnson in speech', Christopher Hope and Ben Riley-Smith, Telegraph Online, 7 October 2015

380 Interview, Theresa May, *The Andrew Marr Show*, BBC1, 1 November 2015

381 *All Out War*, Shipman, op. cit.

382 Ibid.

383 'Now make EU mind up: Cameron U-turn as he gives Cabinet free choice on Brexit', Craig Woodhouse, *The Sun*, 6 January 2016

384 'Will May go all in?', James Forsyth, *The Sun*, 16 January 2016

385 *Unleashing Demons*, Craig Oliver, Hodder & Stoughton, 2016

386 Ibid.

387 Ibid.

388 *All Out War*, Shipman, op. cit.

389 *Unleashing Demons*, Oliver, op. cit.

390 Ibid.

391 Ibid.

392 'May savages Europe then says she still wants us in', James Slack, *Daily Mail*, 25 April 2016

393 *Unleashing Demons*, Oliver, op. cit.

394 *What Does Theresa Really Think?*, Robinson, op. cit.

395 'Theresa May interview: "Red boxes are very much banned from the bedroom"', Woods, op. cit.

396 'But MoS poll shows how May could bowl him out', Simon Walters, *Mail on Sunday*, 26 June 2016

397 'May is Tory favourite after surge in support', Sam Coates, *The Times*, 28 June 2016

398 'Tory leadership peace talks fail after Theresa May refuses to meet Boris Johnson', Tom Newton Dunn, *The Sun*, 28 June 2016

399 'Glum Blond', Tom Newton Dunn, *The Sun*, 1 July 2016

400 *World at One*, BBC Radio 4, 30 June 2016

401 'Brexecuted: Furious Boris backers condemn Gove to "a deep pit in hell" after he knifes Johnson and aims for Number 10', Tom Newton Dunn, Harry Cole and Steve Hawkes, *The Sun*, 30 June 2016

402 *World at One*, 30 June 2016, op. cit.

403 'A party in flames and why it must be Theresa for leader', *Daily Mail*, 1 July 2016

404 'Theresa May's winning high stakes gamble as 60 per cent of Tories say she should be the next PM', David Wooding, *The Sun*, 3 July 2016

405 'PM hopeful Andrea Leadsom stuns Conservative MPs with her "car crash" pitch at hustings', Tom Newton Dunn, *The Sun*, 5 July 2016

406 'Michael Gove's campaign manager makes extraordinary text gaffe in bid to stop Andrea Leadsom becoming premier', Steve Hawkes and Harry Cole, *The Sun*, 7 July 2016

407 'Being a mother gives me edge on May – Leadsom', Rachel Sylvester and Sam Coates, *The Times*, 9 July 2016

408 'I'm sure Theresa will be really sad that she doesn't have children…', Rachel Sylvester, *The Times*, 9 July 2016

409 'I have been under attack, it's been shattering', Allison Pearson, *Daily Telegraph*, 11 July 2016

410 'May's day of the long stiletto: the inside story', Christopher Hope and Tim Ross, *Sunday Telegraph*, 17 July 2016

411 Ibid.

412 'May's day of the long stiletto: the inside story', Hope and Ross, op. cit.

413 *Peston on Sunday*, ITV, 18 September 2016

414 'May in No. 10 peace talks with terrace rage Tories', Glen Owen, *Mail on Sunday*, 24 July 2016

415 'Theresa May's first Prime Minister's Questions: our writers give their verdict', Ayesha Hazarika, *The Guardian*, 20 July 2016

416 'Prime Minister's towering lead over Corbyn in popularity poll', *Daily Express*, 3 September 2016

417 'PM in school fight: Theresa May hits back at ex-education minister who claims grammar school plans will fail poorer kids', Lynn Davidson and Chloe Mayer, *The Sun*, 8 September 2016

418 Interview, Theresa May, *Sophy Ridge on Sunday*, Sky News, 8 January 2017

419 'Inside Team Theresa', Katie Perrior, *Times Magazine*, 15 July 2017

420 'The Blame Game', Joey Jones, PoliticsHome, 10 June 2017

421 'The Prime Minister undone by her gruesome twosome', Alasdair Palmer, *Sunday Times*, 25 June 2017

422 Perrior, op. cit.

423 'Nick Timothy: why the election went wrong and how the Tories can beat Corbyn next time', Gordon Rayner, *Daily Telegraph*, 5 August 2017

424 Perrior, op. cit.

425 Rayner, op. cit.

426 'Where we went wrong', Nick Timothy, *The Spectator*, 14 June 2017

427 'Revealed: How Theresa May's two aides seized control of the Tory election campaign to calamitous effect', Joe Murphy, *London Evening Standard*, 16 June 2017

428 Interview, Grant Shapps, *Daily Politics*, BBC1, 12 June 2017

429 'Conservatives' free breakfast pledge "costed at just 7p per meal"', Jess Staufenberg, *Schoolsweek*, 23 May 2017

430 Palmer, op. cit.

431 Diane Abbott interview, Nick Ferrari, LBC, 2 May 2017

432 Palmer, op. cit.

433 Interview, Theresa May, ITV News, 5 June 2017

434 Timothy, op. cit.

435 Interview, Theresa May, Emma Barnett, Radio 5Live, 13 July 2017

436 Ibid.

437 'From a 'landslide majority' to horse-trading with the DUP: 24 hours that saw Theresa May's sudden collapse of power', Ben Riley-Smith, *Sunday Telegraph*, 10 June 2017

438 Ibid.

439 Rayner, op. cit.

440 Barnett, op. cit.

441 Ibid.

442 'I was staggered by their arrogance', Katie Perrior, *The Times*, 9 June 2017

443 'Queen of Denial', *London Evening Standard*, 9 June 2017

444 'Don't blame us! May's top advisers resign', Glen Owen, *Mail on Sunday*, 11 June 2017

445 Jones, op. cit.

446 Interview, George Osborne, *Andrew Marr Show*, BBC1, 12 June 2017

447 Michael Portillo, *This Week*, BBC1, 15 June 2017

448 '"Shrivelled" PM can't function', Simon Walters, *Mail on Sunday*, 16 July 2017

INDEX